The Oxford Dictionary of
# Literary Terms

**Chris Baldick** is Professor of English at Goldsmiths, University of
London. He edited *The Oxford Book of Gothic Tales* (1992), and is
the author of *The Oxford English Literary History, Volume 10
(1910–1940): The Modern Movement* (2004), *In Frankenstein's
Shadow* (1987), *Criticism and Literary Theory 1890 to the Present*
(1996), and other works of literary history. He has edited, with
Rob Morrison, *Tales of Terror from Blackwood's Magazine*, and
*The Vampyre and Other Tales of the Macabre*, and has written an
introduction to Charles Maturin's *Melmoth the Wanderer*
(available in the Oxford World's Classics series).

(⊕) SEE WEB LINKS

For recommended web links for this title, visit
www.oxfordreference.com/page/litterm when you
see this sign.

The most authoritative and up-to-date reference books for both students and the general reader.

Many of these titles are also available online at www.oxfordreference.com

# The Oxford Dictionary of
# Literary Terms

### FOURTH EDITION

## CHRIS BALDICK

**OXFORD**
UNIVERSITY PRESS

# OXFORD
UNIVERSITY PRESS

Great Clarendon Street, Oxford, OX2 6DP,
United Kingdom

Oxford University Press is a department of the University of Oxford.
It furthers the University's objective of excellence in research, scholarship,
and education by publishing worldwide. Oxford is a registered trade mark of
Oxford University Press in the UK and in certain other countries

First published 1990
First published as a paperback 1991
Second edition published 2001
Second edition published with new covers 2004
Third edition 2008
Fourth edition 2015

Impression: 3

Published in the United States of America by Oxford University Press
198 Madison Avenue, New York, NY 10016, United States of America

British Library Cataloguing in Publication Data
Data available

Library of Congress Control Number: 2014960115

ISBN 978-0-19-871544-3

Printed in Great Britain by
Clays Ltd, St Ives plc

*For Bethany*

# Contents

# Preface

This is a book of hard words alphabetically arranged and briefly explained. It cannot purport to fulfil the functions of a balanced expository guide to literary criticism or to all literary concepts, nor does it attempt to catalogue the entire body of literary terms in use. It offers instead to clarify those twelve hundred terms that are most likely to cause the student or general reader some doubt or bafflement in the context of literary criticism and other discussion of literary works. Rather than include for the sake of encyclopaedic completeness all the most common terms found in literary discussion, I have set aside several that I have judged to be sufficiently well understood in common speech (*anagram, cliché*, and many more), along with a broad category of general concepts such as *art, belief, culture*, etc., which may appear as literary-critical problems but which are not specifically literary terms. This policy has allowed space for the inclusion of many terms generated by the growth of academic literary theory in recent decades, and for adequate attention to the terminology of classical rhetoric, now increasingly revived. Along with these will be found hundreds of terms from literary criticism, literary history, prosody, and drama. The selection is weighted towards literature and criticism in English, but there are many terms taken from other languages, and many more associated primarily with other literatures. Many of the terms that I have omitted from this dictionary are covered by larger or more specialist works; a brief guide to these appears at pages 391–92.

In each entry I have attempted to explain succinctly how the term is or has been used, with a brief illustrative example wherever possible, and to clarify any relevant distinctions of sense. Related terms are indicated by cross-reference, using an asterisk (*) before a term explained elsewhere in the dictionary, or the instruction *see*. I have chosen not to give much space to questions of etymology, and to discuss a term's origin only when this seems genuinely necessary to clarify its current sense. My attention has been devoted more to helping readers to use the terms confidently for themselves. To this end I have displayed the plural forms, adjectival forms, and other derived words relevant to each entry, and have provided pronunciation guides for more than two hundred potentially troublesome terms. The simplified pronunciation system used, closely based on the system devised by Joyce M. Hawkins for the *Oxford Paperback Dictionary*, offers a basic but sufficient indication of the essential features of stress-placing and vowel quality. One of its advantages is that it requires very little checking against the pronunciation key on page ix.

The dictionary in its present form is a thoroughly updated version of the third edition of 2008, which itself was an expanded form of what was formerly the *Concise Oxford Dictionary of Literary Terms* (1990, revised 2001). Concision remains, I trust, a virtue of the entries themselves, but there are now a further 200 of those, extending the book's coverage not only of recently circulated terms but of modern critical and theoretical movements, schools of American poetry, Spanish verse forms, life writing, crime fiction, and much else. The provision of recommended reading has been extended widely, and is now accompanied in fifty entries by recommended web resources for further research.

My work on this dictionary and its predecessors has occupied me intermittently for more than twenty years, during which period I have incurred several debts of gratitude. From the start I was sustained by an inspirational editor at Oxford University Press, the late Kim Scott Walwyn, who first invited me to tackle this work, and whose enthusiasm and professionalism became legendary among the authors lucky enough to work with her. Wise counsel and well-directed advice came also at an early stage from Pamela Jackson, Harriet Barry, and John Simons, along with help on pronunciations from Michael Ockenden and Joyce Hawkins. Michael Hughes, Colin Pickthall, and Hazel Richardson came generously to my aid for particular entries in the first Concise edition. More lately, as I have brought the work up to date, it has benefited from the expertise of many of my colleagues past and present at Goldsmiths, who have borne sudden interrogation cheerfully. These are Alcuin Blamires, Lucia Boldrini, Michael Bruce, Marie-Claude Canova-Green, Helen Carr, Josh Cohen, Elizabeth Crossley, Rick Crownshaw, Hayley Davis, Alan Downie, Russ McDonald, Philip McGowan, Tim Parnell, Jacqueline Rattray, Michael Simpson, and Catherine Spooner. Annika Lindskog has also kindly provided advice on Swedish orthography for this 4th edition.

C.B.

# Pronunciation

Where a term's pronunciation may not be immediately obvious from its spelling, a guide is provided in square brackets following the word or phrase. Words are broken up into small units, usually of one syllable. The syllable that is spoken with most stress in a word of two or more syllables is shown in **bold type**.

The pronunciations given follow the standard speech of southern England. However, since this system is based on analogies rather than on precise phonetic description, readers who use other varieties of spoken English will rarely need to make any conscious adjustment to suit their own forms of pronunciation.

The sounds represented are as follows:

| | | | | | |
|---|---|---|---|---|---|
| a | *as in* cat | i | *as in* pin | s | *as in* sit |
| ă | *as in* ago | ĭ | *as in* pencil | sh | *as in* shop |
| ah | *as in* calm | I | *as in* eye | t | *as in* top |
| air | *as in* hair | j | *as in* jam | th | *as in* thin |
| ar | *as in* bar | k | *as in* kind | *th* | *as in* this |
| aw | *as in* law | l | *as in* leg | u | *as in* cup |
| ay | *as in* say | m | *as in* man | ŭ | *as in* focus |
| b | *as in* bat | n | *as in* not | uu | *as in* book |
| ch | *as in* chin | ng | *as in* sing, finger | v | *as in* voice |
| d | *as in* day | nk | *as in* thank | w | *as in* will |
| e | *as in* bed | o | *as in* top | y | *as in* yes |
| ĕ | *as in* taken | ŏ | *as in* lemon | | *or when preceded* |
| ee | *as in* meet | oh | *as in* most | | *by a consonant* = I |
| eer | *as in* beer | oi | *as in* join | | *as in* cry, realize |
| er | *as in* her | oo | *as in* soon | yoo | *as in* unit |
| ew | *as in* few | oor | *as in* poor | yoor | *as in* Europe |
| ewr | *as in* pure | or | *as in* for | yr | *as in* fire |
| f | *as in* fat | ow | *as in* cow | z | *as in* zebra |
| g | *as in* get | p | *as in* pen | zh | *as in* vision |
| h | *as in* hat | r | *as in* red | | |

The raised n ($^n$) is used to indicate the nasalizing of the preceding vowel sound in some French words, as in *baton* or in *Chopin*. In several French words no syllable is marked for stress, the distribution of stress being more even than in English.

A consonant is sometimes doubled, especially to help show that the vowel before it is short, or when without this the combination of letters might suggest a wrong pronunciation through looking misleadingly like a familiar word.

**abjection** A psychological process of 'casting off', identified and theorized by the Bulgarian-French psychoanalytic philosopher Julia Kristeva as the basis of horror and revulsion, and so subsequently adopted by literary critics in attempted explanation of the imaginative effects of *horror stories, *Gothic fiction, and narratives of monstrosity. In her book *Pouvoirs de l'horreur* (1980; translated as *Powers of Horror*, 1982), Kristeva proposes that we are especially disgusted by anything that is ambiguously located at the physical boundaries of the self, neither clearly inside nor outside us: thus bodily excretions and secretions excite nausea, and so too, in this theory, do babies and indeed mothers. Such unsettling items are described as **abject** or **abjected** insofar as we attempt to maintain our stable sense of self by imaginatively expelling them or projecting them in the form of monstrous aliens, ghosts, or bogeys.

**abridgement** A shorter version of an otherwise lengthy written work; also the process of selective cutting that results in such an **abridged** *edition. Many classic literary works have appeared in abridged versions marketed to children or language students, for example, or in an attempt to make them digestible to the impatience of modern readers: Edward Gibbon's six-volume *The Decline and Fall of the Roman Empire* (1776–88), for instance, was reduced to a one-volume abridgement by D. M. Low in 1960.

**absurd, the** A term derived from the *existentialism of Albert Camus, and often applied to the modern sense of human purposelessness in a universe without meaning or value. Many 20th-century writers of prose fiction stressed the absurd nature of human existence: notable instances are the novels and stories of Franz Kafka, in which the characters face alarmingly incomprehensible predicaments. The critic Martin Esslin coined the phrase **theatre of the absurd** in 1961 to refer to a number of dramatists of the 1950s (led by Samuel Beckett and Eugène Ionesco)

# academic drama

whose works evoke the absurd by abandoning logical form, character, and dialogue together with realistic illusion. The classic work of **absurdist** theatre is Beckett's *En attendant Godot* (*Waiting for Godot*, 1952), which revives some of the conventions of clowning and *farce to represent the impossibility of purposeful action and the paralysis of human aspiration. Other dramatists associated with the theatre of the absurd include Edward Albee, Jean Genet, Harold Pinter, and Václav Havel.

**Further reading:** Neil Cornwell, *The Absurd in Literature* (2006).

**academic drama (school drama)** A dramatic tradition which arose from the *Renaissance, in which the works of Plautus, Terence, and other ancient dramatists were performed in schools and colleges, at first in Latin but later also in *vernacular adaptations composed by schoolmasters under the influence of *humanism. This tradition produced the earliest English comedies, notably *Ralph Roister Doister* (*c*.1552) by the schoolmaster Nicholas Udall.

**acatalectic** Possessing the full number of syllables in the final *foot (of a metrical verse line); not *catalectic. *Noun*: **acatalexis**.

**accent** The emphasis placed upon a syllable in pronunciation. The term is often used as a synonym for *stress, although some theorists prefer to use 'stress' only for metrical accent. Three kinds of accent may be distinguished, according to the factor that accounts for each: etymological accent (or 'word accent') is the emphasis normally given to a syllable according to the word's derivation or *morphology; rhetorical accent (or 'sense accent') is allocated according to the relative importance of the word in the context of a sentence or question; metrical accent (or stress) follows a recurrent pattern of stresses in a verse line (*see* METRE). Where metrical accent overrides etymological or rhetorical accent, as it often does in *ballads and songs (Coleridge: 'in a far coun-*tree*'), the effect is known as a **wrenched accent**. *See also* ICTUS, RECESSIVE ACCENT.

**accentual-syllabic verse** Verse in which the *metre assumes the counting both of stressed syllables and of the total number of syllables in the line. Thus in an English iambic *pentameter we normally expect to hear five stresses within a ten-syllable line, although in practice there are accepted variations affecting the tally. This accentual-syllabic principle has dominated the literary tradition of verse in English since Chaucer. It is distinguished from pure *accentual verse, in which the stresses alone are counted, and from *syllabic verse, which observes only the total syllable count.

**accentual verse** Verse in which the *metre is based on counting only the number of stressed syllables in a line, and in which the number of unstressed syllables in the line may therefore vary. Most verse in Germanic languages (including Old English) is accentual, and much English poetry of later periods has been written in accentual verse, especially in the popular tradition of songs, *ballads, nursery rhymes, and hymns. The predominant English metrical system in the 'high' literary tradition since Chaucer, however, has been that of *accentual–syllabic verse, in which both stressed and unstressed syllables are counted. *See also* ALLITERATIVE METRE.

**acephalous** [a-**sef**-ăl-ŭs] The Greek word for 'headless', applied to a metrical verse line that lacks the first syllable expected according to regular *metre; e.g. an iambic *pentameter missing the first unstressed syllable, as sometimes in Chaucer:

>                 Twenty bookès, clad in blak or reed

*Noun*: **acephalexis**. *See also* TRUNCATION.

**Acmeism** A short-lived (*c.*1911–21) but significant movement in early 20th-century Russian poetry, aiming for precision and clarity in opposition to the alleged vagueness of the preceding *Symbolist movement. Its leaders, Nikolai Gumilev and Sergei Gorodetsky, founded an **Acmeist** 'Poets' Guild' in 1911, and propounded its principles in the magazine *Apollon*. The principal poetic luminaries of this school were Anna Akhmatova (1889–1966) and Osip Mandelstam (1891–1938).

**Further reading:** Justin Doherty, *The Acmeist Movement in Russian Poetry* (1995).

**acrostic** Usually a poem in which the initial letters of each line can be read down the page to spell either an alphabet, a name (often that of the author, a patron, or a loved one), or some other concealed message. Variant forms of acrostic may use middle letters or final letters of lines or, in prose acrostics, initial letters of sentences or paragraphs. There are also acrostic phrases that serve a *mnemonic function: the initial letters of 'Richard of York gave battle in vain' are those of the colours in a rainbow.

**act** A major division in the action of a play, comprising one or more *scenes. A break between acts often coincides with a point at which the action is interrupted before resuming at a later fictional time, or at which it moves to a different venue.

**actant** In the *narratology of A. J. Greimas, one of six basic categories of fictional role common to all stories. The actants are paired in *binary opposition: Subject/Object, Sender/Receiver, Helper/Opponent. A character (or *acteur*) is an individualized manifestation of one or more actants; but an actant may be realized in a non-human creature (e.g. a dragon as Opponent) or inanimate object (e.g. magic sword as Helper, or Holy Grail as Object), or in more than one *acteur*. *Adjective*: **actantial**.

**adage** [ad-ij] Another word for a *proverb or *maxim.

**adaptation** The process of making a work of art upon the basis of elements provided by an earlier work in a different, usually literary, medium; also the secondary work thus produced. Literary works have been **adapted** in many forms: fairy tales as ballets, plays as operas, novels as stage plays (*see* DRAMATIZATION), stage plays as novels or short stories. Since the early 20th century, new entertainment media have encouraged the adaptation of plays and novels as films or as radio (and later, television) dramas, and conversely the 'novelization' of film or television screenplays into books. Distinctions are commonly drawn between 'faithful' adaptations, in which the distinctive elements (characters, settings, plot events, dialogue) of the original work are preserved as far as the new medium allows, and 'free' adaptations, sometimes called 'versions' or 'interpretations', in which significant elements of the original work are omitted or replaced by wholly new material.

**Further reading:** Julie Sanders, *Adaptation and Appropriation* (2005).

**adventure story** A loose but commonly accepted term for a kind of prose *narrative addressed for the most part to boys, in which a hero or group of heroes engages in exotic and perilous exploration. It is a masculinized variety of *romance, one in which the erotic and religious dimensions common to other types are subordinated to or completely

replaced by an emphasis on vigorous outdoor activity and the practical
arts of survival amid unexpected dangers, along with a cultivation
of such virtues as courage and loyalty. Marvellous events may be
witnessed, but usually within a context provided by modern scientific
knowledge. The genre flourished in the later 19th century, its most
influential master being the French writer Jules Verne, whose series of
eighteen *Voyages extraordinaires* include *Voyage au centre de la terre*
(*Journey to the Centre of the Earth*, 1864) and *Vingt mille lieues sous les
mers* (*Twenty Thousand Leagues under the Sea*, 1870). Popular examples
in English included H. Rider Haggard's *King Solomon's Mines* (1886),
Arthur Conan Doyle's *The Lost World* (1912), and P. C. Wren's *Beau
Geste* (1924). Partial overlapping with *science fiction, as in Verne's case,
or with the *thriller and other popular forms, is sometimes found.

**adynaton** A *figure of speech related to *hyperbole that emphasizes
the inexpressibility of some thing, idea, or feeling, either by stating that
words cannot describe it, or by comparing it with something (e.g. the
heavens, the oceans) the dimensions of which cannot be grasped.
An example from Charles Dickens's *Nicholas Nickleby* is 'Language
was not powerful enough to describe the infant phenomenon.' It is often
a rhetorical index of the *sublime.

**Aestheticism** The doctrine or disposition that regards beauty as
an end in itself, and attempts to preserve the arts from subordination
to moral, *didactic, or political purposes. The term is often used
synonymously with the **Aesthetic Movement**, a literary and artistic
tendency of the late 19th century which may be understood as a further
phase of *Romanticism in reaction against *philistine bourgeois values
of practical efficiency and morality. Aestheticism found theoretical
support in the *aesthetics of Immanuel Kant and other German
philosophers who separated the sense of beauty from practical interests.
Elaborated by Théophile Gautier in 1835 as a principle of artistic
independence, aestheticism was adopted in France by Baudelaire,
Flaubert, and the *Symbolists, and in England by Walter Pater, Oscar
Wilde, and several poets of the 1890s, under the slogan *l'art pour l'art*
('*art for art's sake'). Wilde and other devotees of pure beauty—like the
artists Whistler and Beardsley—were sometimes known as **aesthetes**.
*See also* DECADENCE, *FIN DE SIÈCLE*.

**Further reading:** Leon Chai, *Aestheticism* (1990).

**aesthetics (esthetics)** Philosophical investigation into the nature of beauty and the perception of beauty, especially in the arts; the theory of art or of artistic taste. *Adjective*: **aesthetic** or **esthetic**.

**affective** Pertaining to emotional effects or dispositions (known in psychology as 'affects'). Affective criticism or **affectivism** evaluates literary works in terms of the feelings they arouse in audiences or readers (*see* CATHARSIS). It was condemned in an important essay by W. K. Wimsatt and Monroe C. Beardsley (in *The Verbal Icon*, 1954) as the **affective fallacy**, since in the view of these *New Critics such affective evaluation confused the literary work's objective qualities with its subjective results. The American critic Stanley Fish has given the name **affective stylistics** to his form of *reader-response criticism. *See also* INTENTIONAL FALLACY.

**afflatus** A Latin term for poetic inspiration.

**agitprop** [aj-it-prop] A Russian abbreviation of 'agitation and propaganda', applied to the campaign of cultural and political propaganda mounted in the years after the 1917 revolution. The term is sometimes applied to the simple form of *didactic drama which the campaign employed, and which influenced the *epic theatre of Piscator and Brecht in Germany.

**agon** [a-gohn] (plural **agones** [ă-**goh**-niz]) The contest or dispute between two characters which forms a major part of the action in the Greek *Old Comedy of Aristophanes, e.g. the debate between Aeschylus and Euripides in his play *The Frogs* (405 BCE). The term is sometimes extended to formal debates in Greek tragedies, and may be further applied to later forms such as the *psychomachy. In Harold Bloom's theory of the *anxiety of influence, it is applied to the struggle between the new poet and the precursor. *Adjective*: **agonistic**.

*alazon* The *stock character of the braggart in ancient Greek comedies. The same comic type reappears in later dramatic traditions under new names: *see* BRAGGADOCIO.

**alba** *See* AUBADE.

**Alcaics** A Greek verse form using a four-line *stanza in which the first two lines have eleven syllables each, the third nine, and the fourth ten. The *metre, predominantly *dactylic, was used frequently by the Roman poet Horace, and later by some Italian and German poets, but its *quantitative basis makes it difficult to adapt into English—although Tennyson and Clough attempted English Alcaics, and Peter Reading experimented with the form in *Ukulele Music* (1985) and other works.

**aleatory** [ayl-eer-tri] **(aleatoric)** Dependent upon chance. Aleatory writing involves an element of randomness either in composition, as in *automatic writing and the *cut-up, or in the reader's selection and ordering of written fragments, as in B. S. Johnson's novel *The Unfortunates* (1969), a box of 27 separately bound printed sections of which 25 can be read in any order.

**Alexandrianism** The works and styles of the Alexandrian school of Greek poets in the *Hellenistic age (323–31 BCE), which included Callimachus, Apollonius Rhodius, and Theocritus. The Alexandrian style was marked by elaborate artificiality, obscure mythological *allusion, and eroticism. It influenced Catullus and other Roman poets.

**alexandrine (*alexandrin*)** A verse line of twelve syllables adopted by poets since the 16th century as the standard verse form of French poetry, especially dramatic and narrative. It was first used in 12th-century *chansons de geste*, and probably takes its name from its use in Lambert le Tort's *Roman d'Alexandre* (*c.*1200). The division of the line into two groups of six syllables, divided by a *caesura, was established in the age of Racine, but later challenged by Victor Hugo and other 19th-century poets, who preferred three groups of four, in a pattern referred to as the *trimètre* or as the *alexandrin romantique*. The English alexandrine is an iambic *hexameter (thus having six stresses), and is found rarely except as the final line in the *Spenserian stanza, as in Keats's 'The Eve of St Agnes':

> She knelt, so pure a thing, so free from mortal taint.

A rare example of extended alexandrine composition in English is Robert Browning's poem *Fifine at the Fair* (1872).

**alienation effect (A-effect)** The usual English translation of the German *Verfremdungseffekt* or *V-effekt*, a major principle of Bertolt Brecht's theory of *epic theatre. It is a dramatic effect aimed at encouraging an attitude of critical detachment in the audience, rather than a passive submission to realistic illusion; and is achieved by a variety of means, from allowing the audience to smoke and drink to interrupting the play's action with songs, sudden scene changes, and switches of role. Actors are also encouraged to distance themselves from their characters rather than identify with them; ironic commentary by a narrator adds to this 'estrangement'. By reminding the audience of the performance's artificial nature, Brecht hoped to stimulate a rational view of history as a changeable human creation rather than as a fated process to be accepted passively. Despite this theory, audiences still identify emotionally with the characters in *Mother Courage* (1941) and Brecht's other plays. The theory was derived partly from the *Russian Formalists' concept of *defamiliarization.

**allegory** A story or visual image with a second distinct meaning partially hidden behind its literal or visible meaning. The principal technique of allegory is *personification, whereby abstract qualities are given human shape—as in public statues of Liberty or Justice. An allegory may be conceived as a *metaphor that is extended into a structured system. In written narrative, allegory involves a continuous parallel between two (or more) levels of meaning in a story, so that its persons and events correspond to their equivalents in a system of ideas or a chain of events external to the tale: each character and episode in John Bunyan's *The Pilgrim's Progress* (1678), for example, embodies an idea within a pre-existing Puritan doctrine of salvation. Allegorical thinking permeated the Christian literature of the Middle Ages, flourishing in the *morality plays and in the *dream visions of Dante and Langland. Some later allegorists like Dryden and Orwell used allegory as a method of *satire; their hidden meanings are political rather than religious. In the medieval discipline of biblical *exegesis, allegory became an important method of interpretation, a habit of seeking correspondences between different realms of meaning (e.g. physical and spiritual) or between the Old Testament and the New (*see* TYPOLOGY). It can be argued that modern critical interpretation continues this allegorizing tradition. *See also* ANAGOGICAL, EMBLEM, EXEMPLUM, FABLE, PARABLE, PSYCHOMACHY, SYMBOL.

**Further reading:** Jeremy Tambling, *Allegory* (2009).

**alliteration** (head rhyme; initial rhyme) The repetition of the same sounds—usually initial consonants of words or of stressed syllables—in any sequence of neighbouring words: 'Landscape-lover, lord of language' (Tennyson). Now an optional and incidental decorative effect in verse or prose, it was once a required element in the poetry of Germanic languages (including Old English and Old Norse) and in Celtic verse (where alliterated sounds could regularly be placed in positions other than the beginning of a word or syllable). Such poetry, in which alliteration rather than *rhyme is the chief principle of repetition, is known as **alliterative verse**; its rules also allow a vowel sound to **alliterate** with any other vowel. *See also* ALLITERATIVE METRE, ALLITERATIVE REVIVAL, ASSONANCE, CONSONANCE.

**alliterative metre** The distinctive verse form of Old Germanic poetry, including Old English. It employed a long line divided by a *caesura into two balanced half-lines, each with a given number of stressed syllables (usually two) and a variable number of unstressed syllables. These half-lines are linked by *alliteration between both (sometimes one) of the stressed syllables in the first half and the first (and sometimes the second) stressed syllable in the second half. In Old English, the lines were normally unrhymed and not organized in *stanzas, although some works of the later Middle English *alliterative revival used both stanzaic patterns and rhyme. This *metre was the standard form of verse in English until the 11th century, and was still important in the 14th, but declined under the influence of French *syllabic verse. W. H. Auden revived its use in *The Age of Anxiety* (1948), as Richard Wilbur did in his shorter poem 'Junk' (1961). These lines from the 14th-century poem *Piers Plowman* illustrate the alliterative metre:

> Al for love of oure Lord livede wel straite,
> In hope for to have hevene-riche blisse.

*See also* ACCENTUAL VERSE.

**alliterative revival** A term covering the group of late 14th-century English poems written in an *alliterative metre similar to that of Old English verse but less regular (notably in Langland's *Piers Plowman*) and sometimes—as in the anonymous *Pearl* and *Sir Gawain and the Green Knight*—using rhyme and elaborate *stanza structure. This group may represent more a continuation than a revival of the alliterative tradition.

**Further reading:** Thorlac Turville-Petre, *The Alliterative Revival* (1977).

**allusion** An indirect or passing reference to some event, person, place, or artistic work, the nature and relevance of which is not explained by the writer but relies on the reader's familiarity with what is thus mentioned. The technique of allusion is an economical means of calling upon the history or the literary tradition that author and reader are assumed to share, although some poets (notably Ezra Pound and T. S. Eliot) allude to areas of quite specialized knowledge. In his poem 'The Statues' (1939)—

> When Pearse summoned Cuchulain to his side
> What stalked through the Post Office?

—W. B. Yeats **alludes** both to the hero of Celtic legend (Cuchulain) and to the new historical hero (Patrick Pearse) of the 1916 Easter Rising, in which the revolutionaries captured the Dublin Post Office. In addition to such *topical* allusions to recent events, Yeats often uses *personal* allusions to aspects of his own life and circle of friends. Other kinds of allusion include the *imitative* (as in *parody), and the *structural*, in which one work reminds us of the structure of another (as Joyce's *Ulysses* refers to Homer's *Odyssey*). Topical allusion is especially important in *satire. *Adjective*: **allusive**.

**Further reading:** Joseph Pucci, *The Full-Knowing Reader* (1998).

**alterity** A *Latinate term meaning 'otherness', and commonly found in philosophy and literary theory since the 1970s. It often arises in analyses of relations between the self and the other (person), in discussions of encounters between different cultures, and in observations upon the difficulty of understanding the art and thought of past ages.

**ambiguity** Openness to different interpretations; or an instance in which some use of language may be understood in diverse ways. Sometimes known as 'plurisignation' or 'multiple meaning', ambiguity became a central concept in the interpretation of poetry after William Empson, in *Seven Types of Ambiguity* (1930), defended it as a source of poetic richness rather than a fault of imprecision. Ambiguities in everyday speech are usually resolved by their context, but isolated statements ('they are hunting dogs') or very compressed phrases like book titles (*Scouting for Boys*) and newspaper headlines (GENERALS FLY BACK TO FRONT) can remain ambiguous. The verbal compression and uncertain context of much poetry often produce ambiguity: in the first line of Keats's 'Ode on a Grecian Urn',

> Thou still unravish'd bride of quietness,

'still' may mean 'even yet' or 'immobile', or both. The simplest kind of ambiguity is achieved by the use of *homophones in the *pun. On a

larger scale, a character (e.g. Hamlet, notoriously) or an entire story may
display ambiguity. *See also* DOUBLE ENTENDRE, EQUIVOQUE, MULTI-
ACCENTUALITY, POLYSEMY.

**American Renaissance** The name sometimes given to a flourishing
of distinctively American literature in the period before the Civil War.
As described by F. O. Matthiessen in his influential critical work
*American Renaissance* (1941), this renaissance is represented by the
work of Ralph Waldo Emerson, H. D. Thoreau, Nathaniel Hawthorne,
Herman Melville, and Walt Whitman. Its major works are Hawthorne's
*The Scarlet Letter* (1850), Melville's *Moby-Dick* (1851), and Whitman's
*Leaves of Grass* (1855). The American Renaissance may be regarded
as a delayed manifestation of *Romanticism, especially in Emerson's
philosophy of *Transcendentalism.

**amoebean verses** [a-mĕ-**bee**-ăn] A poetic form in which two
characters chant alternate lines, *couplets, or *stanzas, in competition or
debate with one another. This form is found in the *pastoral poetry of
Theocritus and Virgil, and was imitated by Spenser in his *Shepheardes
Calender* (1579); it is similar to the *débat*, and sometimes resembles
*stichomythia. *See also* FLYTING.

**amphibrach** [**am**-fib-rak] A metrical *foot consisting of one stressed
syllable between two unstressed syllables, as in the word 'confession'
(or, in *quantitative verse, one long syllable between two shorts). It is
the opposite of the *amphimacer. It was rarely used in classical verse,
but may occur in English in combination with other feet.

**amphimacer** [am-**fim**-ăsĕ] A Greek metrical *foot, also known as the
cretic foot. The opposite of the *amphibrach, it has one short syllable
between two long ones (thus in English verse, one unstressed syllable
between two stressed, as in the phrase 'bowing down'). Sometimes
used in Roman comedy, it occurs rarely in English verse. Blake's 'Spring'
is an example:

Sound the flute! | Now it's mute; | Birds delight | Day and night.

**amplification** A general term in *rhetoric applied to various ways
of expanding upon and thereby emphasizing an initial statement,
usually by some sort of repetition employing devices such as *anaphora,
*auxesis, *climax, and *epistrophe, but sometimes involving *hyperbole
and other effects of rhetorical expansion.

**anachronism** The misplacing of any person, thing, custom, or event outside its proper historical time. Performances of Shakespeare's plays in modern dress use deliberate anachronism, but many fictional works based on history include unintentional examples, the most famous being the clock in Shakespeare's *Julius Caesar*. Anachronism may be used deliberately as a structural principle of a work, as in T. S. Eliot's poem *The Waste Land* (1922) or in W. H. Auden's 'The Fall of Rome' (1947). *Adjective*: **anachronistic**.

**anachrony** [an-**ak**-rŏni] A term used in modern *narratology to denote a discrepancy between the order in which events of the *story occur and the order in which they are presented to us in the *plot. Anachronies take two basic forms: 'flashback' or *analepsis, and 'flashforward' or *prolepsis. *Adjective*: **anachronic**. *See also* IN MEDIAS RES.

**anacoluthon** [an-ă-kŏ-**loo**-thon] A grammatical term for a change of construction in a sentence that leaves the initial construction unfinished. For example, Mr Micawber in Charles Dickens's *David Copperfield*: 'Accidents will occur in the best-regulated families; and in families not regulated by that pervading influence which sanctifies while it enhances the—a—I would say, in short, by the influence of Woman . . .'. *Adjective*: **anacoluthic**.

**Anacreontics** [ă-nayk-ri-**on**-tiks] Verses resembling, either metrically or in subject matter, those of the Greek poet Anacreon (6th century BCE) or of his later imitators in the collection known as the *Anacreontea*. Metrically, the original Anacreontic line combined long (−) and short (⌣) syllables in the pattern ⌣ ⌣ − ⌣ − ⌣ − −. It was imitated in English by Sir Philip Sidney. More often, though, the term refers to the subject-matter: the celebration of love and drinking. Anacreontics in this sense are usually written in short *trochaic lines, as in Tom Moore's translated *Odes of Anacreon* (1800):

Hither haste, some cordial soul! Give my lips the brimming bowl.

**anacrusis** (plural **-uses**) The appearance of an additional unstressed syllable or syllables at the beginning of a verse line, before the regular metrical pattern begins.

**anadiplosis** [an-ă-di-**ploh**-sis] (plural **-oses**) A *rhetorical figure of repetition in which a word or phrase appears both at the end of one clause, sentence, or stanza, and at the beginning of the next, thus linking the two units, as in the final line of Shakespeare's 36th sonnet:

As thou being mine, mine is thy good report.

*See also* CLIMAX.

**anagnorisis** [an-ag-**nor**-ĭs-is] (plural **-ises**) The Greek word for 'recognition' or 'discovery', used by Aristotle in his *Poetics* to denote the turning point in a drama at which a character (usually the *protagonist) recognizes the true state of affairs, having previously been in error or ignorance. The classic instance is Oedipus' recognition, in *Oedipus Tyrannus*, that he himself has killed his own father Laius, married his mother Jocasta, and brought the plague upon Thebes. The anagnorisis is usually combined with the play's *peripeteia or reversal of fortunes, in comedy as in tragedy. Similarly, the plots of many novels involve crucial anagnorises, e.g. Pip's discovery, in Charles Dickens's *Great Expectations* (1860–61), that Magwitch rather than Miss Havisham has been his secret benefactor. *See also* DÉNOUEMENT.

**Further reading:** Terence Cave, *Recognitions* (1988).

**anagogical** [an-ă-**goj**-ik-ăl] Revealing a higher spiritual meaning behind the literal meaning of a text. Medieval Christian *exegesis of the Bible (*see* TYPOLOGY) reinterpreted many episodes of Hebrew scripture according to four levels of meaning: the literal, the allegorical, the moral, and the anagogical. Of these, the anagogical sense was seen as the highest, relating to the ultimate destiny of humanity according to the Christian scheme of universal history, whereas the allegorical and moral senses refer respectively to the Church and to the individual soul. **Anagogy** or **anagoge** is thus a specialized form of allegorical interpretation, which reads texts in terms of *eschatology. *See also* ALLEGORY.

**analects** A collection of 'gleanings' or fragments of writing and sayings attributed to a given author. The Confucian Analects are *maxims and other sayings attributed to Confucius, who did not leave behind any written works. The term is also applied to selected passages from a published author's various writings.

**analepsis** (plural **-pses**) A form of *anachrony by which some of the events of a story are related at a point in the narrative after later story-events have been recounted. Commonly referred to as retrospection or flashback, analepsis enables a storyteller to fill in background information about characters and events. A narrative that begins *in medias res* will include an **analeptic** account of events preceding the point at which the tale began. *See also* PROLEPSIS.

**analogy** Illustration of an idea by means of a more familiar idea that is similar or parallel to it in some significant features, and thus said to be **analogous** to it. Analogies are often presented in the form of an extended *simile, as in Blake's *aphorism: 'As the caterpillar chooses the fairest leaves to lay her eggs on, so the priest lays his curse on the fairest joys.' In literary history, an **analogue** is another story or plot which is parallel or similar in some way to the story under discussion. *Verb*: **analogize**.

**anapaest** [an-ă-pest] (US **anapest**) A metrical *foot made up of two unstressed syllables followed by a stressed syllable, as in the word 'interrupt' (or, in *quantitative verse, two short syllables followed by a long one). Originally a Greek marching beat, adopted by some Greek and Roman dramatists, the *rising rhythm of **anapaestic** (or **anapestic**) verse has sometimes been used by poets in English to echo energetic movement, notably in Robert Browning's 'How they Brought the Good News from Ghent to Aix' (1845):

> Not a word to each other; we kept the great pace
> Neck by neck, stride by stride, never changing our place.

Others have used anapaestic verse for tones of solemn complaint, as in this famous line from Swinburne's 'Hymn to Proserpine' (1866):

> Thou hast conquered, O pale Galilean; the world has grown grey
> from thy breath.

Lines made up of anapaests alone are rare in English verse, though; more often they are used in combination with other feet. The commonest anapaestic verse form in English, the *limerick, usually omits the first syllable in its first, second, and fifth lines. *See also* METRE, TRIPLE METRE.

**anaphora** [a-**naf**-ŏ-ră] A rhetorical *figure of repetition in which the same word or phrase is repeated in (and usually at the beginning of) successive lines, clauses, or sentences. Found very often in both verse and prose, it was a device favoured by Dickens and used frequently in the *free verse of Walt Whitman. These lines by Emily Dickinson illustrate the device:

> Mine—by the Right of the White Election!
> Mine—by the Royal Seal!
> Mine—by the Sign in the Scarlet prison
> Bars—cannot conceal!

*Adjective*: **anaphoral** or **anaphoric**. *See also* EPISTROPHE.

**anaptyxis** The insertion of an additional syllable in the middle of a word, usually after a stressed initial syllable and before *r* or *l*, as with *Henery* for Henry or *Engerland* for England. Poets sometimes, and songwriters more frequently resort to this device in order to maintain metrical regularity. Dickens produces a similar effect in *Bleak House* when the bombastic preacher Mr Chadband enthuses about 'the light of Terewth', i.e. Truth.

**anatomy** A written analysis of some subject, which purports to be thorough and comprehensive. The famous model for this literary form is Robert Burton's *Anatomy of Melancholy* (1621). The Canadian critic Northrop Frye, in *Anatomy of Criticism* (1957), discusses the anatomy as an important category of fiction similar to the *Menippean satire. A humorous display of extensive and detailed knowledge, as in Melville's account of whaling in *Moby-Dick* (1851) or Thomas Pynchon's rocket-lore in *Gravity's Rainbow* (1973), is characteristic of this *genre.

**Angry Young Men** A term applied by journalists in the 1950s to the authors and *protagonists of some contemporary novels and plays that seemed to sound a note of protest or resentment against the values of the British middle class. The most striking example of the angry young man was Jimmy Porter, the ranting protagonist of John Osborne's play *Look Back in Anger* (1956). Other works then taken to express 'angry' attitudes included Kingsley Amis's *campus novel *Lucky Jim* (1954), and John Braine's novel of social ambition, *Room at the Top* (1957), but the label is more appropriate to the *anti-heroes of these works than to the authors, whose views were hastily misinterpreted as being socially radical.

**Further reading:** Harry Ritchie, *Success Stories* (1988).

***Angst*** The German word for 'anxiety' or 'dread', used by the philosophers of *existentialism—notably the Danish theologian Søren

Kierkegaard in *Begrebet Angst* (*The Concept of Dread*, 1844)—to denote a state of anguish that we feel as we are confronted by the burden of our freedom and the accompanying responsibility to impose values and meanings on an *absurd universe.

**antagonist** The most prominent of the characters who oppose the *protagonist or hero(ine) in a dramatic or narrative work. The antagonist is often a villain seeking to frustrate a heroine or hero; but in those works in which the protagonist is represented as evil, the antagonist will often be a virtuous or sympathetic character, as Macduff is in *Macbeth*.

**antanaclasis** A *figure of speech that makes a *pun or *paronomasia by repeating the same word, or two words sounding alike (*see* HOMOPHONE), but with differing senses.

**anthem** Originally an *antiphon; Wilfred Owen's 'Anthem for Doomed Youth' and W. H. Auden's 'Anthem for St Cecilia's Day' both preserve something of this antiphonal sense. The term is now used more often to denote a song in which the words affirm a collective identity, usually expressing attachment to some nation, institution, or cause. Anthems have been adopted, formally or informally, by states, schools, sports clubs, and social movements of all kinds.

**anthology** A collection of poems or other short writings chosen from various authors, usually as favourite pieces exhibiting the best of their kind. The term is Greek, meaning a garland of flowers. Various early anthologies of Greek *epigrams and other short poems were gathered and consolidated in about 900 CE by the Byzantine scholar Constantine Cephalas into what we now refer to simply as the Greek Anthology, which survives in two medieval manuscript versions. In modern times, various prose anthologies have appeared, exhibiting short stories, speeches, or extracts from longer prose works of all kinds. A compiler of anthologies is an **anthologist**, and a poem or prose piece selected for an anthology is said to have been **anthologized**.

**anticlimax** An abrupt lapse from growing intensity to triviality in any passage of dramatic, narrative, or descriptive writing, with the effect of disappointed expectation or deflated suspense. Where the effect is unintentionally feeble or ridiculous it is known as *bathos; but **anticlimactic** descent from the sublime to the ludicrous can also be used deliberately for comic effect. Byron employs comic anticlimax repeatedly in *Don Juan*, as in these lines from Canto II (1819), which describe the survivors of a shipwreck:

> Though every wave roll'd menacing to fill,
>   And present peril all before surpass'd,
> They grieved for those who perished with the cutter
> And also for the biscuit-casks and butter.

The device is an important feature of W. H. Auden's verse style, used less for comic effect than as part of a deflating *realism of tone.

**anti-hero (anti-heroine)** A central character in a dramatic or narrative work who lacks the qualities of nobility and magnanimity expected of traditional heroes and heroines in *romances and *epics. Unheroic characters of this kind have been an important feature of the Western *novel, which has subjected idealistic heroism to *parody since Cervantes's *Don Quixote* (1605). Flaubert's Emma Bovary (in *Madame Bovary*, 1857) and Joyce's Leopold Bloom (in *Ulysses*, 1922) are outstanding examples of this antiheroic ordinariness and inadequacy. The anti-hero is also an important figure in modern drama, both in the theatre of the *absurd and in the *tragedies of Arthur Miller, notably *Death of a Salesman* (1949). In these plays, as in many modern novels, the *protagonist is an ineffectual failure who succumbs to the pressure of circumstances. The anti-hero should not be confused with the *antagonist or the *villain.

**anti-masque** A comic and grotesque piece of clowning that sometimes preceded the performance of a *masque (hence the alternative spelling, **antemasque**). Ben Jonson introduced this farcical prelude to some of his masques from 1609 onwards, using it as a kind of *burlesque of the main action.

**antimetabole** [anti-me-**tab**-oli] A *figure of speech in which a pair of words is repeated in reverse order: 'Pleasure's a sin, and sometimes sin's a pleasure' (Byron). This figure is a subtype of *chiasmus.

**anti-novel** A form of experimental fiction that dispenses with certain traditional elements of novel-writing like the analysis of characters' states of mind or the unfolding of a sequential *plot. The term is usually associated with the French *nouveau roman* of Alain Robbe-Grillet, Nathalie Sarraute, and Michel Butor in the 1950s, but has since been extended to include other kinds of fictional experiment that disrupt conventional *narrative expectations, as in some works in English by Flann O'Brien, Vladimir Nabokov, B. S. Johnson, and Christine Brooke-Rose. Antecedents of the anti-novel can be found in the blank pages and comically self-defeating digressions of Sterne's *Tristram Shandy* (1759–67) and in some of the innovations of *modernism, like the absence of narration in Virginia Woolf's *The Waves* (1931). *See also* AVANT-GARDE, POSTMODERNISM.

**antiphon** A song, hymn, or poem in which two voices or choruses respond to one another in alternate verses or *stanzas, as is common in verses written for religious services. *Adjective*: **antiphonal** [an-**tif**-ŏn-ăl]. *See also* AMOEBEAN VERSES, ANTHEM.

**antiphrasis** [an-**tif**-ră-sis] A *figure of speech in which a single word is used in a sense directly opposite to its usual meaning, as in the naming of a giant as 'Tiny' or of an enemy as 'friend'; the briefest form of *irony. *Adjective*: **antiphrastic**.

**anti-Stratfordian** Reluctant to accept William Shakespeare (1564–1616) of Stratford-upon-Avon as the true author of the plays and poems published in his name. Despite the fact that several of Shakespeare's own contemporaries, including Ben Jonson and the compilers of the 1623 First *Folio, clearly acknowledged him as the author of those works, a succession of amateur scholars and conspiracy theorists in the 19th and 20th centuries proposed various alternatives as the 'true' author. Although disagreeing among themselves on the central point of attribution, they shared common ground in their refusal to accept that a provincial glover's son lacking any university education and working as an actor could have written such magnificent works himself: all anti-Stratfordian theories attribute the poems and plays to a better-educated or more socially distinguished contemporary, and most of them propose that William Shakespeare was used as a front-man to disguise the true identity of the hidden genius.

The first candidate in this tradition was the English philosopher, essayist, and lawyer Francis Bacon (1561–1627). The Baconian theory, as it became known, of Shakespearian authorship was launched in 1856 by Delia Bacon in an article for *Putnam's Magazine*, and was soon endorsed by Dr William H. Smith's *Bacon and Shakespeare* (1857). Several followers claimed to have discovered in the writings hitherto attributed to Shakespeare elaborate ciphers and numerological codes all pointing to Bacon's authorship. But other hidden hands were detected by similar illogic, including the Cambridge-educated poet-playwright Christopher Marlowe (1564–93), whose death awkwardly predates nearly all of Shakespeare's works; Queen Elizabeth I (1532–1603), whose death predates many of them and whose life left little enough time for secret literary careers; William Stanley, 6th Earl of Derby (1561–1641), who is not known to have had any literary ability; and Edward de Vere, 17th Earl of Oxford (1550–1604), who was at least a theatrical patron and inferior poet, and who became the favoured candidate of anti-Stratfordians in the wake of Thomas J. Looney's book *'Shakespeare' Identified* (1920). The definitive refutation of these theories is to be found in Samuel Schoenbaum's *Shakespeare's Lives* (1970; rev. 1991).

(⊕) SEE WEB LINKS

• Shakespeare Authorship Page: provides evidence for the Stratfordian position.

**antistrophe** [an-**tis**-trŏ-fi] **1.** The returning movement of the Greek dramatic *chorus of dancers, after their first movement or *strophe; hence also the accompanying verse lines recited by the chorus in a *stanza matching exactly the *metre of the preceding strophe. The *odes of Pindar and his imitators conform to a triple structure of strophe, antistrophe, and *epode. **2.** In *rhetoric, antistrophe is also the name given to two rhetorical *figures of repetition: in the first, the order of terms in one clause is reversed in the next ('All for one, and one for all'), this effect being better known as *chiasmus; in the second (also known as *epistrophe), a word or phrase is repeated at the end of several successive clauses, lines, or sentences ('the truth, the whole truth, and nothing but the truth'). *Adjective*: **antistrophic**.

**antithesis** [an-**tith**-ĕ-sis] (plural -**theses**) A contrast or opposition, either rhetorical or philosophical. In *rhetoric, any disposition of words that serves to emphasize a contrast or opposition of ideas, usually by the balancing of connected clauses with parallel grammatical constructions. In Milton's *Paradise Lost* (1667), the characteristics of Adam and Eve are contrasted by antithesis:

> For contemplation he and valour formed,
> For softness she and sweet attractive grace;
> He for God only, she for God in him.

Antithesis was cultivated especially by Pope and other 18th-century poets. It is also a familiar device in prose, as in John Ruskin's sentence, 'Government and cooperation are in all things the laws of life; anarchy and competition the laws of death.' In philosophy, an antithesis is a second argument or principle brought forward to oppose a first proposition or *thesis (*see* DIALECTIC). *Adjective*: **antithetical**.

**antonomasia** [an-ton-ŏ-**may**-ziă] A *figure of speech that replaces a proper name with an *epithet (*the Bard* for Shakespeare), official address (*His Holiness* for a pope), or other indirect description; or one that applies a famous proper name to a person alleged to share some quality associated with it, e.g. *a Casanova, a little Hitler*. Antonomasia is common in *epic poetry: Homer frequently refers to Achilles as Pelides (i.e. son of Peleus). *Adjective*: **antonomastic**. *See also* METONYMY.

**anxiety of influence** In the unusual view of literary history offered by the critic Harold Bloom, a poet's sense of the crushing weight of poetic tradition which he has to resist and challenge in order to make room for his own original vision. Bloom has in mind particularly the mixed feelings of veneration and envy with which the English Romantic poets regarded Milton, as a 'father' who had to be displaced by his 'sons'. This theory represents the development of poetic tradition as a masculine battle of wills modelled on Freud's concept of the Oedipus complex: the 'belated' poet fears the emasculating dominance of the 'precursor' poet and seeks to occupy his position of strength through a process of misreading or *misprision of the parent-poem in the new poem, which is always a distortion of the original. Thus Shelley's 'Ode to the West Wind' is a powerful misreading of Wordsworth's 'Ode: Intimations of Immortality', through which the younger poet seeks to free himself from the hold of his predecessor. Bloom's theory is expounded in *The Anxiety of Influence* (1973), in which he claims that 'the covert subject of most poetry for the last three centuries has been the anxiety of influence, each poet's fear that no proper work remains for him to perform'.

*aperçu* [ap-air-**soo**] An insight. The French word for a 'glimpse', often used to refer to a writer's formulation or discovery of some truth. Also an outline or summary of a story or argument.

**aphorism** A statement of some general principle, expressed memorably by condensing much wisdom into few words: 'Give a man a mask and he will tell you the truth' (Wilde); 'The road of excess leads to the palace of wisdom' (Blake). Aphorisms often take the form of a definition: 'Hypocrisy is a homage paid by vice to virtue' (La Rochefoucauld). An author who composes aphorisms is an **aphorist**. *Adjective*: **aphoristic**. *Verb*: **aphorize**. *See also* APOPHTHEGM, MAXIM, PROVERB.

**apocalyptic** Revealing the secrets of the future through prophecy; or having the character of an **apocalypse** or world-consuming holocaust. Apocalyptic writing is usually concerned with the coming end of the world, seen in terms of a visionary scheme of history, as in Yeats's poem 'The Second Coming' (1920). *See also* ESCHATOLOGY.

**apocrypha** The collective term for writings that were once included among the recognized holy scriptures or among the works of a given author but have since been rejected as inauthentic. In the contexts of Jewish scripture and of the Christian Bible (especially its Protestant versions), the Apocrypha are those texts of various genres, such as the Book of Judith and the Book of Tobit, that have been excluded from the accepted *canon, or relegated to a status beneath it. These are referred to as **apocryphal** writings. Similarly in secular literature, works formerly attributed to a given author but subsequently discredited are called apocryphal. A major instance is the Shakespeare Apocrypha, which includes plays that appeared in the Third *Folio (1664) collection such as *Locrine*, *Sir John Oldcastle*, and *A Yorkshire Tragedy* as well as some plays doubtfully attributed to him at later dates such as *Arden of Faversham* and *Edmund Ironside*.

**Apollonian and Dionysian** Terms for the twin principles which the German philosopher Friedrich Nietzsche detected in Greek civilization in his early work *Die Geburt der Tragödie* (*The Birth of Tragedy*, 1872). Nietzsche was challenging the usual view of Greek culture as ordered and serene, emphasizing instead the irrational element of frenzy found in the rites of Dionysus (the god of intoxication known to the Romans as Bacchus). He associated the Apollonian tendency with the instinct for form, beauty, moderation, and symmetry, best expressed in Greek sculpture, while the Dionysian (or **Dionysiac**) instinct was one of irrationality, violence, and exuberance, found in music. This opposition has some resemblance to that between *classicism and *Romanticism. In Nietzsche's theory of drama, the

Apollonian (in dialogue) and the Dionysian (in choric song) are combined in early Greek tragedy, but then split apart in the work of Euripides; he hoped at first that Wagner's operas would reunite them.

**apologue** Another word for a *fable, usually a *beast fable.

**apology** In the literary sense, a justification or defence of the writer's opinions or conduct, not usually implying (as in the everyday sense) any admission of blame. The major classical precedent is the *Apologia* of Socrates as recorded by Plato (4th century BCE), in which the philosopher defends himself unsuccessfully against the capital charge of impiety before the Athenian court, justifying his role as 'gadfly' to the state. Later writers adopted the title for various kinds of work from literary theory, as in Sidney's *An Apologie for Poetry* (1595), to *autobiography, as in *An Apology for the Life of Mr Colley Cibber, Comedian* (1740) by the much-mocked poet laureate. John Henry Newman's *Apologia Pro Vita Sua* ('apology for his life', 1864) has a greater element of *polemic, justifying his adoption of Roman Catholicism against aspersions cast by Charles Kingsley. An apology is sometimes called an **apologetic**. An **apologist** is more often a defender of some other person's actions, works, or beliefs.

**apophthegm** [ap-ŏ-them] **(apotegm)** An *aphorism or *maxim, especially one of the pithiest kind. Boswell refers to Johnson's famous saying, 'Patriotism is the last refuge of a scoundrel', as an apophthegm. A person who composes apophthegms is an **apophthegmatist**. *Adjective*: **apophthegmatic** or **apothegmatic**.

**aporia** In *rhetoric, a *figure of speech in which a speaker deliberates, or purports to be in doubt about a question, e.g. 'Well, what can one say?', or 'I hardly know which of you is the worse.' Hamlet's famous 'To be or not to be' soliloquy is an extended example. In the critical terminology of *deconstruction, the term is frequently used in the sense of a final impasse or *paradox: a point at which a *text's self-contradictory meanings can no longer be resolved, or at which the text undermines its own most fundamental presuppositions. It is this aporia that deconstructive readings set out to identify in any given work or passage, leading to the claim that the text's meanings are finally 'undecidable'. *Adjective*: **aporetic**.

**aposiopesis** [ap-ŏ-syr-**pee**-sis] (plural **-peses**) A *rhetorical device in which the speaker suddenly breaks off in the middle of a sentence, leaving the sense unfinished. The device usually suggests strong emotion that makes the speaker unwilling or unable to continue. Shakespeare's King Lear is notably given to such unfinished outbursts:

> I will have such revenges on you both
> That all the world shall–

*Adjective*: **aposiopetic**. *See also* ANACOLUTHON.

**apostrophe** [ă-**pos**-trŏ-fi] A rhetorical *figure in which the speaker addresses a dead or absent person, or an abstraction or inanimate object. In classical *rhetoric, the term could also denote a speaker's turning to address a particular member or section of the audience. Apostrophes are found frequently among the speeches of Shakespeare's characters, as when Elizabeth in *Richard III* addresses the Tower of London:

> Pity, you ancient stones, those tender babes
> Whom envy hath immured within your walls.

The figure, usually employed for emotional emphasis, can become ridiculous when misapplied, as in Wordsworth's line

> Spade! with which Wilkinson hath tilled his lands

The apostrophe is one of the *conventions appropriate to the *ode and to the *elegy. The poet's *invocation of a *muse in *epic poetry is a special form of apostrophe. *Verb*: **apostrophize**. *Adjective*: **apostrophic**. *See also* PROSOPOPOEIA.

**Further reading:** William Waters, *Poetry's Touch* (2003).

**apparatus** A collective term (sometimes given in Latin as *apparatus criticus*) for the textual notes, glossary, lists of variant readings, appendices, introductory explanations and other aids to the study of a *text, provided in scholarly editions of literary works or historical documents.

**arbitrary** Lacking any natural basis or substantial justification. In the theory of the *sign elaborated by the Swiss linguist Ferdinand de Saussure, the relationship between the *signifier (the sound-image or written mark) and its *signified (or concept) is described as 'unmotivated' or arbitrary because there is no natural or necessary bond between them, only the convention of a given language. The same applies to the relationship between the sign and the object to which it refers. The **arbitrariness** of these relationships can be shown by comparing the ways in which different languages allocate signifiers to signifieds. Some theorists point out that the sense of randomness attached to the term is misleading, and that the term 'conventional' is preferable.

**Arcadia (Arcady)** An isolated mountainous region of Greece in the central Peloponnese, famed in the ancient world for its sheep and as the home of the god Pan. It was imagined by Virgil in his *Eclogues* (42–37 BCE), and by later writers of *pastorals in the *Renaissance, as an ideal world of rural simplicity and tranquillity. The adjective **Arcadian** can be applied to any such imagined pastoral setting. *See also* IDYLL.

**archaism** [ark-ay-izm] The use of words or constructions that have passed out of the language before the time of writing; or a particular example of such an obsolete word or expression. A common feature of much English poetry from Spenser to Hardy, it rarely appears in prose or in modern verse. Archaism may help to summon up a nostalgic flavour of the past, as in Spenser's use of Chaucerian expressions and in Coleridge's 'Rime of the Ancient Mariner', which imitates old ballads:

> 'There was a ship,' quoth he.
> 'Hold off! unhand me, greybeard loon!'
> Eftsoons his hand dropped he.

Or it may help to maintain metrical regularity, as in the frequent use of the monosyllable *morn* for 'morning'. Keats combines both motives in this line from 'The Eve of St Agnes':

> Though thou forsakest a deceivèd thing

Here the archaic pronunciation maintains the *metre, and supports (with the 'thou') the poem's medieval setting and atmosphere. *See also* DICTION, POETICISM.

**archetype** [ar-ki-typ] A *symbol, theme, setting, or character-type that recurs in different times and places in *myth, *literature, *folklore, dreams, and rituals so frequently or prominently as to suggest (to certain speculative psychologists and critics) that it embodies some essential element of 'universal' human experience. Examples offered by the advocates of *myth criticism include such recurrent symbols as the rose, the serpent, and the sun; common themes like love, death, and conflict;

mythical settings like the paradisal garden; *stock characters like the
*femme fatale*, the hero, and the magician; and some basic patterns of
action and plot such as the quest, the descent to the underworld, or the
feud. The most fundamental of these patterns is often said to be that of
death and rebirth, reflecting the natural cycle of the seasons: the
Canadian critic Northrop Frye put forward an influential model of
literature based on this proposition in *Anatomy of Criticism* (1957).

Archetypal criticism originated in the early 20th century from the
speculations of the British anthropologist J. G. Frazer in *The Golden
Bough* (1890–1915)—a comparative study of mythologies—and from
those of the Swiss psychologist C. G. Jung, who in the 1920s proposed
that certain symbols in dreams and myths were residues of ancestral
memory preserved in the *collective unconscious. More recently, critics
have been wary of the *reductionism involved in the application of such
unverified hypotheses to literary works, and more alert to the cultural
differences that the archetypal approach often overlooks in its search for
universals.

**architectonics** The principle of structure and governing design in an
artistic work, as distinct from its *texture or stylistic details of execution.

**argument** In the specialized literary sense, a brief summary of the
*plot or subject-matter of a long poem (or other work), such as those
prefixed to the books of Milton's *Paradise Lost*; or, in a sense closer to
everyday usage, the set of opinions expounded in a work (especially in
*didactic works) and capable of being *paraphrased as a logical
sequence of propositions.

**Aristotelian** [a-ris-tǒ-**tee**-li-ǎn] Belonging to or derived from the
works of the Greek philosopher Aristotle (384–322 BCE), the most
important of all ancient philosophers in his influence on medieval
science and logic, and on literary theory since the *Renaissance. In his
*Poetics*, Aristotle saw poetry in terms of the imitation or *mimesis of
human actions, and accordingly regarded the *plot or *mythos* as the
basic principle of coherence in any literary work, which must have a
beginning, a middle, and an end. Since the Renaissance, his name has
been associated most often with his concepts of tragic *catharsis,
*anagnorisis, and unity of action (*see* UNITIES). The *Chicago critics were
self-proclaimed Aristotelians in the renewed emphasis they gave to the
importance of plot in literature.

**art for art's sake** The slogan of *Aestheticism in the 19th century, often given in its French form as *l'art pour l'art*. The most important early manifesto for the idea, Théophile Gautier's preface to his novel *Mademoiselle de Maupin* (1835), does not actually use the phrase itself, which is a simplified expression of the principle adopted by many leading French authors and by Walter Pater, Oscar Wilde, and Arthur Symons in England.

**arte mayor** [**ar**-te ma-**yor**] A Spanish metrical term applied to verse employing lines of between eight and fourteen syllables, with four rhythmic stresses in two pairs divided by a *caesura at the middle of the line. The most common form is a twelve-syllable line with the caesura falling after the sixth syllable, the rhythm being predominantly *anapaestic.

**arte menor** [**ar**-te me-**nor**] A Spanish metrical term applied to verse employing lines of between two and eight syllables, with usually only the penultimate syllable being stressed. The term covers a great variety of popular song and verse, mostly rhyming or *assonantal. This kind of verse was deemed the 'minor art' because it is easier to compose than verse in *arte mayor*.

**Arthurian literature** A large body of writings in various languages in the 12th and 13th centuries and thereafter, recounting legends of King Arthur, his sword Excalibur, his queen Guinevere, and his various knights at the court of Camelot. The historical Arthur, if he existed, seems to have been some kind of chieftain in 6th-century Wales. Literary legends about him and his deadly struggle with his treacherous nephew Modred or Mordred began with Geoffrey of Monmouth's *Historia Regum Britanniae* (*c.*1138). The Norman poet Wace expanded this account in his *Roman de Brut* (1155), which introduced the Round Table and the belief in Arthur's eventual resurrection. Wace's story was in turn extended in the early 13th century in the first English version of the legend, the verse history *Brut* by the priest Layamon, who adds the passing of Arthur by boat to Avalon. Meanwhile the French poet Chrétien de Troyes had in his romance *Lancelot* (*c.*1180) developed the romantic story of Sir Lancelot and his adulterous affair with Guinevere. Chrétien also introduced Sir Perceval and the quest for the Holy Grail in his *Perceval* (*c.*1182), as did Wolfram von Eschenbach in his German epic *Parzifal* (*c.*1205).

In the 1220s a further important group of anonymous prose romances appeared in French on the subjects of Lancelot, Merlin, the Holy Grail, and Arthur's death: this body of work, referred to now as the *Vulgate Cycle, formed the chief basis for the major English prose version of the legends, Sir Thomas Malory's *Le Morte Darthur* (completed 1470, published 1485). Malory seems to have drawn also upon two 14th-century English verse narratives, each titled *Morte Arthure*, and upon other sources now lost. In the line from Chrétien to Malory, it is notable that Arthur himself, apart from the episodes of his birth, accession, and death, plays little part and is overshadowed by the loves and adventures of Merlin and of the knights Lancelot, Gawain, Tristram, Perceval, Galahad, and others.

These legends have been adapted and retold in various forms and languages over the centuries, the most ambitious version in English being Alfred Tennyson's sequence of verse narratives published intermittently from 1859 and collected as *Idylls of the King* (1891). *See also* MATTER OF BRITAIN.

**Further reading:** Derek Pearsall, *Arthurian Romance* (2003).

(⊕) SEE WEB LINKS
• Camelot Project, archive of Arthurian materials and links.

**Asclepiad** [as-**klee**-pi-ad]  A Greek poetic *metre named after Asclepiades of Samos (*c*.300 BCE), although it was used earlier in *lyrics and *tragedies. It consists of two or three *choriambs preceded by a *spondee and followed by an *iamb. Employed frequently by Horace and later adopted by the German poet Hölderlin, it is rarely found in English. *Adjective*: **Asclepiadean**.

**aside**  A short speech or remark spoken by a character in a drama, directed either to the audience or to another character, which by *convention is supposed to be inaudible to the other characters on stage. *See also* SOLILOQUY.

**assonance** [ass-ŏn-ăns]  The repetition of identical or similar vowel sounds in the stressed syllables (and sometimes in the following unstressed syllables) of neighbouring words; it is distinct from *rhyme in that the consonants differ although the vowels or *diphthongs match: sw*ee*t dr*ea*ms, h*i*t or m*i*ss. As a substitute for rhyme at the ends of verse lines, assonance (sometimes called vowel rhyme or vocalic rhyme) had a significant function in early Celtic, Spanish, and French *versification (notably in the *chansons de geste*), but in English it has been an optional poetic device used within and between lines of verse for emphasis or musical effect, as in these lines from Tennyson's 'The Lotos-Eaters':

> And round about the keel with faces pale,
> Dark faces pale against that rosy flame,
> The mild-eyed melancholy Lotos-eaters came.

*Adjective*: **assonantal**. *See also* ALLITERATION, CONSONANCE, HALF-RHYME.

**asteismus** A rhetorical term for a facetious reply, usually involving a *pun or pretended misunderstanding of a word used by the previous speaker. A common device of dramatic dialogue, especially in comedies, it was practised relentlessly by Shakespeare, as in the exchange:

POLONIUS:  I did enact Julius Caesar. I was killed i'th'Capitol. Brutus killed me.

HAMLET:    It was a brute part of him to kill so capital a calf there.

*See also* ANTANACLASIS, REPARTEE.

**asyndeton** [a-**sin**-dĕt-on] (plural **-deta**) A form of verbal compression which consists of the omission of connecting words (usually conjunctions) between clauses. The most common form is the omission of 'and', leaving only a sequence of phrases linked by commas, as in these sentences from Conrad's 'Heart of Darkness': 'An empty stream, a great silence, an impenetrable forest. The air was thick, warm, heavy, sluggish.' The most famous example is Julius Caesar's boast, *Veni, vidi, vici* ('I came, I saw, I conquered'). Less common is the omission of pronouns, as in Auden's early poem 'The Watershed': 'two there were | Cleaned out a damaged shaft by hand'. Here the relative pronoun 'who' is omitted. *Adjective*: **asyndetic**. *See also* ELLIPSIS, PARATACTIC.

**Attic style (Atticism)** The style of *oratory or prose writing associated with the speeches of the great Attic (i.e. Athenian) orators of the 5th and 4th centuries BCE, including Lysias and Demosthenes. Later Roman writers distinguished the purity and simplicity of these Attic models from the excessive artifice and ornamentation of the 'Asiatic' style that had since developed among the Greeks in Asia Minor.

**aubade** [oh-**bahd**] Also known by its Provençal name *alba* and in German as *Tagelied* (plural *-lieder*), a song or lyric poem lamenting the arrival of dawn to separate two lovers. The form, which has no fixed

metrical pattern, flourished in the late Middle Ages in France; it was
adopted in Germany by Wolfram von Eschenbach and in England by
Chaucer, whose *Troilus and Criseyde* includes a fine aubade. Later
English examples include Donne's 'The Sunne Rising' and Act III, scene
v of Shakespeare's *Romeo and Juliet*. Modern adaptations of the
tradition include aubades by W. H. Auden, William Empson, and
Philip Larkin.

*Aufklärung*  The German term for the *Enlightenment.

**Augustan Age**  The greatest period of Roman literature, adorned by
the poets Virgil, Ovid, Horace, and Propertius. It is named after the reign
(27 BCE–14 CE) of the emperor Augustus, but many literary historians
prefer to date the literary period from the death of Julius Caesar in
44 BCE, thus including the early works of Virgil and Horace. In English
literary history, the term is usually applied to the period from the
accession of Queen Anne (1702) to the deaths of Pope and Swift
(1744–5), although John Dryden, whose major translation of Virgil's
works appeared in 1697, may also be regarded as part of the English
phenomenon known as **Augustanism**. The Augustans, led by Pope and
Swift, wrote in conscious emulation of the Romans, adopted their
literary forms (notably the *epistle and the *satire), and aimed to create a
similarly sophisticated urban literary milieu: a characteristic preference
in Augustan literature, encouraged by the periodicals of Addison and
Steele, was for writing devoted to the public affairs and coffee-house
gossip of the imperial capital, London. *See also* NEOCLASSICISM.
**Further reading:** Pat Rogers, *The Augustan Vision* (1974).

**aureate diction**  A highly ornate ('gilded') poetic *diction favoured
by the *Scottish Chaucerians and some English poets in the 15th
century, notably John Lydgate. The aureate style, perfected by William
Dunbar, is notable for its frequent use of *internal rhyme and of
*coinages adapted from Latin. *Noun*: **aureation**.

**autobiografiction**  A *portmanteau word revived by Max Saunders
in his book *Self Impression* (2010), which provides both a history of the
term (it had been coined by the English poet Stephen Phillips in 1906)
and a classification of its sub-types. It covers a range of narratives that
are ambiguously located in the borderlands between recognized forms
of *life writing (autobiography, memoir, biography, diary, etc.) and

fiction. These include novels presented in the form of a diary written by the *protagonist, as in Jean-Paul Sartre's *La Nausée* (1938) or Helen Fielding's *Bridget Jones's Diary* (1996); memoirs of the real author purporting to be those of a fictional character, as in Siegfried Sassoon's *Complete Memoirs of George Sherston* (1937); and autobiographies purporting to be biographical accounts written by another real person, as with Gertrude Stein's *Autobiography of Alice B. Toklas* (1933) and Thomas Hardy's *Life of Thomas Hardy* (1928–30, published posthumously under the name of his widow Florence Hardy).

The most common kind of autobiografiction, though, is the 'autobiographical novel' (sometimes called an **autofiction**, a coinage of 1977 by the French writer Serge Doubrouwsky) in which some of the author's own experiences are presented as those of a fictional protagonist, whether in the form of a first-person memoir, as with Marcel Proust's novel-sequence *A la recherche du temps perdu* (1913–27) or as a third-person account, as in Dorothy Richardson's novel-sequence *Pilgrimage* (1915–38). Saunders distinguishes all those kinds of autobiografiction proper from **biografictions**, in which the narrator is ostensibly a biographer attempting to reconstruct the life of one who is evidently an invented person, as in Virginia Woolf's mock-biographical novel *Orlando* (1928), and from imaginary portraits, which are character-sketches of invented subjects, although sometimes with oblique autobiographical reference, as with Walter Pater's *Imaginary Portraits* (1887). Meanwhile, partly in dialogue with Saunders's work, Lucia Boldrini in her book *Autobiographies of Others* (2012) has proposed the term **heterobiography** for the distinct category of novels that are presented in the form of autobiographical reminiscences composed by historical persons who could not be mistaken for the real author, as with Robert Graves's *I, Claudius* (1934) or Peter Ackroyd's *The Last Testament of Oscar Wilde* (1983).

**autobiography** A narrative account of an extended period of some person's life, written by, or presented as having been written by, that person; or the practice of writing such works. Autobiography differs from biography not only in its evidently more subjective narrative point of view but in its inconclusiveness: an **autobiographer** cannot recount her or his own death, whereas a biographer will almost always offer an account of the subject's life to the very end. Many autobiographies indeed restrict their scope to a phase of the author's early life and

conclude at some point long before the time of writing. Autobiography
also differs from other related *genres of *life writing: from the *memoir
in its focus upon the self rather than on notable people and events
that the author has encountered, and from the journal or diary in its
attempt to produce a connected retrospective account.

The term is a modern one, put into circulation in the early
19th century by the English poet Robert Southey, and the genre
itself is predominantly a modern phenomenon, although there are
classic earlier examples of spiritual autobiography relating crises of
conversion, notably the 4th-century *Confessions* of St Augustine, the
mid-16th-century *Vita* of Benvenuto Cellini (published 1728), and
John Bunyan's *Grace Abounding to the Chief of Sinners* (1666). Distinct
from such early 'conversion narratives', the modern and largely secular
tradition of autobiography arose in the late 18th century with the
highly influential *Les Confessions* (1781–8) of Jean-Jacques Rousseau
and in English with the *Memoirs* (1796) of Edward Gibbon. Most
autobiographies are written in prose, but William Wordsworth's *The
Prelude* (1850) is a lengthy account of selected aspects of the poet's
youth written in *blank verse. Since Daniel Defoe's *Moll Flanders*
(1722), many *novels written in the *first-person voice have presented
themselves as autobiographies of fictional persons, as with Charlotte
Brontë's *Jane Eyre: An Autobiography* (1847), and these are often
classified as fictional autobiographies or as pseudo-autobiographical
novels.

The widely used term **autobiographical novel** (often qualified as
'semi-autobiographical'), however, refers not to this pretence but to
a kind of novel, often a *Bildungsroman*, in which the events, settings,
and characters are based upon those of the author's own life: D. H.
Lawrence's *Sons and Lovers* (1913), for example, is told entirely in the
*third person, but its *protagonist, Paul Morel, is clearly a version of
Lawrence's own younger self, and the author's former fiancée Jessie
Chambers easily identified herself as the basis for the fictional 'Miriam'.
So a fictional autobiography such as *Jane Eyre* is a novel disguised as an
autobiography, whereas an autobiographical novel such as *Sons and
Lovers* may be understood to be a kind of autobiography in the form
of a novel.

Not all autobiographies are actually written by their subjects: *The
Autobiography of Malcolm X* (1964), for instance, was written by Alex
Haley on the basis of taped interviews. Such use of a *ghost-writer is now

common in supposed autobiographies by sports stars and other celebrities.

**Further reading:** Linda Anderson, *Autobiography* (2nd edn, 2010); Sidonie Smith and Julia Watson, *Reading Autobiography* (2001).

**automatic writing** A method of composition that tries to dispense with conscious control or mental censorship, transcribing immediately the promptings of the unconscious mind. Some writers in the early days of *Surrealism attempted it, notably André Breton and Philippe Soupault in their work *Les Champs Magnétiques* (1919). W. B. Yeats had earlier conducted similar experiments with Georgie Hyde-Lees after their marriage in 1917; these séances influenced the mystical system of his prose work *A Vision* (1925).

*auto sacramental* (plural *autos sacramentales*) A Spanish form of allegorical religious play in one act performed at the feast of Corpus Christi between the 16th and 18th centuries. These were didactic plays on biblical or historical subjects, usually culminating in the display of a large host and chalice symbolizing the sacrament of the Eucharist; hence the term 'sacramental play'. Performances were provided by civic authorities, as open-air events with scenery on moveable carts. The most important examples are those written by the major playwright Calderón (Pedro Calderón de la Barca, 1600–1681), who claimed to have written more than 70 such pieces, having held for many years a monopoly on their composition in Madrid. The *autos sacramentales* were eventually banned by order of Charles III in 1765.

**autotelic** Having, as an artistic work, no end or purpose beyond its own existence. The term was used by T. S. Eliot in 1923 and adopted by *New Criticism to distinguish the self-referential nature of literary art from *didactic, philosophical, critical, or biographical works that involve practical reference to things outside themselves: in the words of the American poet Archibald MacLeish, 'A poem should not mean | But be'. A similar idea is implied in the theory of the 'poetic function' put forward in *Russian Formalism.

**auxesis** A *figure of speech that lists a series of things in ascending order of importance, as in this line from Shakespeare's *Richard II*:

O'erthrows thy joys, friends, fortune, and thy state

*Adjective*: **auxetic**. *See also* CLIMAX.

**avant-garde** The French military and political term for the vanguard
of an army or political movement, extended since the late 19th century
to that body of artists and writers who are dedicated to the idea of art
as experiment and revolt against tradition. Ezra Pound's view, that
'Artists are the antennae of the race', is a distinctly modern one,
implying a duty to stay ahead of one's time through constant innovation
in forms and subjects. Peter Bürger's book *Theory of the Avant-garde*
(1984) proposed a distinction between modernist innovation in general
and the true *avant-garde*, which for him means those who set out to
destroy the very idea of Art, principally the *Dada group. Some
commentators on *modernism have adopted Bürger's narrower
definition, while others have retained a more inclusive model.

**ballad** A *folk song or orally transmitted poem telling in a direct and dramatic manner some popular story usually derived from a tragic incident in local history or legend. The story is told simply, impersonally, and often with vivid dialogue. Ballads are normally composed in *quatrains with alternating four-stress and three-stress lines, the second and fourth lines rhyming (*see* BALLAD METRE); but some ballads are in *couplet form, and some others have six-line *stanzas. Appearing in many parts of Europe in the late Middle Ages, ballads flourished particularly strongly in Scotland from the 15th century onwards. Since the 18th century, educated poets outside the folk-song tradition—notably Coleridge and Goethe—have written imitations of the popular ballad's form and style: Coleridge's 'Rime of the Ancient Mariner' (1798) is a celebrated example. The art of composing ballads is called **balladry**, as is any large corpus of ballads.

**Further reading:** David Atkinson, *The English Traditional Ballad* (2002).

**((🌐)) SEE WEB LINKS**

• Bodleian Library Broadside Ballads site with international links to other ballad archives.

**ballade** [bal-**ahd**] A form of French *lyric poem that flourished in the 14th and 15th centuries, notably in the work of François Villon. It normally consists of three *stanzas of eight lines rhyming *ababbcbc*, with an *envoi* (i.e. a final half-stanza) of four lines rhyming *bcbc*. The last line of the first stanza forms a *refrain which is repeated as the final line of the subsequent stanzas and of the *envoi*. Conventionally, the *envoi* opens with an address to a prince or lord. Variant forms include the ballade with ten-line stanzas and a five-line *envoi*, and the double ballade with six stanzas and an optional *envoi*. Poets who have used this very intricate form in English include Chaucer and Swinburne.

**ballad metre (ballad stanza)** The usual form of the folk ballad and its literary imitations, consisting of a *quatrain in which the first and third lines have four stresses while the second and fourth have three stresses.

Usually only the second and fourth lines rhyme. The rhythm is basically
*iambic, but the number of unstressed syllables in a line may vary, as
in this *stanza from the traditional 'Lord Thomas and Fair Annet':

> 'O art thou blind, Lord Thomas?' she said,
> 'Or canst thou not very well see?
> Or dost thou not see my own heart's blood
> Runs trickling down my knee?'

This *metre may also be interpreted (and sometimes printed) as a
couplet of seven-stress lines, as in Kipling's 'Ballad of East and West'
(1889):

> The Colonel's son has taken horse, and a raw rough dun was he,
> With the mouth of a bell and the heart of Hell and the head of a
> gallows-tree.

*See also* COMMON MEASURE.

**barcarole** Literally a 'boat song', from the Italian *barca*, but also any
poem or song about boats, rowing, sailing, or the world of water
generally. The best-known English example is Andrew Marvell's
'Bermudas' (1681).

**bard** A poet who was awarded privileged status in ancient Celtic
cultures, and who was charged with the duty of celebrating the laws and
heroic achievements of his people. In modern Welsh usage, a bard is a
poet who has participated in the annual poetry festival known as the
Eisteddfod. The nostalgic mythology of *Romanticism tended to imagine
the bards as solitary visionaries and prophets. Since the 18th century,
the term has often been applied more loosely to any poet, and as a
fanciful title for Shakespeare in particular. *Adjective*: **bardic**.

**bardolatry** [bar-**dol**-ătri] Excessive veneration of Shakespeare. Ben
Jonson said of Shakespeare, 'I loved the man, and do honour his
memory, on this side idolatry, as much as any.' A **bardolater** is one who
goes even further in revering 'the Bard'. *Adjective*: **bardolatrous**.

**baroque** [bă-**rok**] Eccentric or lavishly ornate in style. The term is
used more precisely in music and in art history than it is in literary
history, where it usually refers to the most artificial poetic styles of the
early 17th century, especially those known as *Gongorism and
*Marinism after the Spanish poet Luis de Góngora and the Italian poet
Giovanbattista Marini, and more generally as *conceptismo* in Spanish

and as *concettismo* and *Secentismo* in Italian. In English, the ornate prose style of Sir Thomas Browne may be called baroque, as may the strange *conceits of the *metaphysical poets, especially Richard Crashaw. Some critics have tried to extend the term to Milton and the later works of Shakespeare as well. *See also* MANNERISM, ROCOCO.

**Further reading:** Peter Davidson, *The Universal Baroque* (2008).

**bathos** [bay-thos] A lapse into the ridiculous by a poet aiming at elevated expression. Whereas *anticlimax can be a deliberate poetic effect, bathos is an unintended failure. Pope named this stylistic blemish from the Greek word for 'depth', in his *Peri Bathous, or the Art of Sinking in Poetry* (1727). This example comes from Dryden's *Annus Mirabilis* (1667):

> The Eternal heard, and from the heavenly quire
> Chose out the Cherub with the flaming sword
> And bad him swiftly drive the approaching fire
> From where our naval magazines were stored.

Wordsworth, Whitman, and other poets who seek to dignify humble subjects are especially vulnerable to such lapses. *Adjective*: **bathetic**.

**beast fable** The commonest type of *fable, in which animals and birds speak and behave like human beings in a short tale usually illustrating some moral point. The fables attributed to Aesop (6th century BCE) and those written in verse by Jean de la Fontaine (from 1668) are the best known, along with the fables of Brer Rabbit adapted by the American journalist Joel Chandler Harris from black *folklore in his 'Uncle Remus' stories (from 1879). A related form is the **beast epic**, which is usually a longer tale written in pseudo-*epic style. Pierre de Saint-Cloud's *Roman de Renart* (1173) was an influential beast epic containing the Chanticleer story later adapted by Chaucer in the *Nun's Priest's Tale*. There were many other beast epics of Reynard the Fox in late-medieval France and Germany.

**Further reading:** Jill Mann, *From Aesop to Reynard* (2009).

**Beat writers** A group of American writers in the late 1950s, led by the poet Allen Ginsberg and the novelist Jack Kerouac. Writers of the 'beat generation' dropped out of middle-class society in search of 'beatific' ecstasy through drugs, sex, and Zen Buddhism. Their loose styles favour spontaneous self-expression and recitation to jazz accompaniment. The principal works of the group are Ginsberg's *Howl* (1956) and

Kerouac's *On the Road* (1957). Significant contributions in poetry were Gregory Corso's *Gasoline* (1958) and Gary Snyder's *Riprap* (1959); while in prose, the group's mentor William S. Burroughs published *The Naked Lunch* in 1959. The poet Lawrence Ferlinghetti was another leading figure. The Beats had a strong influence on the 'counter-culture' of the 1960s.

**Further reading:** Ann Charters, *The Portable Beat Reader* (1992).

**belatedness** In Harold Bloom's theory of literary history (*see* ANXIETY OF INFLUENCE), the predicament of the poet who feels that previous poets have already said all that there is to say, leaving no room for new creativity.

**belles-lettres** [bel-**letr**] The French term for 'fine writing', originally used (as in 'fine art') to distinguish artistic literature from scientific or philosophical writing. Since the 19th century, though, the term has more often been used dismissively to denote a category of elegant essay-writing and lightweight literary chatter, of which much was published in Britain in the late 19th and early 20th centuries: Max Beerbohm's essays and Andrew Lang's *Letters to Dead Authors* (1896) are examples. An author of such elegant trifles is a **belletrist**. *Adjective*: **belletristic**.

**bestiary** A description of animal life in verse or prose, in which the characteristics of real and fabulous beasts (like the phoenix or the unicorn) are given edifying religious meanings. This kind of *allegory was popular in the Middle Ages, and survives in some later children's books as well as in the rare modern example of J. L. Borges's *Book of Imaginary Beings* (1969). *See also* BEAST FABLE, EMBLEM.

**Further reading:** Debra Hassig, *Medieval Bestiaries* (1995).

**(⊕) SEE WEB LINKS**
• Aberdeen Bestiary Project, a well-illustrated archive.

**bibliography** The description of books: **1.** A systematic list of writings by a given author or on a given subject. **2.** The study of books as material objects, involving technical analysis of paper, printing methods, bindings, page-numbering, publishing history, and library holdings. A compiler of bibliographies or a practitioner of bibliography is a **bibliographer**. *Adjectives*: **bibliographic**, **bibliographical**.

**Further reading:** Philip Gaskell, *A New Introduction to Bibliography* (2nd edn, 1985).

*Bildungsroman* [bil-duungz-raw-mahn] (plural *-ane*) A kind of
novel that follows the development of the hero or heroine from
childhood or adolescence into adulthood, through a troubled quest for
identity. The term ('formation-novel') comes from Germany, where
Goethe's *Wilhelm Meisters Lehrjahre* (1795–6) set the pattern for later
*Bildungsromane*. Many outstanding novels of the 19th and early 20th
centuries follow this pattern of personal growth: Dickens's *David
Copperfield* (1849–50), for example. When the novel describes the
formation of a young artist, as in Joyce's *A Portrait of the Artist as a
Young Man* (1916), it may also be called a *\*Künstlerroman*.

**Further reading:** Franco Moretti, *The Way of the World* (1987).

**binary opposition** The principle of contrast between two mutually
exclusive terms: on/off, up/down, left/right etc; an important concept
of \*structuralism, which sees such distinctions as fundamental to all
language and thought. The theory of \*phonology developed by Roman
Jakobson uses the concept of 'binary features', which are properties
either present or absent in any \*phoneme: voicing, for example is
present in /z/ but not in /s/. This concept has been extended to
anthropology by Claude Lévi-Strauss (in such oppositions as
nature/culture, raw/cooked, inedible/edible), and to \*narratology
by A. J. Greimas (*see* ACTANT).

**biography** *See* p. 40.

**black comedy** A kind of drama (or, by extension, a non-dramatic
work) in which disturbing or sinister subjects like death, disease, or
warfare, are treated with bitter amusement, usually in a manner
calculated to offend and shock. Prominent in the theatre of the \*absurd,
black comedy is also a feature of Joe Orton's *Loot* (1965). A similar
**black humour** is strongly evident in modern American fiction from
Nathanael West's *A Cool Million* (1934) to Joseph Heller's *Catch-22*
(1961) and Kurt Vonnegut's *Slaughterhouse-Five* (1969).

**Black Mountain poets** A group of American poets of the 1950s
identified as distinctive by Donald Allen in his influential anthology *The
New American Poetry: 1945–1960* (1960). The leading figures in this
group were associated with Black Mountain College, a tiny experimental
academy established in 1933 near Asheville, North Carolina. The
group's leader was Charles Olson, who taught at the College from 1948,
as its Rector from 1951 until its closure in 1956. He derived his poetic

## BIOGRAPHY

A narrative history of the life of some person; or the practice of writing such works. Most biographies provide an account of the life of a notable individual from birth to death, or in the case of living persons from birth to the time of writing; but some treat the connected lives of paired subjects or of groups (known as 'group biography'); and since the late 20th century the term has been stretched to cover accounts of non-human subjects such as houses, cities, or commodities, in which case 'a biography' really means an intimate or gossipy history. The Western tradition of biography originates with the Greek historian Plutarch and his *Bioi paralleloi* (*Parallel Lives*, *c.*100 CE), in which he compares and contrasts the virtues of several Greek leaders with their Roman counterparts. Sir Thomas North's English translation of this work (1579) became a main source for Shakespeare's Roman plays. Medieval **biographical** writing was restricted to works in praise of monarchs or of saints (for the latter, *see* HAGIOGRAPHY). The modern tradition in English, which has generally been more vigorous than in other languages, may be dated from Izaak Walton's *Life of John Donne* (1640), but its most influential founder, as **biographer**, subject, and theorist, was Samuel Johnson (1709–84), who wrote *The Life of Mr Richard Savage* (1744), the important essay 'On the Genius of Biography' (1750), and the long sequence of *Lives of the English Poets* (1779–81) before himself becoming the subject of the most famous biography in the language, James Boswell's *Life of Samuel Johnson* (1791).

In the 19th century biography became a literary industry, consolidated in great national reference works such as the French *Biographie universelle* (ed. L.-G. Michaud, 1811–28) and the British *Dictionary of National Biography* (ed. Leslie Stephen, 1885–90). In reaction against the often turgidly pious works of that age, a new movement emerged from 1918, known as the **new biography**, led by Lytton Strachey in England and André Maurois in France, in which biography was treated as an imaginative art in which invented dialogues, *interior monologues and other techniques borrowed from the *novel were employed. The new biography was also less reverential towards its subjects, notably in Strachey's landmark sequence of biographical essays, *Eminent Victorians* (1918). The 20th century also saw the emergence of *psychobiography, informed by psychoanalytic theories of development, and of sensational biographies exposing the sexual and other personal secrets of famous figures.

Biography has a number of *subgenres, of which the most important is *autobiography, in which the subject and the author are the same person. Other recognized types are distinguished by the walk of life in which the subject was noted, e.g. political, military, artistic, theatrical, scientific, sporting; among these, **literary biography** retains a favoured position. An unusually disreputable minor form, practised mostly in the United States, is the **campaign biography**, a one-sidedly glowing account of a candidate for political office: Nathaniel Hawthorne wrote one in 1852 for his friend Franklin Pierce, who won the US Presidency and rewarded the author with the consulship at Liverpool.

**Further reading:** Hermione Lee, *Biography: A Very Short Introduction* (2009).

principles from the examples of Ezra Pound and William Carlos Williams, and summarized these in his essay 'Projective Verse' (1950). His chief disciples were Robert Creeley, who briefly taught at the College (1954–5), also editing the *Black Mountain Review* (seven issues, 1954–7), and Robert Duncan, who briefly joined the faculty. Among their students were the poets Ed Dorn, Joel Oppenheimer, John Wieners, and John Williams, while a few others who never attended the College, including Paul Blackburn, Larry Eigner, and Denise Levertov, became associated with the group by publishing work in their *Review* or in the sympathetic magazine *Origin* (1951–7). The common feature of their work was a rejection of regular lines, *metres, and *stanzas in favour of a kind of *open form in which the shape and movement of the poem evolve spontaneously in exploratory response to its subject.

**Further reading:** Edward Halsey Foster, *Understanding the Black Mountain Poets* (1994).

**blank verse** Unrhymed lines of iambic *pentameter, as in these final lines of Tennyson's 'Ulysses' (1842):

> One equal temper of heroic hearts,
> Made weak by time and fate, but strong in will
> To strive, to seek, to find, and not to yield.

Blank verse is a very flexible English verse form which can attain rhetorical grandeur while echoing the natural rhythms of speech and allowing smooth *enjambment. First used (*c.*1540) by Henry Howard, Earl of Surrey, it soon became both the standard *metre for dramatic poetry and a widely used form for *narrative and meditative poems. Much of the finest verse in English—by Shakespeare, Milton, Wordsworth, Tennyson, and Stevens—has been written in blank verse. In other languages, notably Italian (in *hendecasyllables) and German, blank verse has been an important medium for poetic drama. Blank verse should not be confused with *free verse, which has no regular metre.

**Further reading:** Robert B. Shaw, *Blank Verse* (2007).

**blazon (blason)** A poetic catalogue of a woman's admirable physical features, common in Elizabethan *lyric poetry: an extended example is Sidney's 'What tongue can her perfections tell?' The *Petrarchan conventions of the blazon include a listing of parts from the hair down, and the use of *hyperbole and *simile in describing lips like coral, teeth like pearls, and so on. These conventions are mocked in the tradition of the **counter-blazon**, of which the best-known example is Shakespeare's 130th sonnet, 'My mistress' eyes are nothing like the sun'.

**block form** The arrangement of lines of verse into a continuous sequence that is not divided into *stanzas or *verse paragraphs. The term is a recent substitute for the traditional category of *stichic verse, although it may be applied to poems employing varying lengths of line, whereas stichic verse is normally expected to follow the same *metre throughout. A poem written in this form is sometimes called a **block poem**.

**Bloomsbury group** A loose *coterie of writers linked by friendship to the homes of Vanessa Stephen (from 1907 Vanessa Bell) and her sister Virginia (from 1912 Virginia Woolf) in Bloomsbury—the university quarter of London near the British Museum—from about 1906 to the late 1930s. In addition to the sisters and their husbands—Clive Bell, the art critic, and Leonard Woolf, a political journalist—the group included the novelist E. M. Forster, the biographer Lytton Strachey, the economist John Maynard Keynes, and the art critic Roger Fry. It had no doctrine or aim, despite a shared admiration for the moral philosophy of G. E. Moore, but the group had some importance as a centre of modernizing liberal opinion in the 1920s, and later as the subject of countless memoirs and biographies.

**Further reading:** S. P. Rosenbaum, *Aspects of Bloomsbury* (1998).

**bluestocking (blue-stocking)** A disparaging term for a woman devoted to literary or scholarly pursuits. The name comes from the Blue Stocking social circle of London intellectuals of the second half of the 18th century, so nicknamed after the unorthodox evening wear of one regular participant, Benjamin Stillingfleet, who wore cheap blue worsted stockings instead of the finer black silk variety. The original Blue Stocking circle was an interlinked network of literary *salons notable for encouraging intelligent conversation among women and men. From the early 1750s, its receptions hosted by Mrs Elizabeth Vesey, Mrs Elizabeth Montagu, Mrs Frances Boscawen, and others substituted conversation and tea-drinking for card-games and alcohol, while also discouraging political talk or swearing. Many of London's leading literary men were regular guests, including Samuel Johnson, Horace Walpole, Samuel Richardson, James Boswell, and the actor-manager David Garrick. The poet and playwright Hannah More (1745–1833) was a significant beneficiary of this group's encouragement, which she repaid by praising its virtues in her poem *Bas Bleu* (1786). The dismissive application of the term to intellectual women in general became current in the 19th century, but died out as attitudes to women's education changed.

**(⊕) SEE WEB LINKS**

• The Bluestocking Archive.

**bob and wheel** A short sequence of rhymed lines that concludes the larger unrhymed *strophes of *Sir Gawain and the Green Knight* and some other Middle English *romances. It consists of one short line (the bob) with a single stress, followed by four three-stress lines (the wheel) of which the second and fourth lines rhyme with the bob.

**bodice-ripper** A popular modern variety of *romance that emphasizes the sexual excitement of seduction and 'ravishment', usually in colourful settings based on the conventions of the *historical novel and peopled by pirates, highwaymen, wenches, etc. A classic example is Kathleen Winsor's best-selling romance, *Forever Amber* (1944).

**bombast** Extravagantly inflated and grandiloquent *diction, disproportionate to its subject. It was a common feature of English drama of Shakespeare's age, and of later *heroic drama. Marlowe is known especially for the **bombastic** ranting of his *Tamburlaine the Great* (1590):

> Our quivering lances, shaking in the air,
> And bullets, like Jove's dreadful thunderbolts,
> Enroll'd in flames and fiery smouldering mists,
> Shall threat the gods more than Cyclopean wars;
> And with our sun-bright armour, as we march,
> We'll chase the stars from heaven, and dim their eyes
> That stand and muse at our admired arms.

*See also* FUSTIAN, HYPERBOLE, RODOMONTADE.

***bouts-rimés*** [boo-**ree**-may] A parlour-game in which a volunteer is provided with a set of rhyming words or phrases and is then challenged to compose lines of verse which make some sort of sense with these as end-rhymes. The term ('rhymed endings') and the craze came from 17th-century France, whence they spread throughout fashionable European society during the 18th and 19th centuries.

***bovarysme*** [bohv-ar-eezm] A disposition towards escapist day dreaming in which one imagines oneself as a heroine or hero of a *romance and refuses to acknowledge everyday realities. This condition (a later version of Don Quixote's madness) can be found in fictional characters before Emma Bovary, the *protagonist of Gustave Flaubert's novel *Madame Bovary* (1857), gave it her name: for example, Catherine Morland in Jane Austen's *Northanger Abbey* (1818) makes similar confusions between fiction and reality. Novelists have often exposed *bovarysme* to ironic analysis, thus warning against the delusive enchantments of the romance tradition.

**bowdlerize** To censor or expurgate from a literary work those passages considered to be indecent or blasphemous. The word comes from Dr Thomas Bowdler, who published in 1818 *The Family Shakespeare*, 'in which those words or expressions are omitted which cannot with propriety be read aloud in a family'. Many oaths and sexually suggestive speeches were cut, and even entire characters like Doll Tearsheet in *Henry IV, Part Two*. Similarly bowdlerized editions of *Gulliver's Travels* and *Moby-Dick* have been produced for children. *Nouns*: **bowdlerization, bowdlerism**.

**brachylogia** [brak-i-**loh**-jǎ] **(brachiologia; brachylogy; brachiology)** Concision of speech or writing; thus also any condensed form of expression, as for example when Antony in Shakespeare's *Antony and Cleopatra* tells a messenger 'Grates me: the sum', meaning 'This is annoying me; get to the point of what you have to say'. The term is most often applied to expressions involving the omission of conjunctions, as in the figure known as *asyndeton.

**braggadocio** [brag-ǎ-**doh**-chi-oh] A cowardly but boastful man who appears as a *stock character in many comedies; or the empty boasting typical of such a braggart. This sort of character was known in Greek comedy as the **alazon*. When he is a soldier, he is often referred to as the *miles gloriosus* ('vainglorious soldier') after the title of a comedy by the Roman dramatist Plautus. The most famous example in English drama is Shakespeare's Falstaff.

**Brechtian** Belonging to or derived from the work of Bertolt Brecht (1898–1956), German poet, playwright, and dramatic theorist. When applied to the work of other dramatists, the term usually indicates their use of the techniques of *epic theatre, especially the disruption of realistic illusion known as the *alienation effect.

**bricolage** [brik-ŏ-lah*zh*] A French term for improvisation or a piece of makeshift handiwork. It is sometimes applied to artistic works in a sense similar to *collage: an assemblage improvised from materials ready to hand, or the practice of transforming 'found' materials by incorporating them in a new work. *Verb*: **bricoler**.

**broadside** A large sheet of paper printed on one side only, often containing a song or *ballad, and sold by wandering pedlars in Britain from the 16th century until the beginning of the 20th century, when they were superseded by mass-circulation newspapers; they also appeared in the USA in the late 19th century. The broadside ballads were intended to be sung to a well-known tune; often they related topical events, and some were adopted as *folk songs. Broadsides are sometimes called broadsheets.

**broken rhyme** The splitting of a word (not in fact of the rhyme) at the end of a verse line, to allow a rhyme on a syllable other than the final one, which is transferred to the following line. It is a liberty taken for comic effect in light verse, and more rarely used in serious works. Hopkins employed it frequently: the first line of 'The Windhover' ends with the first syllable of 'king/dom' to rhyme with 'wing' in line four.

**bucolic poetry** [bew-**kol**-ik] **(bucolics)** Another term for *pastoral poetry, especially for Virgil's *Eclogues* (42–37 BCE) and later imitations. More loosely, any verse on rustic subjects. *See also* ECLOGUE, IDYLL.

**burden** The *refrain or chorus of a song; or the main theme of a song, poem, or other literary work. A burden is sometimes distinguished from a refrain in that it starts the song or poem, and stands separate from the *stanzas (as in many medieval *carols), whereas a refrain usually appears as the final part of each stanza.

**burlesque** [ber-**lesk**] A kind of *parody that ridicules some serious literary work either by treating its solemn subject in an undignified style (*see* TRAVESTY), or by applying its elevated style to a trivial subject, as in Pope's *mock-epic poem *The Rape of the Lock* (1712–14). Often used in the theatre, burlesque appears in Shakespeare's *A Midsummer Night's Dream* (in the Pyramus and Thisbe play, which mocks the tradition of *interludes), while *The Beggar's Opera* (1728) by John Gay burlesques Italian opera. An early form of burlesque is the Greek *satyr play. In the USA, though, burlesque was also a disreputable form of comic entertainment with titillating dances or striptease. *See also* EXTRAVAGANZA, SATIRE.

**Burns stanza (Burns metre)** A six-line *stanza rhyming *aaabab*, the first three lines and the fifth having four *stresses, and the fourth and sixth having two stresses. Although it was used much earlier in medieval English *romances and Provençal poetry, it is named after the Scottish poet Robert Burns (1759–96), who used it frequently, as in 'A Poet's Welcome to his love-begotten Daughter':

> Welcome! My bonie, sweet, wee dochter!
> Though ye come here a wee unsought for;
> And though your comin I hae fought for,
>> Baith Kirk and Queir;
> Yet by my faith, ye're no unwrought for,
>> That I shall swear!

**Byronic** Belonging to or derived from Lord Byron (1788–1824) or his works. The **Byronic hero** is a character-type found in his celebrated narrative poem *Childe Harold's Pilgrimage* (1812–18), his verse drama *Manfred* (1817), and other works; he is a boldly defiant but bitterly self-tormenting outcast, proudly contemptuous of social norms but suffering for some unnamed sin. Emily Brontë's Heathcliff in *Wuthering Heights* (1847) is a later example. *See also* POÈTE MAUDIT.

**Further reading:** Atara Stein, *The Byronic Hero* (2004).

**cacoethes scribendi** [ka-koh-**eth**-ess skri-**ben**-dee] A mania for writing; or writing regarded as an ingrained bad habit. The Latin phrase, derived from Greek, comes from Juvenal's Seventh Satire, and has been found in English writings since the 16th century.

**cacophony** [kǎ-**ko**-fŏni] Harshness or discordancy of sound; the opposite of *euphony. Usually the result of awkward *alliteration as in tongue-twisters, it is sometimes used by poets for deliberate effect, as in these lines from Robert Browning's 'Caliban upon Setebos':

> And squared and stuck there squares of soft white chalk,
> And, with a fish-tooth, scratched a moon on each,
> And set up endwise certain spikes of tree,
> And crowned the whole with a sloth's skull a-top.

*Adjective*: **cacophonous** or **cacaphonic**. *See also* DISSONANCE.

**cadence** [**kay**-dĕns] The rising and falling *rhythm of speech, especially that of the balanced phrases in *free verse or in prose, as distinct from the stricter rhythms of verse *metre. Also the fall or rise in pitch at the end of a phrase or sentence. *Adjective*: **cadent**.

**caesura** [si-**zew**-rǎ] (plural **-as** or **-ae**) A pause in a line of verse, often coinciding with a break between clauses or sentences. It is usually placed in the middle of the line ('medial caesura'), but may appear near the beginning ('initial') or towards the end ('terminal'). In *scansion, a caesura is normally indicated by the symbol ‖. If it follows a stressed syllable, it is known as a 'masculine' caesura, while if it follows an unstressed syllable, it is 'feminine'. The regular placing of the caesura was an important metrical requirement in much Greek and Latin verse, in the Old English and Middle English *alliterative metre, and in the French *alexandrine; but in the English iambic *pentameter there is scope for artful variation between medial, initial, and terminal positions, and a line may have more than one caesura, or none. In Greek and Latin *prosody, the term is also applied to a break between words within a *foot: the opposite of *diaeresis. *Adjective*: **caesural**.

**Cambridge school** The name sometimes given to an influential group of English critics associated with the University of Cambridge in the 1920s and 1930s. The leading figures were I. A. Richards, F. R. Leavis, Q. D. Leavis, and William Empson. Influenced by the critical writings of Coleridge and of T. S. Eliot, they rejected the prevalent biographical and historical modes of criticism in favour of the 'close reading' of texts. They saw poetry in terms of the reintegration of thought and feeling (*see* DISSOCIATION OF SENSIBILITY), and sought to demonstrate its subtlety and complexity, notably in Empson's *Seven Types of Ambiguity* (1930). The Leavises achieved great influence through the journal *Scrutiny* (1932–53), judging literary works according to their moral seriousness and 'life-enhancing' tendency. *See also* LEAVISITES, PRACTICAL CRITICISM.

A second group sometimes referred to in the contexts of *tragedy and *myth as the Cambridge school, although more often known as the Cambridge Ritualists or the myth-and-ritual school, was made up of the classical scholars Jane Harrison, Gilbert Murray, F. M. Cornford, and A. B. Cook, who in the early 20th century applied the anthropological theories of J. G. Frazer's *The Golden Bough* (1890–1915) to the origins of Greek tragedy, arguing that the drama was derived from religious rituals. Their views influenced the development of *myth criticism.

**Further reading:** Robert Ackerman, *The Myth and Ritual School* (1991).

**camp** A style of performance popularly associated with male homosexual behaviour, in which exaggerated gestures and tones of effeminacy are flaunted and serious subjects are reduced flippantly to sexually suggestive mockery. In the early 20th century, the term was used (as adjective, noun, and verb) simply to denote effeminate homosexual mannerisms or their representation by actors; but in the latter part of that century the camp phenomenon came to be regarded by some writers as a larger aesthetic principle: the novelist Christopher Isherwood suggested that most *baroque art could be regarded as 'high' camp in its cultivation of ornate artifice, and the cultural critic Susan Sontag in her influential essay 'Notes on "Camp"' (1965) saw camp as a version of *Aestheticism in its preference for the artificial over the natural. The subsequent growth of gay literary studies and of *Queer theory has led to new interpretations of camp as a 'transgressive' challenge to social norms of gender because it implies that all gendered identities are more or less stylized performances. In literary contexts, ostentatiously flippant styles cultivated by such writers as Oscar Wilde, Saki, Ronald Firbank, and Joe Orton have been described as camp.

**Further reading:** David Bergman (ed.), *Camp Ground* (1993).

**campus novel** A novel, usually comic or satirical, in which the action is set within the enclosed world of a university (or similar seat of learning) and highlights the follies of academic life. Many novels have presented nostalgic evocations of college days, but the campus novel in the usual modern sense dates from the 1950s: Mary McCarthy's *The Groves of Academe* (1952) and Kingsley Amis's *Lucky Jim* (1954) began a significant tradition in modern fiction including John Barth's *Giles Goat-Boy* (1966), David Lodge's *Changing Places* (1975), and Robertson Davies's *The Rebel Angels* (1982).

**Further reading:** Elaine Showalter, *Faculty Towers* (2005).

**canon** A body of writings recognized by authority. Those books of holy scripture which religious leaders accept as genuine are **canonical**, as are those works of a literary author which scholars regard as authentic. The canon of a national literature is a body of writings especially approved by critics or anthologists and deemed suitable for academic study. **Canonicity** is the quality of being canonical. *Verb*: **canonize**. *See also* CORPUS, OEUVRE.

**Further reading:** Christopher Kuipers, *The Canon* (2007).

**cantar** (plural **cantares**) The Spanish term for a poem originally sung or set to music within an *oral tradition. Within this general category, a notable subtype is the *cantar de gesta*, a kind of *epic poem resembling the French *chanson de geste*; of these, the most celebrated is the 12th-century Castilian epic known as the *Cantar de mio Cid* or as the *Poema de mio Cid*.

**cantiga** [kan-**tee**-gǎ] (**cantega**) A kind of song or poem set to music in medieval Portuguese and Galician traditions. *Cantigas* are usually short, typically of twelve lines, and of various types including the *cantiga de amigo* sung by a woman to a man, the *cantiga de amor* sung by a man to a woman, and the *cantiga de burlas*, satirical in subject; there are also *devotional *cantigas*, notably the four hundred *Cantigas de Santa Maria* attributed to King Alfonso X ('el Sabio') of Castile (1221–84).

**canto** A subdivision of an *epic or other narrative poem, equivalent to a chapter in a prose work.

*canzone* [can-**tsoh**-ni] (plural *-oni*) A term covering various kinds of medieval Provençal and Italian *lyric poem. The most influential form was the *Petrarchan *canzone*, which has five or six *stanzas and a shorter concluding *envoi* (or half-stanza); the lengths of the stanzas (equal in each poem) ranged from seven to twenty lines. *See also* CHANSON.

**carnivalization** The liberating and subversive influence of popular humour on the literary tradition, according to the theory propounded by the Russian linguist Mikhail Bakhtin in his works *Problems of Dostoevsky's Poetics* (1929) and *Rabelais and his World* (1965). Bakhtin argued that the overturning of hierarchies in popular carnival—its mingling of the sacred with the profane, the sublime with the ridiculous—lies behind the most 'open' (*dialogic or *polyphonic) literary *genres, notably *Menippean satire and the *novel, especially since the *Renaissance. Carnivalized literary forms allow alternative voices to dethrone the authority of official culture: Rabelais, for example, subverts the asceticism of the medieval Church by giving free rein to the bodily profanity of folk festivities. *Adjective*: **carnivalistic** or **carnivalesque.**

**carol** A song of religious rejoicing, usually associated with Christmas or Easter in the Christian calendar. In the Middle Ages, however, a carol could be a purely secular song of love or *satire. A carol in this earlier sense is a song appropriate for a round dance, composed in regular rhyming *stanzas with a *refrain or *burden: a common form was the four-line stanza rhyming *aaab* with a two-line burden rhyming *bb*.

**Caroline** Belonging to the period 1625–49, when Charles I (Latin, *Carolus*) reigned as king of England, Scotland, and Ireland. This period includes the later *metaphysical poets, the early work of Milton, and the so-called '*Cavalier poets' Thomas Carew, Robert Herrick, Richard Lovelace, and Sir John Suckling.

*carpe diem* [**kar**-pe **dee**-em] A quotation from Horace's *Odes* (I, xi) meaning 'seize the day', in other words 'make the best of the present moment'. A common theme or *motif in European *lyric poetry, in which the speaker of a poem argues (often to a hesitant virgin) that since life is short, pleasure should be enjoyed while there is still time. The most celebrated examples in English are Marvell's 'To His Coy Mistress' (1681) and Herrick's 'To the Virgins, To Make Much of Time' (1648), which begins 'Gather ye rosebuds while ye may'. In some Christian poems and sermons, the *carpe diem* motif warns us to prepare our souls for death, rather than our bodies for bed.

**catachresis** [kat-ă-**kree**-sis] The misapplication of a word (e.g. *disinterested* for 'uninterested'), or the extension of a word's meaning in a surprising but strictly illogical *metaphor. In the second sense, a well-known example from *Hamlet* is 'To take arms against a sea of troubles'. *Adjective*: **catachretic**.

**catalectic** Lacking the final syllable or syllables expected in the regular pattern of a metrical verse line (*see* METRE). The term is most often used of the common English *trochaic line in which the optional final unstressed syllable (or *feminine ending) is not used. Of these lines from Shelley's 'To a Skylark', the second and fourth are catalectic:

> In the golden lightning
>    Of the sunken sun,
>  O'er which clouds are bright'ning,
>    Thou dost float and run

The first and third lines, which have the full number of syllables, are **acatalectic**. Unlike most English adjectives, 'catalectic' and its opposite 'acatalectic' usually follow the nouns they qualify: thus the last of Shelley's lines quoted above would be called a trochaic *trimeter catalectic. A line which is short by more than one syllable is **brachycatalectic**, while a line with one syllable too many is **hypercatalectic**. *Noun*: **catalexis**. *See also* ACEPHALOUS, DEFECTIVE FOOT, TRUNCATION.

**catalogue verse** (US catalog) Verse that records the names of several persons, places, or things in the form of a list. It is common in *epic poetry, where the heroes involved in a battle are often enumerated. Other types of catalogue verse record genealogical or geographical information. Walt Whitman created a new kind of catalogue verse in his *Song of Myself* (1855), which celebrates the huge variety of peoples, places, and occupations in the United States in the form of long lists. Similar effects are found in Allen Ginsberg's poem 'Howl' (1956).

**catastrophe** The final resolution or *dénouement of the plot in a *tragedy, usually involving the death of the *protagonist.

**catharsis** The effect of 'purgation' or 'purification' achieved by tragic drama, according to Aristotle's argument in his *Poetics* (4th century BCE). Aristotle wrote that a *tragedy should succeed 'in arousing pity and fear in such a way as to accomplish a catharsis of such emotions'. There has been much dispute about his meaning, but Aristotle seems to be rejecting Plato's hostile view of poetry as an unhealthy emotional stimulant. His metaphor of emotional cleansing has been read as a solution to the puzzle of audiences' pleasure or relief in witnessing the disturbing events enacted in tragedies. Another interpretation is that it is the *protagonist's guilt that is purged, rather than the audience's feeling of terror. *Adjective*: **cathartic**.

**cauda** A 'tail' (Latin); thus a short final line of a verse *stanza, usually rhyming with a similarly short line earlier in the stanza, as in the *tail-rhyme stanza. A stanza or *verse form employing such a line is said to be **caudate**.

**causerie** The French word for a chat, sometimes used to denote an informal literary essay or article, after the *Causeries du lundi*—the famous weekly articles by the French literary critic Sainte-Beuve published in Parisian newspapers from 1849 to 1869.

**Cavalier poets** A collective term applied by some literary historians to a group of English lyric poets of the *Caroline period, and derived from the popular designation for supporters of King Charles in the Civil War. The principal figures in the group are Thomas Carew, Richard Lovelace, Robert Herrick, and Sir John Suckling. They are noted for their elegantly witty short lyric poems, usually love poems. They were influenced by Ben Jonson, and like him tended to avoid employing the *sonnet form.

**Celtic Revival** A term sometimes applied to the period of Irish literature in English (*c.*1885–1939) now more often referred to as the *Irish Literary Renaissance or Revival. There are other similar terms: Celtic Renaissance, Celtic Dawn, and Celtic Twilight (the last famously mocked by James Joyce as the 'cultic twalette'). These Celtic titles are

misleading as descriptions of the broader Irish Revival, but they indicate
a significant factor in the early phase of the movement: **Celticism**
involves an idea of Irishness based on fanciful notions of innate racial
character outlined by the English critic Matthew Arnold in *On the Study
of Celtic Literature* (1866), in which Celtic traits are said to include
delicacy, charm, spirituality, and ineffectual sentimentality. This image
of Irishness was adopted in part by W. B. Yeats in his attempt to create a
distinctively Irish literature with his dreamy early verse and with *The
Celtic Twilight* (1893), a collection of stories based on Irish folklore and
fairy-tales. Apart from the poet 'AE' (George Russell), the other major
figures in the Irish Literary Revival—Synge, O'Casey, and Joyce—had
little or nothing to do with such Celticism.

**Further reading:** Gregory Castle, *Modernism and the Celtic Revival* (2001).

**cénacle** [say-**nahkl**] A clique or *coterie of writers that assembles
around a leading figure. A characteristic of the hero-worshipping culture
of *Romanticism, *cénacles* appeared in Paris from the 1820s onwards
around Charles Nodier and, most famously, Victor Hugo.

**cento** [**sen**-toh] A written composition made up of fragments taken
from other writers. This may be a prose composition, but the term is
applied most often to poem that is made up of lines from other poems.
*See also* COLLAGE, *GLOSA*, PASTICHE.

**chanson** [shah$^n$-so$^n$] The French word for a song, also applied
specifically to the kind of love song composed by the Provençal
*troubadours of the late Middle Ages. This usually has five or six
matching *stanzas and a concluding *envoi (or half-stanza), and its
subject is *courtly love. The *metres and *rhyme schemes vary greatly, as
the form was seen as a test of technical skills. *See also* CANZONE.

**chanson de geste** [shah$^n$-so$^n$ dĕ zhest] A kind of shorter *epic
poem in Old French, composed between the late 11th century and the
early 14th century, celebrating the historical and legendary exploits
(*gestes*) of Charlemagne (late 8th century) and other Frankish nobles in
holy wars against the Saracens or in internal rebellions. The *chansons de
geste* were sung by *jongleurs* in *strophes of varying length known as
*laisses*, usually composed of 10-syllable lines linked by *assonance (or
by rhyme in later examples). About 80 of these poems survive, of which
the most celebrated is the *Chanson de Roland* (late 11th century).

Some similar *cantares de gesta* appeared in Spain, notably the *Cantar de mio Cid*, a Castilian epic of the 12th or 13th century.

**Further reading:** Sarah Kay, *The Chansons de Geste in the Age of Romance* (1995).

*chant royal* [shah$^n$ rwa-yal] A French verse form normally consisting of five *stanzas of eleven 10-syllable lines rhyming *ababccddede*, followed by an *envoi* (or half-stanza) rhyming *ddede*. The last line of the first stanza is repeated as a *refrain at the end of the succeeding stanzas and of the *envoi*. The pattern is similar to that of the *ballade, but even more demanding. Most *chants royaux* were *allegories on dignified subjects. They appeared in France from the time of Eustache Deschamps (late 14th century) to that of Clément Marot (early 16th century), but very rarely in English.

**chapbook** The name given since the 19th century to a kind of small, cheaply printed book or pamphlet hawked by chapmen (i.e. pedlars) from the 16th century to the early 19th century, and containing *ballads, fairy-tales, old *romances, accounts of famous criminals, and other popular entertainments.

**character** A personage in a *narrative or dramatic work (*see* CHARACTERIZATION); also a kind of prose sketch briefly describing some recognizable type of person. As a minor literary *genre, the character originates with the *Characters* (late 3rd century BCE) of the Greek writer Theophrastus; it was revived in the 17th century, notably by Sir Thomas Overbury in his *Characters* (1614) and by La Bruyère in *Les Caractères* (1688). *See also* HUMOURS, STOCK CHARACTER, TYPE.

**characterization** The representation of persons in *narrative and dramatic works. This may include direct methods like the attribution of qualities in description or commentary, and indirect (or 'dramatic') methods inviting readers to infer qualities from characters' actions, speech, or appearance. Since E. M. Forster's *Aspects of the Novel* (1927) a distinction has often been made between 'flat' and 'two-dimensional' characters, which are simple and unchanging, and 'round' characters, which are complex, 'dynamic' (i.e. subject to development), and less predictable. *See also* STOCK CHARACTER, TYPE.

**Chaucerian stanza** *See* RHYME ROYAL.

**cheville** The French word for a plug, applied to any word or phrase of little semantic importance which is used by a poet to make up the required number of syllables in a metrical verse line (*see* METRE). Chaucer used chevilles with shameless frequency, often plugging his lines with *eek, for sothe, ywis, I gesse, I trowe*, and similar interjections.

**chiasmus** [ky-**az**-mŭs] (plural **-mi**) A *figure of speech by which the order of the terms in the first of two parallel clauses is reversed in the second. This may involve a repetition of the same words ('Pleasure's a sin, and sometimes sin's a pleasure'—Byron), in which case the figure may be classified as *antimetabole, or just a reversed parallel between two corresponding pairs of ideas, as in this line from Mary Leapor's 'Essay on Woman' (1751):

Despised, if ugly; if she's fair, betrayed.

The figure is especially common in 18th-century English poetry, but is also found in prose of all periods. It is named after the Greek letter *chi* ($\chi$), indicating a 'criss-cross' arrangement of terms. *Adjective:* **chiastic**. *See also* ANADIPLOSIS, ANTITHESIS, PARALLELISM.

**Further reading:** William E. Engel, *Chiastic Design in English Literature* (2009).

**Chicago critics** A group of critics associated with the University of Chicago, who contributed to the volume *Critics and Criticisms: Ancient and Modern* (1952) edited by the most prominent figure, R. S. Crane. Other members included W. R. Keast, Elder Olson, and Bernard Weinberg; Wayne C. Booth, the author of *The Rhetoric of Fiction* (1961), was also associated with the group. The Chicago critics were concerned with accounting for the variety of critical approaches to literature in terms of assumptions about the nature of literary works. They also emphasized the larger structures of literary works, following the example of Aristotle, whom they admired for basing his *Poetics* (4th century BCE) on actual examples rather than on preconceptions. Their interest in *plot, structure, and *genre distinguishes them from the *New Critics, who concentrated on the study of *metaphor and *symbol in *lyric verse. *See also* ARISTOTELIAN.

**chick lit** A kind of light commercial fiction addressed to British women readers of the late 1990s and early 2000s and subsequently imitated in the United States and beyond. The term appeared from 1996 as a flippant counterpart to the *lad-lit fiction of that time. The defining model for the genre was Helen Fielding's comic novel *Bridget Jones's Diary* (1996), a widely discussed bestseller in which the heroine, a single working woman, records her frustrations with a succession of unsatisfactory boyfriends while also keeping track of her attempts to lose weight. Chick-lit novels are written by women about the misadventures of contemporary unmarried working women in their 20s or 30s who struggle with multiple pressures from reproachful mothers, inadequate boyfriends, and tyrannical bosses while consoling themselves with shopping trips, chocolate, and erotic daydreams. The stories are commonly told in the first person in tones of humorous self-deprecation. As the boom in this kind of fiction, sometimes referred to as **chic fic**, continued into the early 21st century, new *subgenres emerged, including 'nanny lit' and 'mommy lit'.

**Further reading:** Suzanne Ferriss and Mallory Young (eds.), *Chick Lit: The New Women's Fiction* (2005).

**chivalric romance** [shi-**val**-rik] The principal kind of *romance found in medieval Europe from the 12th century onwards, describing (usually in verse) the adventures of legendary knights, and celebrating an idealized code of civilized behaviour that combines loyalty, honour, and *courtly love. The emphasis on heterosexual love and courtly manners distinguishes it from the *chanson de geste* and other kinds of *epic, in which masculine military heroism predominates. The most famous examples are the *Arthurian romances recounting the adventures of Lancelot, Galahad, Gawain, and the other Round Table knights. These include the *Lancelot* (late 12th century) of Chrétien de Troyes, the anonymous *Sir Gawain and the Green Knight* (late 14th century), and Malory's prose romance *Le Morte Darthur* (1485).

**Further reading:** Lee C. Ramsey, *Chivalric Romances* (1983).

**choral character** A term sometimes applied to a character in a play who, while participating in the action to some degree, also provides the audience with an ironic commentary upon it, thus performing a function similar to that of the *chorus in Greek *tragedy. Two examples are Thersites in Shakespeare's *Troilus and Cressida* and Wong in Brecht's *The Good Woman of Setzuan*.

**choriamb** [kor-i-am] **(choriambus)** A metrical unit combining one *trochee (or 'choree') and one *iamb into a single *foot of four syllables, with two stressed syllables enclosing two unstressed syllables, as in the word *hullabaloo* (or, in *quantitative verse, two long syllables enclosing two shorts). It was used frequently in Greek dramatic choruses and lyrics, and by the Roman poet Horace, and later in some German verse. Usually, as in the *Asclepiad, it is combined with other feet. A rare English example of choriambic verse is Swinburne's 'Choriambics' (1878), in which the line consists of one trochee, three choriambs, and one iamb:

Ah, thy snow-coloured hands! once were they chains, mighty to bind
    me fast;
Now no blood in them burns, mindless of love, senseless of passions past.

**chorus** A group of singers distinct from the principal performers in a dramatic or musical performance; also the song or *refrain that they sing. In classical Greek *tragedy a chorus of twelve or fifteen masked performers would sing, with dancing movements, a commentary on the action of the play, interpreting its events from the standpoint of traditional wisdom. This practice appears to have been derived from the **choral lyrics** of religious festivals. The Greek tradition of choral *lyric includes the *dithyramb, the *paean, and the choral *odes of Pindar. In some Elizabethan plays, like Shakespeare's *Henry V*, a single character called a chorus introduces the setting and action. Except in opera, the group chorus is used rarely in modern European drama: examples are T. S. Eliot's *Murder in the Cathedral* (1935) and Brecht's *The Caucasian Chalk Circle* (1948). The term has also been applied to certain groups of characters in novels, who view the main action from the standpoint of rural tradition, as in some works of George Eliot, Thomas Hardy, and William Faulkner. *See also* CHORAL CHARACTER.

**chrestomathy** [kres-**tom**-ă-thi] A collection or *anthology of passages in prose or verse, often selected for purposes of literary or linguistic study.

**chronicle** A written record of events presented in order of time, and updated regularly over a prolonged period. The chroniclers of the Middle Ages, from the compilers of King Alfred's *Anglo-Saxon Chronicle* (9th to 12th century) onwards, tended to mix *legend and rumour with fact in their accounts. Significant chronicles in the later Middle Ages include those of Matthew Paris (St Albans, late 13th century) and the accounts of the wars against the English written by the French chronicler Jean Froissart (late 14th century). Raphael Holinshed and his collaborators published in 1577 the *Chronicles of England, Scotland, and Ireland* which (in an expurgated edition of 1587) were adapted by Shakespeare and other dramatists in their *chronicle plays.

**chronicle novel** A long novel or connected sequence of novels in which the narrative recounts the fortunes of a family or similar group of recurring characters over many years, usually covering at least two generations. This category of fiction overlaps with the *saga novel, where the emphasis is on changes within a family; but where the story attempts to reflect typical developments in social history over a sustained period, the term 'chronicle novel' may be preferred, especially if the story's events are connected with notably historic dates and events. Significant modern examples in English include John Galsworthy's sequence of Forsyte novels (1906–28) which attempt to chart English social history from the 1880s to 1926, and C. P. Snow's eleven-volume sequence *Strangers and Brothers* (1940–70), which follows its central character through changes in the English governing elite from 1925 to 1964.

**chronicle play** A *history play, especially of the kind written in England in the 1590s and based upon the revised 1587 edition of Raphael Holinshed's *Chronicles*. This group of plays includes Marlowe's *Edward II* (1592) and the three parts of Shakespeare's *Henry VI* (*c.*1590–2). Later historical dramas that may be regarded as chronicle plays include Goethe's *Götz von Berlichingen* (1773) and Noël Coward's *Cavalcade* (1931).

**chronotope** A term employed by the Russian literary theorist Mikhail Bakhtin (1895–1975) to refer to the co-ordinates of time and space invoked by a given *narrative; in other words to the 'setting', considered as a spatio-temporal whole.

**Ciceronian** [sis-e-**rohn**-yăn] Belonging to or characteristic of the Roman statesman, orator, and prose writer Cicero (Marcus Tullius Cicero, 106–43 BCE), especially in relation to prose style; or, as a noun, a follower of Cicero. His style of oratory and prose, marked by logical but elaborately balanced subordinate clauses (*see* PERIODIC SENTENCE), was adopted as the purest model by subsequent writers of Latin, and often imitated to a slavish degree during the *Renaissance, when some dogmatic Ciceronians regarded Latin words and expressions that postdated his writings as impure, thus tending to ossify the language. A few English prose writers of the 16th century, notably Richard Hooker, imitated Cicero's Latin constructions, but this model was largely rejected by later generations as too pompous and inflexible. A **Ciceronianism** is an expression typical of Cicero or his imitators; but a **cicerone** is a guide, usually one who is well acquainted with the antiquities and history of an old city.

**cinquain** [sang-**kayn**] A verse *stanza of five lines, more commonly known as a *quintain. Examples of such stanzas include the English *limerick, the Japanese *tanka, and the Spanish *quintilla; others include the variant *ballad stanza employed intermittently by S. T. Coleridge in his 'The Rime of the Ancient Mariner' (1798), and many more varieties with no name.

**circumlocution** The roundabout manner of referring to something at length rather than naming it briefly and directly, usually known in literary terminology as *periphrasis. The *kenning is a distinctive **circumlocutory** device found especially in Old Norse verse.

**city comedy (citizen comedy)** A kind of comic drama produced in the London theatres of the early 17th century, characterized by its contemporary urban subject-matter and its portrayal, often satirical, of middle-class life and manners. The principal examples are John Marston's *The Dutch Courtezan* (1605), Ben Jonson's *Bartholomew Fair* (1614), and Thomas Middleton's *A Chaste Maid in Cheapside* (1613).

***claque*** [klahk] The French word for a handclap, applied to a group of people hired by a theatre manager to applaud a performance, thus encouraging the paying audience to do likewise. The French writer Villiers de l'Isle-Adam described this widespread corrupt practice in the theatres of 19th-century Paris as 'the avowed symbol of the Public's inability to distinguish by itself the worth of what it is listening to'.

**classic** A work of the highest class, or so exemplary as to be studied as a model in classrooms. A literary classic is a work admired in both these senses, and usually one that is deemed to have stood the test of time and outlasted changes in critical taste; such works may be of relatively recent date, and so regarded as 'modern classics'. **Classics** as an academic subject, however, is the study of ancient Greek and Latin language and literature, often with aspects of Greek and Roman civilization such as mythology and philosophy. The adjective **classical** is in most literary contexts also strongly associated with the works of the greatest Greek and Roman writers or with the periods in which they lived (as with 'classical civilization', 'classical mythology', and so forth). By extension, it may apply to works of later periods that are inspired by or modelled upon the Greek or Roman traditions, so that one may refer to a classical tendency in modern literature, often opposed to a romantic tendency (*see* CLASSICISM). There are, however, some uses of the term that apply to later periods in which some branch of literary art has flourished: thus one may refer to the 17th century as the classical period of French drama, or to the 19th as the classical period of the Western novel; these are loosely equivalent to the usages found in 'classical' music, ballet, economics, etc.

**Further reading:** Frank Kermode, *The Classic* (1975).

**classicism** An attitude to literature that is guided by admiration of the qualities of formal balance, proportion, *decorum, and restraint attributed to the major works of ancient Greek and Roman literature ('the classics') in preference to the irregularities of later *vernacular literatures, and especially (since about 1800) to the artistic liberties proclaimed by *Romanticism. A **classic** is a work of the highest class, and has also been taken to mean a work suitable for study in school classes. During and since the *Renaissance, these overlapping meanings came to be applied to (and to be virtually synonymous with) the writings of major Greek and Roman authors from Homer to Juvenal, which were regarded as unsurpassed models of excellence.

The adjective **classical**, usually applied to this body of writings, has since been extended to outstandingly creative periods of other literatures: the 17th century may be regarded as the classical age of French literature, and the 19th century the classical period of the Western novel, while the finest fiction of the United States in the mid-19th century from Cooper to Twain was referred to by D. H. Lawrence as Classic American Literature (despite the opposition between 'classical' and 'romantic' views of art, a romantic work can now still be a classic).

A classical style or approach to literary composition is usually one that imitates Greek or Roman models in subject-matter (e.g. Greek legends) or in form (by the adoption of *genres like *tragedy, *epic, *ode, or verse *satire), or both. As a literary doctrine, classicism holds that the writer must be governed by rules, models, or conventions, rather than by wayward inspiration: in its most strictly codified form in the 17th and 18th centuries (*see* *neo-classicism), it required the observance of rules

derived from Aristotle's *Poetics* (4th century BCE) and Horace's *Ars
Poetica* (*c*.20 BCE), principally those of decorum and the dramatic
*unities. The dominant tendency of French literature in the 17th and
18th centuries, classicism in a weaker form also characterized the
*Augustan Age in England; the later German classicism of the late 18th
and early 19th centuries was distinguished by its exclusive interest in
Greek models, as opposed to the Roman bias of French and English
classicisms.

After the end of the 18th century, 'classical' came to be contrasted
with 'romantic' in an opposition of increasingly generalized terms
embracing moods and attitudes as well as characteristics of actual
works. While partisans of Romanticism associated the classical with the
rigidly artificial and the romantic with the freely creative, the classicists
condemned romantic self-expression as eccentric self-indulgence, in the
name of classical sanity and order. The great German writer J. W. von
Goethe summarized his conversion to classical principles by defining
the classical as healthy, the romantic as sickly. Since then, literary
classicism has often been less a matter of imitating Greek and Roman
models than of resisting the claims of Romanticism and all that it may be
thought to stand for (Protestantism, liberalism, democracy, anarchy):
the critical doctrines of Matthew Arnold and more especially of
T. S. Eliot are classicist in this sense of reacting against the Romantic
principle of unrestrained self-expression.

**Further reading:** Craig W. Kallendorf (ed.), *A Companion to the Classical
Tradition* (2007).

**clausula** (plural **-ulae**) The closing words of a prose sentence,
especially when characterized by a distinct rhythm or *cadence, as in the
Latin *oratory of Cicero (106–43 BCE) or his imitators.

**clerihew** A form of comic verse named after its inventor, Edmund
Clerihew Bentley (1875–1956). It consists of two metrically awkward
*couplets, and usually presents a ludicrously uninformative 'biography'
of some famous person whose name appears as one of the rhymed
words in the first couplet:

> Geoffrey Chaucer
> Could hardly have been coarser,
> But this never harmed the sales
> Of his *Canterbury Tales*.

**climax** Any moment of great intensity in a literary work, especially in drama (*see also* ANAGNORISIS, CATASTROPHE, CRISIS, DÉNOUEMENT, PERIPETEIA). Also in *rhetoric, a figure of speech in which a sequence of terms is linked by chain-like repetition through three or more clauses in ascending order of importance. A well-known example is Benjamin Franklin's cautionary maxim, 'For want of a nail, the shoe was lost; for want of a shoe the horse was lost; for want of a horse the rider was lost.' This figure uses a repetitive structure similar to that of *anadiplosis. *Adjective*: **climactic**. See also AUXESIS, SCÈNE À FAIRE.

**closed couplet** Two lines of metrical verse in which the *syntax and sense come to a conclusion or a strong pause at the end of the second line, giving the couplet the quality of a self-contained *epigram. The term is applied almost always to rhyming couplets, especially to the *heroic couplet; but whereas the heroic couplets of Chaucer and Keats often allow the sense to run on over the end of the second line (*see* ENJAMBMENT), those written by English poets in the late 17th century and in the 18th are usually *end-stopped, and are thus closed couplets, as in these lines about men from Sarah Fyge Egerton's 'The Emulation' (1703):

> They fear we should excel their sluggish parts,
> Should we attempt the sciences and arts;
> Pretend they were designed for them alone,
> So keep us fools to raise their own renown.

**close reading** A term commonly applied to the detailed analysis of a literary text, usually a short poem or prose excerpt. In a modern tradition inaugurated by Laura Riding and Robert Graves in their book *A Survey of Modernist Poetry* (1927), the close reader typically attempts to account for and justify the presence of all the text's features of sound and sense, usually detecting sonic correspondences such as internal rhyme and *alliteration, along with ambiguities of meaning, and the complex deployment of rhetorical *figures, all integrated into a formal unity. Following the success of William Empson's book *Seven Types of Ambiguity* (1930), written under the influence of Riding and Graves, close reading was often cultivated in the *Cambridge school of criticism, and developed most influentially in the US by the *New Critics and their successors including the school of *deconstruction. Various reactions against this tradition have emerged, ranging from the *Chicago critics' contrary emphasis on *genre and plot, to Franco Moretti's experiments with a new kind of *distant reading.

**closet drama** A literary composition written in the form of a play (usually as a dramatic poem), but intended—or suited—only for reading in a closet (i.e. a private study) rather than for stage performance. *Senecan tragedy is thought to have been written for private recitation, and there are several important examples of closet drama in English, including Milton's *Samson Agonistes* (1671), Byron's *Manfred* (1817), Shelley's *Prometheus Unbound* (1820), and Arnold's *Empedocles on Etna* (1852).

**closure** The sense of completion or resolution at the end of a literary work or part of a work (e.g. a *stanza or *closed couplet); or, in literary criticism, the reduction of a work's meanings to a single and complete sense that excludes the claims of other interpretations. The contrast between 'closed' texts and 'open' texts has been a common topic of modern criticism, as in Roland Barthes's theory of the *lisible*.

**coda** *See* TAIL-RHYME STANZA.

**code** A shared set of rules or *conventions by which *signs can be combined to permit a message to be communicated from one person to another; it may consist of a language in the normal sense (e.g. English, Urdu) or of a smaller-scale 'language' such as the set of hand-signals, horns, grimaces, and flashing lights used by motorists. The code is one of the six essential elements in Roman Jakobson's influential theory of communication (*see* FUNCTION), and has an important place in *structuralist theories, which stress the extent to which messages (including literary works) call upon already coded meanings rather than fresh revelations of raw reality. An important work in this connection is Roland Barthes's *S/Z* (1970), in which a story by Balzac is broken down into five codes, ranging from the 'hermeneutic code' (which sets up a mystery and delays its solution) to the 'cultural code' (which refers to accepted prejudices, stereotypes, and values). *Verbs*: **codify**, **decode**, **encode**.

**codex** (plural **codices**) A book consisting of ancient manuscripts. The study of codices is called **codicology**.

**cohesion** A term used in linguistic analyses of *texts such as those undertaken in *stylistics, in reference to the degrees and kinds of internal connection that link different parts of the same text. Cohesion between one sentence, stanza or other unit, and another may be established by sound-patterns such as *metre, *rhyme, and *alliteration, or by pronominal back-reference (*she, those*, etc.), or by the use of similar syntactical constructions (e.g. *parallelism), or by conjunctions and similar linking phrases (*nor, however, consequently*, etc.). *Adjective*: **cohesive**.

**coinage** A newly invented word or expression. *See also* NEOLOGISM, NONCE WORD.

**collage** [**kol**-ah*zh*] A work assembled wholly or partly from fragments of other writings, incorporating *allusions, quotations, and foreign phrases. Originally applied to paintings with pasted-on elements, the term has been extended to an important kind of *modernist poetry, of which the most significant examples are the *Cantos* of Ezra Pound and T. S. Eliot's *The Waste Land*. The collage technique can also be found sometimes in prose works. *See also* BRICOLAGE, MACARONIC VERSE, PASTICHE.

**collation** A 'bringing together', used in various literary senses. In *textual criticism, collation is the process of comparing differing manuscripts or *editions of the same work in order to establish a corrected text. A new edition of the work may be also be described as a collation if it results from such a comparative exercise. In *bibliography, collation is the process by which the printer or binder brings together the sheets of paper or folded sets of such sheets (known as quires) to make up a book or bound manuscript. A description of the physical make-up of a book, in terms of the number of its quires and the number of sheets per quire, is also called a collation.

**collective unconscious** The term given by the Swiss psychologist C. G. Jung (1875–1961) to the inborn racial memory which he believed to be the primitive source of the *archetypes or 'universal' *symbols found in legends, poetry, and dreams. *See also* MYTH CRITICISM.

**colloquialism** The use of informal expressions appropriate to everyday speech rather than to the formality of writing, and differing in pronunciation, vocabulary, or grammar. An example is Rudyard Kipling's *ballad beginning

When 'Omer smote 'is bloomin' lyre
  He'd 'eard men sing by land and sea;
An' what he thought 'e might require,
  'E went an' took—the same as me!

*See also* DEMOTIC, DICTION.

**colophon** The publisher's imprint or emblem usually displayed on the title page of a book; or (in older books) an inscription placed at the end of a book, naming the printer and the date and place of publication.

**colportage** Cheap popular literature, originally sold by itinerant hawkers called colporteurs. The category includes religious tracts, sensational novels and *romances, *chapbooks, and *broadsides.

***comédie larmoyante*** A 'tearful play', in other words a tear-jerking sentimental drama. A kind of French *sentimental comedy inclining to *melodrama that flourished briefly in the mid-18th century. These plays were usually in verse, and were intricately plotted exhibitions of the virtues of patience and forgiveness. The best-known examples were Nivelle de la Chaussée's *Mélanide* (1741) and Madame de Graffigny's prose play *Cénie* (1750).

**comedy** A play (or other literary composition) written chiefly to amuse its audience by appealing to a sense of superiority over the characters depicted. A comedy will normally be closer to the representation of everyday life than a *tragedy, and will explore common human failings rather than tragedy's disastrous crimes. Its ending will usually be happy for the leading characters. In another sense, the term was applied in the Middle Ages to narrative poems that end happily: the title of Dante's *Divine Comedy* (c.1320) carries this meaning.

As a dramatic form, comedy in Europe dates back to the Greek playwright Aristophanes in the 5th century BCE. His *Old Comedy combines several kinds of mischief, including the satirical mockery of living politicians and writers. At the end of the next century, Menander established the fictional form known as *New Comedy, in which young lovers went through misadventures among other *stock characters; this tradition was later developed in the Roman comedy of Plautus and Terence, and eventually by Shakespeare in England and Lope de Vega in Spain. The great period of European comedy, partly influenced by the **commedia dell' arte**, was the 17th century, when Shakespeare, Lope de

Vega, and Jonson were succeeded by Molière and by the *Restoration comedy of Congreve, Etheredge, and Wycherley. There are several kinds of comedy, including *sentimental comedy, the *romantic comedy of Shakespeare's *A Midsummer Night's Dream* (c.1596), the *satire in Jonson's *Volpone* (1606) or in Molière's *Le Tartuffe* (1669), the sophisticated verbal wit of the *comedy of manners in Wilde's *The Importance of Being Earnest* (1895), and the more topical 'comedy of ideas' in the plays of Bernard Shaw. Among its less sophisticated forms are *burlesque, *pantomime, and *farce.

The adjective **comedic** means 'characteristic of comedy' and is sometimes preferred as more neutral than 'comic' or 'comical' in that it avoids suggesting that the referent is funny. *See also* BLACK COMEDY, COMIC RELIEF, HUMOURS, TRAGICOMEDY.

**Further reading:** Andrew Stott, *Comedy* (2nd edn, 2014).

**comedy of humours** *See* HUMOURS.

**comedy of manners** A kind of *comedy representing the complex and sophisticated code of behaviour current in fashionable circles of society, where appearances count for more than true moral character. Its *plot usually revolves around intrigues of lust and greed, the self-interested cynicism of the characters being masked by decorous pretence. Unlike *satire, the comedy of manners tends to reward its cleverly unscrupulous characters rather than punish their immorality. Its humour relies chiefly upon elegant verbal wit and *repartee. In England, the comedy of manners flourished as the dominant form of *Restoration comedy in the works of Sir George Etherege, William Wycherley (notably *The Country Wife*, 1675), and William Congreve; it was revived in a more subdued form in the 1770s by Goldsmith and Sheridan, and later by Oscar Wilde. Modern examples of the comedy of manners include Noël Coward's *Design for Living* (1932) and Joe Orton's *Loot* (1965).

**Further reading:** David L. Hirst, *Comedy of Manners* (1979).

**comic relief** The interruption of a serious work, especially a *tragedy, by a short humorous episode. The inclusion of such comic scenes, characters, or speeches can have various and complex effects, ranging from relaxation after moments of high tension to sinister ironic brooding. Famous instances are the drunken porter's speech in *Macbeth* (Act II, scene iii), and the dialogues between Hamlet and the gravediggers in *Hamlet* (Act V, scene i). Other playwrights of Shakespeare's time made frequent use of this technique, which can also be found in some prose works like Malcolm Lowry's tragic novel *Under the Volcano* (1947). *See also* SATYR PLAY, SUBPLOT, TRAGICOMEDY.

**coming-of-age novel** An English term adopted as an approximate equivalent to the German *Bildungsroman*, although with an implied distinction in terms of time-span. Whereas a fully developed English *Bildungsroman* or 'education novel' such as Dickens's *David Copperfield* (1849–50) will follow the maturation of the protagonist from infancy—or even from before that, in the case of D. H. Lawrence's *Sons and Lovers* (1913)—to early adulthood, a coming-of-age novel may be devoted entirely to the crises of late adolescence involving courtship, sexual initiation, separation from parents, and choice of vocation or spouse. One among many modern examples is H. G. Wells's *Ann Veronica* (1909), which opens with the *eponymous heroine at the age of 21 and about to run away from her father's home to explore life for herself.

***commedia dell' arte*** The Italian term for 'professional comedy', a form of improvised comic performance popular between the 16th and 18th centuries in Italy, France, and elsewhere in Europe, acted in masks by travelling companies of professional actors each of whom specialized in a *stock character. The plots involved intrigues carried on by young lovers and their servants against the rich father ('Pantaloon') of the leading lady (the 'Inamorata'), and included stock characters like Harlequin, Pulcinella, and Scaramouche, who survive as part of theatrical folklore. This form of comedy had an important influence on later forms of *farce, *pantomime, and light opera, as well as on some major dramatists including Molière and Goldoni. It was also drawn upon by the French *Symbolist poets, notably Paul Verlaine in his collection *Fêtes galantes* (1869).

**common measure (common metre)** A form of verse *quatrain (also called the 'hymnal stanza') often used in hymns. Like the *ballad metre, its first and third lines have four *stresses, and its second and fourth have three; but it tends to be more regularly *iambic, and it more often rhymes not only the second and fourth lines (*abcb*) but the first and third too (*abab*). A variant form is **long measure** or **long metre**, in which all four lines have four stresses, and in which the rhyme scheme *aabb* is sometimes also used. *See also* SHORT MEASURE.

**commonplace book** Not a dull or trite book, as the usual sense of 'commonplace' would suggest, but a writer's notebook in which interesting ideas and quotations are collected for further reflection and possible future use. In this sense, a commonplace is a remark or written passage that is worth remembering or quoting. Notable examples of commonplace books that have been published include Ben Jonson's *Timber* (1640) and W. H. Auden's *A Certain World* (1971).

**companion poem** A poem that is to be understood as paired with another poem, as reply, inversion, contradiction, or similar complementary relation. The best-known examples in English are John Milton's *L'Allegro* and *Il penseroso* (1645). Several examples are also to be found among the contrasting poems of William Blake's *Songs of Innocence and Experience* (1794).

**comparative literature** The combined study of similar literary works written in different languages, which stresses the points of connection between literary products of two or more cultures, as distinct from the sometimes narrow and exclusive perspective of *Eng. Lit. or similar approaches based on one national *canon. Advocates of comparative literature maintain that there is, despite the obvious disadvantages, much to be gained from studying literary works in translation. A scholar engaged in such studies is a **comparatist**.

**Further reading:** Susan Bassnett, *Comparative Literature* (1993).

**competence** The term established by the American linguist Noam Chomsky to denote that unconscious store of linguistic knowledge which enables us to speak and understand our first language properly without having to think about it, permitting us to utter and comprehend sentences that we may never have heard before. Competence is what we know about the language we speak (without having to know that we know it), whereas performance is what we do with this knowledge in practice: that is, actual utterances. The distinction between competence and performance (similar to Saussure's distinction between *langue* and *parole*) is made in order to isolate the proper object of linguistics, which is to make the implicit rules of speakers' competence explicit in the form of grammar. The concept has been extended by theorists of

communication, as 'communicative competence', and also adapted
by some literary theorists who identify a 'literary competence' in
experienced readers' implicit recognition of *narrative structures and
other literary *conventions: a competent audience, for instance, will
recognize the difference between the end of a scene and the end of
the whole play, and so applaud at the right time.

**complaint** A kind of *lyric poem common from the Middle Ages to
the 17th century, in which the speaker bewails either the cruelty of a
faithless lover or the advent of some misfortune like poverty or exile.
This kind of *monologue became highly conventional in love poetry,
as can be seen from 'The Complaint of Chaucer to His Purse', in
which the poet wittily addresses his light purse as if it were a 'light'
(i.e. promiscuous) mistress. Chaucer also wrote serious complaints,
as did Villon, Surrey, and Spenser. *See also* LAMENT.

**conceit** An unusually far-fetched or elaborate *metaphor or *simile
presenting a surprisingly apt parallel between two apparently dissimilar
things or feelings: 'Griefe is a puddle, and reflects not cleare | Your
beauties rayes' (T. Carew). Under *Petrarchan influence, European
poetry of the *Renaissance cultivated fanciful comparisons and conceits
to a high degree of ingenuity, either as the basis for whole poems
(notably Donne's 'The Flea') or as an incidental decorative device.
Poetic conceits are prominent in Elizabethan love *sonnets, in
*metaphysical poetry, in the French dramatic verse of Corneille and
Racine, and in the Italian and Spanish styles known respectively as
*concettismo* and *conceptismo*. Conceits often employ the devices of
*hyperbole, *paradox, and *oxymoron.

**conceptismo** [kon-thep-**teez**-moh] A Spanish term for 'conceitism',
i.e. a cultivation in poetry of *conceits or elaborate *metaphors and
paradoxical images that challenge the reader to notice occult relations
among things. This became something of slogan among some early
17th-century Spanish poets, who on this account became known as
**conceptistas**, notably Alonso de Ledesma Buitrago in his three-volume
*Conceptos espirituales* (1600–12) and the more important figure of
Quevedo. The doctrine of *conceptismo* was theorized in terms of *wit
(*agudeza*) and of the combined virtues of obscurity and brevity by the
prose writer Baltasar Gracián y Morales in his critical treatise *Agudeza y
arte de ingenio* (1648). There are some parallels here with the practice of

the English *metaphysical poets, and more clearly with the equivalent Italian movement of *concettismo*. *See also* BAROQUE, MANNERISM.

**concettismo** An Italian word for 'conceitism', or the cult of strikingly ingenious *conceits, *metaphors, *paradoxes, and *wit (*ingegno*) in both prose and verse of the early 17th century. Its most prominent exponent was the poet Giovanbattista Marino (1569–1625), whose elaborate and surprising metaphors won many imitators, and whose name eventually provided the term *Marinism that came in literary history to replace both the original *concettismo* and the disparaging *Secentismo*. The use of far-fetched metaphor found in *concettismo* came to be justified and theorized by Matteo Peregrini in *Delle acutezze* (1639) and later by Emanuele Tesauro in *Il cannocchiale aristotelico* (1654), but by this time the movement was fading. The equivalent trend in Spanish poetry is known as *conceptismo*. *See also* BAROQUE, MANNERISM.

**concordance** An alphabetical index of all the significant words used in a text or related group of texts, indicating all the places in which each word is used. Concordances to the Bible and to the complete works of Shakespeare have been followed, especially since the advent of computers, by similar reference books on other works.

**concrete poetry** A kind of picture made out of printed type, and regarded in the 1950s and 1960s, when it enjoyed an international vogue, as an experimental form of poetry. It usually involves a punning kind of typography in which the visual pattern enacts or corresponds in some way to the sense of the word or phrase represented: a well-known early example is Guillaume Apollinaire's poem 'Il pleut' ('It rains', 1918), in which the words appear to be falling down the page like rain. The Scottish artist and poet Ian Hamilton Finlay was one of the few significant practitioners in English; his works come closer to sculpture than to two-dimensional art. Most concrete poems are apprehended instantaneously by the viewer as visual shapes, since they dispense with the linear sequence demanded by language; these therefore have little claim to the status of poetry. Others are closer to the traditional form of *pattern poetry, in which typographical presentation supports an already coherent poem.

((⊕)) SEE WEB LINKS
• Provides bibliography and links.

**confessional poetry** An autobiographical mode of verse that reveals the poet's personal problems with unusual frankness. The term and its cognate **confessionalism** are usually applied to certain poets of the United States from the late 1950s to the late 1960s, notably Robert Lowell, whose *Life Studies* (1959) and *For the Union Dead* (1964) deal with his divorce and mental breakdowns. Lowell's candour had been encouraged in part by that of the gay poet Allen Ginsberg in *Howl* (1956) and by the intensely personal poetry of Theodore Roethke. Other important examples of confessional poetry are Anne Sexton's *To Bedlam and Part Way Back* (1960) and *All My Pretty Ones* (1962), including poems on abortion and life in mental hospitals; John Berryman's *Dream Songs* (1964–8) on alcoholism and insanity; Sylvia Plath's poems on suicide in *Ariel* (1965); and W. D. Snodgrass's *Heart's Needle* (1959) on his divorce. The term is sometimes used more loosely to refer to any personal or autobiographical poetry, but its distinctive sense depends on the candid examination of what were at the time of writing virtually unmentionable kinds of private distress. The genuine strengths of confessional poets, combined with the pity evoked by their high suicide rate (Berryman, Sexton, and Plath all killed themselves), encouraged in the reading public a romantic confusion between poetic excellence and inner torment. Poets of later generations who have written on similar topics under the apparent influence of the original confessional poets are sometimes referred to as **neo-confessional**: the work of Sharon Olds in *Satan Says* (1980) and later volumes has often been placed under that description.

**Further reading:** Adam Kirsch, *The Wounded Surgeon* (2005).

**confidant(e)** A minor or secondary character in a play (or other literary work), in whom the *protagonist confides, revealing his or her state of mind in dialogue rather than in *soliloquies. Commonly the trusted servant of the leading lady in drama has the role of confidante: Charmian, for example, in Shakespeare's *Antony and Cleopatra. See also* FICELLE, SOUBRETTE.

**connotation** The range of further associations that a word or phrase suggests in addition to its straightforward dictionary meaning (the primary sense known as its **denotation**); or one of these secondary meanings. A word's connotations can usually be formulated as a series of qualities, contexts, and emotional responses commonly associated with its *referent (that to which it refers). Which of these will be activated by the word will depend on the context in which it is used, and to some degree on the reader or hearer. *Metaphors are made possible by the fact that the two terms they identify both have overlapping connotations. For example, the word *worm* denotes a small, slender invertebrate; but its connotation of slow burrowing activity also allows an ingratiating person to be described metaphorically as 'worming his way into favour', while other connotations based on emotional response (sliminess, insignificance) permit a person to be described simply as 'a worm'. *Adjective*: **connotative**. *Verb*: **connote**.

**consonance** The repetition of identical or similar consonants in neighbouring words whose vowel sounds are different (e.g. *coming home, hot foot*). The term is most commonly used, though, for a special case of such repetition in which the words are identical except for the stressed vowel sound (*group/grope, middle/muddle, wonder/wander*); this device, combining *alliteration and terminal consonance, is sometimes known more precisely as 'rich consonance', and since *c.*1920 has frequently been used at the ends of verse lines as an alternative to full rhyme (*see* PARARHYME). Consonance may be regarded as the counterpart to the vowel-sound repetition known as *assonance. The adjective **consonantal** is sometimes ambiguous in that it also means, more generally, 'pertaining to consonants'.

**conte** The French word for a tale, applied since the 19th century to *short stories, but previously used to denote a more fanciful kind of short prose fiction, especially that deriving from *oral tradition. Among the kinds of conte are the *folktale or *conte populaire*, the *fairy tale (*conte merveilleux* or *conte de fées*), and the *nursery rhyme or *conte rimé*. In the more literary manner is the *conte philosophique*, of which Voltaire's *Zadig* (1747) and *Candide* (1759) are major examples. A storyteller is a *conteur*.

**content** The term commonly used to refer to what is said in a literary work, as opposed to how it is said (that is, to the *form or *style). Distinctions between form and content are necessarily abstractions made for the sake of analysis, since in any actual work there can be no content that has not in some way been formed, and no purely empty form. The indivisibility of form and content, though, is something of a critical truism which often obscures the degree to which a work's matter can survive changes in its manner (in *revisions, translations, and *paraphrases); and it is only by positing some other manner in which this matter can be presented that one is able in analysis to isolate the specific form of a given work.

**context** Those parts of a *text preceding and following any particular passage, giving it a meaning fuller or more identifiable than if it were read in isolation. The context of any statement may be understood to comprise immediately neighbouring *signs (including punctuation such as quotation marks), or any part of—or the whole of—the remaining text, or the biographical, social, cultural, and historical circumstances in which it is made (including the intended audience or reader). The case of *irony shows clearly how the meaning of a statement can be completely reversed by a knowledge of its context. An interpretation of any passage or text that offers to explain it in terms of its context is sometimes said to **contextualize** it. *Adjective*: **contextual**.

**convention** An established practice—whether in technique, style, structure, or subject-matter—commonly adopted in literary works by customary and implicit agreement or precedent rather than by natural necessity. The clearest cases of the 'unnatural' devices known as conventions appear in drama, where the audience implicitly agrees to suspend its disbelief and to regard the stage as a battlefield or kitchen, the actors as historical monarchs or fairy godmothers; likewise author and audience observe an unwritten agreement that a character speaking an *aside cannot be heard by other characters on stage. But conventions are, in less immediately striking ways, essential to poetry and to prose fiction as well: the use of *metre, *rhyme, and *stanzaic forms is conventional, as are the *narrative techniques of the *short story (e.g. the neat or surprising ending) and the *novel (including chronological presentation and *point of view), and the *stock characters of both fiction and drama. Some dramatic and literary forms are clearly composed of very elaborate or very recognizable conventions: opera, *melodrama, *kabuki, the pastoral *elegy, the *chivalric romance, the *detective story, and the *Gothic novel are instances. In these and other cases an interrelated set of conventions in both *form and *content has constituted a *genre.

Since the advent of *Romanticism and of *realism in the 19th century, however, it has become less apparent (although no less true) that literature is conventional, because realism—and later, *naturalism—attempted as far as possible to diminish or conceal those conventions considered unlifelike while Romanticism tried to discard those that were insincere, thus giving rise to that pejorative sense of 'conventional' which devalues traditionally predictable forms. As much modern criticism has to argue, such rebellions against conventions are fated to generate new conventions of their own, which may be less elaborate and less noticeable in their time. This does not render innovation futile, since the new conventions will often be appropriate to changed conditions, but it does mean that while some literary works may be 'unconventional', none can be conventionless. Literary theorists (notably those influenced by *structuralism) tend to confirm the inevitability of conventions by appealing to modern linguistics, which claims that languages can produce meanings only from '*arbitrary' or conventional *signs.

**conversation poem**  The term often applied to certain important *blank-verse poems written by Samuel Taylor Coleridge in the late 1790s. These are addressed to close friends, and are characterized by an informal but serious manner of deliberation that expands from a particular setting. Apart from 'The Nightingale' (1798)—which Coleridge subtitled 'A Conversation Poem'—the group of poems includes 'This Lime-Tree Bower My Prison', 'Frost at Midnight' (addressed to his infant son), and 'Fears in Solitude'. There are some equivalents among the poems of his friend William Wordsworth—most importantly 'Tintern Abbey' (1798). Sometimes the term 'conversation poem' or 'conversation piece' is applied more generally to informal verse *epistles by other poets.

**copy-text**  The specific *text used as the basis for a later *edition of a given work. The scholarly editor of a literary work by a deceased author will decide upon the copy-text and reproduce this, accompanied by lists of variant readings found in other editions (or manuscripts) of the same work. Standard editorial procedure is to adopt as the copy-text the last edition of the work that was published during the author's lifetime; but there may be strong reasons for preferring the first published edition, or a manuscript version, or a set of proofs corrected by the author.

**coronach** [ko-ro-nak]  A Gaelic funeral song or *dirge.

**corpus**  A related 'body' of writings, usually sharing the same author or subject-matter. *See also* CANON, *OEUVRE*.

**coterie** [**koh**-tě-ri]  A small group of writers (and others) bound together more by friendship and habitual association than by a common literary cause or style that might unite a school or movement. The term often has pejorative connotations of exclusive cliquishness. The *Bloomsbury group is one well-known example. The term **coterie verse** is sometimes applied to poems that seem to address the poet's intimate circle of friends, making use of private references that may be obscure to readers outside such circles. *See also* CÉNACLE, SALON, *VERS DE SOCIÉTÉ*.

**country house poem**  A minor genre of poetry which has some importance in 17th-century English verse. It is defined by its subject-matter, which is the fruitfulness and stability of a patron's country estate, and the patron's own conservative virtues. Ben Jonson's 'To Penshurst' (1616) is the model in English, based partly on Latin poems by Martial and Horace. Later examples include Thomas Carew's 'To Saxham' (1640), and Andrew Marvell's 'Upon Appleton House' (written *c*.1652).

**Further reading:** Malcolm Kelsall, *The Great Good Place: The Country House in English Literature* (1993).

***coup de théâtre*** [koo dě tay-**ahtr**]  A sudden, surprising turn of events that gives a new twist to the plot of a play. Typical *coups de théâtre* involve the unveiling of a disguised character or the reappearance of one assumed by the audience to be dead. *See also* PERIPETEIA.

**couplet** [**kup**-lit]  A pair of rhyming verse lines, usually of the same length; one of the most widely used verse forms in European poetry. Chaucer established the use of couplets in English, notably in the *Canterbury Tales*, using rhymed iambic *pentameters later known as *heroic couplets: a form revived in the 17th century by Ben Jonson, Dryden and others, partly as the equivalent in *heroic drama of the *alexandrine couplets which were the standard verse form of French drama in that century. Alexander Pope followed Dryden's use of heroic couplets in non-dramatic verse to become the master of the form, notably in his use of *closed couplets. The octosyllablic couplet (of 8-syllable or 4-stress lines) is also commonly found in English verse. A couplet may also stand alone as an *epigram, or form part of a larger *stanza, or (as in Shakespeare) round off a *sonnet or a dramatic *scene. *See also* DISTICH.

**courtesy book** A book that gives advice to aspiring young courtiers in etiquette and other aspects of behaviour expected at royal or noble courts. This kind of work—sometimes written in verse—first became popular in various parts of Europe in the late Middle Ages. In the *Renaissance, some important courtesy books expanded more philosophically on the nature of the ideal gentleman and his varied accomplishments. The most influential of these was Baldessare Castiglione's *Il Libro del Cortegiano* (1528), a sequence of dialogues on court life and platonic love. English examples include Henry Peacham's *The Compleat Gentleman* (1622).

**courtly love** A modern term (coined by the French scholar Gaston Paris in 1883, as *amour courtois*) for the literary cult of heterosexual love that emerged among the French aristocracy from the late 11th century onwards, with a profound effect on subsequent Western attitudes to love. Probably influenced by Arabic love poetry, the *troubadours of southern France were followed by northern French *trouvères,* by German *Minnesänger,* and by Dante, Petrarch, and other Italian poets in converting sexual desire from a degrading necessity of physical life into a spiritually ennobling emotion, almost a religious vocation. An elaborate code of behaviour evolved around the tormented male lover's abject obedience to a disdainful, idealized lady, who was usually his social superior. Some of these conventions may derive from misreadings of the Roman poet Ovid, but this form of adoration also imitated both feudal servitude and Christian worship, despite celebrating the excitements of clandestine adultery (as in stories of Lancelot and Guinevere) rather than the then merely economic relation of marriage.

The most important literary treatments of courtly love appear in Chrétien de Troyes's *romance *Lancelot* (late 12th century), and in the first part of the 13th-century allegorical poem, the *Roman de la Rose* by Guillaume de Lorris, later translated by Chaucer. Middle English literature shows less enthusiasm for, or understanding of, courtly love: Chaucer treated the cult sceptically, if sympathetically, but its later influence, established and modified through the *Petrarchan tradition, is strong in 16th-century English *lyrics.

**Further reading:** David Burnley, *Courtliness and Literature in Medieval England* (1998).

**Cowleyan ode** *See* ODE.

**crambo** A versifying game in which players are challenged to produce rhymes for given words or lines (*see also* BOUTS-RIMÉS); or a poem written in response to such a challenge. In a more specialized sense, the term denotes a poem in which all the words that could rhyme with some person's name are accumulated to the point of absurdity. A notable English example is *Molly Mog, or The Fair Maid of the Inn* (1726), a *ballad attributed to John Gay and his drinking partners, who seem to have encouraged each other to rhyme upon the name of an attractive barmaid. In a more general sense, the term is applied to any unimpressively repetitious use of rhyming.

**cretic** *See* AMPHIMACER.

**crisis** A decisive point in the plot of a play or story, upon which the outcome of the remaining action depends, and which ultimately precipitates the *catastrophe or *dénouement. *See also* ANAGNORISIS, CLIMAX, PERIPETEIA.

**criterion** [kry-**teer**-iŏn] (plural **-eria**) A standard or principle by which literary works can be judged or compared.

**Critical Theory** The term adopted by the *Frankfurt School for its intellectual project, essentially one of understanding the relation between freedom and reason in the modern world in the light of an independent form of Marxism revised under influences from sociology (e.g. Max Weber), psychology (Freud), and philosophy (Hegel, Nietzsche). The term when used in this specific sense is often capitalized as here in order to distinguish it from the confusingly similar 'critical theory' in the more general sense of theory pertaining to (literary or aesthetic) criticism: this latter is less confusingly designated as *metacriticism or simply literary theory.

**(⊕) SEE WEB LINKS**
• Illuminations: a Critical Theory site at University of Texas.

**criticism** The reasoned discussion of literary works, an activity which may include some or all of the following procedures, in varying proportions: the defence of *literature against moralists and censors, classification of a work according to its *genre, interpretation of its meaning, analysis of its structure and style, judgement of its worth by comparison with other works, estimation of its likely effect on readers, and the establishment of general principles by which literary works (individually, in categories, or as a whole) can be evaluated and understood. Contrary to the everyday sense of criticism as 'fault-finding', much modern criticism (particularly of the academic kind) assumes that the works it discusses are valuable; the functions of judgement and analysis having to some extent become divided between the market (where reviewers ask 'Is this worth buying?') and the educational world (where academics ask 'Why is this so good?').

The various kinds of criticism fall into several overlapping categories: theoretical, practical, *impressionistic, *affective, *prescriptive, or descriptive. Criticism concerned with revealing the author's true motive or intention (sometimes called 'expressive' criticism) emerged from *Romanticism to dominate much 19th- and 20th-century critical writing, but has tended to give way to 'objective' criticism, focusing on the work itself (as in *New Criticism and *structuralism), and to a shift of attention to the reader in *reader-response criticism. Particular schools of criticism also seek to understand literature in terms of its relations to history, politics, gender, social class, mythology, linguistic theory, or psychology, as with *psychoanalytic criticism, *Marxist criticism, *feminist criticism, *myth criticism, *ecocriticism, and others. *See also* EXEGESIS, HERMENEUTICS, HIGHER CRITICISM, METACRITICISM, POETICS, TEXTUAL CRITICISM.

**critique** A considered assessment of a literary work, usually in the form of an essay or review. Also, in philosophy, politics, and the social sciences, a systematic inquiry into the nature of some principle, idea, institution, or ideology, usually devoted to revealing its limits or self-contradictions. *Verb:* **critique**.

**crossed rhyme** The rhyming of one word in the middle of a long verse line with a word in a similar position in the next line. Sometimes found in rhyming *couplets, crossed rhyme has the effect of making the couplet sound like a *quatrain rhyming *abab*, as in Swinburne's 'Hymn to Proserpine' (1866):

Will ye bridle the deep sea with reins, will ye chasten the high sea with rods?
Will ye take her to chain her with chains, who is older than all ye Gods?

**crown**  A linked sequence of *lyric poems (usually *sonnets), in which the last line of each poem is repeated as the first line of the next, until the final line of the last (usually the seventh) poem repeats the opening line of the first. An Italian form of poetic tribute to the person addressed, the crown of sonnets was used in English by John Donne in the introductory sequence of his *Holy Sonnets* (1633). Sir Philip Sidney had earlier written a crown of *dizains in his *Arcadia* (1590).

**crux** (plural **cruces**)  A difficult or ambiguous passage in a literary work, upon which interpretation of the rest of the work depends.

*culteranismo*  See GONGORISM.

**cultural materialism**  An approach to the analysis of literature, drama, and other cultural forms, adopted by some critics, mainly in Britain, since the early 1980s. Its principles, derived from western traditions of *Marxist criticism, were outlined most influentially by Raymond Williams in his later writings, notably *Problems in Materialism and Culture* (1980) and *Culture* (1981). Here the orthodox Marxist model of an economic 'base' determining a cultural (and political, religious, etc.) 'superstructure' is challenged and replaced by a more flexible model in which cultural activities themselves are regarded as 'material' and productive processes. Cultural materialist approaches to literature emphasize the social and economic contexts (publishing, theatre, education) in which it is produced and consumed. They are also interested in the ways in which the meanings of literary and dramatic works are remade in new social and institutional contexts, especially in re-stagings of Shakespeare. Critics who have identified their work as cultural materialist include Alan Sinfield, Catherine Belsey, and Jonathan Dollimore. Their approach has been distinguished from the somewhat similar school of *new historicism in that they hold a less pessimistic view of the prospects of cultural dissidence and resistance to established powers.

**Further reading:** John Brannigan, *New Historicism and Cultural Materialism* (1998).

**Cultural Studies**  An academic field of interdisciplinary research that grew out of literary studies in the early 1960s in Britain and extended its investigations of culture, language, and social meanings into neighbouring realms of cinema, television, print journalism, advertising, and fashion as well as popular literature and drama. In reaction against the alleged narrowness of literary studies, with their concentration on a *canon of 'high' literary art, it aimed to take a much wider range of cultural productions as its object of study, and it helped to generate further academic ventures in the form of Film Studies and Media Studies. As a distinct enterprise, Cultural Studies first became visible with the foundation by Richard Hoggart of the Centre for Contemporary Cultural Studies (CCCS) at the University of Birmingham in 1964, at first within the Department of English and then from 1972 as an independent unit. In its early phase, Cultural Studies at Birmingham and elsewhere was broadly an extension of the *sociology of literature inspired by Raymond Williams's *The Long Revolution* (1961), combined with 'communications studies' of media and advertising, and with social history of working-class subcultures. Under Stuart Hall's directorship of the CCCS (1969–79) and thereafter, the new discipline came increasingly under the influence of French *structuralist, *poststructuralist, and neo-Marxist theories, and devoted itself to showing how 'discursive practices' (Hollywood movies, TV advertisements, etc.) constructed 'subject positions' that held their viewers in thrall to capitalism. Cultural Studies remains a recognized academic term, less for the study of culture or cultures than for the cultivation of *Theory as applicable equally to literary and non-literary cultural productions and processes, all being counted as 'texts' to be decoded.

**Further reading:** Graeme Turner, *British Cultural Studies: An Introduction* (3rd edn, 2003).

(⊕) SEE WEB LINKS
• Culturemachine: searchable database of free texts.

**cunto** [**kuun**-toh] (plural **cunti**) A Neapolitan dialect word for a tale or short story (in Italian, *novella*), as in the title of Giambattista Basile's *Lo cunto de li cunti* (1634–6), an important early collection of *fairy tales and other *folktales within a *frame narrative, more widely known as the *Pentamerone* and translated into Italian in 1747.

**curtain-raiser** A brief dramatic entertainment, usually a light one-act play, preceding the full-length drama that formed the main part of a theatre's programme. A common form in the late 19th-century theatre, although now obsolete.

**curtal sonnet** The name given by the English poet Gerard Manley
Hopkins (1844–89) to a curtailed form of the *sonnet which he invented.
The curtal sonnet has ten lines with an additional half-line at the end.
Hopkins wrote two of these: 'Peace' and 'Pied Beauty'.

**cut-up** A technique used by the novelist William S. Burroughs in some
passages of his works, notably *The Ticket That Exploded* (1962), whereby
a pre-existing written text is cut into segments which are reshuffled
at random before being printed in the resulting accidental order.
*See also* ALEATORY, COLLAGE.

**cyberpunk** A phase of American *science fiction in the 1980s and
1990s most often associated with William Gibson's novel *Neuromancer*
(1984) and its sequels, and with the work of Bruce Sterling, who edited
*Mirrorshades: The Cyberpunk Anthology* (1986). By contrast with
earlier mainstream science fiction, which commonly implied a utopian
confidence in technological progress, cyberpunk fiction is influenced
by the gloomier world of *hard-boiled detective fiction and by *film
*noir* thrillers; it foresees a near future in which sinister multinational
corporations dominate the 'cyberspace' (that is, the world computerized
information network) upon which an impoverished metropolitan
populace depends. In a broader sense, the term refers to a larger
body of work in the 1980s and after—including such films as Ridley
Scott's *Blade Runner* (1982)—in which the interpenetration of human
and technological or electronic realms, in androids or in 'virtual'
reality, is taken as the basis of fictional speculation, usually
*dystopian.
**Further reading:** Larry McCaffery (ed.), *Storming the Reality Studio* (1992).

**cycle** A group of works, usually narrative poems, that either share a
common theme or subject (e.g. the Trojan war, Charlemagne, the
Knights of the Round Table), or are linked together as a sequence. In
addition to *epics, *sagas, *romances, and *chansons de geste*, which
scholars have categorized into different cycles, the *mystery plays of the
Middle Ages that were performed as a sequence during the same festival
at a particular place are referred to as the York Cycle, the Chester Cycle,
etc. The term is also applied to sequences of sonnets by the same author,
and sometimes to sequences of novels or stories (*see* ROMAN-FLEUVE).
*Adjective*: **cyclic**.

**cynghanedd** [kung-**han**-ĕth] An elaborate system of sound-correspondences employed by poets in the Welsh language since the 14th century. Its conventions, formally adopted by an assembly of *bards (*Eisteddfod*) in 1523, govern the positions of stressed syllables and *caesurae in different kinds of verse line, from which are generated various patterns of internal rhyme and *alliteration. In one such pattern, for example, the second part of a tripartite line will rhyme with the first part while its sequence of consonants will be repeated in the third part.

**dactyl** A metrical unit (*foot) of verse, having one stressed syllable followed by two unstressed syllables, as in the word *carefully* (or, in *quantitative verse, one long syllable and two short ones). Dactylic *hexameters were used in Greek and Latin *epic poetry, and in the elegiac *distich, but **dactylic verse** is rare in English: Tennyson's 'The Charge of the Light Brigade' uses it, as does Thomas Hardy's 'The Voice', which begins

> Woman much missed, how you call to me, call to me

*See also* FALLING RHYTHM, METRE, TRIPLE METRE.

**Dada (Dadaism)** An *avant-garde* movement of anarchic protest against bourgeois society, religion, and art, founded in 1916 in Switzerland by Tristan Tzara, a Romanian-born French poet. From 1919 the Dadaist group assembled in Paris, issuing nihilistic manifestos against the culture which had been discredited by the 1914–18 war, and experimenting with anti-logical poetry and *collage pictures and sculptures. The group included the artists Marcel Duchamp and Man Ray, the poet-sculptor Hans Arp, and the young poets André Breton, Paul Éluard, and Louis Aragon. Dada was short-lived, but it ushered in the *Surrealism which superseded it from 1922.

**Further reading:** David Hopkins, *Dada and Surrealism* (2004).

**(⊕) SEE WEB LINKS**

• International Dada Archive at University of Iowa.

**death of the author** A slogan launched by the French literary theorist Roland Barthes in an influential essay of 1968, 'La mort de l'auteur', in which he proclaimed the corresponding 'birth of the reader'. In partial imitation of Friedrich Nietzsche's announcement of the 'death of God' in the late 19th century, Barthes sought to topple the supposedly godlike authority of the writer over the possible meanings of his or her work, and to grant more freedom of interpretation to readers; he thereby gave important encouragement to *reader-response criticism. He drew upon *structuralist principles, according to which the meanings of texts derive from pre-existing linguistic and cultural *codes which the author may combine or activate but does not originate. Barthes was reacting both against a *Romantic cult of genius and originality, in which authors are creative while readers are essentially receptive, and against academic tendencies to grant conclusive authority in the determination of literary meaning to biographical sources such as prefaces or letters written by an author about the work in question. The argument that the author had in principle no such authority had been advanced twenty years earlier by some of the American *New Critics (*see* INTENTIONAL FALLACY), without resort to bloodthirsty metaphors. Barthes's phrase has become widely identified with the iconoclastic tendencies of structuralist and *post-structuralist theory.

**Further reading:** Sean Burke, *The Death and Return of the Author* (1992).

**débat** [day-bah] A poem in the form of a debate between two characters, who are usually *personifications of opposed principles or qualities: body and soul, water and wine, winter and summer, etc. The *débat* was much practised in Europe during the 12th and 13th centuries, both in Latin and in the *vernacular languages. The outstanding English example is the early 13th-century poem *The Owl and the Nightingale*, in which the two birds—probably representing religious and secular poetry respectively—dispute over the benefits they bring to mankind. In French, François Villon later wrote a *débat* between the heart and the body. The *débat* commonly ends with an inconclusive reference of the issue to a judge. The form has some classical precedents in the *agon of Aristophanes' comedies and the *eclogues of Theocritus; and it may in turn have influenced the structures of later medieval drama. *See also* AMOEBEAN VERSES, DIALOGUE.

**decadence** A state of decay shown in either the inferior literary quality or the looser moral standards of any period's works compared with a preceding period, as with *Hellenistic Greek or post-*Augustan Latin literatures; or the 19th-century literary movement in Paris, London, and Vienna that cultivated the exhausted refinement and artificiality it admired in the 'decadent' ages of Greek and Latin literature. Although the term has various unfavourable connotations ranging from simple inferiority to moral 'degeneracy', several writers in the late 19th century accepted the description proudly, thus implying a shocking parallel between their imperial societies and the decline of the Roman empire. The Decadent movement, closely associated with the doctrines of *Aestheticism, can be traced back to the writings of Théophile Gautier and Edgar Allan Poe in the 1830s, but became a significant presence only after the publication of Charles Baudelaire's influential collection of poems, *Les Fleurs du mal* (1857), and culminated in the *fin-de-siècle* culture of the 1880s and 1890s.

The basic principle of this decadence, expounded in the 1860s by Gautier and Baudelaire, was complete opposition to Nature: hence its systematic cultivation of drugs, cosmetics, Catholic ritual, supposedly 'unnatural' sexual practices, and sterility and artificiality in all things. A complete decadent way of life is portrayed in Joris-Karl Huysmans's novel *A Rebours* (*Against the Grain* or *Against Nature*, 1884), upon which Oscar Wilde's *The Picture of Dorian Gray* (1891) is partly based. In France, decadence became almost synonymous with the work of the *Symbolists, some of whom were associated in the 1880s with the journal *Le Décadent*. In England, it emerged from the *Pre-Raphaelite circle, in the poetry of D. G. Rossetti and in Swinburne's scandalous *Poems and Ballads* (1866), leading to the work of Wilde, Ernest Dowson, and Arthur Symons in the 1890s, until Wilde's imprisonment in 1895 suddenly ended the decadent episode. Symons, in his essay 'The Decadent Movement in Literature' (1893), described the phenomenon as 'an interesting disease' typical of an over-luxurious civilization, characterized by 'an intense self-consciousness, a restless curiosity in research, an over-subtilizing refinement upon refinement, a spiritual and moral perversity'.

**Further reading:** George C. Schoolfield, *A Baedeker of Decadence* (2003).

**decastich** [dek-ă-stik] A *stanza or poem of ten lines, for example the stanza used by Keats in his 'Ode to a Nightingale' and 'Ode on a Grecian Urn' (both 1820), or the Spanish *décima*.

**decasyllabic** Made up of ten syllables. In English verse, the iambic *pentameter is normally decasyllabic, although it sometimes becomes *hendecasyllabic with the addition of an eleventh syllable. On the other hand, the hendecasyllabic line (*endecasyllabo*) of Italian verse employed by Dante and Petrarch may in practice be decasyllabic if no further

unstressed syllables follow the stressed tenth syllable (*see* VERSO
TRONCO).

**décima** [deth-i-mă]  A Spanish verse *stanza of ten *octosyllabic lines
rhyming *abbaaccddc*. It is sometimes referred to as an *espinela* after one
of its notable practitioners, Vicente Espinel (1550–1624), whose
contemporaries mistakenly believed he had invented the form.

**deconstruction**  A philosophically sceptical approach to the
possibility of coherent meaning in language, initiated by the French
philosopher Jacques Derrida (1930–2004) in a series of works published
in 1967 (later translated as *Speech and Phenomena*, *Of Grammatology*,
and *Writing and Difference*), and adopted by several leading literary
critics in the United States—notably at Yale University—from the early
1970s onwards. Derrida's claim is that the dominant Western tradition
of thought has attempted to establish grounds of certainty and truth
by repressing the limitless instability of language. This '*logocentric'
tradition sought some absolute source or guarantee of meaning
(a 'transcendental signified') which could centre or stabilize the
uncertainties of signification, through a set of 'violent hierarchies'
privileging a central term over a marginal one: nature over culture,
male over female, and most importantly speech over writing. The
'*phonocentric' suspicion of writing as a parasite upon the authenticity
of speech is a crucial target of Derrida's subversive approach to Western
philosophy, in which he inverts and dissolves conceptual hierarchies
to show that the repressed or marginalized term has always already
contaminated the privileged or central term. Thus, drawing on
Saussure's theory of the *sign, Derrida argues that the stable self-identity
which we attribute to speech as the authentic source of meaning is
illusory, since language operates as a self-contained system of internal
differences rather than of positive terms or presences: writing, distrusted
in the Western 'metaphysics of presence' because it displays the absence
of any authenticating voice, is in this sense logically prior to speech.
    Derrida's central concept (although in principle it ought not to occupy
such a 'hierarchical' position) is presented in his coining of the term
*différance*, a French *portmanteau word combining 'difference' with
'deferral' to suggest that the differential nature of meanings in language
ceaselessly defers or postpones any determinate meaning: language is
an endless chain or 'play of *différance'* which logocentric discourses try
vainly to fix to some original or final term that can never be reached.

Deconstructive readings track down within a *text the *aporia or internal contradiction that undermines its claims to coherent meaning; or they reveal how texts can be seen to deconstruct themselves. Derrida's difficult and paradoxical attitude to the metaphysical tradition seeks to subvert it while also claiming that there is no privileged vantage-point from which to do this from outside the instabilities of language.

Deconstruction thus undermines its own radical scepticism by admitting that it leaves everything exactly as it was; it is an unashamedly self-contradictory effort to think the 'unthinkable', often by recourse to strange *neologisms, *puns, and other word-play. Although initially directed against the scientific pretensions of *structuralism in the human sciences, it was welcomed enthusiastically into literary studies at Yale University and elsewhere in the English-speaking world, partly because it seemed to place literary problems of *figurative language and interpretation above philosophers' and historians' claims to truth, and partly because it opened up limitless possibilities of interpretation. The writings of Paul de Man, Barbara Johnson, J. Hillis Miller, and Geoffrey Hartman in the 1970s and 1980s applied and extended Derrida's concepts to critical questions of interpretation, tending to challenge the status of the author's intention or of the external world as a source of meaning in texts, and questioning the boundary between criticism and literature. This '*Yale school' and other deconstructionists came under fierce attack for dogmatic nihilism and wilful obscurity. *See also* DISSEMINATION, INDETERMINACY, POST-STRUCTURALISM.

**Further reading:** Nicholas Royle (ed.), *Deconstructions: A User's Guide* (2000).

**decorum** [di-**kor**-ŭm]  A standard of appropriateness by which certain styles, characters, forms, and actions in literary works are deemed suitable to one another within a hierarchical model of culture bound by class distinctions. Derived from Horace's *Ars Poetica* (*c.*20 BCE) and other works of classical criticism, decorum was a major principle of late *Renaissance taste and of *neoclassicism. It ranked and fixed the various literary *genres in 'high', 'middle', and 'low' stations, and expected the style, characters, and actions in each to conform to its assigned level: thus a *tragedy or *epic should be written in a high or 'grand' style about high-ranking characters performing grand deeds, whereas a *comedy should treat humble characters and events in a 'low' or colloquial style. The mixture of high and low levels, as in Shakespeare, was seen as indecorous, although it could be exploited for humorous effect in *burlesques and *mock-heroic works. The strict application of these principles of decorum was overturned by the advent of *Romanticism; although in a general sense writers always suit style to subject-matter according to their purposes. *See also* CONVENTION, DICTION, STYLE.

**deep structure** The underlying structure of meaning in any utterance, as opposed to the observable arrangement (the **surface structure**) in which it is presented. The distinction between deep structure and surface structure is a major principle of the revolution in grammatical theory led by the American linguist Noam Chomsky in the 1960s, and has been adopted by some theorists of *narratology. According to Chomsky, the deep structure of a sentence is its underlying semantic content, an abstraction decoded from the actual syntactic sequence of its surface structure (*see* SEMANTICS, SYNTAX). Thus the sentence *The mariner shot the albatross* differs in surface structure from *The albatross was shot by the mariner*, but shares the same deep structure. The distinction is broadly similar to that between *content and *form. Some narratologists have attempted to define the deep structures of narratives on the model of linguistic analyses of sentences: thus A. J. Greimas distinguishes the underlying *binary oppositions between basic roles (or *actants) from their surface realization as contrasts between characters in a sequential *plot.

**defamiliarization** The distinctive effect achieved by literary works in disrupting our habitual perception of the world, enabling us to 'see' things afresh, according to the theories of some English Romantic poets and of *Russian Formalism. Samuel Taylor Coleridge in *Biographia Literaria* (1817) wrote of the 'film of familiarity' that blinds us to the wonders of the world, and that Wordworth's poetry aimed to remove. P. B. Shelley in his essay 'The Defence of Poetry' (written 1821) also claims that poetry 'makes familiar objects be as if they were not familiar' by stripping 'the veil of familiarity from the world'. In modern usage, the term corresponds to Viktor Shklovsky's use of the Russian word *ostranenie* ('making strange') in his influential essay 'Poetry as Technique' (1917). Shklovsky argued that art exists in order to recover for us the sensation of life which is diminished in the 'automatized' routine of everyday experience. He and the other Formalists set out to define the devices by which literary works achieve this effect, usually in terms of the '*foregrounding' of the linguistic medium. Brecht's theory of the *alienation effect in drama starts from similar grounds. *See also* LITERARINESS.

**defective foot** An incomplete *foot in a line of metrical verse. The term, sometimes applied to *catalectic lines, is misleadingly pejorative, since the deficiency is usually not in the verse itself but rather in the metrical analysis that attempts to make the *metre conform to an abstract scheme of feet. *See also* ACEPHALOUS, TRUNCATION.

**deixis** A term used in linguistics to denote those aspects of an utterance that refer to and depend upon the situation in which the utterance is made. **Deictic** words indicate the situational 'co-ordinates' of person (*I/you, us/them*), place (*here/there, this/that*), and time (*now/then, yesterday/today*).

**demotic** [di-**mot**-ik] Derived from or using the language of the common people rather than the more formal style of a priesthood or other educated élite. *See also* COLLOQUIALISM, VERNACULAR.

**demotion** The use of a stressed syllable in an 'offbeat' position in a metrical verse line that would normally be occupied by an unstressed syllable. An important means of variation in English verse, demotion usually has the effect of slowing the rhythm of the line, as in the *iambic verse of Tennyson's 'Ulysses':

> The long day wanes, the slow moon climbs; the deep
> Moans round with many voices

where 'day', 'moon', and 'Moans' are all demoted to offbeat positions. This does not mean that they should be read as unstressed: in fact the effect depends upon their retaining at least some of their normal *stress. The demotion rules formulated by Derek Attridge in *The Rhythms of English Verse* (1982) permit a stressed syllable to realize an offbeat between two other stressed syllables or at the beginning of a line before a stressed syllable. In similar positions in *triple metre, a stressed syllable may realize an offbeat, either on its own, or with an unstressed syllable, or (more rarely) with another stressed syllable. The concepts of demotion and *promotion account more successfully for those metrical variations that traditional *prosody described in terms of *substitution. *See also* METRE.

**denotation** *See* CONNOTATION.

**dénouement** [day-**noo**-mah[n]] The clearing up or 'untying' of the complications of the *plot in a play or story; usually a final scene or chapter in which mysteries, confusions, and doubtful destinies are clarified. *See also* CATASTROPHE.

**detective story** *See* p. 94.

***deus ex machina*** [**day**-uus eks **mak**-ină] The 'god from a machine' who was lowered on to the stage by mechanical contrivance in some ancient Greek plays (notably those of Euripides) to solve the problems of the *plot at a stroke. A later example is Shakespeare's introduction of Hymen into the last scene of *As You Like It* to marry off the main characters. The term is now used pejoratively for any improbable or unexpected contrivance by which an author resolves the complications of the plot in a play or novel, and which has not been convincingly prepared for in the preceding action: the discovery of a lost will was a favourite resort of Victorian novelists. *See also* COUP DE THÉÂTRE, DÉNOUEMENT, MACHINERY.

**device** An all-purpose term used to describe any literary technique deliberately employed to achieve a specific effect. In the theories of *Russian Formalism and *Brechtian theatre, the phrase 'baring the device' refers to the way that some works expose or highlight the means (linguistic or theatrical) by which they operate on us, rather than conceal them. *See also* FOREGROUNDING, METADRAMA.

**devotional poetry** Poetry expressing religious worship or prayer. This is a large and varied category of verse, distinguished from secular poetry of all kinds, especially in the study of medieval lyrics. A secular love poem may express devotion to the beloved, but it would still not be classed as devotional poetry.

**diachronic** [dy-ă-**kron**-ik] Relating to historical change over a span of time. The revolution in linguistics begun by Ferdinand de Saussure in the *Cours de linguistique générale* (1915) is founded partly on the distinction between the diachronic study of linguistic features evolving in time and the *synchronic study of a language as a complete system operating at a given moment. Saussure argued, against the historical bias of 19th-century *philology, that the synchronic dimension or 'axis' must be given precedence. *Noun*: **diachrony**.

**diacritic**  A mark placed above or below a letter or syllable to specify its distinctive sound value. Diacritics commonly found are the acute accent (é), grave accent (è), circumflex (ô), umlaut (ö), and cedilla (ç). Diacritical markings commonly used in *scansion include the macron (−) for long syllables, the breve (⌣) for short syllables, the acute accent or the virgule (') for stressed syllables, and the ˟ symbol for unstressed syllables.

**diaeresis** [dy-**err**-ĕsis] **(dieresis)** (plural **-eses**)  A Greek word for 'division', used in three different senses: **1.** In classical *prosody, the coincidence of a word ending with the end of a *foot. **2.** The separation of two adjacent vowels into distinct sounds (e.g. Zoë, coöperate), also the umlaut mark which indicates this. **3.** In *rhetoric, a *figure by which the parts or attributes of anything are enumerated.

**dialect**  A distinctive variety of a language, spoken by members of an identifiable regional group, nation, or social class. Dialects differ from one another in pronunciation, vocabulary, and (often) in grammar. Traditionally they have been regarded as variations from a 'standard' educated form of the language, but modern linguists point out that standard forms are themselves dialects which have come to predominate for social and political reasons. The study of variations between different dialects is known as **dialectology**. *Adjective*: **dialectal**.

**dialectic**  **1.** The art of formal reasoning, especially the procedure of seeking truth through debate or discussion. **2.** The reasoning or logical structure that holds together a continuous argument or exposition. **3.** The interplay of contradictory principles or opposed forces, as understood in the European tradition of philosophy influenced by G. W. F. Hegel and including Marx and Engels. Some schematic versions of **dialectical** philosophy speak of a unification of opposites in which the *thesis* is opposed by the *antithesis* but united with it in a higher *synthesis*.

**dialogic (dialogical)**  Characterized or constituted by the interactive, responsive nature of *dialogue rather than by the single-mindedness of *monologue. The term is important in the writings of the Russian theorist Mikhail Bakhtin, whose book *Problems of Dostoevsky's Poetics* (1929) contrasts the dialogic or *polyphonic interplay of various

## DETECTIVE STORY

A story in which the principal action and focus of interest is the investigation of a crime or apparently criminal enigma by a detective figure, either professional or amateur. The centrality of this detective figure distinguishes the detective story proper from some other kinds of crime fiction in which the emphasis lies upon the actions of a crime's perpetrator or victim (*see also* THRILLER, SENSATION NOVEL). Conventionally, the crime should be an especially baffling case that requires the uncommon ingenuity of the detective to find a solution and identify or pin the blame on the true perpetrator, who commonly has an apparently safe alibi or has left a false trail incriminating others. Various kinds of crime are possible subjects, although murder, and preferably multiple murder involving the elimination of witnesses to the original crime, has been found to be the most appetizing to readers addicted to the *genre—tax evasion and non-lethal motoring offences, for instance, being passed over as insufficiently colourful. The superior insight of the detective is often contrasted with the gullibility of others in the story, usually unimaginative police officers self-blinded by routines and habitual assumptions.

Detective fiction comes in two sizes: the *short story and the short or mid-length *novel (lengthy novels are rare in this genre). From the origins of detective fiction in the mid-19th century until the 1920s, the short story tended to be more important, from Edgar A. Poe's founding tale 'The Murders in the Rue Morgue' (1841) and Arthur Conan Doyle's stories in the *Strand* magazine collected in *The Adventures of Sherlock Holmes* (1892) and several later volumes, to the Father Brown stories (1911–35) of G. K. Chesterton. The full-length detective novel was inaugurated in France by Emile Gaboriau's *L'Affaire Lerouge* (1866), and grew in importance in the early 20th century with the success of such major practitioners as Agatha Christie (from her first novel, *The Mysterious Affair at Styles*, 1920) and the Belgian author Georges Simenon (from his first Maigret novel, *Pietr-le-Letton*, 1931).

Various *subgenres of detective story are recognized by its devotees, among them the 'locked room mystery' involving an apparently impossible crime perpetrated within an enclosed space with ostensibly no exit or entrance (Poe's Rue Morgue story being an example); and the 'police procedural', in which the investigation is conducted by a professional team employing normal methods, as in Ed McBain's series (from 1956) set in the offices of the 87th Precinct of the New York Police Department. Otherwise detective stories are divided loosely according to kinds of detective figure (amateur, private eye, police) or according to their settings (railway, village, ship, or the favourite English country house) or professional mileux (ecclesiastical, medical, academic, theatrical, etc.). Certain major traditions or schools are also well recognized in the history of the genre, the most important being *Golden-Age detective writing and the *hard-boiled school.

**Further reading:** Julian Symons, *Bloody Murder* (3rd edn, 1992); T. J. Binyon, *Murder Will Out* (1991).

 SEE WEB LINKS

• Crimeculture: web resource for academic study of crime fiction.

characters' voices in Dostoevsky's novels with the 'monological' subordination of characters to the single viewpoint of the author in Tolstoy's . In the same year, *Marxism and the Philosophy of Language* (probably by Bakhtin, although published under the name of V. N. Voloshinov) argued, against Saussure's theory of *la \*langue*, that actual utterances are 'dialogic' in that they are embedded in a context of dialogue and thus respond to an interlocutor's previous utterances and/or try to draw a particular response from a specific auditor. *See also* CARNIVALIZATION, MULTI-ACCENTUALITY. *Noun*: **dialogism**.

**Further reading:** Michael Holquist, *Dialogism* (1990).

**(⊕) SEE WEB LINKS**

• Site of the Bakhtin Centre, University of Sheffield.

**dialogue** Spoken exchanges between or among characters in a dramatic or narrative work; or a literary form in prose or verse based on a debate or discussion, usually between two speakers. Dialogue is clearly a major aspect of drama, and is usually a significant component of prose fictions and of some narrative poetry, as in the \*ballad. As a literary form, the dialogue was much favoured in ancient Greek and Latin literature for \*didactic and \*satirical purposes as well as in \*pastoral poetry. The \*Socratic dialogues of Plato (4th century BCE) are the most influential ancient works in dialogue form; a modern counterpart is Wilde's *The Critic as Artist* (1891). The \**débat* and the \*flyting are special varieties of verse dialogue. In modern poetry, W. B. Yeats often used the dialogue form, as in 'Michael Robartes and the Dancer' (1921). *See also* AMOEBEAN VERSES.

**diction** The choice of words used in a literary work. A writer's diction may be characterized, for example, by \*archaism, or by \*Latinate or Anglo-Saxon derivations; and it may be described according to the oppositions formal/colloquial, abstract/concrete, and literal/figurative. For the specific \*conventions of diction in poetry, *see* POETIC DICTION.

**didactic** [dy-**dak**-tik] Instructive; designed to impart information, advice, or some doctrine of morality or philosophy. Much of the most ancient surviving literature is didactic, containing genealogies, proverbial wisdom, and religious instruction. Most European literary works of the Middle Ages have a strong didactic element, usually expounding doctrines of the Church. Practical advice has often been presented in verse, as in the *Georgics* (37–30 BCE) of Virgil, which give

advice on farming, and in the imitative *georgics of the 18th century.
Since the ascendancy of *Romanticism and *Aestheticism in the 19th
century, didactic writing has been viewed unfavourably as foreign to
true art, so that the term **didacticism** refers (usually pejoratively) to the
use of literary means to a doctrinal end. Some imaginative works still
contain practical information, however: Robert Pinsky's verse sequence
'Tennis' (1975) offers practical tips on service, backhand shots, and
other relevant skills. The boundaries of didactic literature are open
to dispute, since both the presence and the prominence of doctrinal
content are subject to differing interpretations. In the broadest sense,
most *allegories and *satires implying a moral or political view may be
regarded as didactic, along with many other kinds of work in which the
*theme embodies some philosophical or other belief of the author. A
stricter definition would confine the term to those works that explicitly
tell readers what they should do. *See also* PROPAGANDISM.

**diegesis** [dy-ĕ-**jee**-sis] An analytic term used in modern *narratology
to designate the narrated events or *story (French, *histoire*) as a 'level'
distinct from that of the *narration. The **diegetic** level of a narrative is
that of the main story, whereas the 'higher' level at which the story is
told is **extradiegetic** (i.e. standing outside the sphere of the main story).
An *embedded tale-within-the-tale constitutes a lower level known as
**hypodiegetic**. In an older sense outlined in Aristotle's *Poetics*, diegesis
is the reporting or narration of events, contrasted with *mimesis, which
is the imitative representation of them: so a character in a play who
performs a certain action is engaged in mimesis, but if she recounts
some earlier action, she is practising diegesis. The distinction is often
cast as that between 'showing' and 'telling'.

**dieresis** *See* DIAERESIS.

**différance** [dif-air-ah$^n$s] A term coined by the philosopher Jacques
Derrida to combine two senses of the French verb *différer* (to differ, and
to defer or postpone) in a noun which is spelt differently from *différence*
but pronounced in the same way. The point of this *neologism is to
indicate simultaneously two senses in which language denies us the full
presence of any meaning: first, that no linguistic element (according to
Saussure's theory of the *sign) has a positive meaning, only an effect
of meaning arising from its differences from other elements; second,
that presence or fullness of meaning is always deferred from one sign

to another in an endless sequence. Thus if you look up a word in a dictionary, all it can give you is other words to explain it; so—in theory, at least—you will then have to look these up, and so on without end. *Différance*, then, may be conceived as an underlying principle of non-identity which makes signification possible only by 'spacing out' both *signifiers and concepts (*signifieds) so that meaning appears merely as a 'trace' of other terms within or across any given term. Derrida tried to avoid placing *différance* as a fixed concept, preferring to use it as an unstable term, although it is fundamental to his philosophy of *deconstruction. *See also* DISSEMINATION.

**digression** A temporary departure from one subject to another more or less distantly related topic before the discussion of the first subject is resumed. A valuable technique in the art of storytelling, digression is also employed in many kinds of non-fictional writing and *oratory. *Adjective*: **digressive**. *See also* EXCURSUS.

**dime novel** A cheap and usually violently sensational *novel, so called because of its price (a dime being ten US cents) in the late 19th century, although in fact many of these books were cheaper still at five cents. The dime novel flourished from the 1860s to the 1890s, and provided tales of adventure about war, crime, or life on the Western frontier, featuring characters such as the real-life frontiersman Deadwood Dick or the entirely fictional New York detective Nick Carter.

**(⊕) SEE WEB LINKS**
• Dime Novel and Story Paper Collection at Stanford University, a large archive.

**dimeter** [**dim**-it-er] A line of verse consisting of two metrical feet (*see* FOOT). In English verse, this means a line with two main *stresses. The term originally referred, in classical *prosody, to a line of two *dipodies, i.e. four feet.

**Dionysian** *See* APOLLONIAN.

**diphthong** A vowel sound that changes noticeably in quality during the pronunciation of a syllable, as in the English words *wide*, *late*, *beer*, or *round*. Diphthongs are thus distinguished from simple vowels (*cat*, *feed*, etc.), which are referred to by phoneticians as **monophthongs**. *Adjective*: **diphthongal**.

**dipody** [**dip**-ŏdi] A pair of metrical feet (*see* FOOT) considered as a single unit. **Dipodic** verse, commonly found in *ballads and nursery rhymes, is characterized by the pairing together of feet, in which one usually has a stronger *stress.

**dirge**  A song of lamentation in mourning for someone's death; or a poem in the form of such a song, and usually less elaborate than an *elegy. An ancient *genre employed by Pindar in Greek and notably by Propertius in Latin, the dirge also occurs in English, most famously in Ariel's song 'Full fathom five thy father lies' in Shakespeare's *The Tempest*.

**dirty realism**  A critical label attached since the early 1980s to a group of American short-story writers, of whom the best-known are Raymond Carver, Jayne Anne Phillips, and Tobias Wolff. The term refers to a tendency for their stories to recount incidents of impoverished life among blue-collar workers in small-town America, in a bare, unsensational style.

*discours* [dis-koor]  The French word for *discourse or conversation. When it appears in this form in modern theoretical writings in English, it usually carries a special sense given to it by the linguist Émile Benveniste in his *Problèmes de linguistique générale* (1966), in which he distinguishes *discours* as a 'subjective' mode of speech (or writing) from *histoire*, which is apparently 'objective'. In *discours*, the present situation of speech or writing is indicated by signs of *deixis (e.g. the pronouns *I* and *you*, the adverbs *here*, *now*, *there*, etc.) and by the use of tense (*she has gone* rather than *she went*). While *discours* thus displays its nature as an enunciation involving a relationship between a speaker/writer and a listener/reader, *histoire* conceals this by its concentration on the enounced (*see ÉNONCÉ*). Confusingly, another distinction is made between these two terms in *narratology, where *histoire* is *story, and *discours* is language or *narration.

**discourse**  Any extended use of speech or writing; or a formal exposition or dissertation. In linguistics, discourse is the name given to units of language longer than a single sentence; **discourse analysis** is the study of *cohesion and other relationships between sentences in written or spoken discourse. In modern cultural theory, especially in the *post-structuralism associated with the French historian Michel Foucault, the term has been used to denote any coherent body of statements that produces a self-confirming account of reality by defining an object of attention and generating concepts with which to analyse it (e.g. medical discourse, legal discourse, aesthetic discourse). The specific discourse in which a statement is made will govern the kinds of connections that can be made between ideas, and will involve certain assumptions about the kind of person(s) addressed. By extension, as a free-standing noun ('discourse' as such), the term denotes language in actual use within its social and ideological context and in institutionalized representations of the world called **discursive** practices. In general, the increased use of this term in modern cultural theory arises from dissatisfaction with the rather fixed and abstract term 'language' (*see* LANGUE); by contrast, 'discourse' better indicates the specific contexts and relationships involved in historically produced uses of language. *See* DISCOURS for a further sense. *See also* EPISTEME, RHETORIC.

**Further reading:** Sara Mills, *Discourse* (2nd edn, 2004).

**discovery**  A term sometimes used as an English equivalent for *anagnorisis, that is, a point in a play or story at which a character recognizes the true state of affairs. *See also* DÉNOUEMENT.

**discussion play**  A kind of drama in which debate and discussion are more important than plot, action, or character. Some of Bernard Shaw's plays are of this kind, notably *Misalliance* (1910) and *Heartbreak House* (1919). *See also* PROBLEM PLAY.

**disintegration**  A term coined by E. K. Chambers, in his day the leading authority on the history of English theatre, in his British Academy lecture *The Disintegration of Shakespeare* (1924), characterizing the efforts of earlier scholars (principally F. G. Fleay and J. M. Robertson) to attribute some of the plays of Shakespeare wholly or partly to other Elizabethan and Jacobean playwrights such as Christopher Marlowe, George Chapman, and Ben Jonson. The **disintegrators**, as Chambers called them, had based their reattributions upon supposedly scientific analyses of the plays' versification, and upon unsupported assumptions that Shakespeare had revised plays written by others. Chambers's arguments against the disintegration of the Shakespeare *canon were generally accepted, although scholars do now broadly agree that a few of the plays did involve partial collaboration with John Fletcher and Thomas Middleton. Disintegration is a phenomenon entirely distinct from the *anti-

Stratfordian conspiracy theories, which usually deny Shakespeare the authorship of any of the works published in his name.

**dissemination** In the terminology of *deconstruction, the dispersal of meanings among infinite possibilities; the effect of *différance* in the 'free play' of signification beyond the control of concepts or stable interpretation. Whereas *ambiguity usually involves a limited number of possible meanings, dissemination is an endless proliferation of possibilities. *See also* INDETERMINACY.

**dissociation of sensibility** The separation of thought from feeling, which T. S. Eliot diagnosed as the weakness of English poetry from the Revolution of the 1640s until his own time. In his influential essay 'The Metaphysical Poets' (1921), Eliot argued that whereas in Donne and other pre-Revolutionary poets 'there is a direct sensuous apprehension of thought, or a recreation of thought into feeling', from the time of Milton and Dryden 'a dissociation of sensibility set in, from which we have never recovered'. This view had some influence in British and American criticism in the mid-20th century, notably in the *Cambridge school and among the *New Critics, but it has frequently been challenged as a misleading simplification of literary history.

**dissonance** Harshness of sound and/or rhythm, either inadvertent or deliberate. The term is nearly equivalent to *cacophony, but tends to denote a lack of harmony between sounds rather than the harshness of a particular sound in isolation. Browning, Hopkins, and many other poets have made deliberate use of dissonance. *Adjective*: **dissonant**.

**distant reading** A provocative slogan launched by the Italian literary historian Franco Moretti in his article 'Conjectures on World Literature' (2000; later reprinted with related pieces in his collection *Distant Reading*, 2013). Coined in direct opposition to the tradition of *close reading cultivated in the English-speaking academic world, Moretti's phrase indicates his apparently perverse attempts to discover what may be learned about novels without actually reading them. His research projects have included quantitative bibliometric analyses of thousands of forgotten novels, for example, detecting trends in the length of their titles as listed in catalogues.

**distich** [**dis**-tik]  A pair of verse lines, usually making complete sense, as in the *closed couplet. The term is most often applied to the Greek verse form in which a dactylic *hexameter is followed by a 'pentameter' (actually composed of two dactylic half-lines of two-and-a-half feet each). This form, known as the **elegiac distich** or **elegiac couplet**, was used in Greek and Latin verse for *elegies and *epigrams, and later by some German poets including Goethe.

*dit* [dee]  A late-medieval French term for a kind of poem distinguished neither by verse-form (although octosyllabic couplets are common), nor by subject-matter (the *dit* could be erotic, satirical, devotional etc.), but by its first-person voice. This element of personal testimony separates the narrative *dit* from the third-person voice of the contemporary *lai* or of the verse *romance, while the non-narrative *dit* is distinguished from the *lyric in that it presents itself not as song but as spoken or written composition. There are many examples from the 13th and 14th centuries, including Rutebeuf's scurrilous narrative *Dit de frère Denise* (1262), Guillaume de Machaut's *Dit du Lyon* (1342), and Jean Froissart's *Joli Buisson de Jonece* (1373).

**dithyramb** [**dith**-i-ram]  A form of *hymn or choral *lyric in which the god Dionysus was honoured in Greek religious festivities from about the 7th century BCE onwards. Later in Athenian competitions, dithyrambs were composed—by Pindar among others—on episodes from myths of other gods, and the arrangement in matched *strophes came to be relaxed. Dithyrambs seem to have been performed by a large *chorus of singers, possibly dressed as satyrs, to flute accompaniment. A rare English imitation is Dryden's *Alexander's Feast* (1697). The adjective **dithyrambic** is sometimes applied to *rhapsodies, or wildly impassioned chants.

**divan (diwan)**  A Persian—and later, Arabic and Turkish—word of numerous senses, among which the specialized literary meaning is that of a collection of poems, usually the complete shorter poems of an individual author. Joseph Hammer-Purgstall's 1812 German translation of the *Divan* of the 14th-century Persian poet Hafiz brought the term, along with the Persian verse tradition, to the attention of Goethe, who composed his own collection of orientally inspired poems, partly in collaboration with Marianne von Willemer, publishing this as the *West-östlicher Divan* (1819).

***dizain*** [dee-ze$^n$]  A French verse *stanza of ten lines, of which each normally has ten syllables, or more rarely eight. The *dizain* was employed by French poets of the 15th and 16th centuries either as an independent poem rhyming *ababbccded* or as a stanza of the *ballade or *chant royal*. In English, Sir Philip Sidney wrote a *crown of *dizains* rhyming *ababbcacdd*.

**docudrama**  A term dating from the 1960s for a kind of television *documentary that incorporates semi-fictional or imagined sequences played by actors, e.g. representing historical persons or recently convicted criminals. A loosely related genre from the 1990s is the **docusoap**, a documentary in several episodes showing the lives of real people, usually in a specific working environment, such that viewers can follow the fortunes of these 'characters' as they would those of a fictional TV soap opera.

**documentary**  Usually a non-fiction film that offers an informative view of some aspect of nature or society. The term occasionally has literary uses, too: some kinds of travel writing and *memoir, for example, have been called documentaries, as have some essays in sociological investigation. George Orwell's book about poverty in northern England, *The Road to Wigan Pier* (1937), could be counted as one. Certain kinds of fiction, too, are described as exhibiting 'documentary *realism' if they include accurately researched factual information about places and ways of life, as with some of the novels of Emile Zola, or Upton Sinclair's novel *The Jungle* (1906), which exposed real problems of exploitation in the Chicago meat-packing industry; and a novel may be said to have a documentary element on the same basis, as with the cetology (whale-lore) exhibited in many chapters of Herman Melville's *Moby-Dick* (1851). Documentary poems are also possible, at least as contributions to film documentaries: a notable instance is W. H. Auden's 'Night Mail' (1938), which formed part of the soundtrack for a film of the same title praising the wonders of the British postal system. A maker of documentaries is a **documentarist**.

**Further reading:** Barbara Foley, *Telling the Truth: The Theory and Practice of Documentary Fiction* (1986).

**doggerel**  Clumsy verse, usually monotonously rhymed, rhythmically awkward, and often shallow in sentiment, as in greetings cards. The notoriously irregular verses of William McGonagall (?1830–1902) are doggerel. Some poets, like Skelton and Stevie Smith, have deliberately imitated doggerel for comic effect. *See also* CLERIHEW, HUDIBRASTIC, LIGHT VERSE, SKELTONICS.

**dolce stil novo (nuovo)** A new style of Italian lyric love poetry practised in the late 13th century by Guido Cavalcanti, Dante Alighieri, and Cino da Pistoia, along with some imitators. The name ('sweet new style') comes from a dialogue in Dante's *Purgatorio* (xxiv. 57). This style is marked mainly by praise of the beloved in religious terms as an embodiment of divine grace, an attitude seemingly influenced by *troubadour poetry and the codes of *courtly love. The practitioners and partisans of this kind of lyric are sometimes referred to as *stilnovisti*.

**domestic tragedy** A kind of *tragedy in which the leading characters belong to the middle class rather than to the royal or noble ranks usually represented in tragic drama, and in which the action concerns family affairs rather than public matters of state. A few English verse plays from Shakespeare's time belong to this category: the chief examples are the anonymous *Tragedy of Mr Arden of Feversham* (1592), Thomas Heywood's *A Woman Killed with Kindness* (1603), and *A Yorkshire Tragedy* (1608, of uncertain authorship). Domestic tragedy was revived in prose by George Lillo with *The London Merchant* (1732) and his new version of *Arden of Feversham* (1759). Lillo's influence led to the appearance of 'domestic' prose dramas in Germany with G. E. Lessing's tragedy *Miss Sara Sampson* (1755), and in France with Diderot's *drames*. This tradition was renewed by the late 19th-century plays of Henrik Ibsen and subsequently in the American tragedies of Tennessee Williams and Arthur Miller. Domestic tragedy is sometimes known as 'bourgeois tragedy'.

**donnée** A French word for something 'given', sometimes used to refer to the original idea or starting-point from which a writer elaborates a complete work. This initial choice of subject-matter may be a very simple situation or a basic relationship between two characters which is then complicated as the work takes shape.

**double dactyl** A form of humorous light verse in two stanzas of four lines each, with ponderous dactylic rhythm. In each stanza the first three lines are double *dactyls, i.e. of six syllables with the stress on the first and fourth, while the final line is truncated to four syllables (the first and fourth again stressed). These final lines rhyme with each other, all

the other lines being unrhymed. The devilish rules of this verse form
additionally require that the first line should be a compound nonsense
phrase (e.g. *higgledy-piggledy*), the second line the name of some
person who happens to be blessed with a doubly dactylic appellation
(e.g. *Christopher Isherwood*), and the sixth line a single six-syllable
word (e.g. *elephantiasis*); otherwise it is all very simple.

**Further reading:** *Jiggery-Pokery*, eds. A. Hecht and J. Hollander (1967).

**double entendre** [doo-blah^n-tah^ndr] A French phrase for 'double
meaning', adopted in English to denote a *pun in which a word or
phrase has a second, usually sexual, meaning, as in Elizabethan uses of
the verb 'die' referring both to death and to orgasm. Modern French
usage prefers the form **double entente**. *See also* AMBIGUITY,
EQUIVOQUE.

**double rhyme** A *rhyme on two syllables, the first stressed and
the second unstressed (e.g. *tarry/marry*, *adore us/chorus*), also known
as *feminine rhyme, and opposed to *masculine rhyme, which
matches single stressed syllables.

**drama** The general term for performances in which actors
impersonate the actions and speech of fictional or historical characters
(or non-human entities) for the entertainment of an audience, either
on a stage or by means of a broadcast; or a particular example of this
art, i.e. a play. Drama is usually expected to represent stories showing
situations of conflict between characters, although the *monodrama is a
special case in which only one performer speaks. Drama is a major
*genre of literature, but includes non-literary forms (in *mime), and has
several dimensions that lie beyond the domain of the literary **dramatist**
or playwright (*see* MISE EN SCÈNE). The major dramatic genres in the
West are *comedy and *tragedy, but several other kinds of dramatic
work fall outside these categories (*see* DRAME, HISTORY PLAY, MASQUE,
MELODRAMA, MORALITY PLAY, MYSTERY PLAY, TRAGICOMEDY). **Dramatic
poetry** is a category of verse composition for theatrical performance;
the term is now commonly extended, however, to non-theatrical poems
that involve a similar kind of impersonation, as in the *closet drama
and the *dramatic monologue.

**Further reading:** Simon Shepherd and Mick Wallis, *Drama/Theatre/
Performance* (2004); John Lennard and Mary Luckhurst, *The Drama
Handbook* (2002).

**dramatic irony** *See* IRONY.

**dramatic monologue** A kind of poem in which a single fictional or historical character other than the poet speaks to a silent 'audience' of one or more persons. Such poems reveal not the poet's own thoughts but the mind of the impersonated character, whose personality is revealed unwittingly; this distinguishes a dramatic monologue from a *lyric, while the implied presence of an auditor distinguishes it from a *soliloquy. Major examples of this form in English are Tennyson's 'Ulysses' (1842), Browning's 'Fra Lippo Lippi' (1855), and T. S. Eliot's 'The Love Song of J. Alfred Prufrock' (1917). Some plays in which only one character speaks, in the form of a *monologue or soliloquy, have also been called dramatic monologues; but to avoid confusion it is preferable to refer to these simply as monologues or as *monodramas.

**Further reading:** Glennis Byron, *Dramatic Monologue* (2003).

***dramatis personae*** [**dram**-ă-tis per-**soh**-ny] The Latin phrase for 'persons of the play', used to refer collectively to the characters represented in a dramatic work (or, by extension, a *narrative work). This phrase is the conventional heading for a list of characters published in the text of a play or in a theatrical programme.

**dramatization** The process of *adaptation whereby a stage play or film drama is created from major elements (plot, characters, settings) derived from a non-dramatic literary or historical work, usually a novel, romance, short story, or biography; or the new dramatic work thereby created. This commonly involves some degree of simplification, e.g. by the omission of some minor characters or episodes, or the reduction in the number of settings; and sometimes it involves substantial transformations to the plot of the original work, e.g. by making a happy ending from a plot that originally lacked one. A second, more general and figurative sense of this term is the 'bringing to life' of some element of a written work by the use of any technique that involves the reader more closely with the story, e.g. by narration in the present tense or by prominent use of dialogue. These techniques are deemed dramatic in the sense that they give readers the impression of the story unfolding as 'live' action, as it would if presented as a stage play, rather than being recounted from the distance of retrospect. Since the late 19th century, critical discussion of the techniques of the novel, especially under the influence of Henry James, has often recommended that novelists

**dramatize** their stories in such ways; and similar devices are used by historians and biographers.

**dramaturgy** [**dram**-ă-ter-ji] The theory and practice of *drama, now usually called dramatics. A **dramaturge** or **dramaturgist** is a playwright, or in some contexts (especially German) a literary adviser or theatrical director. *Adjective*: **dramaturgic** or **dramaturgical**.

*drame* [dramm] The French word for drama, applied more specifically by Denis Diderot and later writers to plays that are intermediate between *comedy and *tragedy. Diderot outlined his theory of the *drame* in the prefaces to his plays *Le Fils naturel* (1757) and *Le Père de famille* (1758), which both exemplify this moralizing blend of *sentimental comedy with *domestic tragedy, being serious in content but still ending happily. The category of *drames* came to include both the *drame bourgeois* of contemporary domestic problems in the middle classes, and, closer to tragedy and *melodrama, the *drame romantique* of the 19th century, of which Victor Hugo's *Hernani* (1830) was an influential example. *See also* TRAGICOMEDY.

**dream vision (dream allegory)** A kind of *narrative (usually but not always in verse) in which the narrator falls asleep and dreams the events of the tale. The story is often a kind of *allegory, and commonly consists of a tour of some marvellous realm, in which the dreamer is conducted and instructed by a guide, as Dante is led through hell by Virgil in his *Divine Comedy* (*c.*1320)—the foremost example of the form. The dream vision was much favoured by medieval poets, most of them influenced by the 13th-century *Roman de la rose* by the French poets Guillaume de Lorris and Jean de Meung. In English, Chaucer devoted much of his early work to dream visions, including *The Parlement of Foules*, while Langland wrote the more substantial *Piers Plowman*; another fine 14th-century example is the anonymous poem *Pearl*. Some later poets have adopted the *conventions of the dream vision, as in Shelley's *The Triumph of Life* (1824) and Wilfred Owen's 'The Show' (1919). Significant examples in prose include Bunyan's *The Pilgrim's Progress* (1678) and William Morris's vision of socialism in *News from Nowhere* (1890).

**dub poetry** A kind of poetry that emerged in Jamaica and England during the early 1970s, influenced by the rhythms of reggae music. The term was at first applied to the improvised 'rapping' of the Jamaican disc-jockeys known as 'toasters', who sang or recited their own words over the dub versions of reggae records (i.e. the purely instrumental re-mixed versions on the B-sides); but it has come to be adopted as a collective label for a tradition of popular poetry in the Jamaican (and black British) *vernacular or 'Patwah', inaugurated by Mutabaruka and Oku Onuora in Jamaica and by Linton Kwesi Johnson in England. Dub poetry includes *lyrics and *narrative poems on various subjects including protest against racism and police brutality, the celebration of sex, music, and ganja, and Rastafarian religious themes. Although primarily an oral poetry for public performance, it has increasingly appeared in print, notably in Johnson's *Dread Beat and Blood* (1975) and Benjamin Zephaniah's *The Dread Affair* (1985). Other leading dub poets include Michael Smith, Jean Binta Breeze, and Levi Tafari.

**dumb show** A short piece of silent action or *mime included in a play. A common device in Elizabethan and *Jacobean drama, it was sometimes used to summarize the succeeding spoken scene, as in the dumb show preceding the players' main performance in *Hamlet* (Act III, scene ii).

**duodecimo** [dew-oh-**des**-i-moh] A small size of book in which the page size results from folding a standard printer's sheet of paper into twelve leaves (i.e. 24 pages). Abbreviated as 12mo, it is thus sometimes called 'twelvemo'. *See also* FOLIO, OCTAVO, QUARTO.

**duple metre** A term covering poetic *metres based upon a *foot of two syllables (a **duple foot**), as opposed to *triple metre, in which the predominant foot has three syllables. Most English metrical verse is in duple metre, either *iambic or *trochaic, and thus displays an alternation of stressed syllables with single unstressed syllables (*see* STRESS). In the context of classical Greek and Latin poetry, however, the term often refers to verse composed of *dipodies.

**dystopia** [dis-**toh**-piă] A modern term invented as the opposite of *utopia, and applied to any alarmingly unpleasant imaginary world, usually of the projected future. The term is also applied to fictional works depicting such worlds. A significant form of *science fiction and of modern *satire, dystopian writing is exemplified in H. G. Wells's *When the Sleeper Wakes* (1899), George Orwell's *Nineteen Eighty-Four* (1949), and Russell Hoban's *Riddley Walker* (1980).

**early modern period** A period of European history broadly
equivalent to that of the 16th and 17th centuries. The term has since
the 1980s been increasingly adopted by historians, including literary
historians, in preference to the once customary term *Renaissance.
This is for a number of reasons: in part because 'Renaissance' tends
to overemphasize the flourishing of art and learning in the Italian
city-states of the 14th and 15th centuries at the expense both of
non-artistic developments and of later developments beyond Italy
(e.g. printing, Protestantism, and the European exploration of the
Americas); in part also because 'Renaissance' carries with it an implied
disparagement of the so-called 'Middle Ages', which the *humanists
of the 16th century invented as a supposedly benighted period of
ignorance between classical antiquity and their own time. So 'early
modern' has been preferred as both more neutral and in chronological
terms more precise. In literary terminology, this has meant that
Shakespeare and others who were once habitually classed as
Renaissance dramatists are now more often called **early-modern**
dramatists.

**eclogue** [ek-log] A short *pastoral poem, often in the form of a
shepherds' *dialogue or a *soliloquy. The term was first applied to the
'bucolic' poems of Virgil, written in imitation of the *idylls of Theocritus;
Virgil's work became known as the *Eclogues* (42–37 BCE). The form was
revived in the Italian *Renaissance by Dante, Petrarch, and Boccaccio,
and appears in English in Spenser's *The Shephearde's Calender* (1579).
Some later poets have extended the term to include non-pastoral poems
in dialogue form.

**ecocriticism** A new subfield of literary and cultural enquiry that
emerged in the 1980s and 1990s, devoted to the investigation of relations
between literature and the natural world and to the rediscovery and
reinterpretation of 'nature writings' such as those of H. D. Thoreau and

the poets of *Romanticism (sometimes categorized as 'environmental literature') in the light of recent ecological concerns. Ecocriticism is not a method of analysis or interpretation but a redefined area of research and rediscovery. Most of this work has been pursued in the USA, where a special emphasis has been given to Native American folklore and literature; but much **ecocritical** work has also been devoted to the English Romantic tradition, notably by the British literary historian Jonathan Bate in his books *Romantic Ecology* (1991) and *The Song of the Earth* (2000). Special varieties within this field include **ecofeminist criticism**.

**Further reading:** Greg Garrard, *Ecocriticism* (2nd edn, 2011).

(((⊕))) SEE WEB LINKS

• Association for the Study of Literature and Environment.

**écriture** [ay-kri-tewr] The French word for 'writing'. Where it appears in this form in English texts, it refers to one or more specific senses used by modern French theorists: **1.** Writing as style, in Roland Barthes's book *Le Degré Zéro de l'Écriture* (*Writing Degree Zero*, 1953), which attacks the illusion of a blank or neutral writing on the grounds that all writing has some style or *discourse that shapes our view of the world. **2.** Writing as an intransitive activity, as proposed in Barthes's later essay 'Écrivains et écrivants' ('Writers and Authors', 1960) which contrasts *écrivants* writing 'about' something for an ulterior purpose with *écrivains* for whom writing is self-directed, about itself as language. **3.** Writing as *différance* as opposed to the illusory authenticity of speech (*see* LOGOCENTRISM) according to Jacques Derrida's philosophy of *deconstruction. **4.** *Écriture féminine*, or specifically gendered women's writing, as conceived by Hélène Cixous, whose works of the 1970s discuss the sense in which women's writing overflows the *binary oppositions of patriarchal logic.

**Edda** The Old Norse name given to two important collections of early Icelandic writing. The Elder or Poetic Edda is a collection of poems written down in the late 13th century but including works from an oral tradition going back to the 9th century; it contains heroic *narrative poems about Sigurd and other heroes, along with mythological tales of the Norse gods. The Younger or Prose Edda is a handbook of *poetics by Snorri Sturluson, written in the early 13th century; it also contains mythological lore. *Adjective*: **Eddaic**.

**edition** A printed version of a given work that may be distinguished from other versions either by its published format (e.g. paperback edition, popular edition, abridged edition), or by its membership of a complete batch of copies printed from the same setting of type, usually at the same time and place. These batches come to be numbered as first, second, third, etc. editions, each time a new version is set again from fresh type; where the same type is used to run off further copies, the batches are known as second, third, fourth, etc. 'printings' or 'impressions' of the relevant edition. The term is also applied rather differently to the works of an author as edited by a particular scholar or by a team of scholars sharing the same procedures, e.g. Christopher Ricks's edition of Tennyson, or the Arden editions of Shakespeare. *See also* VARIORUM EDITION.

**Edwardian** Belonging to or characteristic of the period from January 1901 to May 1910, when Edward VII was King of England, following the end of the *Victorian age. This at least is the chronologically strict sense of the term; but it is not unusual to find it extended to reach up to the next major historical landmark, the outbreak of the Great War in August 1914, or even beyond that. For example, Sandra Kemp and her co-editors in their reference work *Edwardian Fiction* (1997) in practice cover the period up to 1915. Since Edward's reign was a comparatively short one, it does not have such a distinct literary identity as the *Elizabethan or Victorian ages do, and there are hardly any 'Edwardian writers' who were not also late-Victorian writers beforehand or *Georgian writers afterwards. Literary history therefore tends to treat the period either as a late extension of Victorian literature or as an interregnum before the arrival of *modernism. Influential essays by Virginia Woolf in the 1920s disparaged several of the foremost writers of the period, tending to use 'Edwardian' as a dismissive insult. The writers who flourished during this reign or whose work is most often associated with it include W. B. Yeats, Joseph Conrad, John Galsworthy, Arnold Bennett, H. G. Wells, E. M. Forster, Bernard Shaw, J. M. Barrie, Rudyard Kipling, G. K. Chesterton, Hilaire Belloc, and John Masefield.

**Further reading:** Anthea Trodd, *A Reader's Guide to Edwardian Literature* (1991).

**egotistical sublime** The phrase by which John Keats, in a letter to Richard Woodhouse (27 Oct. 1818), criticized what he felt to be the excessively self-centred quality of Wordsworth's poetry, in contrast with his own ideal of *negative capability, which he found in the more anonymous imagination of Shakespeare. *See also* SUBLIME.

**eiron** [I-ron] A *stock character in Greek *comedy, who pretends to be less intelligent than he really is, and whose modesty of speech contrasts with the boasting of the stock braggart or *alazon*. Our word *irony derives from the pretence adopted by the *eiron*.

**ekphrasis (ecphrasis)** (plural **-ases**) A verbal description of, or meditation upon, a non-verbal work of art, real or imagined, usually a painting or sculpture. In classical literature, the most famous case is the lengthy description in the 18th book of Homer's *Iliad* of the decorated shield made for Achilles by the god Hephaestos, which in turn is the basis of W. H. Auden's **ekphrastic** poem 'The Shield of Achilles' (1952). Auden's earlier poem 'Musée des Beaux Arts' (1939), a meditation on Brueghel's *Fall of Icarus*, is a celebrated modern example, as is John Ashbery's 'Self-Portrait in a Convex Mirror' (1975; on a curious painting by Parmigianino). An earlier English classic of this genre is John Keats's 'Ode on a Grecian Urn' (1820). Ekphrastic passages can be found in prose writings, too: for example, the nineteenth chapter of Charlotte Brontë's novel *Villette* (1853) includes description of a painting of Cleopatra, whose voluptuous semi-nudity offends the heroine, Lucy Snowe.

**Further reading:** Murray Krieger, *Ekphrasis* (1992).

**elegy** An elaborately formal *lyric poem lamenting the death of a friend or public figure, or reflecting seriously on a solemn subject. In Greek and Latin verse, the term referred to the *metre of a poem (alternating dactylic *hexameters and *pentameters in couplets known as **elegiac** *distichs), not to its mood or content: love poems were often included. Likewise, John Donne applied the term to his amorous and satirical poems in *heroic couplets. But since Milton's 'Lycidas' (1637), the term in English has usually denoted a *lament (although Milton called his poem a 'monody'), while the adjective 'elegiac' has come to refer to the mournful mood of such poems. Two important English elegies that follow Milton in using *pastoral conventions are Shelley's 'Adonais' (1821) on the death of Keats, and Arnold's 'Thyrsis' (1867). This tradition of the **pastoral elegy**, derived from Greek poems by Theocritus and other Sicilian poets in the 3rd and 2nd centuries BCE,

evolved a very elaborate series of *conventions by which the dead friend
is represented as a shepherd mourned by the natural world; pastoral
elegies usually include many mythological figures such as the nymphs
who are supposed to have guarded the dead shepherd, and the *muses
invoked by the **elegist**. Tennyson's *In Memoriam A. H. H.* (1850) is a
long series of elegiac verses (in the modern sense) on his friend Arthur
Hallam, while Whitman's 'When Lilacs Last in the Dooryard Bloom'd'
(1865) commemorates a public figure—Abraham Lincoln—rather than a
friend; Auden's 'In Memory of W. B. Yeats' (1939) does the same. In a
broader sense, an elegy may be a poem of melancholy reflection upon
life's transience or its sorrows, as in Gray's 'Elegy Written in a Country
Churchyard' (1751), or in Rilke's *Duino Elegies* (1912–22). The **elegiac
stanza** is a *quatrain of iambic pentameters rhyming *abab*, named after
its use in Gray's Elegy. In an extended sense, a prose work dealing with a
vanished way of life or with the passing of youth may sometimes be
called an elegy. *See also* DIRGE, GRAVEYARD POETRY, MONODY, THRENODY.
**Further reading:** David Kennedy, *Elegy* (2007).

**elision**  The slurring or suppression of a vowel sound or syllable,
usually by fusing a final unstressed vowel with a following word
beginning with a vowel or mute *h*, as in French *l'homme* or in
Shakespeare's 'Th'expense of spirit'. In poetry, elision is used in order
to fit the words to the *metre of a verse line (*see* SYNAERESIS). Another
form of contraction sometimes distinguished from elision is *syncope,
in which a letter or syllable within a word is omitted (e.g. *o'er* for
over, *heav'n* for heaven). *Verb*: **elide**. *See also* HIATUS.

**Elizabethan**  Belonging to or characteristic of the period 1558–1603
when Elizabeth I reigned as Queen of England, continuing the Tudor
dynasty of her father Henry VIII but also bringing that dynasty to a close
by dying childless. Despite attempts to revive the term at the start of
the reign of Queen Elizabeth II (1952– ), it has not been widely adopted
as a designation for the late 20th and early 21st centuries, so the name
remains unambiguously applicable to the late 16th century. In English
literature, that period has long been celebrated as an outstanding
one in poetry, both dramatic and non-dramatic: it includes the work
of Edmund Spenser, Sir Philip Sidney, and Christopher Marlowe,
along with the early work of Ben Jonson and the greater portion of
Shakespeare's (including all the English *history plays and most of

the comedies along with *Hamlet*, but excluding the other great tragedies, which belong to the succeeding *Jacobean period). Landmarks in prose writing include the earlier works of Sir Francis Bacon, notably the *Essays* of 1597. A scholar whose work is devoted to this period is an **Elizabethanist**.

**((⊕)) SEE WEB LINKS**

• Renaissance: The Elizabethan World: links to a range of study resources.

**ellipsis (ellipse)** (plurals **-pses**) The omission from a sentence of a word or words that would be required for complete clarity but which can usually be understood from the context. A common form of compression both in everyday speech and in poetry (e.g. Shakespeare, 'I will [go] to Ireland'), it is used with notable frequency by T. S. Eliot and other poets of *modernism. The sequence of three dots ( . . . ) employed to indicate the omission of some matter in a text is also known as an ellipsis. *Adjective*: **elliptical** or **elliptic**. *See also* ASYNDETON, LACUNA, PARATACTIC.

*éloge* [ay-lohzh] The French term for a eulogy or *encomium, and in literary contexts especially for a solemn speech, usually published later as a kind of obituary tribute, given to one of the great French Academies (Académie Française, Académie des Sciences, etc.) in praise of a recently deceased academician; or, usually as a competitive exercise in pursuit of an academic prize, in commemoration of some illustrious person of a past age. A notable 18th-century practitioner was Antoine-Léonard Thomas, who won several prizes for *éloges* on historical figures, and wrote a study of this genre, the *Essai sur les éloges* (1773). Better-known French authors who composed *éloges* include Condorcet and d'Alembert.

**embedded** Enclosed within a *frame narrative as a tale-within-the-tale, like the pilgrims' stories in the *Canterbury Tales*, which are embedded within Chaucer's account of the journey to Canterbury.

**emblem** A picture with a symbolic meaning, as in heraldry or visual *allegory; or a simple kind of literary *symbol with a fixed and relatively clear significance. In the 16th and 17th centuries the term was applied to a popular kind of woodcut or engraving accompanied by a motto and a short verse explanation of its meaning. The vogue for the **emblem books** in which these were found began with Andrea Alciato's

*Emblemata* (1531) and culminated in England with the *Emblems* (1635) of Francis Quarles. Poets of this period often drew upon such works for their *imagery. The term **emblem poem** is sometimes applied to *pattern poems. *Adjective*: **emblematic**.

**(⊕) SEE WEB LINKS**
• University of Glasgow Emblem archive.

**emendation** A correction made to a *text in the belief that the author's original wording has been wrongly altered, e.g. by scribal error, printer's misreading, or the intervention of censorship. Unlike an amendment, which creates a fresh wording, an emendation aims to restore a lost original.

**encomium** [in-**koh**-mi-ŭm] (plural **-mia**) A composition in prose or verse written in praise of some person, event, or idea; a eulogy. Originally denoting a Greek choral song in praise of a victorious athlete, the term was later extended to include prose compositions devoted to praise, usually involving elaborate *rhetoric. Many *odes and *elegies are wholly or partly **encomiastic**. An author of encomia is an **encomiast**. *See also* PANEGYRIC.

***Encyclopédistes*** The group of writers and philosophers led by Denis Diderot and Jean d'Alembert who contributed to the *Encyclopédie ou Dictionnaire raisonnée des sciences, des arts et des métiers* which began to appear in 1751 under Diderot's editorship, eventually running to 35 volumes including indexes. Other leading contributors were Condillac, Helvétius, Voltaire, and the Baron d'Holbach, who played host to the meetings of this loose association. The *Encyclopédistes* were the leading spirits of the *Enlightenment, hoping through this ambitious project to sweep away the superstitions of Church and State by offering a rational account of the universe. *See also* PHILOSOPHES.

**(⊕) SEE WEB LINKS**
• The Encyclopedia of Diderot & d'Alembert Collaborative Translation Project at University of Michigan, offering selected articles in English.

***endecasyllabo*** (plural *-syllabi*) The Italian hendecasyllabic verse line, the standard line for *epic verse, *sonnets, and many other forms including *blank verse, known in Italian as *endecasyllabi sciolti* ('free hendecasyllables'). Italian versification counts the syllables of a verse line up to the last stressed syllable, which in the *endecasyllabo* is the tenth, and assumes one further unstressed syllable (*see* VERSO PIANO); so although the usual form of the line is truly hendecasyllabic, there are accepted ten- and twelve-syllable variants (*see* VERSO TRONCO). Apart from the required stress on the tenth syllable, a stress is expected on either the fourth or the sixth syllable, or both.

**end-rhyme** Rhyme occurring at the ends of verse lines, as opposed to *internal rhyme and 'head-rhyme' (*alliteration); the most familiar kind of rhyming.

**end-stopped** Brought to a pause at which the end of a verse line coincides with the completion of a sentence, clause, or other independent unit of *syntax. End-stopping, the opposite of *enjambment, gives verse lines an appearance of self-contained sense; it was favoured especially by Pope and other 18th-century poets in English in their *heroic couplets, and by the classical French poets in their *alexandrines. *See also* CLOSED COUPLET.

**Eng. Lit.** A common abbreviation for English Literature as an academic subject or as a *canon of 'set texts' for study. This abbreviated usage often implies a disrespectful attitude to the traditional limits of the canon or to the routine examination cramming that has beset the subject.

**enjambment (enjambement)** The running over of the sense and grammatical structure from one verse line or couplet to the next without a punctuated pause. In an **enjambed** line (also called a 'run-on line'), the completion of a phrase, clause, or sentence is held over to the following line so that the line ending is not emphasized as it is in an *end-stopped line. Enjambment is one of the resources available to poets in English *blank verse, but it appears in other verse forms too, even in *heroic couplets: Keats rejected the 18th-century *closed couplet by using frequent enjambment in *Endymion* (1818), of which the first and fifth lines are end-stopped while the lines in between are enjambed.

> A thing of beauty is a joy for ever:
> Its loveliness increases; it will never
> Pass into nothingness; but still will keep
> A bower quiet for us, and a sleep
> Full of sweet dreams, and health, and quiet breathing.

**Enlightenment, the**  A general term applied to the movement of intellectual liberation that developed in Western Europe from the late 17th century to the late 18th (the period often called the 'Age of Reason'), especially in France and Switzerland. The Enlightenment culminated with the writings of Jean-Jacques Rousseau and the *Encyclopédistes, the philosophy of Immanuel Kant, and the political ideals of the American and French Revolutions, while its forerunners in science and philosophy included Bacon, Descartes, Spinoza, Newton, and Locke. Its central idea was the need for (and the capacity of) human reason to clear away ancient superstition, prejudice, dogma, and injustice. Kant defined enlightenment (*die Aufklärung*) as man's emancipation from his self-incurred immaturity. Enlightenment thinking encouraged rational scientific inquiry, humanitarian tolerance, and the idea of universal human rights. In religion, it usually involved the sceptical rejection of superstition, dogma, and revelation in favour of 'Deism'—a belief confined to those universal doctrines supposed to be common to all religions, such as the existence of a venerable Supreme Being as creator. The advocates of enlightenment tended to place their faith in human progress brought about by the gradual propagation of rational principles, although their great champion Voltaire, more militant and less optimistic, waged a bitter campaign against the abuses of the *ancien régime* under the virtually untranslatable slogan *écrasez l'infâme!* (for which a rough equivalent would be 'smash the system!').

In English, the attitudes of the Enlightenment are found in the late 18th century, in the historian Edward Gibbon and the political writers Thomas Paine and William Godwin, as well as in the feminist Mary Wollstonecraft. The flourishing of philosophy and science in Edinburgh and Glasgow in the 18th century is known as the **Scottish Enlightenment**; its leading figures included David Hume and Adam Smith. *See also* PHILOSOPHES.

**Further reading:** Norman Hampson, *The Enlightenment* (1968); Roy Porter, *Enlightenment* (2000).

**énoncé** and **énonciation**  Terms of a distinction observed in *structuralist theory, between what is said (the *énoncé*) and the act or process of saying it (the *énonciation*). The linguist Émile Benveniste defined *énonciation* as a process by which a speaker (or writer) adopts a position within language as an 'I' addressing a 'you' and perhaps referring to a 'they'. Whenever I say 'I', however, the I who speaks can be distinguished (as the 'subject of the *énonciation*') from the 'I' that is thus spoken of (the 'subject of the *énoncé*'). This splitting of the subject by language has been of great interest to theorists of *post-structuralism, notably the psychoanalyst Jacques Lacan. In literary analysis, the distinction leads to a further differentiation between *discours*, in which first- and second-person pronouns and other markers of the situation of the *énonciation* are evident (*see* DEIXIS), and the more 'objective' mode of *histoire* in which the *énonciation* seems to have disappeared into or behind the *énoncé*. So while a *first-person narrative will show a split between the narrating I of the *énonciation* and the younger 'I' spoken of (*énoncé*) in the narrative, a *third-person narrative will often be able to disguise the distinction between the process of narration and its result.

**entremés** (plural -**meses**)  The Spanish term for a short comical performance presented between the acts of a more serious drama. This form flourished on the Spanish stage in the first half of the 17th century. Numerous *entremeses* are attributed to Lope de Vega (1562–1635) and his associates, and a few to Cervantes.

**envelope**  A structural device in poetry, by which a line or *stanza is repeated either identically or with little variation so as to enclose between its two appearances the rest (or part) of the poem: a stanza may begin and end with the same line, or a poem may begin and end with the same line or stanza. A well-known example is Blake's poem 'The Tiger', in which the opening stanza is repeated as the last with only one change of wording. The effect of an envelope pattern is subtly different from that of a *refrain. The term **envelope stanza** has also been applied to stanzas not involving repeated lines but having a symmetrical *rhyme scheme (almost always *abba*) which encloses one set of rhymes within another, as in the *In Memoriam* stanza.

**envoi** (**envoy**)  The additional half-stanza that concludes certain kinds of French poetic form, principally the *ballade but also the *chant royal* and the *sestina. Its length is usually four lines in a ballade, five or seven in a *chant royal*, and three in a sestina. In the ballade and *chant royal* it repeats the *metre and *rhyme scheme of the previous half-stanza, along with the poem's *refrain, and is conventionally addressed to a prince or other noble personage.

**epanalepsis** A *figure of speech in which the initial word of a sentence or verse line reappears at the end. *See also* PLOCE.

***épater les bourgeois*** [ay-pat-ay lay boor-*zh*wah] A French phrase that can be translated only rather clumsily, as 'to shock the (respectable) middle-class citizens'. This has often been the conscious aim of the literary and artistic *avant-garde in Europe since the late 19th century, especially in the movements of *decadence, *Dada, and *Surrealism.

**epic** A long *narrative poem celebrating the great deeds of one or more legendary heroes, in a grand ceremonious style. The hero, usually protected by or even descended from gods, performs superhuman exploits in battle or in marvellous voyages, often saving or founding a nation—as in Virgil's *Aeneid* (30–20 BCE)—or the human race itself, in Milton's *Paradise Lost* (1667). Virgil and Milton wrote what are called 'secondary' or literary epics in imitation of the earlier 'primary' or traditional epics of Homer, whose *Iliad* and *Odyssey* (*c*.8th century BCE) are derived from an oral tradition of recitation. They adopted many of the *conventions of Homer's work, including the *invocation of a muse, the use of *epithets, the listing of heroes and combatants, and the beginning **in medias res* (for other epic conventions, *see* EPIC SIMILE, FORMULAIC, MACHINERY). The Anglo-Saxon poem *Beowulf* (8th century CE) is a primary epic, as is the oldest surviving epic poem, the Babylonian *Gilgamesh* (*c*.3000 BCE). In the *Renaissance, epic poetry (also known as 'heroic poetry') was regarded as the highest form of literature, and was attempted in Italian by Tasso in *Gerusalemme Liberata* (1575), and in Portuguese by Camoëns in *Os Lusiadas* (1572). Other important national epics are the Indian *Mahābhārata* (3rd or 4th century CE) and the German *Nibelungenlied* (*c*.1200). The action of epics takes place on a grand scale, and in this sense the term has sometimes been extended to long *romances, to ambitious *historical novels like Tolstoy's *War and Peace* (1863–9), and to some large-scale film productions on heroic or historical subjects.

**Further reading:** Paul Innes, *Epic* (2013).

(⊕) SEE WEB LINKS
• Hyperepos: a resource for the study of epic.

**epic simile** An extended *simile elaborated in such detail or at such length as to eclipse temporarily the main action of a *narrative work, forming a decorative *digression. Usually it compares one complex action (rather than a simple quality or thing) with another: for example, the approach of an army with the onset of storm-clouds. Sometimes called a **Homeric simile** after its frequent use in Homer's epic poems, it was also used by Virgil, Milton, and others in their literary epics.

**epic theatre** A revolutionary form of drama developed by the German playwright Bertolt Brecht from the late 1920s under the influence of Erwin Piscator. It involved rejecting the *Aristotelian models of dramatic unity in favour of a detached *narrative (hence 'epic') presentation in a succession of loosely related episodes interspersed with songs and commentary by a *chorus or narrator. As a Marxist, Brecht turned against the bourgeois tradition of theatre in which the audience identifies emotionally with psychologically rounded characters in a *well-made play; he aimed instead for an *alienation effect which would keep the audience coolly reflective and critical, partly by setting his plays in remote times and places, and also by stressing the contrived nature of the drama. The best examples of this drama are Brecht's plays *The Threepenny Opera* (1928), *Mother Courage* (1941), and *The Good Woman of Setzuan* (1943).

**epideictic** Intended for display at public occasions. Epideictic *oratory was one of the three branches of classical *rhetoric, differing from legal argument or political persuasion in being devoted to public praise (or blame), as in funeral orations, *panegyrics, etc. Epideictic poetry is verse for special occasions, such as *epithalamia, many *odes, and other kinds of poem now usually referred to as *occasional verses. *See also* ENCOMIUM.

**epigone (epigon)** [ep-ig-ohn] (plural **-oni** or **-ones**) An inferior or derivative follower of some more distinguished writer.

**epigram** A short poem with a witty turn of thought; or a wittily condensed expression in prose. Originally a form of monumental inscription in ancient Greece, the epigram was developed into a literary form by the poets of the *Hellenistic age and by the Roman poet Martial, whose *Epigrams* (86–102 CE) were often obscenely insulting. This epigram by Herrick is adapted from Martial:

> Lulls swears he is all heart, but you'll suppose
> By his proboscis that he is all nose.

The art of the epigram was cultivated in the 17th and 18th centuries in France and Germany by Voltaire, Schiller, and others. In English, epigrams have been written by several poets since Ben Jonson's *Epigrams* (1616), and are found in the prose of Oscar Wilde and other authors, who are thus known as **epigrammatists**. Some of the more pointed *closed couplets of Pope are called epigrams although they are not independent poems. *Adjective*: **epigrammatic**. *See also* APHORISM.

**epigraph** A quotation or motto placed at the beginning of a book, chapter, or poem as an indication of its theme. The term can also refer to an inscription on a monument or coin. **Epigraphy** is the collective term for any body of epigraphs in either sense, and for the study of epigraphs. *Adjective*: **epigraphic**.

**epilogue** [ep-i-log] A concluding section of any written work. At the end of some plays in the age of Shakespeare and Jonson, a single character would address the audience directly, begging indulgence and applause; both the speech and the speaker were known as the epilogue, as in Rosalind's closing address in *As You Like It*. Some novels have epilogues in which the characters' subsequent fates are briefly outlined. *Verb*: **epilogize**. *Adjective*: **epilogistic**.

**epinicion (epinikion; epinicium; epinician ode)** A kind of Greek *ode composed in honour of a victor in the Olympic Games or equivalent festivals at Delphi and Corinth. Such odes were sung in chorus in a triadic structure of *strophe, antistrophe, and epode, by custom upon the return of the victor to his home city. They praised the city and the victor's family along with him, also adding mythological narrative and some moral reflections. Examples survive by Pindar (*see* PINDARIC) and by his rival Bacchylides, sometimes praising the same victor (e.g. of the Delphic chariot-race of 470 BCE).

**epiphany** [i-**pif**-ăni] The term used in Christian theology for a manifestation of God's presence in the world. It was taken over by James Joyce to denote secular revelation in the everyday world, in an early version of his novel *A Portrait of the Artist as a Young Man* (1916) later published as *Stephen Hero* (1944). Here Joyce defined an epiphany as 'a sudden spiritual manifestation' in which the 'whatness' of a common object or gesture appears radiant to the observer. Much of Joyce's fiction is built around such special moments of sudden insight, just as Wordsworth's long autobiographical poem *The Prelude* (1850) is constructed around certain revelatory 'spots of time'. *Adjective*: **epiphanic**.

**Further reading:** Morris Beja, *Epiphany in the Modernist Novel* (1971).

**episodic** Constructed as a narrative by a succession of loosely connected incidents rather than by an integrated *plot. *Picaresque novels and many medieval *romances have an episodic structure in which the only link between one episode and the next is the presence of the same central character.

**episteme** [ep-is-teem] (*épistème* [ay-pi-stem]) The accepted mode of acquiring and arranging knowledge in a given period. An episteme unites the various *discourses (legal, scientific, etc.) and guarantees their coherence within an underlying structure of implicit assumptions about the status of knowledge. The term has gained currency from the work of the French historian Michel Foucault, especially his *Les Mots et les choses* (*The Order of Things*, 1966). Foucault attempted to show how an episteme based on the detection of resemblances was replaced in the 17th century by a new episteme of differences and distinctions, while the 19th century introduced a further episteme of historical evolution. *Adjective*: **epistemic**.

**epistle** [ip-iss-ŭl] A letter. As a literary form, the **verse epistle** is a poem in the form of a letter to a friend or patron in a familiar, conversational style. The theme of the most common kind (the *Horatian, moral, or familiar epistle) is usually some moral, philosophical, or literary subject. The chief classical model is Horace's *Epistulae* (*c*.15 BCE), written in *hexameters and treating various matters from the pleasures of his rural retreat to the state of Roman literature. The Horatian epistle was a favoured form among poets from the *Renaissance to the 18th century: Jonson's 'Epistle to Elizabeth, Countess of Rutland' (1616) and Pope's *Epistle to Dr Arbuthnot* (1735) are fine examples; more recent epistles in English include Auden's *New Year Letter* (1940) and Derek Mahon's 'Beyond Howth Head' (1975). A distinct tradition of 'sentimental' epistles derives from Ovid's *Heroides* (*c*.20 BCE); these are in the form of letters imagined as being addressed by heroines of legend to their husbands or lovers, and were imitated in English by Drayton in *England's Heroical Epistles* (1597). Pope's 'Eloisa to Abelard' is a later Ovidian epistle. *Adjective*: **epistolary**.

**epistolary novel** A novel written in the form of a series of letters exchanged among the characters of the story, with extracts from their journals sometimes included. A form of narrative often used in English and French novels of the 18th century, it has been revived only rarely since then, as in John Barth's *Letters* (1979). Important examples include Richardson's *Pamela* (1740–1) and *Clarissa* (1747–8), Rousseau's *La Nouvelle Héloïse* (1761), and Laclos's *Les Liaisons dangereuses* (1782).

**Further reading:** Joe Bray, *The Epistolary Novel* (2003).

**epistrophe** [i-**pis**-trŏfi] A rhetorical *figure by which the same word or phrase is repeated at the end of successive clauses, sentences, or lines, as in Whitman's *Song of Myself* (1855):

The moth and the fish-eggs are in their place,
The bright suns I see and the dark suns I cannot see are in their place,
The palpable is in its place and the impalpable is in its place.

*Adjective*: **epistrophic.** *See also* ANAPHORA, ANTISTROPHE.

**epitaph** A form of words in prose or verse suited for inscription on a tomb—although many facetious verses composed as epitaphs have not actually been inflicted on their victims' graves. Epitaphs may take the form of appeals from the dead to passers-by, or of descriptions of the dead person's merits. Many ancient Greek epitaphs survive in the *Greek Anthology* (*c.*920 CE), and both Johnson and Wordsworth wrote essays on the epitaph as an art. *Adjective*: **epitaphic.** *See also* LAPIDARY.

**epithalamion** [epi-thă-**lay**-mion] (**epithalamium**) (plural **-amia**) A song or poem celebrating a wedding, and traditionally intended to be sung outside the bridal chamber on the wedding night. Some epithalamia survive from ancient literature, notably by Catullus, but the form flourished in the Renaissance: Edmund Spenser's 'Epithalamion' (1595) is the most admired English model, but others were written by Sidney, Donne, Jonson, Marvell and Dryden. Later examples are those by Shelley and Auden. *Adjective*: **epithalamic.**

**epithet** An adjective or adjectival phrase used to define a characteristic quality or attribute of some person or thing. Common in historical titles (Catherine the Great, Ethelred the Unready), 'stock' epithets have been used in poetry since Homer. The **Homeric epithet** is an adjective (usually a compound adjective) repeatedly used for the same thing or person: *the wine-dark sea* and *rosy-fingered Dawn* are famous examples. In the **transferred epithet** (or *hypallage), an adjective appropriate to one noun is attached to another by association: thus in the phrase *sick room* it is not strictly the room that is sick but the person in it. *Adjective*: **epithetic**. *See also* ANTONOMASIA.

**epizeuxis** A rhetorical *figure by which a word is repeated for emphasis, with no other words intervening:

> Break, break, break,
> On thy cold gray stones, O Sea!
> (Tennyson)

**epode** [ep-ohd] The third part of the triadic structure used in the Pindaric *ode and in Greek dramatic *choruses, following the *strophe and *antistrophe and differing from them in length and metrical form. The term was also used for a Greek *metre invented by Archilochus (7th century BCE), in which a longer line was followed by a shorter one (e.g. a *trimeter followed by a *dimeter); in this metre, adopted in Latin by Horace, the shorter line can also be called the epode. *Adjective*: **epodic**.

**eponymous** [ip-on-imŭs] Name-giving: a term applied to a real or fictitious person after whom a place, thing, institution, meal, or book is named. Thus Anna Karenina is called the eponymous heroine of Tolstoy's novel *Anna Karenina*. The term is often extended beyond its strict sense to describe a character who is referred to indirectly (i.e. not by name) in the title of a work: thus Michael Henchard is called the eponymous hero of Hardy's *The Mayor of Casterbridge*. An **eponym** is a name transferred from a person to a place or thing, either in its original form or as adapted (e.g. Bolivar or Bolivia). *See also* ANTONOMASIA.

**epos** The *epic poetry of an early oral tradition.

**epyllion** (plural -llia) A miniature *epic poem, resembling an epic in *metre and/or style but not in length. The term dates from the 19th century, when it was applied to certain shorter *narrative poems in Greek and Latin, usually dealing with a mythological love story in an elaborately digressive and allusive manner, as in Catullus' poem on Peleus and Thetis. The nearest equivalents in English poetry are the Elizabethan erotic narratives such as Marlowe's *Hero and Leander* (1598) and Shakespeare's *Venus and Adonis* (1593), although the term

has also been applied to later non-erotic works including Arnold's
*Sohrab and Rustum* (1853).

**equivoque** [ek-wi-vohk]  A *pun or deliberately ambiguous expression.
*Adjective*: **equivocal**. *Verb*: **equivocate**. *See also* AMBIGUITY, *DOUBLE
ENTENDRE*, PARONOMASIA.

**erasure**  The placing of a concept under suspicion by marking the
word for it as crossed (e.g. ~~philosophy~~), in order to signal to readers that
it is both unreliable and at the same time indispensable. The device of
placing words *sous rature* ('under erasure') has sometimes been
adopted in modern philosophy and criticism, notably in
*deconstruction.

***erlebte Rede***  The German term for *free indirect style.

***ermetismo***  *See* HERMETICISM.

**erotica**  The collective term for materials of an erotic nature, and
particularly for prose or verse narratives of sexual fantasy ranging from
explicitly *pornographic novels to jocular poems on sexual subjects,
whether or not these are illustrated pictorially. The term was for a long
time a booksellers' euphemism for such forbidden materials. Within this
broad category are works of genuine literary distinction categorized
as **erotic poetry**, including some of the poems of Catullus and Ovid,
Marlowe's narrative poem *Hero and Leander* (completed by George
Chapman, 1598), Shakespeare's narrative poem *Venus and Adonis*
(1593), and several French lyrics by Paul Verlaine. Erotic fiction in
English includes John Cleland's *Memoirs of a Woman of Pleasure*
(1748–9; popularly known as *Fanny Hill*), once an underground classic
but now legitimately published in scholarly editions for students;
and D. H. Lawrence's novel *Lady Chatterley's Lover* (1928), a banned
book until a landmark legal verdict in an obscenity trial in 1960. The
much-disputed boundary between erotica and pornography is not
open to settlement by dictionary definitions, but shifts according to the
climate of public opinion. Since the 1960s, written texts have been not
only less subject to sexual censorship but increasingly marginal to the
image-dominated pornography industry proper; so that fiction that
would once have counted as pornographic is now called erotica, and
more than ever marketed in anthologies addressed to lesbians and
heterosexual women as well as to men.

**Erziehungsroman** Another term for *Bildungsroman*.

**eschatology** [esk-ă-**tol**-ŏji] The theological study or artistic representation of the end of the world. **Eschatological** writing is found chiefly in religious *allegories, but also in some *science fiction. The term should not be confused with *scatology, which is the scientific or humorous consideration of excrement. *See also* ANAGOGICAL, APOCALYPTIC.

**espinela** [es-pin-**ay**-ă] (*espinella*) Another name for the Spanish *decastich more often known as the *décima*.

**essay** A short written composition in prose that discusses a subject or proposes an argument without claiming to be a complete or thorough exposition. A minor literary form, the essay is more relaxed than the formal academic dissertation. The term ('trying out') was coined by the French writer Michel de Montaigne in the title of his *Essais* (1580), the first modern example of the form. Francis Bacon's *Essays* (1597) began the tradition of essays in English, of which important examples are those of Addison, Steele, Hazlitt, Emerson, D. H. Lawrence, and Virginia Woolf. The verse essays of Pope and of Robert Pinsky are rare exceptions to the prose norm.

**esthetics** *See* AESTHETICS.

**estrangement** *See* DEFAMILIARIZATION.

**euphony** [**yoo**-fŏni] A pleasing smoothness of sound, perceived by the ease with which the words can be spoken in combination. The use of long vowels, liquid consonants ($l$, $r$), and semi-vowels ($w$, $y$), contributes to euphony, along with the avoidance of adjacent stresses; the meaning of the words, however, has an important effect too. Euphony is the opposite of *cacophony. *Adjective*: **euphonious**.

**euphuism** [**yoo**-few-izm] An elaborately ornate prose style richly decorated with rhetorical *figures. The term comes from the popularity of two prose romances by John Lyly: *Euphues: The Anatomy of Wit* (1578), and its sequel *Euphues and His England* (1580). Lyly's style, later parodied by Shakespeare among others, is marked by the repeated use of *antitheses reinforced by *alliteration, along with *rhetorical questions and various figures of repetition. It is also notable for its frequent use of *sententiae and elaborate *similes drawn from real and fabulous birds and beasts. This example comes from a *soliloquy spoken by the character Euphues:

> Ah Euphues, into what misfortune art thou brought! In what sudden misery art
> thou wrapped! It is like to fare with thee as with the eagle, which dieth neither
> for age nor with sickness but with famine, for although thy stomach hunger,
> thy heart will not suffer thee to eat. And why shouldst thou torment thyself for
> one in whom is neither faith not fervency? Oh the counterfeit love of women!
> Oh inconstant sex! I have lost Philautus. I have lost Lucilla. I have lost that
> which I shall hardly find again: a faithful friend. Ah, foolish Euphues! Why
> didst thou leave Athens, the nurse of wisdom, to inhabit Naples, the nourisher
> of wantonness? Had it not been better for thee to have eaten salt with the
> philosophers in Greece than sugar with the courtiers in Italy?

*Adjective*: **euphuistic**.

**exclamatio** A rhetorical *figure in which high emotion is expressed in the form of a sudden exclamation, which is often an *apostrophe: 'O Richard! York is too far gone with grief' (Shakespeare, *Richard II*).

**excursus** (plural **-suses**) A *digression in which some point is discussed at length; or an appendix devoted to detailed examination of some topic held over from the main body of the text. *Adjective*: **excursive**.

**exegesis** [eks-ĕ-**jee**-sis] (plural **-geses**) The interpretation or explanation of a *text. The term was first applied to the interpretation of religious scriptures (or oracles and visions), but has been borrowed by literary *criticism for the analysis of any poetry or prose. Literary scholars have likewise inherited some of the procedures of biblical exegesis, for instance the decoding of *allegories (*see* TYPOLOGY). A person who practises exegesis is an **exegete**. *Adjective*: **exegetic** or **exegetical**.

**exemplum** (plural **-pla**) A short tale used as an example to illustrate a moral point, usually in a sermon or other *didactic work. The form was cultivated in the late Middle Ages, for instance in Robert Mannyng of Brunne's *Handlyng Synne* (early 14th century) and in Chaucer's *Pardoner's Tale* and *Nun's Priest's Tale*, as well as in many prose collections for the use of preachers. *See also* ALLEGORY, FABLE, PARABLE.

**existentialism** [eksi-**stench**-ăl-izm] A current in European philosophy distinguished by its emphasis on lived human existence. Although it had an important precursor in the Danish theologian

Søren Kierkegaard in the 1840s, its impact was fully felt only in the mid-20th century in France and Germany: the German philosophers Martin Heidegger and Karl Jaspers prepared some of the ground in the 1920s and 1930s for the more influential work of Jean-Paul Sartre and the other French existentialists including Simone de Beauvoir, Albert Camus, and Maurice Merleau-Ponty. In terms of its literary impact, the thought of Sartre has been the most significant, presented in novels (notably *La Nausée* (*Nausea*), 1938) and plays (including *Les Mouches* (*The Flies*), 1943) as well as in the major philosophical work *L'Être et le néant* (*Being and Nothingness*), 1943).

Sartrean existentialism, as distinct from the Christian existentialism derived from Kierkegaard, is an atheist philosophy of human freedom conceived in terms of individual responsibility and authenticity. Its fundamental premiss that 'existence precedes essence', implies that we as human beings have no given essence or nature but must forge our own values and meanings in an inherently meaningless or *absurd world of existence. Obliged to make our own choices, we can either confront the anguish (or *Angst) of this responsibility, or evade it by claiming obedience to some determining convention or duty, thus acting in 'bad faith'. Paradoxically, we are 'condemned to be free'. Similar themes can be found in the novels and essays of Camus; both authors felt that the absurdity of existence could be redeemed through the individual's decision to become *engagé* ('committed') within social and political causes opposing fascism and imperialism. Some of the concerns of French existentialism are echoed in English in Thom Gunn's early collection of poems, *The Sense of Movement* (1957), and in the fiction of Iris Murdoch and John Fowles. *See also* PHENOMENOLOGY.

**Further reading:** Kevin Aho, *Existentialism: An Introduction* (2014).

**exordium** The first part of a speech, according to the structure recommended in classical *rhetoric; or the introductory section of a written work of argument or exposition. *Adjective*: **exordial**.

**experimentalism** The commitment to exploring new concepts and representations of the world through methods that go beyond the established *conventions of literary tradition. Experimentalism was an important characteristic of 20th-century literature and art, in which successive *avant-garde* movements arose in continual reaction against what they regarded as decayed or ossified forms of expression. For examples, *see* DADA, EXPRESSIONISM, FUTURISM, MODERNISM, *NOUVEAU ROMAN*, SURREALISM, VORTICISM.

**explication** The attempt to analyse a literary work thoroughly, giving full attention to its complexities of form and meaning. The term has usually been associated with the kind of analysis practised in the USA by *New Criticism and in Britain under the name of *practical criticism or *close reading. Explication in this sense is normally a detailed explanation of the manner in which the language and formal structure of a short poem work to achieve a unity of *form and *content; such analysis tends to emphasize ambiguities and complexities of the text while putting aside questions of historical or biographical context. A less thorough form of analysis is the French school exercise known as *explication de texte*, in which students give an account of a work's meaning and its stylistic features. *Adjective*: **explicatory** or **explicative**. *See also* CRITICISM, EXEGESIS, HERMENEUTICS.

**exposition** The setting forth of a systematic explanation of or argument about any subject; or the opening part of a play or story, in which we are introduced to the characters and their situation, often by reference to preceding events. *Adjective*: **expository**. *Verb*: **expound**.

**expressionism** A general term for a mode of literary or visual art which, in extreme reaction against *realism or *naturalism, presents a world violently distorted under the pressure of intense personal moods, ideas, and emotions: image and language thus express feeling and imagination rather than represent external reality. Although not an organized movement, expressionism was an important factor in the painting, drama, poetry, and cinema of German-speaking Europe between 1910 and 1924. The term did not come into use until 1911, but has since been applied retrospectively to some important forerunners of expressionist technique, going as far back as Georg Büchner's plays of the 1830s and Vincent Van Gogh's paintings of the 1880s; other significant precursors include the Norwegian painter Edvard Munch, the Swedish playwright August Strindberg (in his *Dream Play*, 1902), and the German playwright Frank Wedekind. Within the period 1910–24, consciously expressionist techniques of abstraction were promoted by Wassily Kandinsky and the 'Blue Rider' group of painters, while in drama various anti-naturalist principles of abstract characterization and structural discontinuity were employed in the plays of Ernst Toller,

Georg Kaiser, and Walter Hasenclever; these had some influence on the
early plays of Bertolt Brecht, notably *Baal* (1922). The poetry of Georg
Trakl, Gottfried Benn, August Stramm, and Franz Werfel displayed
comparable distortions of accepted structures and syntax in favour of
symbolized mood. The nightmarish labyrinths of Franz Kafka's novels
are the nearest equivalent in prose fiction.

German expressionism is best known today through the wide
influence of its cinematic masterpieces: Robert Wiene's *The Cabinet of
Dr Caligari* (1920), F. W. Murnau's *Nosferatu* (1922), and Fritz Lang's
*Metropolis* (1926). Along with their much-imitated visual patterns of
sinister shadows, these films reveal a shared obsession with
automatized, trance-like states, which appears in expressionist literature
too: a common concern of expressionism is with the eruption of
irrational and chaotic forces from beneath the surface of a mechanized
modern world. Some of its explosive energies issued into *Dada,
*Vorticism, and other *avant-garde* movements of the 1920s. In the
English-speaking world, expressionist dramatic techniques were
adopted in some of the plays of Eugene O'Neill and Sean O'Casey, and
in the 'Circe' episode of James Joyce's novel *Ulysses* (1922); in poetry,
T. S. Eliot's *The Waste Land* (1922) may be considered expressionist in
its fragmentary rendering of postwar desolation. In a further sense, the
term is sometimes applied to the belief that literary works are essentially
expressions of their authors' moods and thoughts; this has been the
dominant assumption about literature since the rise of *Romanticism.

**Further reading:** Neil H. Donahue (ed.), *A Companion to the Literature of
German Expressionism* (2002).

**expurgate** To remove objectionable (especially sexual or politically
sensitive) passages from a text. *Noun*: **expurgation**. *See also*
BOWDLERIZE, UNEXPURGATED.

**extempore** [iks-**tem**-pŏ-ri] Composed on the spur of the moment,
without preparation. Some kinds of oral poetry involve a degree of
extemporization. *Verb*: **extemporize**.

**extravaganza** A theatrical entertainment consisting of a mild
*burlesque of some *myth or fairy tale enlivened by *puns, music, dance,
and elaborate spectacle. The form was made popular in the mid-19th
century by J. R. Planché, and influenced the development both of

*pantomime and of the light operas of Gilbert and Sullivan. The term is now applied to any lavishly staged musical *revue.

**eye rhyme** A kind of *rhyme in which the spellings of paired words appear to match but without true correspondence in pronunciation: *dive/give, said/maid*. Some examples, like *love/prove*, were originally true rhymes but have become eye rhymes through changes in pronunciation: these are known as 'historical rhymes'. *See also* CONSONANCE, HALF-RHYME, POETIC LICENCE.

e

**fable** A brief tale in verse or prose that conveys a moral lesson, usually by giving human speech and manners to animals and inanimate things (*see* BEAST FABLE). Fables often conclude with a moral, delivered in the form of an *epigram. A very old form of story related to *folklore and *proverbs, the fable in Europe descends from tales attributed to Aesop, a Greek slave in the 6th century BCE: his fable of the fox and the grapes has given us the phrase 'sour grapes'. An Indian collection, the *Bidpai*, dates back to about 300 CE. The French **fabulist** La Fontaine revived the form in the 17th century with his witty verse adaptations of Greek fables. More recent examples are Rudyard Kipling's *Just So Stories* (1902), James Thurber's *Fables of Our Time* (1940), and George Orwell's *Animal Farm* (1945). *Adjectives*: **fabular, fabulous**. *See also* ALLEGORY, EXEMPLUM.

**fabliau** [**fab**-li-oh] (plural **-liaux**) A coarsely humorous short story in verse, dealing in a bluntly realistic manner with *stock characters of the middle class involved in sexual intrigue or obscene pranks. Fabliaux flourished in France in the 12th and 13th centuries, and were usually written in *octosyllabic couplets; some 150 French examples survive, most of them anonymous. They were imitated in English by Chaucer (in rhyming *pentameters), notably in his *Miller's Tale* and *Reeve's Tale*. Many fabliaux involve *satire against the clergy. A standard plot is the cuckolding of a slow-witted husband by a crafty and lustful student.

**Further reading:** John Hines, *The Fabliau in English* (1993).

**fabula** The term used in *Russian Formalism for the 'raw material' of *story events as opposed to the finished arrangement of the *plot (or *sjuzet*); the distinction reappears in later French *narratology as that between *histoire* (story) and *récit* (account). In Latin literature, *fabula* (plural -*lae*) is also the general name for various kinds of play, of which the most significant *genres are *fabula Atellana* or Atellan *farce, and *fabula palliata* or Roman *New Comedy.

**fabulation** A term used by some modern critics for a mode of modern fiction that openly delights in its self-conscious verbal artifice, thus departing from the conventions of *realism. Robert Scholes in his book *The Fabulators* (1967) describes fabulation in the works of John Barth, Kurt Vonnegut, and others as an essentially comic and *allegorical mode of fiction that often adopts the forms of *romance or of the *picaresque novel. *See also* MAGIC REALISM, METAFICTION, POSTMODERNISM.

**faction** A short-lived *portmanteau word denoting works that present verifiably factual contents in the form of a fictional novel, as in Norman Mailer's *The Armies of the Night* (1968). Although still sometimes used by journalists, the term suffers from the disadvantage of already meaning something else (i.e. a conspiratorial group within a divided organization), so the preferred term is *New Journalism.

**fairy tale (fairy story)** A traditional *folktale adapted and written down for the entertainment of children, usually featuring *marvellous events and characters, although fairies as such are less often found in them than princesses, talking animals, ogres, and witches. The term is a direct translation of the French *conte de fée*, the writing down of fairy tales having emerged from a fad for such stories among the French aristocracy of the late 17th century. Many of these stories are of incalculable antiquity, some deriving from Sanskrit, Chinese, Arabic, and Persian traditions, and a few had appeared in early *chapbooks and *romances, but the first major literary collection was Charles Perrault's *Histoires, ou contes du temps passé* (1697, better known as *Contes de ma mère l'Oye* or *Mother Goose's Tales*), containing 'The Sleeping Beauty', 'Cinderella', 'Little Red Riding-Hood', 'Bluebeard', 'Puss in Boots', and others. 'Beauty and the Beast' appeared in 1756 from the pen of Marie de Beaumont, a French governess working in England. Such stories began to be used as the basis for *pantomimes from the late 18th century, and were soon joined by the anonymous early 19th-century English tale 'Jack and the Beanstalk'.

The fairy-tale canon was expanded in the early 19th century by Jacob and Wilhelm Grimm, whose researches into folklore resulted in their written versions of 200 *Kinder- und Hausmärchen* (1812–14) (*see* MÄRCHEN), including 'Rapunzel', 'Snow White and the Seven Dwarves', 'Hansel and Gretel', and 'Rumpelstiltskin'. The third major author of modern fairy tales was the Danish writer Hans Christian Andersen, who published his first collection in 1835, following this with 'The Ugly Duckling' (1845) and dozens of others in a cycle completed in 1874. Andrew Lang then collected various fairy tales from around the world in his series of *Fairy Books* (1899–1910).

**Further reading:** Andrew Teverson, *Fairy Tale* (2013).

**falling rhythm (descending rhythm)** A rhythmical effect often found in metrical verse in which the unstressed syllables are perceived as being attached to the preceding stressed syllables rather than to those following. In the terms of classical *prosody, lines composed of *dactyls or *trochees may be marked by falling rhythm, although this is not inevitable. Falling rhythm is less common in English verse than its opposite, *rising rhythm.

**fancy** The mind's ability to produce new combinations of images or ideas, usually in a more limited, superficial, or whimsical manner than that achieved by the *imagination proper. Before S. T. Coleridge's distinction between the faculties of fancy and imagination, the terms were often synonymous, 'fancy' being an abbreviation of 'fantasy'. Coleridge, in *Biographia Literaria* (1817), argued that the fancy was merely 'a mode of memory emancipated from the order of time and space' and was thus able to combine and reassemble ready-made images in new spatial and temporal arrangements, but not able to dissolve and unite them in new creations as the imagination could.

**fantastic, the** A mode of fiction in which the possible and the impossible are confounded so as to leave the reader (and often the narrator and/or central character) with no consistent explanation for the story's strange events. Tzvetan Todorov, in his *Introduction à la littérature fantastique* (1970; translated as *The Fantastic*, 1973), argues that fantastic narratives involve an unresolved hesitation between the supernatural explanation available in *marvellous tales and the natural or psychological explanation offered by tales of the *uncanny. The literature of the fantastic flourished in 19th-century ghost stories and related fiction: Henry James's mysterious tale *The Turn of the Screw* (1898) is a classic example.

**fantasy** A general term for any kind of fictional work that is not primarily devoted to realistic representation of the known world. The category includes several literary *genres (e.g. *dream vision, *fable, *fairy tale, *romance, *science fiction) describing imagined worlds in which magical powers and other impossibilities are accepted. Recent theorists of fantasy have attempted to distinguish more precisely between the self-contained magical realms of the *marvellous, the psychologically explicable delusions of the *uncanny, and the inexplicable meeting of both in the *fantastic.

**Further reading:** Brian Attebery, *Strategies of Fantasy* (1992).

**farce** A kind of *comedy that inspires hilarity mixed with panic and cruelty in its audience through an increasingly rapid and improbable series of ludicrous confusions, physical disasters, and sexual innuendos among its *stock characters. Farcical episodes of buffoonery can be found in European drama of all periods since Aristophanes, notably in medieval France, where the term originated to describe short comic *interludes; but as a distinct form of full-length comedy farce dates from the 19th century, in the works of Eugène Labiche in the 1850s, and of A. W. Pinero and Georges Feydeau in the 1880s and 1890s. Brandon Thomas's *Charley's Aunt* (1892) is recognized as a classic of the *genre. The bedroom farce, involving bungled adultery in rooms with too many doors, has had prolonged commercial success in London's *West End since the 1920s, when Ben Travers perfected the genre at the Aldwych Theatre. Joe Orton used its *conventions to create a disturbing kind of *satire in *What the Butler Saw* (1969), while the Italian playwright-activist Dario Fo used them for political satire in his *Morte accidentale di un anarchico* (1970). A writer of farces is sometimes called a **farceur**, although in everyday French usage this usually means a joker.

**Further reading:** Jessica Milner Davis, *Farce* (2nd edn, 2003).

***Fastnachtspiel*** (plural ***-spiele***) A kind of short popular drama performed by townsfolk in Germany during the Shrove Tuesday (*Fastnacht*) festivals in the 16th century. Most surviving examples are from Nuremburg, where Hans Sachs (1494–1576) was the foremost author of such plays.

**feminine ending** The ending of a metrical verse line on an unstressed syllable, as in the regular *trochaic line. In English iambic *pentameters, a feminine ending involves the addition of an eleventh syllable, as in Shakespeare's famous line

>            To be, or not to be; that is the question

In French, a feminine line is one ending with a mute *e*, *es*, or *ent*. A feminine *caesura is a pause following an unstressed syllable, usually in the middle of a line. *See also* METRE, STRESS.

**feminine rhyme (double rhyme)** A *rhyme on two syllables, the first stressed and the second unstressed (e.g. *mother/another*), commonly found in many kinds of poetry but especially in humorous verse, as in Byron's *Don Juan*:

> Christians have burned each other, quite persuaded
> That all the Apostles would have done as they did.

*Masculine rhyme, on the other hand, does not employ unstressed syllables. Where more than one word is used in one of the rhyming units, as in the example above, the rhyme is sometimes called a 'mosaic rhyme'. In French verse, the alternation of masculine and feminine rhymes became the norm during the 16th century.

**feminist criticism** *See* p. 138.

**Festschrift** (plural **-iften**) A volume of essays written by the disciples of an eminent scholar or writer, to whom it is presented as a tribute on a special occasion such as a birthday or retirement. The custom and the term ('celebration-writing') originated in German universities in the 19th century.

**feuilleton** [fer-yĕ-to$^n$] A French term for the literary section of a daily newspaper: originally the lower part of the front page, devoted to drama criticism, but later a separate page or pages. The *roman-feuilleton* is a novel *serialized in a newspaper; this form flourished in France in the 1840s, bringing great financial rewards to Balzac, George Sand, Dumas *père*, and other authors.

**fiaba** (plural **fiabe**) The Italian word for a *fable or *folktale, often with the more specific sense of a *fairy tale, as in Italo Calvino's much-admired retelling of *Fiabe italiane* (1956).

**ficelle** [fi-sell] The term used by Henry James in the prefaces to some of his novels to denote a fictional character whose role as *confidant or confidante is exploited as a means of providing the reader with information while avoiding direct address from the *narrator: in James's novel *The Ambassadors* (1903), Maria Gostrey is the *ficelle* to whom the *protagonist Lambert Strether discloses confidentially his opinions about the complex state of affairs in which he is involved. In French, the

## FEMINIST CRITICISM

A mode of literary and cultural discussion and reassessment
inspired by modern feminist thought, from which has developed
since the 1970s not a method of interpretation but an arena of
debate about the relations between literature and the socio-cultural
subordination borne by women as writers, readers, or fictional
characters within a male-dominated ('patriarchal') social order.
This tradition, mostly American and British, honours certain earlier
pioneers of such discussion, notably Rebecca West, Virginia Woolf
(in her long essays *A Room of One's Own* (1929) and *Three Guineas*
(1938), sometimes regarded as the founding documents of the
movement), and Simone de Beauvoir (whose *Le Deuxième Sexe*
(1949, translated as *The Second Sex*) enjoys a similar status). In its
recognizable modern form, however, the founding texts are Mary
Ellmann's *Thinking About Women* (1968), a wittily satirical survey
of male writers' stereotypes of women, and Kate Millett's *Sexual
Politics* (1970), an enraged polemic against the alleged misogyny of
D. H. Lawrence and other modern male authors. These works
inspired others to extend the variety of feminist criticism that came
to be known as 'Images-of-Women' study, e.g. in the essays
collected in Susan K. Cornillon (ed.), *Images of Women in Fiction*
(1972) or in Judith Fetterley's *The Resisting Reader* (1978).

A major redirection of attention away from the sins of male
authors and towards the virtues of women's writing (often regarded
as having been unjustly neglected by a patriarchal critical
establishment) was soon launched by a second wave of critics and
literary historians, notably Ellen Moers in *Literary Women* (1976),
Elaine Showalter in *A Literature of Their Own* (1977), and Sandra M.
Gilbert with Susan Gubar in *The Madwoman in the Attic* (1979).
This form of feminist criticism, termed '*gynocritics' by Showalter,
attempts to reconstruct an occluded tradition of women's writing
in which female authors are inspired by their 'foremothers'
rather than by male authors; it meanwhile reinterprets women's
writings as coded expressions of their rage or frustration against
patriarchy.

Since the 1980s, these early styles of American feminist criticism,
based on 'female experience' and literary fidelity or infidelity to

it, have come under some challenge both from women critics speaking for ethnic and sexual minorities with different experiences, and from feminist scholars more inclined to draw upon Marxist, psychoanalytic, or *poststructuralist thinking (despite counter-charges that such *Theory is in effect 'male' theory). In this latter group, some preferred to pursue the distinct agenda of so-called 'French feminism' in the writings of Julia Kristeva, Luce Irigaray, and Hélène Cixous (who were usually wary of styling themselves as feminists), with their theories of gendered language and of *écriture feminine; others grew sceptical of what they saw as 'essentialist' models of sexual difference (see GYNESIS). Feminist criticism and the allied project of feminist literary history have thus become highly variegated and hyphenated (as ecofeminist criticism, vegetarian-feminist criticism, etc.).

**Further reading:** Mary Eagleton (ed.), *Feminist Literary Theory* (2nd edn, 1995); Ruth Robbins, *Literary Feminisms* (2000); Ellen Rooney (ed.), *The Cambridge Companion to Feminist Literary Theory* (2006).

(🌐) SEE WEB LINKS

• Feminist theory site at Virginia Tech.

word denotes a string used to manipulate a puppet, or more broadly, any underhand trick.

**fiction** The general term for invented stories, now usually applied to novels, short stories, novellas, romances, fables, and other *narrative works in prose, even though most plays and narrative poems are also fictional. The adjective **fictitious** tends to carry the unfavourable sense of falsehood, whereas 'fictional' is more neutral, and the archaic adjective **fictive**, revived by the poet Wallace Stevens and others, has a more positive sense closer to 'imaginative' or 'inventive'. *Verb*: **fictionalize**. *See also* METAFICTION.

**figure (figure of speech)** An expression that departs from the accepted literal sense or from the normal order of words, or in which an emphasis is produced by patterns of sound. Such **figurative language** is an especially important resource of poetry, although not every poem will use it; it is also constantly present in all other kinds of speech and writing, even though it usually passes unnoticed. The ancient theory of *rhetoric named and categorized dozens of figures, drawing a rough and often disputed distinction between those (known as *tropes or figures of thought) that extend the meaning of words, and those that merely affect their order or their impact upon an audience (known as figures of speech, schemes, or rhetorical figures). The most important tropes are *metaphor, *simile, *metonymy, *synecdoche, *personification, and *irony; others include *hyperbole (overstatement), *litotes (understatement), and *periphrasis (circumlocution). The minor rhetorical figures can emphasize or enliven a point in several different ways: by placing words in contrast with one another (*antithesis), by repeating words in various patterns (*anadiplosis, *anaphora, *antistrophe, *chiasmus), by changing the order of words (*hyperbaton), by missing out conjunctions (*asyndeton), by changing course or breaking off in mid-sentence (*anacoluthon, *aposiopesis), or by assuming special modes of address (*apostrophe) or enquiry (*rhetorical question). A further category of figures, sometimes known as 'figures of sound', achieves emphasis by the repetition of sounds, as in *alliteration, *assonance, and *consonance.

**Further reading:** Anthony Quinn, *Figures of Speech* (1982).

**(⊕) SEE WEB LINKS**

• Silva Rhetoricae (The Forest of Rhetoric): lists and describes a huge number of figures.

***fin de siècle*** [faⁿ dĕ si-**airkl**]  The French phrase ('end of century')
often used to refer to the characteristic world-weary mood of European
culture in the 1880s and 1890s, when writers and artists like Oscar Wilde,
Aubrey Beardsley, and the French *symbolists, under the slogan '*art
for art's sake', adopted a 'decadent' rejection of any moral or social
function for art. Reacting against *realism and *naturalism, they sought
a pure beauty entirely removed from the imperfections of nature and
from the drabness of contemporary society. *See also* AESTHETICISM,
DECADENCE.

**first-person narrative**  A narrative or mode of storytelling in
which the *narrator appears as the 'I' recollecting his or her own
part in the events related, either as a witness of the action or as an
important participant in it. The term is most often used of novels
such as Charlotte Brontë's *Jane Eyre* (1847), in which the narrator
is also the central character. The term does not mean that the
narrator speaks only in the first person, of course: in discussions
of other characters, the third person will be used. *See also*
AUTOBIOGRAFICTION.

**fit**  An obsolete term for a *canto or division of a long poem. The
14th-century English poem *Sir Gawain and the Green Knight* is
composed of four fits.

**fixed forms**  The general term covering the various kinds of poem in
which the *metre and *rhyme scheme are governed by a prescribed
pattern. The term usually refers to a class of medieval French verse
forms including the *ballade, *chant royal*, *rondeau, *sestina, *triolet,
and *villanelle; but there are some other fixed poetic forms, the most
significant being the *sonnet, the *haiku, and the *limerick. Various
established *stanza forms such as *ottava rima* and *rhyme royal may
also be considered as 'fixed'.

**flashback**  *See* ANALEPSIS.

**flyting**  A slanging match in verse, usually between two poets who
insult each other alternately in profanely abusive verses. The finest
example from the strong Scottish tradition is the early 16th-century
*Flyting of Dunbar and Kennedie*. The term has also been applied to the
boasting matches between warriors in some *epic poems. *See also*
AMOEBEAN VERSES, *DÉBAT*, INVECTIVE.

**focalization** The term used in modern *narratology for '*point of view'; that is, for the kind of perspective from which the events of a story are witnessed. Events observed by a traditional *omniscient narrator are said to be non-focalized, whereas events witnessed within the story's world from the constrained perspective of a single character, the focalizer, are 'internally focalized'. The nature of a given narrative's focalization is to be distinguished from its narrative 'voice', as seeing is from speaking.

**foil** A character whose qualities or actions serve to emphasize those of the *protagonist (or of some other character) by providing a strong contrast with them. Thus in Charlotte Brontë's *Jane Eyre*, the passive obedience of Jane's school-friend Helen Burns makes her a foil to the rebellious heroine.

**folio** A large size of book in which the page size results from folding a standard printer's sheet of paper in half, forming two leaves (i.e. four pages). The collected editions of Shakespeare's plays published after his death, as distinct from the earlier unauthorized *quarto editions, are often referred to as the Folios: the First Folio was published by his colleagues Heming and Condell in 1623, as *Mr. William Shakespeares Comedies, Histories, & Tragedies. Published according to the true Originall Copies*, and three others followed in 1632, 1663, and 1685.

(((⊕))) SEE WEB LINKS
• The Bodleian First Folio: digital facsimile.

**folklore** A modern term for the body of traditional customs, superstitions, stories, dances, and songs that have been adopted and maintained within a given community by processes of repetition not reliant on the written word. Along with *folk songs and *folktales, this broad category of cultural forms embraces all kinds of *legends, *riddles, jokes, *proverbs, games, charms, omens, spells, and rituals, especially those of pre-literate societies or social classes. Those forms of verbal expression that are handed on from one generation or locality to the next by word of mouth are said to constitute an *oral tradition. *Adjective*: **folkloric**.

**folk song** A song of unknown authorship that has been passed on, preserved, and adapted (often in several versions) in an *oral tradition before later being written down or recorded. Folk songs usually have an easily remembered melody and a simple poetic form such as the *quatrain. The most prominent categories are the narrative *ballad and the *lyric love-song, but the term also covers lullabies, *carols, and various songs to accompany working (e.g. the sea shanty), dancing, and drinking.

**folktale** A story passed on by word of mouth rather than by writing, and thus partly modified by successive re-tellings before being written down or recorded. The category includes *legends, *fables, jokes, *tall stories, and *fairy tales or *Märchen. Many folktales involve mythical creatures and magical transformations.

**SEE WEB LINKS**
• Folklore and Mythology Electronic Texts: large archive of folktales at University of Pittsburgh.

**foot** (plural **feet**) A group of syllables taken as a unit of poetic *metre in traditional *prosody, regardless of word-boundaries. As applied to English verse, the foot is a certain fixed combination of syllables, each of which is counted as being either stressed (●) or unstressed (○); but in Greek and Latin *quantitative verse, from which the various names of feet are derived, it is a combination of long (−) and short (◡) syllables. While the concept of the foot is clearly applicable to the quantitative principles of Greek and Latin verse, its widespread use in the analysis of the very different stress-based patterns of English verse is often very unhelpful and misleading, especially in *accentual verse. It is worth remembering that the foot is only an abstract unit of analysis in *scansion, not a substantial rhythmic entity.

The most common feet in English prosody are the *iamb (○●: *to be*) and the *trochee (●○: *beat it*); these disyllabic or 'duple' feet are the units of metrical lines described as iambic and trochaic respectively, according to the perceived predominance of one or other foot in the line. Less common in English are the trisyllabic or 'triple' feet known as the *dactyl (●○○: *heavenly*) and the *anapaest (○○●: *to the wall*); again, these feet when predominant in a line give their names to dactylic and anapaestic metres. Two other feet are sometimes referred to in English prosody, although they do not form the basis for whole lines: these are the *spondee (●●: *home-made*) and the *pyrrhic (○○: *in a*), which are both regarded as devices of metrical *substitution. There are several other Greek quantitative feet, for which equivalents are occasionally found or fabricated in English: these include the *amphibrach (◡−◡), the *amphimacer or cretic (− ◡ −), the *choriamb (− ◡◡ −), the *ionic ($\smile\smile--$ or $--\smile\smile$), the *paeon ($-\smile\smile\smile$ or $\smile\smile\smile-$), and the epitrite ($-\smile--$ or $--\smile-$). In traditional prosody, it is the number of feet in a line that determines the description of its length: thus a line of four feet is called a *tetrameter, while a line of five feet is a *pentameter.

**foregrounding** Giving unusual prominence to one element or property of a *text, relative to other less noticeable aspects. According to the theories of *Russian Formalism, literary works are special by virtue of the fact that they foreground their own linguistic status, thus drawing attention to how they say something rather than to what they say: poetry 'deviates' from everyday speech and from prose by using *metre, surprising *metaphors, *alliteration, and other devices by which its language draws attention to itself. *See also* DEFAMILIARIZATION, LITERARINESS.

**foreword** A short introductory essay placed at the beginning of a book, and usually written by somebody other than the book's author, e.g. by a translator or by a better-known writer introducing a new author to the public. Sometimes such a piece is placed at the book's end and is, logically, called an afterword.

**form** A critical term with a confusing variety of meanings. It can refer to a *genre (e.g. 'the short story form'), or to an established pattern of poetic devices (as in the various *fixed forms of European poetry), or, more abstractly, to the structure or unifying principle of design in a given work. Since the rise of *Romanticism, critics have often contrasted the principle of *organic form, which is said to evolve from within the developing work, with 'mechanic form', which is imposed as a predetermined design. When speaking of a work's **formal** properties, critics usually refer to its structural design and patterning, or sometimes to its style and manner in a wider sense, as distinct from its *content.

**Further reading:** Angela Leighton, *On Form* (2007).

**formalism** In the most general sense, the cultivation of artistic technique at the expense of subject-matter, either in literary practice or in criticism. The term has been applied, often in a derogatory sense, to several kinds of approach to literature in which *form is emphasized in isolation from a work's meanings or is taken as the chief criterion of aesthetic value. In modern critical discussion, however, the term frequently refers more specifically to the principles of certain Russian and Czech theorists: for this sense, *see* RUSSIAN FORMALISM. In the context of modern American poetry, the term has the specific sense of adherence to traditional metres and verse forms, as with the work of Howard Nemerov, Richard Wilbur, and the later poets of the *New Formalism, in contrast with the more widely adopted use of *free verse.

**formulaic** Characterized by the repetition of certain stock phrases, known as **formulae**. Many orally composed poems, especially *epics, are formulaic in that they repeatedly use the same *epithets and the same forms of introduction to episodes and speeches. In another sense, a work may be called formulaic if it conforms in a predictable way to the established patterns of a *genre.

**four-hander** A play written for only four speaking parts, such as Harold Pinter's *No Man's Land* (1975).

**fourteener** A line of verse containing fourteen syllables. It usually has seven stresses in an *iambic metre, in which case it can also be called an iambic *heptameter. Fourteeners, usually in rhyming *couplets or *poulter's measure, were often used by English poets in the 15th and 16th centuries, but rarely after George Chapman's famous translation of the *Iliad* (1611), from which this fourteener comes:

> So Agamemnon did sustain the torment of his wound.

In couplets, fourteeners strongly resemble the *ballad metre.

**frame narrative (frame story)** A story in which another story is enclosed or *embedded as a 'tale within the tale', or which contains several such tales. Prominent examples of frame narratives enclosing several tales are Boccaccio's *Decameron* (1353) and Chaucer's *Canterbury Tales* (*c.*1390), while some novels such as Mary Shelley's *Frankenstein* (1818) and Emily Brontë's *Wuthering Heights* (1847) employ a narrative structure in which the main action is relayed at second hand through an enclosing frame story. *See also* DIEGESIS.

**Frankfurt School** A group of neo-Marxist social theorists and philosophers associated with the Institut für Sozialforschung (Institute for Social Research) which was established at Frankfurt University in 1923, driven into exile in 1933, with a base at Columbia University, New York, from 1936, and returned to Frankfurt in 1950. The group espoused a non-dogmatic version of Marxism that it called *Critical Theory, incorporating various influences from modern traditions of philosophy, sociology, and psychology. Early members of the group included Max Horkheimer, Theodor Adorno, Erich Fromm, and Herbert Marcuse. More marginal but supported by the Institute and later regarded as a major figure was the essayist Walter Benjamin (1892–1940), whose influence in literary theory has generally been felt more strongly than that of the rest of the group, notably through his essays selected in English as *Illuminations* (1968). Adorno's influence has been felt in part through his analyses of the 'culture industry' as a means of social control. In the post-1950 phase of the school, the leading figure has been the philosopher Jürgen Habermas, who has been notable for defending the tradition of the *Enlightenment against the inroads of *postmodernism.

**Further reading:** Rolf Wiggershaus, *The Frankfurt School* (1994).

**free indirect style (free indirect discourse)** A manner of presenting the thoughts or utterances of a fictional character as if from that character's point of view by combining grammatical and other features of the character's 'direct speech' with features of the narrator's 'indirect' report. Direct discourse is used in the sentence *She thought, 'I will stay here tomorrow'*, while the equivalent in indirect discourse would be *She thought that she would stay there the next day*. Free indirect style, however, combines the person and tense of indirect discourse ('she would stay') with the indications of time and place appropriate to direct discourse ('here tomorrow'), to form a different kind of sentence: *She would stay here tomorrow*. This form of statement allows a *third-person narrative to exploit a first-person *point of view, often with a subtle effect of *irony, as in the novels of Jane Austen. Since Flaubert's celebrated use of this technique (known in French as *le style indirect libre*) in his novel *Madame Bovary* (1857), it has been widely adopted in modern fiction.

**free verse** (French, *vers libre*) A kind of poetry that does not conform to any regular *metre: the length of its lines is irregular, as is its use of rhyme—if any. Instead of a regular metrical pattern it uses more flexible *cadences or rhythmic groupings, sometimes supported by *anaphora and other devices of repetition. Now the most widely practised verse form in English, it has precedents in translations of the biblical Psalms and in some poems of Blake and Goethe, but established itself only in the late 19th and early 20th centuries with Walt Whitman, the French

*Symbolists, and the poets of *modernism. Free verse should not be confused with *blank verse, which does observe a regular metre in its unrhymed lines. A writer of free verse is sometimes called a *verslibriste*.

**Further reading:** H. T. Kirby-Smith, *The Origins of Free Verse* (1996).

**Fugitives** A group of American poets and critics in the 1920s associated with Vanderbilt University, Tennessee and more directly with the bimonthly poetry magazine *The Fugitive* (1922–5). The group had no strict doctrine, but tended to insist on poetry as an act of adult intelligence, and to scorn the *local color tradition of Southern US writing. The developing critical positions of some of its members eventually helped to shape the highly influential *New Criticism. The most prominent members were Donald Davidson, John Crowe Ransom, Allen Tate, Merrill Moore, Laura Riding, and Robert Penn Warren.

**Further reading:** Charlotte H. Beck, *The Fugitive Legacy* (2001).

**function** A concept employed in *structuralist literary theory in two senses: either as a kind of use to which language can be directed, or as an action contributing towards the development of a *narrative. The first sense is employed in the influential model of communication outlined in Roman Jakobson's 'Closing statement: linguistics and poetics' (1960). Here Jakobson defines six linguistic functions according to the element of the communicative act that each function makes predominant. Thus the *emotive* function orients the communication towards the 'addresser' (i.e. speaker or writer), expressing an attitude or mood; the *conative* (or connotative) function orients a communication towards its 'addressee' or recipient, as in commands; the most commonly used function, the *referential*, orients a message towards a context beyond itself, conveying some information; the *phatic* function is oriented to the 'contact' between addresser and addressee, maintaining or confirming their link (e.g., in conversation, 'well, here we are, then'; or by radio, 'receiving you loud and clear'); the *metalingual* function is oriented towards the *code, usually to establish that it is shared by both parties (e.g. 'understood?' or 'it depends what you mean by . . .'); finally, the *poetic* function is oriented towards the 'message' itself, that is, to the communication's linguistic features of sound, *syntax, and *diction (*see also* FOREGROUNDING). The second sense of 'function' is used in *narratology, denoting a fundamental component of a tale: an action performed by a character that is significant in the unfolding of the story. Vladimir Propp, in his *Morphology of the Folktale* (1928), described 31 such narrative functions in Russian fairy tales, claiming that their order of appearance is invariable, although not every function will appear in one tale. Thus the 11th function ('the hero leaves home') necessarily precedes the 18th ('the villain is defeated') and the 20th ('the hero returns').

**fustian** Pretentiously inflated or pompous language. *See also* BOMBAST, RODOMONTADE.

**Futurism** A short-lived *\*avant-garde* movement in European art and literature launched in 1909 by the Italian poet Filippo Marinetti in the first of many Futurist *manifestos. Futurism violently rejected all previous artistic traditions and conventions along with accepted grammatical rules, in an attempt to express the dynamism and speed of the 20th-century machine age. Its new poetic techniques included typographic experiments and the composition of poems made up of meaningless sounds. Marinetti's aggressive masculine cult of machinery and warfare was eventually exploited by Mussolini as part of official Fascist culture in Italy, although a distinct revolutionary socialist group of Futurists also appeared in Russia in 1912, led by the poet and playwright Vladimir Mayakovsky. Elsewhere in Europe, Futurism influenced the French poet Guillaume Apollinaire and the *Dada movement, and provoked the emergence of *Vorticism. The adjective **futuristic** usually has no reference to this movement, but is applied to fictional works (usually of *science fiction or *utopian fantasy) that describe some imagined future society.

**Further reading:** John J. White, *Literary Futurism* (1990).

**SEE WEB LINKS**
• Italian Futurism site, including English versions of all the manifestos.

**gaff** A 19th-century term for a rudimentary kind of theatre offering cheap entertainment, usually in the form of *melodrama; such theatres were often referred to as 'penny gaffs', on the basis of the admission price.

**galliambics** Verses written in a Greek *metre associated with the Galli, who were the eunuch priests of the goddess Cybele. Used in Greek by Callimachus, and more famously in Latin by Catullus, the galliambic line is a variant of the *ionic tetrameter. A rare adaptation of this metre into English stress-patterns is Tennyson's poem 'Boadicea', written in awkwardly long lines of between 16 and 18 syllables:

> Lash the maiden into swooning, me they lash'd and humiliated.

**gazal** *See* GHAZAL.

**Geneva school** A group of critics associated with the University of Geneva from the 1940s to the 1960s. Its most prominent figure was the Belgian critic Georges Poulet, while in the USA J. Hillis Miller was a significant practitioner of the school's methods before he adopted those of *deconstruction; others include Jean Rousset, Jean Starobinski, and Jean-Pierre Richard. Drawing on the philosophical tradition of *phenomenology, these 'critics of consciousness' (as they have sometimes been called) saw the critic's task as one of identifying, and fully identifying *with*, the unique mode of consciousness pervading a given author's works. Thus an author's particular sense of time and space would be seen as the unifying source of his or her entire *oeuvre*, regardless of the differences between individual works. Although related to some of the assumptions of biographical criticism, the 'phenomenological' approach of the Geneva critics differs in that it works back from the texts to the mind behind them, not from the life to the texts. An impressive example of this approach at work in English is J. Hillis Miller's *Charles Dickens: The World of his Novels* (1959).

**genre** [*zh*ah$^n$r] The French term for a type, species, or class of composition. A literary genre is a recognizable and established category of written work employing such common *conventions as will prevent readers or audiences from mistaking it for another kind. Much of the confusion surrounding the term arises from the fact that it is used simultaneously for the most basic modes of literary art (*lyric, *narrative, dramatic); for the broadest categories of composition (poetry, prose fiction), and for more specialized sub-categories, which are defined according to several different criteria including formal structure (*sonnet, *picaresque novel), length (*novella, *epigram), intention (*satire), effect (*comedy), origin (*folktale), and subject-matter (*pastoral, *science fiction). While some genres, such as the pastoral *elegy or the *melodrama, have numerous conventions governing subject, style, and form, others—like the *novel—have no agreed rules, although they may include several more limited *subgenres. *Adjective*: **generic**. *See also* DECORUM, FORM, MODE, TYPE.

**Further reading:** John Frow, *Genre* (2005).

**genre fiction** The broad class of fiction that is easily identifiable as belonging within any of the recognized *genres, especially of popular novel or *romance, such as *science fiction, *detective story, *thriller, western, historical romance, or love story. Genre fiction, then, is the kind of story that offers readers more or less what they would expect upon the basis of having read similar books before, whereas its presumed opposite, now increasingly referred to as 'literary fiction', is expected to go beyond generic boundaries and offer more original imaginative exploration.

**Further reading:** Ken Gelder, *Popular Fiction* (2004).

**Georgian poetry** A body of English verse published in the first half of George V's reign (1910–36) in five anthologies edited by Edward Marsh as *Georgian Poetry* (1912–22). The group of poets represented here included Rupert Brooke, Walter de la Mare, John Drinkwater, James Elroy Flecker, John Masefield, and J. C. Squire. They are now usually regarded as minor poets, quietly traditional in form and devoted to what Robert Graves called 'uncontroversial subjects' of rural and domestic life. The term **Georgianism** is sometimes used in a slightly extended sense to embrace this group along with other more or less traditional poets of the time (e.g. Edward Thomas) in contrast with the contemporary movement of *modernism in English verse. The term Georgian is only rarely applied to the literature of the period of the first four Georges (1714–1830).

**Further reading:** Rennie Parker, *The Georgian Poets* (1999).

**georgic** [jor-jik] A *didactic poem giving instruction on farming, husbandry, or some comparable pursuit, often involving praise of rural life. The earliest Greek example is Hesiod's *Works and Days* (8th century BCE), but the most influential work was the *Georgics* (37–30 BCE) of the Roman poet Virgil, which includes advice on bee-keeping and vines. Several English poets in the 18th century produced banal georgics in imitation of Virgil, including John Dyer in *The Fleece* (1757) and James Grainger in *The Sugar-Cane* (1759). Apart from its didactic intention, the georgic is distinguished from the *pastoral in that it regards nature in terms of necessary labour, not of harmonious idleness.

**ghazal** (ghasel; gazal; ghazel) A short *lyric poem written in *couplets using a single rhyme (*aa*, *ba*, *ca*, *da*, etc.), sometimes mentioning the poet's name in the last couplet. The ghazal is an important lyric form in Arabic, Persian, Turkish, and Urdu poetry, often providing the basis for popular love songs. Its usual subject-matter is amatory, although it has been adapted for religious, political, and other uses. Goethe and other German poets of the early 19th century wrote some imitations of the Persian ghazal, and the form has been adopted by a number of modern American poets, notably Adrienne Rich.

**ghost story** A modern form of *short story designed to provoke dread and unease in its readers by bringing about a crisis in which fictional characters are confronted terrifyingly by spirits of the returning dead. Such stories draw upon ancient traditions of *folklore concerning ghosts, but their narrative conventions date from the mid-19th century, when the Anglo-Irish writer J. Sheridan LeFanu perfected the required manipulation of suspense in his *Ghost Stories and Tales of Mystery* (1851) and later collections. Other popular Victorian writers took part in this new craze, notably Charles Dickens (as in his 'The Signalman', 1866) and Amelia B. Edwards (in 'The Phantom Coach', 1864), while magazine editors adopted the habit of publishing such works in their Christmas numbers. The classic age of the ghost story in English lasted through the early 20th century, when the recognized master of the genre was M. R. James, author of *Ghost Stories of an Antiquary* (1904) and other collections. The ghost story may be distinguished from its apparent near neighbour the Gothic tale (derived from the longer *Gothic novel) in one of two ways: it often employs settings that are distinctly non-Gothic in their apparently rational modernity; and it must exhibit a ghost, which need not actually appear in a Gothic tale.

**Further reading:** Julia Briggs, *Night Visitors* (1977).

**ghost-writer (ghostwriter)** A term used since the 1920s to designate a writer who is paid to produce books or articles that are presented as being written by somebody else. Typically this will be a sports journalist who writes a newspaper column or an entire *autobiography in the name of a well-known athlete whose own literary talents are insufficient for the task; but there are equivalent cases of **ghost-writing** in the worlds of cinema, music, politics, etc. *Adjective*: **ghost-written**.

***glosa*** (in English, **glose; gloss**) A poem composed as an amplification of lines taken from an earlier and usually better-known poem, although not literally as a *gloss in the explanatory sense. The standard form begins with a sequence of lines—commonly a *quatrain—from the source-poem, following this with a sequence of stanzas each ending with one (in variant forms, two) of these lines in succession. The term is Spanish, this kind of poem having been devised by Spanish courtiers in the early 15th century. There are English examples in the recent work of the American poet Marilyn Hacker, whose *Essays on Departure* (2006) includes poems entitled 'Glose', all developing four quoted lines from earlier poets into four rhymed stanzas.

**gloss** An explanation or translation of a difficult word or phrase, usually added to a text by a later copyist or editor, as in many modern editions of Chaucer. When placed between the lines of a text, it is known as an 'interlinear gloss', but it may appear in the margin, or as a footnote, or in an appendix, and may form an extended commentary. A rare example of a poem that includes the author's own marginal glosses is Coleridge's 'The Rime of the Ancient Mariner' (1798; glosses added 1817). A special poetic sense of the term is that of a poem developed from selected lines of an earlier poem, the English equivalent of the Spanish *glosa*. A **glossary** is a list of difficult words and phrases with accompanying explanations. *Verb*: **gloss**.

**gnomic** [**noh**-mik] Characterized by the expression of popular wisdom in the condensed form of *proverbs or *aphorisms, also known as **gnomes**. The term was first used of the 'Gnomic Poets' of 6th-century Greece, although there are older traditions of gnomic writing in Chinese, Egyptian, and other cultures; the Hebrew book of Proverbs is a well-known collection. The term is often extended to later writings in which moral truths are presented in maxims or aphorisms. *See also* SENTENTIA.

**Golden Age** In Classical mythology, variously resumed by writers of the *Renaissance, the earliest period of humanity, imagined as one of uncomplicated harmony and happiness, particularly in *pastoral writing. In Spanish, the term refers to the greatest period of literature in that language, usually taken to be from about 1500 to the death of Calderón in 1681.

**Golden-Age detective writing** In the context of the *detective story, a term denoting (not without some ironic exaggeration) a period of uncomplicated happiness for devotees of such fiction, usually associated with the period 1920–39 in England, although some date it back to 1913. This was the period in which appeared such major new talents as Agatha Christie (from 1920 with her series detective Hercule Poirot and from 1930 with Miss Marple), Dorothy L. Sayers (from 1923 with Lord Peter Wimsey), Margery Allingham (from 1929 with Albert Campion), Gladys Mitchell (from 1929 with Mrs Lestrange Bradley), and Nicholas Blake (from 1935 with Nigel Strangeways). The distinctive new feature of detective fiction in the Golden Age was the cultivation of the murder-mystery narrative as a light-hearted intellectual puzzle, no longer as a sensational treatment of bloody outrages. A new kind of detective figure also appears in this period, noted for a self-mocking strain of humour and for aesthetic connoisseurship of criminal enigmas, by contrast with the earnest dedication to battling crime shown by Sherlock Holmes. These detectives delight in exposing violent hatreds behind the apparently orderly and harmless appearances of an English village or country house, and Golden-Age fiction is especially associated with clichés of English social hierarchy, although in fact there were also some significant American contributors to this phase, including S. S. Van Dine (from 1926 with Philo Vance) and 'Ellery Queen' (from 1929).

**Further reading:** Lee Horsley, *Twentieth-Century Crime Fiction* (2005).

**goliardic verse** [gohli-**ard**-ik] A kind of medieval lyric poetry typically celebrating love and drink, attributed to the **goliards**, who were supposedly wandering scholars in France, Germany, and England in the 12th and 13th centuries. Some of the goliardic lyrics also contain *satire against the clergy. The most famous examples of goliardic verse appear in the *Carmina Burana*, a 13th-century collection of Latin and German poems discovered in a Bavarian monastery in the 19th century.

**Gongorism (*Gongorismo*)** An artificial poetic style cultivated by the major Spanish poet Góngora (Luis de Góngora y Argote, 1561–1627), especially in his *Fábula de Polifemo y Galatea* (1613) and in his unfinished *Soledades* (1627). It is remarkable for its *Latinate syntax and diction, *archaism, mythological allusions, and sumptuously colourful imagery. In the heated debates over style in the early 17th century, Gongorism was mocked relentlessly by the poet's younger rival Quevedo, who characterized it as a kind of *culteranismo*, i.e. an over-refined or affected manner. *See also* BAROQUE, MANNERISM.

**Gothic novel (Gothic romance)** A story of terror and suspense, usually set in a gloomy old castle or monastery (hence 'Gothic', a term applied to medieval architecture and thus associated in the 18th century with superstition). Following the appearance of Horace Walpole's *The Castle of Otranto* (1764), the Gothic novel flourished in Britain from the 1790s to the 1820s, dominated by Ann Radcliffe, whose *Mysteries of Udolpho* (1794) had many imitators. She was careful to explain away the apparently supernatural occurrences in her stories, but other writers, like M. G. Lewis in *The Monk* (1796), made free use of ghosts and demons along with scenes of cruelty and horror. The fashion for such works, ridiculed by Jane Austen in *Northanger Abbey* (1818), gave way to a vogue for *historical novels, but it contributed to the new emotional climate of *Romanticism. In an extended sense, many novels that do not have a medievalized setting, but which share a comparably sinister, *grotesque, or claustrophobic atmosphere, have been classed as Gothic: Mary Shelley's *Frankenstein* (1818) is a well-known example; and there are several important American tales and novels with strong Gothic elements in this sense, from Poe to Faulkner and beyond. A popular modern variety of women's *romance dealing with endangered heroines in the manner of Charlotte Brontë's *Jane Eyre* (1847) and Daphne du

Maurier's *Rebecca* (1938) is also referred to as Gothic. *See also* FANTASTIC, HORROR STORY, PREROMANTICISM.

**Further reading:** Fred Botting, *Gothic* (2nd edn, 1996).

**grammatology** The title adopted by the French philosopher Jacques Derrida, in his book *De la grammatologie* (1967), for the general theory of writing; this is a mode of inquiry involving the critique of *phonocentrism, rather than a science with a known object. *See* *deconstruction.

***Grand Guignol*** [grah^n gween-**yol**] A popular French form of *melodrama featuring bloody murders, rapes, and other sensational outrages, presented in lurid and gruesome detail. It is named after Guignol, a French puppet-character similar to Mr Punch. The term is now often applied to horror movies; while in late 20th-century fiction, several of Angela Carter's stories are studies in *Grand Guignol*.

**grand narrative** A term imperfectly translated from Jean-François Lyotard's influential account of *postmodernism in *La Condition postmoderne* (1979), in which he condemns big bad 'totalizing' theories and systems of thought, principally Marxism and Hegelianism. These are 'big stories' (*grands récits*) which claim to explain everything, whereas the postmodern condition, by which Lyotard means the hoped-for next phase of thought, will be characterized by a rejection of such systems in favour of harmless micro-narratives (*petits récits*) that do not make any claim to anything so 'authoritarian' as truth. A literary narrative characterized by grandeur, however, is simply called an *epic.

**grapheme** The smallest meaningful unit of a written language. As with the concept of the *phoneme, a grapheme is defined negatively by its differences from other units of writing. Thus the letter *b* makes a difference in meaning because it differs from the letter *d*, so *big* and *dig* mean different things. The study of graphic signs in a given language is known as **graphemics** or **graphology**.

**graphic novel** A book-length narrative in comic-strip form. The genre has been known by other names such as 'picture novel' and 'comic-strip novel', but graphic novel, a term first found in the 1960s, has more often been adopted since the 1980s. The term is also being applied retrospectively to the bound versions of narratives originally *serialized in newspapers, such as the many books comprising *Les*

*Aventures de Tintin* (1929–76) by the Belgian cartoonist Hergé. The graphic novel attained literary recognition in the later 20th century with the critical praise accorded to Raymond Briggs's *When the Wind Blows* (1982) and especially with the award of the Pulitzer Prize (1992) to Art Spiegelman's Holocaust narrative *Maus* (2 vols., 1986, 1991).

**Further reading:** Jan Baetens and Hugo Frey, *The Graphic Novel: An Introduction* (2014).

**graveyard poetry** The term applied to a minor but influential 18th-century tradition of meditative poems on mortality and immortality, often set in graveyards. The so-called 'graveyard school' of poets in England and Scotland was not in fact an organized group. The best-known examples of this melancholic kind of verse are 'A Night-Piece on Death' (1721) by the Irish poet Thomas Parnell, Edward Young's *Night Thoughts* (1742–6), the Scottish clergyman Robert Blair's *The Grave* (1743), and the culmination of this tradition in English, Thomas Gray's 'Elegy written in a Country Churchyard' (1751; usually called 'Gray's Elegy'). These works had many imitators in Europe, and constitute a significant current of *preromanticism.

**greater Romantic lyric** A term devised by the American scholar M. H. Abrams in his essay 'Structure and Style in the Greater Romantic Lyric' (1965; reprinted in Abrams's book *The Correspondent Breeze*, 1984), to denote an extended *lyric poem of description and serious meditation, as practised by some of the English Romantic poets (S. T. Coleridge, William Wordsworth, P. B. Shelley, and John Keats). Abrams justified this new term on the grounds that although several examples are called *odes, others are not, despite exhibiting the ode's expected serious meditative development. The earliest examples, indeed, are Coleridge's *conversation poems. Other central examples that do not identify themselves as odes are Wordsworth's 'Tintern Abbey' (i.e. 'Lines Composed a few miles above Tintern Abbey, on revisiting the banks of the Wye during a tour. July 13, 1798') and Shelley's 'Stanzas Written in Dejection'. The word 'greater' in this term derives from the older custom of referring to the *Pindaric ode as the 'greater ode' by comparison with the less elevated *Horatian kind; so it is not an assertion of artistic greatness. Abrams's general claim about this verse genre is that it was a new form developed by the English Romantics, remarkable for its integration of local description and general moral or philosophical meditation. Abrams also indicates that there are later examples of the genre, by Tennyson, Auden, and Stevens, among others of the post-Romantic generations.

**griot** [gree-oh] A kind of *bard or itinerant minstrel found in western African societies, who usually sings of local legends, histories, genealogies, or heroic deeds.

**grotesque** Characterized by bizarre distortions, especially in the exaggerated or abnormal depiction of human features. The literature of the grotesque involves freakish caricatures of people's appearance and behaviour, as in the novels of Dickens. A disturbingly odd fictional character may also be called a grotesque.

**Further reading:** Justin Edwards and Runo Graulund, *Grotesque* (2013).

**Grub Street** A street in London (now renamed Milton Street) off Chiswell Street by Finsbury Square, which was occupied in the 18th century by impoverished writers reduced to turning out third-rate poems, reference books, and histories to make a living. The term now covers any such underworld of literary penury and its products, as in George Gissing's novel *New Grub Street* (1891). Its writers are known as 'hacks', an abbreviation of 'hackney', a hired horse.

**gynesis** A term coined by the American feminist theorist Alice Jardine as part of her attempt to bring together certain *post-structuralist ideas with those of *feminist criticism in her book *Gynesis: Configurations of Woman and Modernity* (1985). Writing partly under the influence of Julia Kristeva (some of whose works she translated) and of other leaders of 'French' feminism, she suggested that the contemporary crisis in Western thought was intimately related to the emergence of new concepts that could be gendered as feminine (e.g. 'madness' in the work of Michel Foucault). In this extremely abstract sense, 'woman' (not to be confused with any real woman) was undermining old intellectual certainties. This may help to elucidate Jardine's definition of gynesis (which, etymologically, should mean 'woman-process') as the 'putting into discourse of "woman"'. In practice, neither the term nor Jardine's argument achieved any lasting circulation.

**gynocritics** The branch of modern feminist literary studies that focuses on women as writers, as distinct from the feminist critique of male authors. The term was coined by Elaine Showalter in her article

'Toward a Feminist Poetics' (1979), in which she explains that gynocritics is concerned 'with woman as the producer of textual meaning, with the history, themes, genres, and structures of literature by women'. It thus includes critical works like Showalter's *A Literature of Their Own* (1977), Sandra Gilbert and Susan Gubar's *The Madwoman in the Attic* (1979), and several other such studies published since the mid-1970s. Some writers have amended the term to 'gynocriticism', using 'gynocritics' to denote instead the practitioners of this kind of feminist study. *Adjective*: **gynocritical**.

g

**hagiography** [hag-i-**og**-răfi] Writing devoted to recording and glorifying the lives of saints and martyrs. This form of Christian propaganda was much practised in the Middle Ages but has few modern literary equivalents apart from Bernard Shaw's play *Saint Joan* (1923). By extension, the term is now often applied to modern *biographies that treat their subjects reverentially as if they were saints. A writer of such works is a **hagiographer**. *Adjective*: **hagiographic**.

**haiku** [**hy**-koo] A form of Japanese *lyric verse that encapsulates a single impression of a natural object or scene, within a particular season, in seventeen syllables arranged in three unrhymed lines of five, seven, and five syllables. Arising in the 16th century, it flourished in the hands of Bashō (1644–94) and Buson (1715–83). At first an opening *stanza of a longer sequence (*haikai*), it became a separate form in the modern period under the influence of Masaoka Shiki (1867–1902). The haiku *convention whereby feelings are suggested by natural images rather than directly stated has appealed to many Western imitators since *c.*1905, notably the *Imagists. *See also* TANKA.

**Further reading:** Stephen Addiss, *The Art of Haiku* (2012).

(((●))) SEE WEB LINKS
• Site of the Haiku Society of America.

**half-rhyme** An imperfect *rhyme (also known by other names including near rhyme and slant rhyme) in which the final consonants of stressed syllables agree but the vowel sounds do not match; thus a form of *consonance (*cape/deep*). For the variant form of half-rhyme employing 'rich' consonance, in which the preceding consonants also correspond (*cape/keep*), *see* PARARHYME. Employed regularly in early Icelandic, Irish, and Welsh poetry, half-rhyme appeared only as an occasional *poetic licence in English verse until the late 19th century, when Emily Dickinson and G. M. Hopkins made frequent use of it. The example provided by W. B. Yeats and Wilfred Owen has encouraged its increasingly widespread use in English since the early 20th century. *See also* EYE RHYME.

**hamartia** The Greek word for error or failure, used by Aristotle in his *Poetics* (4th century BCE) to designate the false step that leads the *protagonist in a *tragedy to his or her downfall. The term has often been translated as 'tragic flaw', but this misleadingly confines the cause of the reversal of fortunes to some personal defect of character, whereas Aristotle's emphasis was rather upon the protagonist's *action*, which could be brought about by misjudgement, ignorance, or some other cause. *See also* HUBRIS, PERIPETEIA.

**hapax legomenon** A now archaic term of scholarly commentary derived from the Greek ('once-only expression') and applied to a word or phrase of which only one recorded example has been found, also known as a *nonce word.

**hard-boiled** A term applied both to a certain kind of detective character, usually a world-weary private investigator, and to a special tradition of American *detective story in which these characters are prominent, sometimes also known as 'tough-guy' fiction. The tradition of hard-boiled fiction, often contrasted with the gentility of the *Golden Age tradition, arose from the violent short stories of the popular magazine *Black Mask* in the 1920s, and flourished from the 1930s to the 1950s in the hands of Dashiell Hammett (as in *The Maltese Falcon*, 1930), Raymond Chandler (as in *The Big Sleep*, 1939 and *Farewell, My Lovely*, 1940), and Mickey Spillane (as in *Kiss Me Deadly*, 1952). These works are realistic in their presentation of the underworlds of urban crime and in their avoidance of far-fetched methods of murder, and they are fatalistic in their assumption that everybody is either corrupt or readily corruptible, with only the 'hard-boiled' hero, e.g. Sam Spade in the stories of Hammett, holding to an individual code of integrity. This solitary investigative hero, sometimes allied with an alluring 'dame', is typically pitted against a shadowy group that enjoys protection from powerful quarters, and he will take violent and illegal measures to outwit it. *See also* NOIR.

**Further reading:** Sean McCann, *Gumshoe America* (2000).

**Harlem Renaissance** A notable phase of black American writing centred in Harlem (a predominantly black area of New York City) in the

1920s. Announced by Alain Locke's anthology *The New Negro* (1925), the movement included the poets Langston Hughes, Jean Toomer, Countee Cullen, and Claude McKay, continuing into the 1930s with the novels of Zora Neale Hurston and Arna Bontemps. It brought a new self-awareness and critical respect to black literature in the United States.

**Further reading:** George Hutchinson, *The Harlem Renaissance in Black and White* (1995).

**Hellenistic** The term designating a period of Greek literature and learning from the death of Alexander the Great (323 BCE) to that of Cleopatra (31 BCE), when the centre of Greek culture had shifted to the settlements of the eastern Mediterranean, notably the great library of Alexandria. This period includes the poetry of Callimachus and Theocritus, the philosophy of Epicurus and the Stoics, and the scientific achievements of Aristarchus, Archimedes, and Euclid (*see also* ALEXANDRIANISM). A **Hellenist** is a student or admirer of Greek civilization, or, in a special sense promoted by Matthew Arnold in *Culture and Anarchy* (1869), a devotee of **Hellenism** (the life of intellect and beauty), which Arnold contrasted with Hebraism (the life of moral obedience) in his sketch of the two contending ideals within Western culture. Phrases or constructions derived from the Greek language (e.g. *hoi polloi*) are also called Hellenisms.

**Further reading:** Kathryn Gutzwiller (ed.), *A Guide to Hellenistic Literature* (2006).

**hemistich** [hem-i-stik] A half-line of verse, either standing as an unfinished line for dramatic or other emphasis, or forming half of a complete line divided by a *caesura. In the second sense, the hemistich is an important structural unit of the early Germanic *alliterative metre. In verse drama, *dialogue in which characters exchange short utterances of half a line is known as **hemistichomythia** (*see* STICHOMYTHIA). *Adjective*: **hemistichic**.

**hendecasyllabics** Verses written in lines of eleven syllables. Hendecasyllabic verse is found in some ancient Greek works, and was used frequently by the Roman poet Catullus. The **hendecasyllable** or *endecasyllabo* later became the standard line of Italian verse, both in *sonnets and in *epic poetry, and was also used by some Spanish poets. It is very rare in English, although Tennyson and Swinburne attempted

imitations of Catullus' *metre, as in this line from Swinburne's
'Hendecasyllabics' (1866):

> Sweet sad straits in a soft subsiding channel

**hendiadys** [hen-**dy**-ă-dis] A *figure of speech described in traditional
*rhetoric as the expression of a single idea by means of two nouns
joined by the conjunction 'and' (e.g. *house and home* or *law and order*),
rather than by a noun qualified by an adjective. The commonest English
examples, though, combine two adjectives (*nice and juicy*) or verbs
(*come and get it*). Shakespeare uses this figure quite often in his later
works, as in the first part of this line from *Hamlet*:

> The flash and outbreak of a fiery mind

**heptameter** [hep-**tamm**-ĕt-er] A metrical verse line composed of
seven feet (*see* FOOT). In the context of English verse, in which a
heptameter is a seven-stress line, it is often referred to as a *fourteener. It
is sometimes known as a septenary. Examples of English poems written
in heptameters include William Blake's 'Holy Thursday' (1789) and
Louis MacNeice's 'Bagpipe Music' (1937).

**heptastich** [**hep**-tă-stik] A poem or *stanza of seven lines, such as
the *rhyme royal stanza. Also known as a *septet.

**hermeneutic circle** A model of the process of interpretation, which
begins from the problem of relating a work's parts to the work as a
whole: since the parts cannot be understood without some preliminary
understanding of the whole, and the whole cannot be understood
without comprehending its parts, our understanding of a work must
involve an anticipation of the whole that informs our view of the parts
while simultaneously being modified by them. This problem, variously
formulated, has been a recurrent concern of German philosophy since
the work of the theologian Friedrich Schleiermacher in the early 19th
century. The writings of Hans-Georg Gadamer in the 1960s tackled a
similar hermeneutic circle in which we can understand the present
only in the context of the past, and vice versa; his solutions to this
puzzle have influenced the emergence of *reception theory.

**hermeneutics** The theory of interpretation, concerned with general
problems of understanding the meanings of texts. Originally applied
to the principles of *exegesis in theology, the term has been extended

since the 19th century to cover broader questions in philosophy and
*criticism, and is associated in particular with a tradition of German
thought running from Friedrich Schleiermacher and Wilhelm Dilthey
in the 19th century to Martin Heidegger and Hans-Georg Gadamer
in the 20th. In this tradition, the question of interpretation is posed
in terms of the *hermeneutic circle, and involves basic problems such as
the possibility of establishing a determinate meaning in a text, the role
of the author's intention, the historical relativity of meanings, and the
status of the reader's contribution to a text's meaning. A significant
modern branch of this hermeneutic tradition is *reception theory.
*See also* PHENOMENOLOGY.

**Further reading:** Peter Szondi, *Introduction to Literary Hermeneutics* (1995).

**hermeticism** [her-**met**-iss-izm] A tendency towards obscurity in
modern poetry, involving the use of private or occult *symbols and
the rejection of logical expression in favour of musical suggestion.
Hermetic poetry is associated primarily with the French *Symbolists
and the poets influenced by them, notably the Italians Giuseppe
Ungaretti, Eugenio Montale, and Salvatore Quasimodo, who are
sometimes grouped together as exponents of *ermetismo*.

**hero (heroine)** The main character in a narrative or dramatic work.
The more neutral term *protagonist is often preferable, to avoid
confusion with the usual sense of heroism as admirable courage or
nobility, since in many works (other than *epic poems, where such
admirable qualities are required in the hero), the leading character may
not be morally or otherwise superior. When our expectations of heroic
qualities are strikingly disappointed, the central character may be
known as an *anti-hero or anti-heroine.

**heroic couplet** A rhymed pair of iambic *pentameter lines:

> Let Observation with extensive View
> Survey Mankind, from China to Peru   (Johnson)

Named from its use by Dryden and others in the *heroic drama of
the late 17th century, the heroic couplet had been established much
earlier by Chaucer as a major English verse form for narrative and other
kinds of non-dramatic poetry; it dominated English poetry of the 18th
century, notably in the *closed couplets of Pope, before declining in
importance in the early 19th century.

**heroic drama** A kind of *tragedy or *tragicomedy that came into vogue with the Restoration of the English monarchy in 1660. Influenced by French classical tragedy and its dramatic *unities, it aimed at *epic (thus 'heroic') grandeur, usually by means of *bombast, exotic settings, and lavish scenery. The noble hero would typically be caught in a conflict between love and patriotic duty, leading to emotional scenes presented in a manner close to opera. The leading English exponent of heroic drama was John Dryden: his *The Conquest of Granada* (1670–71) and *Aureng-Zebe* (1675) were both written in *heroic couplets.

**Further reading:** Derek Hughes, *English Drama, 1660–1700* (1996).

**heroic poetry** Another name for *epic poetry. The kind of verse line used for epic poetry in a given language is known as the **heroic line**: the dactylic *hexameter in Greek and Latin, the iambic *pentameter in English, the *alexandrine in French, the *hendecasyllabic line in Italian. The **heroic quatrain** or **heroic stanza** is not used for epics, but is so named because it employs the English heroic line: it consists of four pentameters rhyming *abab*, as in Gray's 'Elegy written in a Country Churchyard' (1751), or *aabb*.

**heteroglossia** The existence of conflicting *discourses within any field of linguistic activity, such as a national language, a novel, or a specific conversation. The term appears in translations of the writings of the Russian linguistic and literary theorist Mikhail Bakhtin (1895–1975), as an equivalent for his Russian term *raznorechie* ('differentspeechness'). In Bakhtin's works, this term addresses linguistic variety as an aspect of social conflict, as in tensions between central and marginal uses of the same national language; these may be echoed in, for example, the differences between the narrative voice and the voices of the characters in a novel. *Adjectives*: **heteroglot**, **heteroglossic**.

**heterometric** Varied in *metre. The term is applied to *verse forms and *stanzas or *strophes in which lines of different lengths are found, usually arranged in a consistent order of variation and rhyming pattern (although verse in *open form is also by definition heterometric, as are some unrhymed forms including the *haiku). Some kinds of poem, such as the *limerick, the *clerihew, and the standard form of the *ballad, are expected to be heterometric; and variation in line length is often found in the *ode. Certain stanza forms, including the *Burns

stanza, the *Spenserian stanza, and the quatrain in *common measure
or *short measure, display heterometric patterns. The opposite kind
of poem or stanza in unvaried metre is called *isometric. *Noun*:
**heterometry**.

**hexameter** [hek-**samm**-ĕt-er]  A metrical verse line of six feet (*see*
FOOT). Its most important form is the *dactylic hexameter used in Greek
and Latin *epic poetry and in the elegiac *distich: this *quantitative
metre permitted the substitution of any of the first four dactyls (and
more rarely of the fifth) by a *spondee, and was *catalectic in that the
final foot was either a spondee or a *trochee. Although successfully
adapted to the stress-based metres of German, Russian, and Swedish
verse (by, among others, Goethe and Pushkin), the dactylic hexameter
has not found an established place in English or French verse, except
in some rather awkward experiments such as A. H. Clough's *The Bothie
of Tober-na-Vuolich* (1848), from which this hexameter comes:

This was the final retort from the eager, impetuous Philip.

The *iambic hexameter in English is more usually known as an
*alexandrine.

**hiatus** [hy-**ay**-tus]  **1.** A break in pronunciation between two adjacent
vowels, either within a word (forming two distinct syllables, as in *doing*,
rather than a *diphthong as in *joint*) or between the end of one word
and the beginning of the next (e.g. *the expense* rather than the *elision
of *th'expense*). **2.** Any gap or omission in a sentence, verse, or logical
argument. *See also* DIAERESIS, ELLIPSIS, LACUNA.

**higher criticism**  The name given in the 19th century to a branch of
biblical scholarship concerned with establishing the dates, authorship,
sources, and interrelations of the various books of the Bible, often with
disturbing results for orthodox Christian dogma. It was 'higher' not in
status but in the sense that it required a preliminary basis of 'lower'
*textual criticism, which reconstructed the original wording of biblical
texts from faulty copies.

***histoire*** [ees-twah]  The French word for story or history, used in
modern *narratology to denote the *story, that is, the narrated events as
distinct from the form of *narration in which they are presented: thus
the *histoire* is the sequence of narrated events as reconstructed by
readers in a chronological order that may differ from the order in which

the *plot arranges them (*see also* FABULA). In another sense, linguists have used the term to designate an apparently 'objective' way of relating events without *deixis, that is, without reference to the speaker or writer, to the auditor or reader, or to their situation, as in most kinds of historical writing and *third-person narrative; in this sense, *histoire* is contrasted with **discours*. See also ÉNONCÉ.

**historical novel** A *novel in which the action takes place during a specific historical period well before the time of writing (often one or two generations before, sometimes several centuries), and in which some attempt is made to depict accurately the customs and mentality of the period. The central character—real or imagined—is usually subject to divided loyalties within a larger historic conflict of which readers know the outcome. The pioneers of this *genre were Walter Scott and James Fenimore Cooper; Scott's historical novels, starting with *Waverley* (1814), set the pattern for hundreds of others: outstanding 19th-century examples include Victor Hugo's *Notre Dame de Paris* (1831), Dumas *père's Les Trois Mousquetaires* (1844), Flaubert's *Salammbô* (1862), and Tolstoy's *War and Peace* (1863–9). While the historical novel attempts a serious study of the relationship between personal fortunes and social conflicts, the popular form known as the historical or 'costume' *romance tends to employ the period setting only as a decorative background to the leading characters.

**Further reading:** Jerome de Groot, *The Historical Novel* (2009).

**historicism** An intellectual tendency, found in philosophy, sociology, and many other disciplines since the 19th century, that stresses the importance of historical contexts to the understanding of any social or cultural phenomenon; in particular it insists that the meanings and values of human artefacts and systems of thought are to be understood in relation to the historical circumstances of their production, and not according to later (especially present-day) standards. Historicism is thus in this narrow sense the theory of historical relativism, and a vigilant opponent of *anachronism. In a broader sense, the term is applied to any emphasis upon the importance of historical explanations or historical understanding in general. Thus in literary contexts a historicist approach to poetry, for example, is one that starts from an attempted historical account of the production and reception of poems at a given time, not from a description of a given poem's formal or aesthetic features. The verb **historicize** means to place anything within its historical contexts. The school of literary and cultural study known since the 1980s as *new historicism is not simply a renovated kind of historicism.

**Further reading:** Paul Hamilton, *Historicism* (1996).

**history play** A play representing events drawn wholly or partly from recorded history. The term usually refers to *chronicle plays, especially those of Shakespeare, but it also covers some later works such as Schiller's *Maria Stuart* (1800) and John Osborne's *Luther* (1961). In a somewhat looser sense, it has been applied also to some plays that take as their subject the impact of historical change on the lives of fictional characters: David Hare's *Licking Hitler* (1978) has been reprinted with two other works under the title *The History Plays* (1984).

**Further reading:** Matthew H. Wikander, *The Play of Truth and State: Historical Drama from Shakespeare to Brecht* (1986).

**hokku** Another name for a *haiku, originally applied to the first *stanza in a longer poem known as a *haikai*, before the haiku became an independent form.

**holograph** A document written entirely in the author's own handwriting. *Adjective*: **holographic**.

**Homeric** [hoh-**merr**-ik] Characteristic of or resembling the Greek *epic poems the *Iliad* and the *Odyssey* (*c*.8th century BCE), which are by custom attributed to 'Homer', a figure about whom nothing is known. For **Homeric simile**, *see* EPIC SIMILE; for **Homeric epithet**, *see* EPITHET. The **Homeric Hymns** are a group of 33 ancient Greek poems of various dates from the 8th century BCE onwards and of unknown authorship (although some were formerly attributed to Homer); they celebrate the qualities of various Greek deities, sometimes in the form of prolonged *invocations.

**homily** A sermon or morally instructive lecture. An author of homilies is a **homilist**, while the art of composing homilies is known as **homiletics**. *Adjective*: **homiletic**.

**homology** A correspondence between two or more structures. The Marxist critic Lucien Goldmann developed a theory of the relations between literary works and social classes in terms of homologies. In his *Le Dieu Caché* (1959), he observed a homology between the underlying structure of Racine's tragedies and that of the world-view held by a particular group in the French nobility. This method was extended to the modern novel in Goldmann's *Pour une sociologie du roman* (1964). An example of something that bears a resemblance to something else is called a **homologue**, and is said to be **homologous** with it.

**homonym** A word that is identical in form with another word, either in sound (as a *homophone) or in spelling (as a **homograph**), or in both, but differs from it in meaning: *days/daze*, or *lead* (guide)/*lead* (metal), or *pitch* (throw)/*pitch* (tar). Identity of form between two or more words is known as **homonymy**. *Adjective*: **homonymic**.

**homophone** A word that is pronounced in the same way as another word but differs in meaning and/or in spelling; thus a kind of *homonym. Examples of this identity of sound, known as **homophony**, include *maid/made* and *left* (opposite of right)/*left* (abandoned). Homophony is often exploited in *puns. *Adjective*: **homophonic**.

**homostrophic** Composed of *stanzas that all share the same form, with identical numbers of lines of corresponding lengths, and with identical *rhyme schemes. Nearly all stanzaic verse is homostrophic. The term is used chiefly to distinguish the *Horatian ode, which is homostrophic, from the *Pindaric and irregular ode forms, which are not.

**Horatian** Characteristic of or derived from the work of the Roman poet Quintus Horatius Flaccus (65–8 BCE), usually known as Horace. The **Horatian ode**, as distinct from the *Pindaric ode, is *homostrophic and usually private and reflective in mood: Keats's odes (1820) are English examples of this form. **Horatian satire**, often contrasted with the bitterness of *Juvenalian satire, is a more indulgent, tolerant treatment of human inconsistencies and follies, ironically amused rather than outraged. Pope's verse satires, some of them directly modelled upon Horace's work, are generally Horatian in tone. For **Horatian epistle**, *see* EPISTLE. *See also* ODE, SATIRE.

**horizon of expectations** A term used in the *reception theory of Hans Robert Jauss to designate the set of cultural norms, assumptions, and criteria shaping the way in which readers understand and judge a literary work at a given time. It may be formed by such factors as the prevailing *conventions and definitions of art (e.g. *decorum), or current moral codes. Such 'horizons' are subject to historical change, so that a later generation of readers may see a very different range of meanings in the same work, and revalue it accordingly.

**horror story** A kind of fictional narrative designed to inspire feelings of revulsion in its readers. Since the late 18th century, before which there were no horror stories in the modern sense, a distinction has been recognized between stories of this kind that rely upon physical horror and 'tales of terror' that inspire a more psychological apprehension and suspense, although in practice the boundaries have proved hard to draw. In general, the tale of terror is devoted to the evocation of the ghostly or supernatural (*see* GHOST STORY, FANTASTIC), while the horror story focuses upon the violation of physical taboos. The typical materials of horror fiction are decomposing corpses (rather than ethereal ghosts), vermin, bodily mutilations or tortures, monstrous transformations, cannibalism, blood-sucking, incest, and the great empire of slime. *Gothic fiction is commonly although not necessarily horrific in these terms, as in some episodes of M. G. Lewis's novel *The Monk* (1794). Vampire fiction, which originated in 1819 with John Polidori's story 'The Vampyre' and achieved its classic form in Bram Stoker's *Dracula* (1897), is a mild *subgenre within the horror tradition, tinged with fetishistic eroticism. The mainstream is occupied by tales of grave-robbing and the violation of corpses, as in the central episodes of Mary Shelley's *Frankenstein* (1818; rev. 1831), and of monstrous reversions, as in Robert Louis Stevenson's *Strange Case of Dr Jekyll and Mr Hyde* (1886). The American author H. P. Lovecraft invented his own fantastical subgenre, relying upon a bombastic mythography of primeval slime. For one psychoanalytic theory (by no means universally credited) of such effects, *see* ABJECTION. *See also* GROTESQUE, *GRAND GUIGNOL*.

**Further reading:** David Punter, *The Literature of Terror* (2nd edn, 1996).

**hubris** [**hew**-bris] **(hybris)** The Greek word for 'insolence' or 'affront', applied to the arrogance or pride of the *protagonist in a *tragedy in which he or she defies moral laws or the prohibitions of the gods. The protagonist's transgression or *hamartia leads eventually to his or her downfall, which may be understood as divine retribution or *nemesis. Hubris is commonly translated as 'overweening (i.e. excessively

presumptuous) pride'. In proverbial terms, hubris is thus the pride
that comes before a fall. *Adjective*: **hubristic**.

**Hudibrastic verse** [hew-di-**bras**-tik] **(Hudibrastics)** A kind of comic
verse written in *octosyllabic couplets with many ridiculously forced
*feminine rhymes. It is named after the long *mock-heroic poem
*Hudibras* (1663–78), a *satire on Puritanism by the English poet Samuel
Butler. These lines from Canto III give some impression of the style:

> He would an elegy compose
> On maggots squeez'd out of his nose;
> In lyric numbers write an ode on
> His mistress, eating a black-pudden;
> And, when imprison'd air escap'd her,
> It puft him with poetic rapture.

Several poets, including Jonathan Swift, wrote Hudibrastic verse in
imitation, and the form became popular in poetic *burlesques. *See also*
DOGGEREL, LIGHT VERSE.

*huitain* [wee-teⁿ] A French *stanza form consisting of eight lines of
either 8 or 10 syllables each, usually rhyming *ababbcbc* or *abbaacac*.
It may form an independent poem or part of a longer work such as a
*ballade. The *huitain* was used by François Villon in his *Lais* (1456)
and in his famous *Testament* (1461). In English, the stanza used earlier
by Chaucer in his *Monk's Tale* has the same form.

**humanism** A 19th-century term for the values and ideals of the
European *Renaissance, which placed a new emphasis on the expansion
of human capacities. Reviving the study of Greek and Roman history,
philosophy, and arts, the Renaissance **humanists** developed an image
of 'Man' more positive and hopeful than that of medieval ascetic
Christianity: rather than being a miserable sinner awaiting redemption
from a pit of fleshly corruption, 'Man' was a source of infinite
possibilities, ideally developing towards a balance of physical, spiritual,
moral, and intellectual faculties. Most early humanists like Erasmus and
Milton in the 16th and 17th centuries combined elements of Christian
and classical cultures in what has become known as **Christian
humanism**, but the 18th-century *Enlightenment began to detach the
ideal of human perfection from religious supernaturalism, so that by
the 20th century humanism came to denote those moral philosophies
that abandon theological dogma in favour of purely human concerns.

While being defined against theology on the one side, humanism came also to be contrasted with scientific materialism on the other: from the mid-19th century onwards, Matthew Arnold and others (including the **New Humanists** in the United States, led by Paul More and Irving Babbitt in the 1920s) opposed the claims of science with the ideal of balanced human perfection, self-cultivation, and ethical self-restraint. This Arnoldian humanism, which has enjoyed wide influence in Anglo-American literary culture, is one variety of the prevalent **liberal humanism**, which centres its view of the world upon the notion of the freely self-determining individual. In modern literary theory, liberal humanism (and sometimes all humanism) has come under challenge from *post-structuralism, which replaces the unitary concept of 'Man' with that of the 'subject', which is gendered, 'de-centred', and no longer self-determining.

**Further reading:** Tony Davies, *Humanism* (2nd edn, 2007).

**humours**  The bodily fluids to which medieval medicine attributed the various types of human temperament, according to the predominance of each within the body. Thus a preponderance of blood would make a person 'sanguine', while excess of phlegm would make him or her 'phlegmatic'; too much choler (or yellow bile) would give rise to a 'choleric' disposition, while an excess of black bile would produce a 'melancholic' one. The **comedy of humours**, best exemplified by Ben Jonson's play *Every Man in His Humour* (1598), and practised by some other playwrights in the 17th century, is based on the eccentricities of characters whose temperaments are distorted in ways similar to an imbalance among the bodily humours.

**hybris**  *See* HUBRIS.

**hymn**  A song (or *lyric poem set to music) in praise of a divine or venerated being. The title is sometimes given to a poem on an elevated subject, like Shelley's 'Hymn to Intellectual Beauty' (1816), or praising a historical hero, like MacDiarmid's 'First Hymn to Lenin' (1931). The term **hymnody** is used to refer either to a particular body of hymns or to the art of hymn-writing, while a composer of hymns is called a **hymnodist** or **hymnist**. *See also* ANTIPHON, ODE, PSALM.

**hypallage**  [hy-**pal**-ăji]  A *figure of speech by which an *epithet is transferred from the more appropriate to the less appropriate of two nouns: so at the eighth line of Allen Ginsberg's poem 'Howl' (1956), which employs hypallage plentifully, the phrase 'who cowered in unshaven rooms' transfers the adjective *unshaven* from the people described to the rooms they occupied. Similarly in everyday speech, a person with a *blind dog* is more likely to be blind than the dog is. The term has sometimes also been applied to other constructions in which the elements of an utterance exchange their normal positions (*see* HYPERBATON). *Adjective*: **hypallactic**.

**hyperbaton** [hy-**per**-bǎ-ton] A *figure of speech by which the normal order of words in a sentence is significantly altered. A very common form of *poetic licence, of which Milton's *Paradise Lost* affords many spectacular examples:

> Him the Almighty Power
> Hurled headlong flaming from th'ethereal sky

*See also* INVERSION.

**hyperbole** [hy-**per**-bǒli] Exaggeration for the sake of emphasis in a *figure of speech not meant literally. An everyday example is the complaint 'I've been waiting here for ages.' Hyperbolic expressions are common in the inflated style of dramatic speech known as *bombast, as in Shakespeare's *Antony and Cleopatra* when Cleopatra praises the dead Antony:

> His legs bestrid the ocean: his reared arm
> Crested the world.

**hypermetrical (hypercatalectic)** Having an extra syllable or syllables in excess of the normal length of a specified metrical verse line. *See also* ANACRUSIS, FEMININE ENDING.

**hypertext** A term used since 1965 in the discussion of computerized text, now referring to the realm of electronically interlinked texts and multimedia resources found on the World Wide Web (from 1990) and on CD-ROM reference sources. Hypertext is sometimes distinguished from 'linear' printed text in terms of the reader's changed experience of moving around and among texts. In a different sense, the term is also applied, in discussions of *intertextuality, to a text that in some way derives from an earlier text (the 'hypotext') as a *parody of it, a sequel to it, etc.

**Further reading:** George P. Landow, *Hypertext 3.0* (2006).

**hypotactic** Marked by the use of connecting words between clauses or sentences, explicitly showing the logical or other relationships between them: 'I am tired *because* it is hot.' Such use of syntactic subordination of one clause to another is known as **hypotaxis**. The opposite kind of construction, referred to as *paratactic, simply juxtaposes clauses or sentences: 'I am tired; it is hot'. *See also* SYNTAX.

**hysterical realism** A term coined by British critic James Wood in a review of Zadie Smith's novel *White Teeth* in 2000 (since reprinted in Wood's essay-collection *The Irresponsible Self*, 2004) and in some later articles, to describe an ambitious kind of late 20th-century *postmodernist novel that follows in the wake of *magic realism. Wood's complaint against such novels by Thomas Pynchon, Don DeLillo, David Foster Wallace, and Salman Rushdie is that they pursue 'vitality at all costs' through an unconvincing profusion of intertwined stories underpinned by minutely detailed research and involving 'vivacious caricatures' rather than credible human figures, all presented with a 'false zaniness' of style. Wood identifies the historical model for such fiction as the work of Charles Dickens, with its multitude of cartoonishly grotesque characters. Other critics in broad agreement have identified symptoms of this hysterical realism in the work of novelists not named by Wood himself, including Richard Powers and Dave Eggers. Zadie Smith's own fiction since *White Teeth* has meanwhile shown a calmer tone of sobriety.

**iamb** [I-am or I-amb] **(iambus)** A metrical unit (*foot) of verse, having one unstressed syllable followed by one stressed syllable, as in the word 'beyond' (or, in Greek and Latin *quantitative verse, one short syllable followed by one long syllable). Lines of poetry made up predominantly of iambs are referred to as **iambics** or as **iambic verse**, which is by far the most common kind of metrical verse in English. Its most important form is the 10-syllable iambic *pentameter, either rhymed (as in *heroic couplets, *sonnets etc.) or unrhymed in *blank verse:

> Beyond the utmost bound of human thought. (Tennyson)

The iambic pentameter permits some variation in the placing of its five *stresses; thus it may often begin with a stressed syllable followed by an unstressed syllable (a reversal called trochaic *inversion or *substitution) before resuming the regular iambic pattern:

> Oft she rejects, but never once offends (Pope)

The 8-syllable iambic *tetrameter is another common English line:

> Come live with me, and be my love (Marlowe)

Iambic tetrameters were also used in ancient Greek dramatic dialogue. The English iambic *hexameter or six-stress line is usually referred to as the *alexandrine. *See also* METRE.

**ibid.** The commonly abbreviated form of *ibidem* (Latin, 'in the same place'), a term widely used in scholarly footnotes and endnotes when these provide bibliographical references for quotations or facts cited. In these contexts, 'ibid.' means 'in the same work already mentioned', usually referring back to the immediately preceding note or to a previous reference to a work by a specified author, and followed by the relevant page number from that work. It does not automatically refer precisely to the same page as before: for this purpose, the customary Latin abbreviation is *loc. cit.

**Ibsenite (Ibsenist)** A defender, partisan supporter, or imitator of Norwegian dramatist Henrik Ibsen (1828–1906), a writer whose plays provoked international controversy when translated into English and other languages from 1877. In the English-speaking world the first leading Ibsenites were the Scottish drama critic William Archer, who collected his early translations in *Henrik Ibsen's Prose Dramas* (1890–91), and the dramatist Bernard Shaw, whose polemical essay *The Quintessence of Ibsenism* (1890, rev. ed. 1913) has sometimes been accused of expounding Shaw's own dramatic principles rather than Ibsen's.

**icon** [I-kon] **(iconic sign)** In the *semiotics of the American philosopher C. S. Peirce, a sign that stands for its object mainly by resembling or sharing some features (e.g. shape) with it; such resemblance having a status called **iconicity**. A photograph or diagram of an object is iconic, but the signs of language (apart from a few *onomatopoeic words) have a merely conventional or *arbitrary relation to their objects: in Peirce's terminology, they are not icons but *symbols. *See also* INDEX.

**ictus** (plural **-uses**) The *stress or *accent that is placed on a syllable in a line of verse, as distinct from the stressed syllable itself. *Adjective*: **ictal**.

**idiolect** [id-i-oh-lekt] The particular variety of a language used by an individual speaker or writer, which may be marked by peculiarities of vocabulary, grammar, and pronunciation. *Adjective*: **idiolectal** or **idiolectic**. *See also* DIALECT.

**idiom** A phrase or grammatical construction that cannot be translated literally into another language because its meaning is not equivalent to that of its component words. Common examples, of which there are thousands in English, include *follow suit, hell for leather, flat broke, on the wagon, well hung,* etc. By extension, the term is sometimes applied more loosely to any style or manner of writing that is characteristic of a particular group or movement. *Adjective*: **idiomatic**.

**idyll** [id-il] **(idyl)** A short poem describing an incident of country life in terms of idealized innocence and contentment; or any such episode in a poem or prose work. The term is virtually synonymous with *pastoral poem, as in Theocritus' *Idylls* (3rd century BCE). The title of Tennyson's *Idylls of the King* (1842–85), a sequence of Arthurian *romances, bears little relation to the usual meaning. Browning in *Dramatic Idyls* (1879–80) uses the term in another sense, as a short self-contained poem. *Adjective*: **idyllic**. *See also* BUCOLIC POETRY, ECLOGUE.

**illocutionary act**   An utterance that accomplishes something in the act of speaking. In the *speech act theory proposed by J. L. Austin in *How to Do Things with Words* (1962), an utterance involves not only the simple 'locutionary' act of producing a grammatical sentence, but also an 'illocutionary force' of effectiveness either as an affirmation or as a promise, a threat, a warning, a command, etc. The most explicit illocutionary acts are the *performatives, which accomplish the very deed to which they refer, when uttered by authorized speakers in certain conditions: 'I arrest you in the name of the law'; 'I hereby renounce the Devil and all his works'; 'I promise to defend and uphold the constitution.' *See also* PERLOCUTIONARY.

**imagery**   A rather vague critical term covering those uses of language in a literary work that evoke sense-impressions by literal or *figurative reference to perceptible or 'concrete' objects, scenes, actions, or states, as distinct from the language of abstract argument or exposition. The imagery of a literary work thus comprises the set of **images** that it uses; these need not be mental 'pictures', but may appeal to senses other than sight. The term has often been applied particularly to the figurative language used in a work, especially to its *metaphors and *similes. Images suggesting further meanings and associations in ways that go beyond the fairly simple identifications of metaphor and simile are often called *symbols. The critical emphasis on imagery in the mid-20th century, both in *New Criticism and in some influential studies of Shakespeare, tended to glorify the supposed concreteness of literary works by ignoring matters of structure, convention, and abstract argument: thus Shakespeare's plays were read as clusters or patterns of 'thematic imagery' according to the predominance of particular kinds of image (of animals, of disease, etc.), without reference to the action or to the dramatic meaning of characters' speeches. *See also* MOTIF.

**Imaginary, the**   *See* SYMBOLIC.

**imagination**   The mind's capacity to generate images of objects, states, or actions that have not been felt or experienced by the senses. In the discussion of psychology and art prior to *Romanticism, imagination was usually synonymous with *fancy, and commonly opposed to the

faculty of reason, either as complementary to it or as contrary to it.
S. T. Coleridge's famous distinction between fancy and imagination in
his *Biographia Literaria* (1817) emphasized the imagination's vitally
creative power of dissolving and uniting images into new forms, and
of reconciling opposed qualities into a new unity. This freely creative
and transforming power of the imagination was a central principle
of Romanticism.

**Further reading:** Richard Kearney, *The Wake of Imagination* (1988).

**Imagism** The doctrine and poetic practice of a small but influential
group of American and British poets calling themselves Imagists or
Imagistes between 1912 and 1917. Led at first by Ezra Pound, and then—
after his defection to *Vorticism—by Amy Lowell, the group rejected
most 19th-century poetry as cloudy verbiage, and aimed instead at a
new clarity and exactness in the short *lyric poem. Influenced by the
Japanese *haiku and partly by ancient Greek lyrics, the Imagists
cultivated concision and directness, building their short poems
around single images; they also preferred looser *cadences to traditional
regular rhythms. Apart from Pound and Lowell, the group also included
Richard Aldington, 'H.D.' (Hilda Doolittle), F. S. Flint, D. H. Lawrence,
Ford Madox Ford, and William Carlos Williams. Imagist poems and
manifestos appeared in the American magazine *Poetry* and the London
journal *The Egoist*. Pound edited *Des Imagistes: An Anthology* (1914),
while the three further anthologies (1915–17), all entitled *Some
Imagist Poets*, were edited by Lowell. *See also* MODERNISM.

**Further reading:** Andrew Thacker, *The Imagist Poets* (2007).

**imperfect rhyme** *See* HALF-RHYME.

**implied author** A term coined by Wayne C. Booth in *The Rhetoric
of Fiction* (1961) to designate that source of a work's design and meaning
which is inferred by readers from the text, and imagined as a personality
standing behind the work. As an imaginary entity, it is to be
distinguished clearly from the real author, who may well have written
other works implying a different kind of *persona or implied author
behind them. The implied author is also to be distinguished from the
*narrator, since the implied author stands at a remove from the narrative
voice, as the personage assumed to be responsible for deciding what
kind of narrator will be presented to the reader; in many works this
distinction produces an effect of *irony at the narrator's expense.

**implied reader**  A term used by Wolfgang Iser and some other theorists of *reader-response criticism to denote the hypothetical figure of the reader to whom a given work is designed to address itself. Any *text may be said to presuppose an 'ideal' reader who has the particular attitudes (moral, cultural, etc.) appropriate to that text in order for it to achieve its full effect. This implied reader is to be distinguished from *actual* readers, who may be unable or unwilling to occupy the position of the implied reader: thus, most religious poetry presupposes a god-fearing implied reader, but many actual readers today are atheists. The implied reader is also not the same thing as the *narratee, who is a figure imagined within the text as listening to—or receiving a written narration from—the narrator (e.g. the Wedding Guest in Coleridge's 'The Rime of the Ancient Mariner').

**impressionism**  In the literary sense borrowed from French painting, a rather vague term applied to works or passages that concentrate on the description of transitory mental impressions as felt by an observer, rather than on the explanation of their external causes. Impressionism in literature is thus neither a school nor a movement but a kind of subjective tendency manifested in descriptive techniques. It is found in *Symbolist and *Imagist poetry, and in much modern verse, but also in many works of prose fiction since the late 19th century, as in the novels of Joseph Conrad, Ford Madox Ford, and Virginia Woolf.
**Impressionistic criticism** is the kind of *criticism that restricts itself to describing the critic's own subjective response to a literary work, rather than ascribing intrinsic qualities to it in the light of general principles. Walter Pater's defence of such criticism, in the Preface to his *Studies in the History of the Renaissance* (1873), was that 'in aesthetic criticism the first step towards seeing one's object as it really is, is to know one's own impression as it really is, to discriminate it, to realise it distinctly'. The most common kind of impressionistic criticism is found in theatre and book reviews: 'I laughed all night'; 'I couldn't put it down'.

**Further reading:** Jesse Matz, *Literary Impressionism and Modernist Aesthetics* (2001).

***in medias res*** [in **med**-i-ahs rayss]  The Latin phrase meaning 'into the middle of things', applied to the common technique of storytelling by which the *narrator begins the story at some exciting point in the middle of the action, thereby gaining the reader's interest before

explaining preceding events by *analepses ('flashbacks') at some later
stage. It was conventional to begin *epic poems *in medias res*, as Milton
does in *Paradise Lost*. The technique is also common in plays and in
prose fiction: for example, Katherine Mansfield's short story 'A Dill
Pickle' (1920) begins *in medias res* with the sentence 'And then, after
six years, she saw him again.' *See also* ANACHRONY.

***In Memoriam* stanza**   A *stanza of four iambic *tetrameter lines
rhyming *abba*, used by Tennyson in the sequence of lyrics making up
his *In Memoriam A. H. H.* (1850). This was the most notable English use
of this *envelope stanza, although not the first. *See also* QUATRAIN.

**incantation**   The chanting or reciting of any form of words deemed to
have magical power, usually in a brief rhyming spell with an insistent
rhythm and other devices of repetition; or the form of words thus
recited. Incantation is characteristic of magical charms, curses,
prophecies, and the conjuring of spirits: a famous literary example is the
witches' chant, 'Double, double, toil and trouble', in *Macbeth*. Poetry
that resembles such chants may be called **incantatory**.

**incremental repetition**   A modern term for a device of repetition
commonly found in *ballads. It involves the repetition of lines or
*stanzas with small but crucial changes made to a few words from one
to the next, and has an effect of *narrative progression or suspense.
It is found most often in passages of dialogue, as in the traditional
Scottish ballad, 'Lord Randal':

> 'What d' ye leave to your mother, Lord Randal, my son?
> What d' ye leave to your mother, my handsome young man?'
> 'Four and twenty milk kye; mother, mak my bed soon,
> For I'm sick at the heart, and I fain wad lie down.'
>
> 'What d' ye leave to your sister, Lord Randal, my son?
> What d' ye leave to your sister, my handsome young man?'
> 'My gold and my silver; mother, mak my bed soon,
> For I'm sick at the heart, and I fain wad lie down.'

**incunabula** [ink-yu-**nab**-yu-lǎ]   The collective term for books dating
from the earliest (pre-1500) phase of the history of printing. Literally,
it means 'swaddling-clothes', and is thus suggestive of the 'infancy' of
the art of printing. The singular form **incunabulum** is only rarely found

in reference to a particular book from that period. *Adjective*:
**incunabular**.

**indeterminacy** **1.** In *reader-response criticism, any element of a
*text that requires the reader to decide on its meaning (*see also*
AMBIGUITY, CRUX, *SCRIPTIBLE*). **2.** In *deconstruction, a principle of
uncertainty invoked to deny the existence of any final or determinate
meaning that could bring to an end the play of meanings between the
elements of a text (*see* DIFFÉRANCE). To proclaim the ultimate
indeterminacy of meaning need not mean that no decisions can be
made about the meaning of anything (or at least it cannot be determined
that it means this), only that there is no final arbiter of such decisions.
Some deconstructionists, however, have the habit of calling the
meanings of literary works 'undecidable'. *See also* APORIA.

**index** (plural **-dices** or **-dexes**) In the *semiotics of the American
philosopher C. S. Peirce, a *sign that is connected to its object by a
concrete relationship, usually of cause and effect. A finger or signpost
pointing to an object or place is **indexal**; so, in more clearly causal ways,
are many kinds of symptom, mark, or trace: scars, footprints, crumpled
bedclothes, etc. Thus smoke may be seen as an index of fire. Peirce
distinguished the index from two other kinds of sign: the *icon and the
*symbol.

**Index, the** The name commonly given to the *Index Librorum
Prohibitorum*, a list of the titles of those books that the Catholic Church
forbade its followers to read, from the 16th century to 1966. A second
list, the *Index Expurgatorius*, specified those passages that must be
expurgated from certain works before they could be read by Catholics.

**(⊕) SEE WEB LINKS**

• Beacon for Freedom of Expression: lists all the banned books from final (1948) edition
 of *Index Librorum*.

**induction** An older word for the *prologue or introduction to a work.
The introductory episode of Shakespeare's *The Taming of the Shrew*,
for example, is called the induction.

**inflection (inflexion)** The modification of words according to their
grammatical functions, usually by employing variant word-endings to
indicate such qualities as tense, gender, case, and number (*see also*
MORPHOLOGY). English uses inflection for the past tense of many verbs

(usually with the ending -*ed*), for degrees of adjectives (-*er* and -*est*), for plurals (usually -*es* or -*s*), and other functions; but since the transition from *Old English to *Middle English it has been relatively 'uninflected' by comparison with the so-called **inflected languages** such as Latin, in which the use of inflection is far more extensive. In a second sense, the term is sometimes used to denote a change of pitch in the pronunciation of a word (*see* INTONATION).

**inkhorn** (ink-horn) A small portable container for carrying ink. The word was used by some 16th-century writers as a *metonym for book learning and thus pedantry. Accordingly an **inkhorn term** was a word or phrase derived from old books or from Latin rather than from the living English language, and a style 'smelling of the inkhorn' was similarly bookish or remote from spoken English.

**inscape** and **instress** Two terms coined by the English poet Gerard Manley Hopkins (1844–89) in a not wholly successful attempt to elucidate his poetic method and religious philosophy. Inscape is the unique quality or essential 'whatness' of a thing, while instress is the divine energy that both supports the inscape of all things and brings it alive to the senses of the observer.

**intentional fallacy** The name given by the American *New Critics W. K. Wimsatt Jr and Monroe C. Beardsley to the widespread assumption that an author's declared or supposed intention in writing a work is the proper basis for deciding on the meaning and the value of that work. Where that assumption becomes a principle, it is known as **intentionalism**. In their 1946 essay 'The Intentional Fallacy' (reprinted in Wimsatt's *The Verbal Icon*, 1954), these critics argue that a literary work, once published, belongs in the public realm of language, which gives it an objective existence distinct from the author's original idea of it: 'The poem is not the critic's own and not the author's (it is detached from the author at birth and goes about the world beyond his power to intend about it or control it). The poem belongs to the public.' Thus any information or surmise we may have about the author's intention cannot in itself determine the work's meaning or value, since it still has to be verified against the work itself. Many other critics have pointed to the unreliability of authors as witnesses to the meanings of their own works, which often have significances wider than their intentions in composing them: as D. H. Lawrence wrote in his *Studies* *in Classic American Literature* (1923), 'Never trust the artist. Trust the tale.' A similar principle is involved in theories of the *death of the author.

**interior monologue** The written representation of a character's inner thoughts, impressions, and memories as if directly 'overheard' without the apparent intervention of a summarizing and selecting *narrator. The term is often loosely used as a synonym for *stream of consciousness. However, some confusion arises about the relationship between these two terms when critics distinguish them: some take 'stream of consciousness' as the larger category, embracing all representations of intermingled thoughts and perceptions, within which interior monologue is a special case of 'direct' presentation; others take interior monologue as the larger category, within which stream of consciousness is a special technique emphasizing continuous 'flow' by abandoning strict logic, *syntax, and punctuation. The second of these alternatives permits us to apply the term 'interior monologue' to that large class of modern poems representing a character's unspoken thoughts and impressions, as distinct from the spoken thoughts imagined in the *dramatic monologue: Browning's 'Soliloquy of the Spanish Cloister' (1842) is an early example. More often, though, the term refers to prose passages employing stream-of-consciousness techniques: the most celebrated instance in English is the final chapter of James Joyce's *Ulysses* (1922). Joyce acknowledged Édouard Dujardin's novel *Les Lauriers sont coupées* (1888) as a precedent in the use of interior monologue. *See also* MONOLOGUE.

**interlude** A short play, of a kind believed to have been performed by small companies of professional actors in the intervals of banquets and other entertainments before the emergence of the London theatres. This rather loose category includes several types of play that are regarded as transitional between the *morality play and Elizabethan comedy: some resemble the morality plays in *didactic intent and are sometimes called 'moral interludes', while others are closer to *farce. Interludes flourished in England from the end of the 15th century to the late 16th century. An early example is Henry Medwall's *Fulgens and Lucres* (1497). The foremost author of interludes was John Heywood, who wrote *The Play of the Weather* (1533) among other works.

**internal rhyme** A poetic device by which two or more words rhyme within the same line of verse, as in Kipling's reactionary poem 'The City of Brass' (1909):

> Men swift to see done, and outrun, their extremest commanding—
> Of the tribe which describe with a jibe the perversions of Justice—
> Panders avowed to the crowd whatsoever its lust is.

A special case of internal rhyme between words at the middle and the end of certain lines is *leonine rhyme. *See also* CROSSED RHYME.

**interpolation** A passage inserted into a text by some later writer, usually without the authority of the original author; or the act of introducing such additional material. For example, it was once believed by many critics that the obscene jokes of the drunken porter in Shakespeare's *Macbeth* must have been interpolated by some inferior playwright.

**intertextuality** A term coined by Julia Kristeva to designate the various relationships that a given *text may have with other texts. These **intertextual** relationships include anagram, *allusion, adaptation, translation, *parody, *pastiche, imitation, and other kinds of transformation. In the literary theories of *structuralism and *post-structuralism, texts are seen to refer to other texts (or to themselves as texts) rather than to an external reality. The term **intertext** has been used variously for a text drawing on other texts, for a text thus drawn upon, and for the relationship between both.

**Further reading:** Graham Allen, *Intertextuality* (2nd edn, 2011).

**intonation** The pattern of variation in pitch during a spoken utterance. Intonation has important expressive functions, indicating the speaker's attitudes (of astonishment, sarcasm, etc.), but it also signals the grammatical status of an utterance, for instance by showing relations between clauses or by marking the difference between a simple statement and a question: in English, a simple assertion like *We are going* can be changed into a question simply by reversing its intonation from a lowering of pitch to a raising of pitch.

**intrigue** An older term for the *plot of a play or story, or for its most complicated portion. In another sense closer to modern usage, the term may also refer to the secret scheme ('plot' in the other sense, as conspiracy) that one character or group of characters devises in order to outwit others. Much European comedy of the 17th century is based on complex plots about plotters, and is sometimes called the **comedy of intrigue**, especially where intricacy of plot overshadows the development of character or of satiric theme.

**intrusive narrator** An *omniscient narrator who, in addition to reporting the events of a novel's story, offers further comments on characters and events, and who sometimes reflects more generally upon the significance of the story. A device used frequently by the great *realist novelists of the 19th century, notably George Eliot and Leo Tolstoy, the intrusive narrator allows the novel to be used for general moral commentary on human life, sometimes in the form of brief digressive essays interrupting the narrative. An earlier example is the narrator of Henry Fielding's *Tom Jones* (1749).

**invective** The harsh denunciation of some person or thing in abusive speech or writing, usually by a succession of insulting *epithets. Among many memorable examples in Shakespeare is Timon's verbal assault upon his false friends in *Timon of Athens*:

> Most smiling, smooth, detested parasites,
> Courteous destroyers, affable wolves, meek bears,
> You fools of fortune, trencher-friends, time's flies,
> Cap-and-knee slaves, vapours, and minute-jacks!

*Verb*: **inveigh**. *See also* FLYTING, JUVENALIAN SATIRE, LAMPOON.

**inversion** The reversal of the normally expected order of words: or, in *prosody, the turning around of a metrical *foot. Inversion of word order (*syntax), also known in rhetoric as *hyperbaton, is a common form of *poetic licence allowing a poet to preserve the *rhyme scheme or the *metre of a verse line, or to place special emphasis on particular words. Common forms of inversion in English are the placing of an adjective after its noun (*his fiddlers three*), the placing of the grammatical subject after the verb (*said she*), and the placing of an adverb or adverbial phrase before its verb (*sweetly blew the breeze*). Stronger forms of inversion, where the grammatical object precedes the verb and even the subject, are found in *Latinate styles, notably Milton's. In prosody, the term is applied to a kind of *substitution whereby one foot is replaced by another in which the positions of stressed and unstressed (or of long and short) syllables are exactly reversed: the most common type of **inverted foot** is the *trochee substituted for an *iamb at the beginning of a line.

**invocation**  An appeal made by a poet to a *muse or deity for help in composing the poem. The invocation of a muse was a *convention in ancient Greek and Latin poetry, especially in the *epic; it was followed later by many poets of the *Renaissance and *neoclassical periods. Usually it is placed at the beginning of the poem, but may also appear in later positions, such as at the start of a new *canto. The invocation is one of the conventions ridiculed in *mock-epic poems: Byron begins the third Canto (1821) of *Don Juan* with the exclamation 'Hail, Muse! *et cetera*'. In terms of *rhetoric, the invocation is a special variety of *apostrophe.

**in-yer-face theatre**  A term coined by Aleks Sierz in his book *In-Yer-Face Theatre: British Drama Today* (2001), to refer to a new wave of British drama of the 1990s that was notable for its provocative uses of obscene language, nudity, violence, and taboo subject-matter. This feature of new 1990s drama had been noted before, and referred to by theatre critics as 'the new brutalism' among other labels. The leading dramatists of this new wave were Mark Ravenhill, Sarah Kane, and Anthony Neilson, and its defining works included Kane's *Blasted* (1995), Ravenhill's *Shopping and Fucking* (1996), Neilson's *Penetrator* (1993), Jez Butterworth's *Mojo* (1995), Patrick Marber's *Closer* (1997), and Harry Gibson's *Trainspotting* (1994; an adaptation of Irvine Welsh's 1993 novel). Although predominantly British, this school included some American playwrights, notably Tracy Letts (author of *Killer Joe*, 1994) and Phyllis Nagy (*The Strip*, 1995).

**ionic** [I-on-ik]  A Greek metrical *foot consisting of two long syllables followed by two short syllables (known as the greater ionic or ionic *a majore*) or of two short syllables followed by two long syllables (the lesser ionic or ionic *a minore*). Associated with the early religious verse of the Ionians in Asia Minor (now Turkey), the *metre was used by several Greek *lyric poets, by the dramatist Euripides, and in Latin by Horace. It is hardly ever found in English as the basis for whole lines: the Epilogue to Robert Browning's *Asolando* (1889) provides a rare example of the lesser ionic metre adapted to English stresses:

At the midnight in the silence of the sleep-time

**Irish Literary Renaissance (Irish Revival, Celtic Revival)** The
great period of modern Irish writing, mostly in the English language and
to a significant extent written outside Ireland, from about 1885 to the
death of William Butler Yeats in 1939. The twin highlights of this period
are the poetic career of Yeats himself, indisputably the greatest poet in
the English language in his time, and the spectacular talent of James
Joyce, who made himself the master of modern English prose and
a formidably original leader of international *modernism. The literary
achievements in this period of the playwrights J. M. Synge and Sean
O'Casey are also noteworthy.

**irony** A subtly humorous perception of inconsistency, in which an
apparently straightforward statement or event is undermined by its
*context so as to give it a very different significance. In various forms,
irony appears in many kinds of literature, from the *tragedy of Sophocles
to the novels of Jane Austen and Henry James, but is especially
important in *satire, as in Voltaire and Swift. At its simplest, in **verbal
irony**, it involves a discrepancy between what is said and what is really
meant, as in its crude form, sarcasm; for the *figures of speech exploiting
this discrepancy, *see* ANTIPHRASIS, LITOTES, MEIOSIS. The more
sustained **structural irony** in literature involves the use of a naïve or
deluded hero or *unreliable narrator, whose view of the world differs
widely from the true circumstances recognized by the author and
readers; literary irony thus flatters its readers' intelligence at the expense
of a character (or fictional narrator). A similar sense of detached
superiority is achieved by **dramatic irony**, in which the audience knows
more about a character's situation than the character does, foreseeing
an outcome contrary to the character's expectations, and thus ascribing
a sharply different sense to some of the character's own statements; in
*tragedies, this is called **tragic irony**. The term **cosmic irony** is
sometimes used to denote a view of people as the dupes of a cruelly
mocking Fate, as in the novels of Thomas Hardy. A writer whose works
are characterized by an ironic tone may be called an **ironist**.
**Further reading:** Claire Colebrook, *Irony* (2003).

**irregular ode** *See* ODE.

**isometric** Unvaried in *metre. The term is applied to *verse forms and
*stanzas which employ only one kind of line, so they are consistent in
line length and, allowing for accepted local variations, in metrical

pattern. *Heroic poetry, *blank verse, and *sonnets are all expected to be isometric, as are poems written in rhyming *couplets, in *terza rima, and in certain stanza forms such as *rhyme royal, *ottava rima, and the *quatrain form known as long measure (see COMMON MEASURE). The opposite kind of poem or stanza in which lines of different lengths are found is called *heterometric. Noun: **isometry**.

**Italian sonnet** See SONNET.

**Jacobean** [jakŏ-**bee**-an]  Belonging to the period 1603–25, when James VI of Scotland reigned as King James I of England. The term is formed from the Latin equivalent of his name: *Jacobus*. As a literary period it marks a high point of English drama, including the later plays of Shakespeare (notably *Macbeth*, *King Lear*, *Othello*, *Antony and Cleopatra*, and *The Tempest*), the *masques and major plays of Ben Jonson, and significant works by several other playwrights, notably John Webster's *The Duchess of Malfi* (1623). In non-dramatic poetry, it includes the publication of Shakespeare's *Sonnets* (1609) and of Jonson's *The Forest* (1616). Next to the publication of the First *Folio edition of Shakespeare's plays (1623), the most important literary legacy of this period is the King James Bible (often called the Authorized Version) of 1611, a translation produced by a committee of scholars at James's command. The *portmanteau word **Jacobethan** is sometimes found as shorthand for '*Elizabethan and Jacobean', as several developments in literature, including the career of Shakespeare, run over the 1603 boundary between the two periods.

**jeremiad** [je-ri-**my**-ad]  Either a prolonged lamentation or a prophetic warning against the evil habits of a nation, foretelling disaster. The term comes from the name of the Hebrew prophet Jeremiah: the second sense refers to his dire warnings of Jerusalem's coming destruction (fulfilled in 586 BCE) and to his threats against the Egyptians, Chaldeans, Ammonites, Moabites, Philistines, and others, as recorded in the biblical book of Jeremiah; the first sense refers to the sequence of *elegies on Jerusalem's fall in the book of Lamentations. The term has been applied to some literary works that denounce the evils of a civilization: many of the writings of Thomas Carlyle, H. D. Thoreau, or D. H. Lawrence would fit this description.

***jeu d'esprit*** [*zher* des-**pri**] (plural ***jeux***)  A French phrase meaning literally 'play of spirit', perhaps better translated as 'flight of fancy'.

The term is applied to light-hearted witticisms and *epigrams such as those of Oscar Wilde, and more generally to any clever piece of writing dashed off in a spirit of fun, such as a *limerick or a short comic novel.

**jingle** A brief set of verses with strong, repetitive rhythm and emphatic rhymes, usually similar to a nursery rhyme in being memorable but nonsensical (e.g. 'With a hey, and a ho, and a hey nonino'). Jingles are now used in radio and TV advertisements, but the term was used before the rise of broadcasting to refer, usually unfavourably, to poems—like those of Edgar Allan Poe—that sacrifice meaning to showy effects of sound. *See also* NONSENSE VERSE.

***jongleur*** [zho$^n$-**gler**] The French term for a kind of wandering entertainer in medieval Europe, especially one who sang or recited works composed by others, such as *chansons de geste*. The term also covered jugglers and acrobats, as did the profession itself—many *jongleurs* seem to have combined various forms of entertainment. Although they appear to have been active across Europe for several hundreds of years before, the *jongleurs* flourished in the 13th century, by which time they were distinguished (not always sharply) from the *troubadours and *trouvères*, who were writers but not necessarily performers, and from the *minstrels, who often had more settled positions at noble courts. One notable *jongleur* is the 13th-century French satirical poet Rutebeuf.

***jouissance*** [zhwee-sah$^n$s] The French word for 'enjoyment' (often used in a sexual sense), employed by the critic Roland Barthes in his *Le Plaisir du texte* (1973) to suggest a kind of response to literary works that is different from ordinary *plaisir* (pleasure). Whereas *plaisir* is comfortable and reassuring, confirming our values and expectations, *jouissance*—usually translated as 'bliss' to retain its erotic sense—is unsettling and destabilizing. The distinction seems to stand in parallel with Barthes's preference for those fragmentary or dislocated texts which he called *scriptible rather than *lisible, that is, those that challenge the reader to participate in creating them rather than just consume them.

**Juvenalian** Characteristic of or written in the manner of the Roman poet Juvenal (Decimus Junius Juvenalis, *c.*65–*c.*135 CE), whose sixteen verse *satires are fierce denunciations of his fellow-Romans in general and of women in particular for their mercenary lives. Juvenalian satire is the kind of satire that bitterly condemns human vice and folly, in contrast with the milder and more indulgent kind known as *Horatian satire. In English, Samuel Johnson's poems *London* (1738) and *The Vanity of Human Wishes* (1749) are both imitations of Juvenal, but the satires of Jonathan Swift come closer to Juvenal's uncompromisingly disgusted tone.

**juvenilia** [joo-vě-**nil**-iă]  The collective term for those works written during an author's youth. Use of the term commonly implies that the faults of such writings are to be excused as the products of immaturity or lack of experience.

**kabuki** [ka-**boo**-ki] A Japanese form of theatrical entertainment which is more popular than the aristocratic *\*nō* plays, and combines song, dance, and stylized gesture in a prolonged spectacle set on a low stage. Scenery and costumes are elaborate, and the female roles are all played by men. Unlike the *nō* actor, the kabuki performer does not make use of masks, but employs heavy make-up. Kabuki plays are usually based on well-known \*legends and \*myths.

> **SEE WEB LINKS**
> • Kabuki21: extensive summaries of plays, details of actors, etc.

**katabasis** [kat-ă-**bay**-sis] (plural **–ases**) A descent into the underworld, or a literary account of such a journey to the land of the dead, constituting a temporary visit followed by an anabasis (ascent). A conventional component of classical \*epic, katabasis is found in the eleventh book of Homer's *Odyssey*, in the sixth book of Virgil's *Aeneid*, and more briefly in the story of Orpheus and Eurydice recounted by Ovid in the tenth book of his *Metamorphoses*. In medieval literature, the outstanding example is Dante's *Inferno*. In modern literature, katabasis arises either in \*burlesque forms such as the episode of Paddy Dignam's funeral in James Joyce's *Ulysses* (1922), or in retellings of the Orpheus-Eurydice story such as Mick Imlah's poem 'The Ayrshire Orpheus' (2008), or in imaginatively extended senses: Doris Lessing's novel *Briefing for a Descent into Hell* (1971) concerns a man undergoing a nervous breakdown; while Seamus Heaney's verse sequence *Station Island* (1984) involves a pilgrimage to Lough Derg in which the speaker converses with various spirits of the dead. *Adjective*: **katabatic**.

**Further reading:** Rachel Falconer, *Hell in Contemporary Literature* (2004).

**kenning** (plural **-ings** or **-ingar**) A stock phrase of the kind used in Old Norse and Old English verse as a poetic \*circumlocution in place of a more familiar noun. Examples are *banhus* (bonehouse) for 'body', and *saewudu* (sea-wood) for 'ship'. Similar \*metonymic compounds appear in colloquial speech, e.g. *fire-water* for 'whisky'. A famous Shakespearean example is *the beast with two backs* for 'copulation'. *See also* PERIPHRASIS.

**kitchen-sink drama** A rather condescending title applied from the late 1950s onwards in Britain to the then new wave of realistic drama depicting the family lives of working-class characters, on stage and in broadcast plays. Such works, by Arnold Wesker, Alun Owen, and others, were at the time a notable departure from the conventions of middle-class drawing-room drama. Wesker's play *Roots* (1959) actually does begin with one character doing the dishes in a kitchen sink.

**Further reading:** Stephen Lacey, *British Realist Theatre* (1995).

**kitsch** Rubbishy or tasteless pseudo-art of any kind. It is most easily recognizable in the products of the souvenir trade, especially those attempting to capitalize on 'high' art (Mona Lisa ashtrays, busts of Beethoven, etc.) or on religion (flesh-coloured Christs that glow in the dark); and is found in many forms of popular entertainment—the films of Cecil B. De Mille, much 'Easy Listening' music. It is harder to identify in written works, but the sentimental *doggerel found in greetings cards is one obvious example, while the trashier end of the science-fiction and sword-and-sorcery fiction markets provide many more pretentious cases.

*Knittelvers* (plural **-erse**) A German verse form consisting of four-stress lines rhymed as *couplets. Found in the popular poetry of the 15th and 16th centuries either in *accentual metre or in regular *octosyllabic lines, it was rejected by 17th-century poets as too clumsy (the word literally means 'cudgel-verse'), but was revived in the 18th century by Gottsched, Schiller, and Goethe.

*Künstlerroman* (plural **-mane**) The German term (meaning 'artist-novel') for a novel in which the central character is an artist of any kind, e.g. the musical composer Leverkühn in Thomas Mann's *Doktor Faustus* (1947), or the painter Lantier in Zola's *L'Oeuvre* (1886). Although this category of fiction often overlaps with the *Bildungsroman* in showing the protagonist's development from childhood or adolescence—most famously in Joyce's *A Portrait of the Artist as a Young Man* (1916)—it also includes studies of artists in middle or old age, and sometimes of historical persons: in David Malouf's *An Imaginary Life* (1978), for example, the central character and narrator is the Roman poet Ovid (43 BCE–17 CE).

**lacuna** [lă-kew-nă] (plural **-unae** or **-unas**) Any gap or missing element in a text, usually in a manuscript. *Adjective*: **lacunal** or **lacunose**. *See also* ELLIPSIS, HIATUS.

**lad lit** A marketing term of the 1990s in Britain, referring to a new kind of popular fiction concerning the 'lad' of that period, a supposedly carefree hedonist devoted to football, beer, music, and casual sex: a figure created in contrast to the feminist-defined 'New Man' of previous decades. Some publishers believed that such fiction would open up a lucrative new lad readership, but they discovered that although lads bought glossy magazines pitched to them at that time (*Arena, FHM, Loaded*), they hardly ever bought books. The key texts of this genre were the early novels of Nick Hornby, *Fever Pitch* (1992) and *High Fidelity* (1995), each of which has a protagonist dominated by a typically masculine obsession (Arsenal Football Club, a record collection) that highlights his inability to communicate with women. Other authors associated with this new wave of fictions about inadequate young British masculinities include Tony Parsons (*Man and Boy*, 1991), Tim Lott, and Mike Gayle. The term has sometimes been extended retrospectively to cover earlier fictions about selfish young men, including Martin Amis's *The Rachel Papers* (1973) and even the American novelist Bret Easton Ellis's *Less Than Zero* (1985). Since British lad lit arrived in the USA slightly later than the more successful first wave of *chick lit, it was mistakenly believed to be a backlash against the *Bridget Jones* phenomenon; in fact the correct answer to the question 'which came first, the chick or the lad?' is: the lad. *Adjective*: **lad-lit**.

***lai*** (lay) A term from Old French meaning a short *lyric or *narrative poem. The *Contes* (*c*.1175) of Marie de France were narrative *lais* of *Arthurian legend and other subjects from Breton folklore, written in *octosyllabic couplets. They provided the model for the so-called 'Breton lays' in English in the 14th century, which include Chaucer's

*Franklin's Tale* and the anonymous *Sir Orfeo*. Since the 16th century, the term has applied to songs in general, and to short narrative poems, as in T. B. Macaulay's *Lays of Ancient Rome* (1842).

**laisse** [less] A subdivision within a medieval French *chanson de geste*. In such poems, the *laisses* were *verse paragraphs of unequal length. *See also* STROPHE.

**Lake poets (Lake school)** A term applied in the 19th century to a group of English poets, namely William Wordsworth, Samuel Taylor Coleridge, and Robert Southey, all resident in the Lake District of northern England, Coleridge briefly (1800–04) and the others permanently. The term appears in journals from 1817, and became established through the publication of Thomas De Quincey's memoir *Recollections of the Lake Poets* (1834–9), in which he denied that they constituted a school. Other poets of the time wrote about lakes, notably Walter Scott in *The Lady of the Lake* (1810; set in Loch Katrine, Perthshire), but this did not qualify them to be called lake poets.

**lament** Any poem expressing profound grief or mournful regret for the loss of some person or former state, or for some other misfortune. *See also* COMPLAINT, DIRGE, ELEGY, JEREMIAD, MONODY, THRENODY, *UBI SUNT*.

**lampoon** An insulting written attack upon a real person, in verse or prose, usually involving caricature and ridicule. Among English writers who have indulged in this maliciously personal form of *satire are Dryden, Pope, and Byron. The laws of libel have restricted its further development as a literary form. *See also* FLYTING, INVECTIVE.

**Language poetry** An avant-garde movement in American poetry and poetics since the 1970s, with roots in both San Francisco and New York City and an academic centre at the State University of New York, Buffalo. It is a highly theorized tendency that draws not only upon late *modernist traditions of American *free verse (Zukofsky, Olson, Creeley) and upon the inspiration of the *New York school but upon *post-structuralist arguments about language and representation in support of its central emphases on the self-referential nature of language and the incoherence of the authorial self. As with other avant-garde groups, it claimed to be undermining the linguistic pillars of bourgeois power, such as *closure, meaning, etc. The principal figures

in this movement have been Bruce Andrews, Charles Bernstein, Lyn
Hejinian, Susan Howe, and Ron Silliman; others associated with the
movement were Michael Palmer, Clark Coolidge, and Bob Perelman.
An important vehicle for their essays and poems was the journal
L=A=N=G=U=A=G=E (1978–82) edited by Bruce Andrews
and Charles Bernstein, who later selected an anthology of its materials
as *The L=A=N=G=U=A=G=E Book* (1984). Bernstein's book *A Poetics*
(1992) is an important restatement of the group's aims.

**Further reading:** Linda Reinfeld, *Language Poetry* (1992).

(⊕) SEE WEB LINKS
• Archive of early issues of L=A=N=G=U=A=G=E.

*langue* [lahng]  The French word for language or tongue, which has
had a special sense in linguistics since the Swiss linguist Ferdinand de
Saussure, in his *Cours de linguistique générale* (1915), distinguished
*langue* from *parole*. In this sense, *langue* refers to the rules and
conventions of a given language—its phonological distinctions, its
permitted grammatical combinations of elements, etc.—whereas *parole*
('speech') refers to the sphere of actual linguistic events, i.e. utterances.
Saussure proposed that because *langue* underlies and makes possible
the infinitely varied forms of *parole*, it should be the primary object of
linguistic science. The *langue/parole* distinction is one of the theoretical
bases of *structuralism, although some structuralist writings have
encouraged a confusion between *langue* (the rules of a specific
language) and Saussure's distinct third term *langage* (the concept
'language' as such): the power attributed to 'Language' in this tradition
has little to do with Saussure's notion of *langue*, and owes more to
abstract conceptions of *langage* as a universal 'system'.

**lapidary**  Suitable for engraving in stone. A lapidary inscription is
one that is actually carved in stone, while a style of writing—especially
in verse—may be called lapidary if it has the dignity or the concision
expected of such inscriptions, or otherwise deserves to be passed on
to posterity. As a noun, the term also applies to a book about gems,
or to a jeweller. *See also* EPIGRAM.

**Latinate**  Derived from or imitating the Latin language. Latinate
*diction in English is the use of words derived from Latin rather
than those originating in Old English, e.g. *suspend* rather than *hang*.
A Latinate style may also be marked by prominent syntactic *inversion,

especially the delaying of the main verb: while the normal English word order is subject-verb-object, Milton frequently uses the Latin order object-subject-verb in his poem *Paradise Lost* (1667), as in the line

His far more pleasant garden God ordained

Milton's is the most notoriously Latinate style in English verse. In English prose, especially of the 18th century, Latinate style appears both in diction and in the *periodic sentence, which delays the completion of the sense through a succession of subordinate clauses, as in this sentence from Edward Gibbon's *Memoirs* (1796):

> It was at Rome, on the 15th of October, 1764, as I sat musing amidst the ruins of the Capitol, while the barefooted friars were singing vespers in the Temple of Jupiter, that the idea of writing the decline and fall of the city first started to my mind.

Particular instances of words, phrases, or constructions taken from the Latin are called **Latinisms**.

**Latinity** Proficiency in the Latin language, or a tendency to use *Latinate diction or style. In the first sense, Latinity may be an individual acquisition or a feature of an entire educational culture. A serious student of Latin language and literature is a **Latinist**, but an incompetent or fraudulent one may be called a **Latinitaster**, or in the worst case completely **Latinless**.

**lay** *See* LAI.

**Leavisites** The name given to followers of the English literary critic F. R. Leavis, who achieved an extensive influence in mid-20th-century British culture as co-editor of the journal *Scrutiny* (1932–53), as a teacher in Cambridge, and as the author of *New Bearings in English Poetry* (1932), *Revaluation* (1936), *The Great Tradition* (1948), and several other books. Leavis's attitude to literature and society, strongly influenced by his wife Q. D. Leavis's book *Fiction and the Reading Public* (1932), was marked by an intense moral seriousness and a militant hostility both to Marxism and to the utilitarian values of modern 'commercialism'. He saw the critic's task as one of preserving the values of the best literature—identified with those of 'Life'—against the hostile cultural environment of 'mass' society. His harshly exclusive literary judgements were influenced partly by T. S. Eliot's rejection of 19th-century poetry in favour of the *metaphysical poets, and partly by admiration for the work of D. H. Lawrence. Many of his pronouncements on the decline of English culture followed Eliot's hypothesis of the *dissociation of sensibility. The Leavisite influence on the teaching of English literature (which Leavis saw as central to cultural survival) was strong in Britain during the 1950s and 1960s, and produced a detailed version of English literary history in *The Pelican Guide to English Literature* (ed. Boris Ford, 7 vols., 1954–61), but it has declined sharply since Leavis's death in 1978. The Leavisites, including L. C. Knights, Denys Thompson, and Derek Traversi, are sometimes referred to as 'Scrutineers', after the name of their journal. The adjective **Leavisian** is applied more neutrally to ideas characteristic of Leavis's work. *See also* CAMBRIDGE SCHOOL.

**Further reading:** Christopher Hilliard, *English as a Vocation* (2012).

**legend** A story or group of stories handed down through popular *oral tradition, usually consisting of an exaggerated or unreliable account of some actually or possibly historical person—often a saint, monarch, or popular hero. Legends are sometimes distinguished from *myths in that they concern human beings rather than gods, and sometimes in that they have some sort of historical basis whereas myths do not; but these distinctions are difficult to maintain consistently. The term was originally applied to accounts of saints' lives (*see* HAGIOGRAPHY), but is now applied chiefly to fanciful tales of warriors (e.g. King Arthur and his knights), criminals (e.g. Faust, Robin Hood), and other sinners; or more recently to those bodies of biographical rumour and embroidered anecdote surrounding dead film stars and rock musicians (Judy Garland, John Lennon, etc.). *Adjective*: **legendary**. *See also* FOLKLORE.

**leitmotif** [lyt-moh-teef] **(leitmotiv)** A frequently repeated phrase, image, *symbol, or situation in a literary work, the recurrence of which usually indicates or supports a *theme. The term (German, 'leading motif') comes from music criticism, where it was first used to describe the repeated musical themes or phrases that Wagner linked with particular characters and ideas in his operatic works. The repeated references to rings and arches in D. H. Lawrence's novel *The Rainbow* (1915) are examples of the use of a leitmotif; the repetition of set phrases in the novels of Muriel Spark is another example. *See also* MOTIF.

**lemma** (plural **lemmata**) A heading or title, especially in a glossary (*see* GLOSS), textual commentary, footnote, or dictionary. So in a dictionary such as this one, the word or phrase appearing in bold type at the start of each entry is the lemma (or 'headword'), and the remainder of the entry is the commentary upon it. *Adjective*: **lemmatical** or **lemmatic**.

**leonine rhyme** A form of *internal rhyme in which a word or syllable(s) in the middle of a verse line rhymes with the final word or syllable(s) of the same line, as in the opening line of Edgar Allan Poe's 'The Raven' (1845):

Once upon a midnight dreary, while I pondered, weak and weary

The term was once restricted to a particular variety of such rhymes as used by medieval poets in Latin *hexameters and *pentameters, with the first rhyming word immediately preceding the medial *caesura, but it now often refers to similar rhymes in other kinds of line.

*letrilla* [let-**ree**-yǎ] A kind of Spanish lyric poem in short lines (of eight syllables or fewer), with a one-line *refrain (*estribillo*) at the end of each stanza. There are many *lettrillas* from the classical age of Spanish poetry, by Lope de Vega, Góngora, Quevedo, and others. They vary in subject from the religious to the satirical and erotic.

**lexis** A term used in linguistics to designate the total vocabulary of a language, or sometimes the vocabulary used in a particular text (*see* DICTION). The adjective **lexical** means 'of vocabulary' or sometimes 'of dictionaries'. A **lexicon** is a dictionary, while a **lexicographer** is a person who compiles dictionaries and is thus a practitioner of **lexicography**.

**libretto** (plural **-etti** or **-ettos**) The Italian word for a booklet, applied in English to the text of an opera, operetta, or oratorio, that is, to the words as opposed to the music; thus a kind of dramatic work written for operatic or other musical performance. A writer of libretti, such as W. S. Gilbert or W. H. Auden, is known as a **librettist**.

**life writing** A modern term meant to cover the general realm of non-fictional writings about the lives, experiences, and memories of individual people or small groups of people. Thus although excluding most other kinds of history or ethnology it includes *autobiography,

*biography, *hagiography, *apology, and *memoir, along with certain kinds of diary, journal, letter, *travelogue, and personal *essay.

**light verse** The general term for various kinds of verse that have no serious purpose and no solemnity of tone. They may deal with trivial subjects, or bring a light-hearted attitude to more serious ones. Light verse is often characterized by a display of technical accomplishment in the handling of difficult rhymes, *metres, and *stanza forms. The many forms of light verse include *Anacreontics, *clerihews, *epigrams, *jingles, *limericks, *mock epics, *nonsense verse, *parodies, and *vers de société.

**limerick** [**limm**-ĕ-rik] An English verse form consisting of five *anapaestic lines rhyming *aabba*, the third and fourth lines having two *stresses and the others three. Early examples, notably those of Edward Lear in his *Book of Nonsense* (1846), use the same rhyming word at the end of the first and last lines, but most modern limericks avoid such repetition. The limerick is almost always a self-contained, humorous poem, and usually plays on rhymes involving the names of people or places. First found in the 1820s, it was popularized by Lear, and soon became a favourite form for the witty obscenities of anonymous versifiers. The following is one of the less offensive examples of the coarse limerick tradition:

> There was a young fellow named Menzies
> Whose kissing sent girls into frenzies;
>    But a virgin one night
>    Crossed her legs in a fright
> And fractured his bi-focal lenses.

**lipogram** A written composition that deliberately avoids using a particular letter of the alphabet. Examples have been found in ancient Greek poetry, but the most extravagant curiosities of this pointless game include Alonso Alcalá y Herrera's *Varios effectos de amor* (1641)—a sequence of five novellas each eschewing a different vowel, J. R. Ronden's play *La Pièce sans A* (1816), and Georges Perec's novel *La Disparition* (1969; later translated into English as *A Void*), which dispenses with *e*. Lipograms are extremely rare in English, although one Ernest Wright managed a 50,000-word novel, *Gadsby* (1939), without using *e*.

**lira** A five-line Spanish *stanza form of Italian origin, combining seven-syllable and eleven-syllable lines in the order 7,11,7,7,11, with the standard *rhyme scheme *ababb*. Its name ('lyre') comes from the final word of the opening line in a well-known such stanza by the early 16th-century poet Garcilaso de la Vega, whose exile in Naples led to his influential importation of Italian verse forms into Spanish. The art of the Spanish *lira* was perfected later in that century in the religious verse of Luis de León and Juan de la Cruz.

**lisible** [liz-eebl] The French word for 'legible', used in a specific sense by the critic Roland Barthes in his book *S/Z* (1970), and usually translated as 'readerly' or 'readable'. Barthes applies this term to texts (usually of the *realist tradition) that involve no true participation from the reader other than the consumption of a fixed meaning. A readerly text can be understood easily in terms of already familiar *conventions and expectations, and is thus reassuringly 'closed'. By contrast, the *texte* **scriptible* ('writerly' text, usually *modernist) challenges the reader to produce its meanings from an 'open' play of possibilities. *See also* JOUISSANCE.

**litany** [litt-ăni] A kind of prayer consisting of a long sequence of chanted supplications and responses; also, by extension, any prolonged or repetitive speech or written composition. Some kinds of *catalogue verse and *incantation resemble the repetitive forms of litany. *Adjective*: **litaneutical**.

**literal** Confined to the simplest primary meaning of a word, statement, or text, as distinct from any figurative sense (*see* FIGURE) which it may carry—whether *ironic, *allegorical, *metaphoric, or *symbolic. Thus the literal sense of a text is its most straightforward meaning. **Literalism** is a tendency to interpret texts according to their most obvious meaning, often disregarding their *connotations as well as their figurative senses. A **literal translation** is one that tries as far as possible to transfer each element of a text from one language into the other, without allowance for differences of *idiom between the two languages.

**literariness** The sum of special linguistic and formal properties that distinguish literary texts from non-literary texts, according to the theories of *Russian Formalism. The leading Formalist Roman Jakobson declared in 1919 that 'the object of literary science is not literature but *literariness*, that is, what makes a given work a literary work'. Rather than seek abstract qualities like *imagination as the basis of literariness, the Formalists set out to define the observable 'devices' by which literary texts—especially poems—*foreground their own language, in *metre, rhyme, and other patterns of sound and repetition. Literariness was understood in terms of *defamiliarization, as a series of deviations from 'ordinary' language. It thus appears as a relation between different uses of language, in which the contrasted uses are liable to shift according to changed contexts. *See also* FUNCTION, LITERATURE.

**literary criticism** *See* CRITICISM.

**literary history** The practice of recounting in narrative form some process of change in a given body of *literature (e.g. in a national literature or in a *genre such as drama); or an example of such an account of literary developments. Literary history as we know it dates from the 18th century, and was at first strongly associated with the antiquarian and *bibliographic cataloguing of rare manuscripts and books in a given country or language. With the development of 19th-century nationalism, it lent itself increasingly to the rediscovery and celebration of the literary treasures (understood to disclose the essential national 'spirit') of a given nation or linguistic community, e.g. the German- or English- or Spanish-speaking peoples. In the early 20th century it came under some challenge for its habits of tracing sources, influences, and movements on the larger scale without addressing the unique value of the individual literary work; and its former prestige in the academic study of literature suffered under the rival claims of *criticism and *Theory. Classic modern examples in English include C. S. Lewis's *English Literature in the Sixteenth Century* (1954) and Ian Watt's *The Rise of the Novel* (1957).

**literati** [litt-ĕ-**rah**-ti] The collective term for educated people, especially those involved in studying, writing, or criticizing literary works. The term is often used disrespectfully. The singular forms, literatus (masculine) and literata (feminine), are rarely used; the French term *littérateur* is more frequently found.

**literature** A body of written works related by subject-matter (e.g. the literature of computing), by language or place of origin (e.g. Russian literature), or by prevailing cultural standards of merit. In this last sense, 'literature' is taken to include oral, dramatic, and broadcast compositions that may not have been published in written form but which have been (or deserve to be) preserved. Since the 19th century, the broader sense of literature as a totality of written or printed works has given way to more exclusive definitions based on criteria of imaginative, creative, or artistic value, usually related to a work's absence of factual or practical reference (*see* AUTOTELIC). Even more restrictive has been the academic concentration upon poetry, drama, and fiction. Until the mid-20th century, many kinds of non-fictional writing—in philosophy, history, biography, *criticism, topography, science, and politics—were counted as literature; implicit in this broader usage is a definition of literature as that body of works which—for whatever reason—deserves to be preserved as part of the current reproduction of meanings within a given culture (unlike yesterday's newspaper, which belongs in the disposable category of ephemera). This sense seems more tenable than the later attempts to divide literature—as creative, imaginative, fictional, or non-practical—from factual writings or practically effective works of propaganda, *rhetoric, or *didactic writing. The *Russian Formalists' attempt to define *literariness in terms of linguistic deviations is important in the theory of *poetry, but has not addressed the more difficult problem of the non-fictional prose forms. *See also* BELLES-LETTRES, CANON, PARALITERATURE.

**Further reading:** Peter Widdowson, *Literature* (1998).

**litotes** [**ly**-toh-teez] A *figure of speech by which an affirmation is made indirectly by denying its opposite, usually with an effect of understatement: common examples are *no mean feat* and *not averse to a drink*. This figure is *not uncommon* in all kinds of writing. For example, William Wordsworth in his autobiographical poem *The Prelude* (1850) frequently uses the phrase 'not seldom' to mean 'fairly often'. *See also* MEIOSIS.

**littérateur** [lit-er-at-**er**] A person occupied with literature, usually as a professional writer or critic. The term is often used with a disparaging suggestion of pretentiousness. *See also* LITERATI.

**little magazine** A magazine, usually of literature and art, that has only a small circulation. It is the tiny readership that makes it little, not its physical size as a publication: some little magazines, for example *Blast* (1914–15), have been rather large in format. During the heyday of such magazines, approximately 1890–1950, several of them enjoyed a literary influence out of proportion to their commercial fragility: one of the earliest, *The Yellow Book* (London, 1894–7), became a legend in helping to define the temperament of its time. Others, such as *The Egoist* (London, 1914–19), *Dial* (New York, 1916–29), and *Scrutiny* (Cambridge, 1932–53), were important shapers of modern critical opinion.

**Further reading:** Robert Scholes and Clifford Wulfman, *Modernism in the Magazines: An Introduction* (2010).

**((⊕)) SEE WEB LINKS**

• Modernist Journals Project at Brown and Tulsa universities, with archive of early modernist journals.

**liturgical drama** A form of religious drama performed within a church as an extension of the liturgy (i.e. the established form of Christian worship in the Mass or Eucharist). In medieval Europe, the introduction of chanted responses to the Easter services seems to have evolved into a more recognizably dramatic form of *passion play, while the Christmas service gave rise to the first Nativity plays. Liturgical drama is generally thought to be the origin of *mystery plays and *miracle plays, which came to be performed by lay actors in sites away from the churches themselves, and in the *vernacular rather than in Latin.

**loc. cit.** Common abbreviation for *loco citato* (Latin, 'in the place cited'), a phrase employed in scholarly footnotes and endnotes to indicate that a quotation just given is from the same place (i.e. the same page or paragraph) as the previous quotation given from that work. This is a more specific direction than '*ibid.' or '*op. cit.', which indicate that the quotation comes from the same article or book.

**local color writing** A kind of fiction that came to prominence in the USA in the late 19th century, and was devoted to capturing the unique customs, manners, speech, folklore, and other qualities of a particular regional community, usually in humorous short stories. The most famous of the local colorists was Mark Twain; others included Bret Harte, George Washington Cable, Joel Chandler Harris, Kate Chopin, and Sarah Orne Jewett. The trend has some equivalents in European fiction, notably in the attention given by Zola and Hardy to the settings of their stories.

**loco-descriptive** *See* TOPOGRAPHICAL POETRY.

**logocentrism** The term used by Jacques Derrida and other
exponents of *deconstruction to designate the desire for a centre or
original guarantee of all meanings, which in Derrida's view has
characterized Western philosophy since Plato. The Greek word *logos* can
just mean 'word', but in philosophy it often denotes an ultimate
principle of truth or reason, while in Christian theology it refers to the
Word of God as the origin and foundation of all things. Derrida's critique
of logocentric thinking shows how it attempts to repress difference
(*see* DIFFÉRANCE) in favour of identity and presence: the philosophical
'metaphysics of presence' craves a 'transcendental signified' or
ultimately self-sufficient meaning (e.g. God, Man, Truth). The most
significant case of logocentrism is the enduring *phonocentrism that
privileges speech over writing because speech is held to guarantee
the full 'presence' and integrity of meaning.

**log-rolling** A disreputable form of collusion in the reviewing of
books, whereby one author writes a glowing appraisal of his or her
friend's book, and the friend repays the favour by endorsing the first
author's books too. The term arises from the proverbial phrase 'You
roll my log and I'll roll yours'. *See also* CLAQUE.

**long measure (long metre)** *See* *common measure.

**longueur** [long-ger] The French word for 'length', applied to any
tediously prolonged passage or scene in a literary work.

**lost generation** A phrase sometimes applied to the younger
American writers and intellectuals of the 1920s, on the grounds of their
supposed disillusionment and loss of moral bearings in the wake of the
First World War. It derives from a remark made by Gertrude Stein to
Ernest Hemingway and recorded as the *epigraph to his novel *The Sun
Also Rises* (1926): 'You are all a lost generation'. The more general
reference is usually to writers born, like Hemingway, in the late 1890s,
e.g. Edmund Wilson, John Dos Passos, F. Scott Fitzgerald, William
Faulkner, and Hart Crane.

**lyric** [li-rik] In the modern sense, any fairly short poem expressing the
personal mood, feeling, or meditation of a single speaker (who may
sometimes be an invented character, not the poet). In ancient Greece, a
lyric was a song for accompaniment on the lyre, and could be a **choral
lyric** sung by a group (*see* CHORUS), such as a *dirge or *hymn; the

modern sense, current since the *Renaissance, often suggests a song-like quality in the poems to which it refers. Lyric poetry is the most extensive category of verse, especially after the decline—since the 19th century in the West—of the other principal kinds: *narrative and dramatic verse. Lyrics may be composed in almost any *metre and on almost every subject, although the most usual emotions presented are those of love and grief. Among the common lyric forms are the *sonnet, *ode, *elegy, *haiku, and the more personal kinds of hymn. **Lyricism** is the emotional or song-like quality, the **lyrical** property, of lyric poetry. A writer of lyric poems may be called a **lyric poet**, a **lyricist**, or a **lyrist**. In another sense, **the lyrics** of a popular song or other musical composition are the words as opposed to the music; these may not always be lyrical in the poetic sense (e.g. in a narrative song like a *ballad).

**Further reading:** Scott Brewster, *Lyric* (2007).

**macaronic verse** Poetry in which two or more languages are mixed together. Strictly, the term denotes a kind of comic verse in which words from a *vernacular language are introduced into Latin (or other foreign-language) verses and given Latin *inflections; such verse had a vogue among students in Europe in the 16th and 17th centuries, but is rare in English. More loosely, the term is applied to any verses in which phrases or lines in a foreign language are frequently introduced: several medieval English poems have Latin *refrains or alternating Latin and English lines, and in modern times the poems of Ezra Pound and T. S. Eliot have been called macaronic for their use of lines in several languages. *Noun*: **macaronism**.

**Machiavel** [**mak**-yă-vel] A type of stage *villain found in Elizabethan and *Jacobean drama, and named after the Florentine political theorist Niccolò Machiavelli, whose notorious book *Il Principe* (*The Prince*, 1513) justified the use of dishonest means to retain state power. Exaggerated accounts of Machiavelli's views led to the use of his name— sometimes directly referred to in speeches—for a broad category of ruthless schemers, atheists, and poisoners. Shakespeare's Iago and Richard III are the most famous examples of the type.

**machinery** The collective term applied since the 18th century to the supernatural beings—gods, angels, devils, nymphs, etc.—who take part in the action of an *epic or *mock-epic poem or in a dramatic work. The term is taken from the Greek dramatic convention of the *deus ex machina*, and is also applied in a more familiar sense to the cranes, moving sets, and other contraptions used in the theatre.

**madrigal** A short *lyric poem, usually of love or *pastoral life, often set to music as a song for several voices without instrumental accompaniment. As a poetic form, it originated in 14th-century Italy, but it was revived and adopted by composers throughout Europe in the 16th century; the English madrigal flourished from the 1580s to the

1620s. There is no fixed metrical form or *rhyme scheme, but the
madrigal usually ends with a rhyming *couplet. *Adjective*: **madrigalian**.

**magic realism (magical realism)** A kind of modern fiction in which
fabulous and fantastical events are included in a *narrative that
otherwise maintains the 'reliable' tone of objective realistic report. The
term was once applied to a trend in German fiction of the early 1950s,
but is now associated chiefly with certain leading novelists of Central
and South America, notably Miguel Ángel Asturias, Alejo Carpentier,
and Gabriel García Márquez. The latter's *Cien años de soledad* (*One
Hundred Years of Solitude*, 1967) is often cited as a leading example,
celebrated for the moment at which one character unexpectedly ascends
to heaven while hanging her washing on a line. The term has also been
extended to works from very different cultures, designating a tendency
of the modern novel to reach beyond the confines of *realism and draw
upon the energies of *fable, *folktale and *myth while retaining a strong
contemporary social relevance. Thus Günter Grass's *Die Blechtrommel*
(*The Tin Drum*, 1959), Milan Kundera's *The Book of Laughter and
Forgetting* (1979), and Salman Rushdie's *Midnight's Children* (1981)
have been described as magic realist novels along with Angela Carter's
*Nights at the Circus* (1984) and Rushdie's *The Satanic Verses* (1988).
The fantastic attributes given to characters in such novels—levitation,
flight, telepathy, telekinesis—are among the means that magic realism
adopts in order to encompass the often phantasmagoric political
realities of the 20th century. *See also* FABULATION, HYSTERICAL REALISM.

**Further reading:** Maggie Ann Bowers, *Magic(al) Realism* (2004).

**malapropism** [**mal**-ă-prop-izm] A confused, comically inaccurate
use of a long word or words. The term comes from the character
Mrs Malaprop (after the French *mal à propos*, 'inappropriately') in
Sheridan's play *The Rivals* (1775): her bungled attempts at learned
speech include a reference to another character as 'the very pine-apple
of politeness', instead of 'pinnacle'. This kind of joke, though, is older
than the name: Shakespeare's Dogberry in *Much Ado About Nothing*
(*c.*1598) makes similar errors. *Adjective*: **malapropian**. *Verb*: **malaprop**.

**manifesto** (plural **-festos** or **-festoes**) A public self-justification or
proclamation of intentions, usually issued by a political authority or
party. Literary and artistic groups since the 19th century, especially
those of the *avant-garde* associated with *modernism, borrowed this

political genre for their own purposes, usually to declare the obsolescence of some previous artistic movement and the arrival of a new era based upon their own new principles. The most famous political model for the genre is Karl Marx's and Friedrich Engels's *Communist Manifesto* (1848), itself a modern rhetorical masterpiece. Notable literary examples include André Breton's *Manifeste du Surréalisme* (1924) and the many manifestos (no fewer than five were issued between 1909 and 1913) of *Futurism. Less celebrated now is the Italian philosopher Giovanni Gentile's *Manifesto degli intellettuali fascisti* (1925).

**Further reading:** Janet Lyon, *Manifestoes: Provocations of the Modern* (1999).

**mannerism** A vague term for the self-conscious cultivation of peculiarities of style—usually elaborate, ingenious, and ornate—in literary works of any period. Like the *baroque, with which it often overlaps, mannerism is a concept more clearly defined in art history than in literary studies: art historians have marked out a Mannerist period (roughly 1520–1610) between the High Renaissance and the Baroque, characterized by distortions of figure and perspective. Clear equivalents in English literature of this period would be the **mannered** style of *euphuism and the elaborate *conceits of the Elizabethan *sonnet. In Spanish literature, the term can apply to *conceptismo* and *Gongorism; in Italian to *concettismo* and *Marinism. But mannered styles can be found in many later periods, from the *Latinate style of Milton to the far-fetched similes of Raymond Chandler. A common indicator of literary mannerism is that the elaborate manner is maintained, whatever the nature of the matter treated.

**Further reading:** John H. Steadman, *Redefining a Period Style* (1990).

**Märchen** [**mairh**-yen] The German term for tales of enchantment and marvels, usually translated as '*fairy tales' despite the absence of actual fairies from most examples; also for a single such tale (the singular and plural forms being the same). *Märchen* have been divided into two categories: the *Volksmärchen* are *folktales of the kind collected by Jacob and Wilhelm Grimm in their celebrated *Kinder- und Hausmärchen* (1812–14), while *Kunstmärchen* are 'art tales', that is, literary creations like the uncanny tales of E. T. A. Hoffmann.

**marginalia** A term coined by S. T. Coleridge to denote material written into the margins of a book or manuscript, these usually being annotations upon the main text within the margins. A notable literary example is the series of exasperated comments written by the poet-artist William Blake in his copy of the *Works* of Sir Joshua Reynolds, objecting vehemently to the latter's aesthetic principles. There is no singular form except **marginal note**. To add marginalia to a text is to **marginate** it or simply to **marginalize** (although the latter form is now more often found to mean 'push something to the margins', by back-formation from the noun 'marginalization'). A 'marginalist', however, is an adherent of the important school of economic theory known as marginalism. *Adjective*: **marginalic**.

**Marinism (*marinismo*)** The term given by later literary historians to a deliberately startling new poetic style inaugurated by the Italian poet Giovanbattista Marino (1569–1625) and his many followers, originally referred to as *concettismo*. It cultivated powerful sense-impressions and especially the far-fetched *conceit or extended metaphor that connects hitherto remote things, sometimes on the basis of new scientific knowledge or exotic explorations. The style is exhibited most fully in Marino's erotic *epic *Adone* (1623) but is visible in the widely-read collection of shorter poems *Rime* (1602); among the lesser **Marinists** who imitated it in the early 17th century were Marcello Macedonio and Giovan Leone Sempronio. It is one of several stylistic manifestations of the European *baroque cult of ingenuity, and has some parallels with the Spanish poetic movement of *conceptismo* and with the practice of the English *metaphysical poets. *See also* MANNERISM, *SECENTISMO*.

**Martian poets** The term applied in the 1980s to a small group of poets in Britain whose work is marked by the prominence of surprising visual *metaphors, *similes, and *conceits. The leading figures are Christopher Reid and Craig Raine, who both published important collections in 1979: Reid's *Arcadia* and Raine's *A Martian Sends a Postcard Home* both transform everyday objects, in a playful kind of *defamiliarization. The term comes from the title poem of Raine's book, in which we are shown familiar earthly sights through the inexperienced eyes of a visiting Martian ('Rain is when the earth is television'). Similar effects are achieved by David Sweetman in *Looking Into the Deep End* (1981) and by Oliver Reynolds in *Skevington's Daughter* (1985). This tendency has been called **Martianism**.

**marvellous, the** (US **marvelous**) A category of fiction in which supernatural, magical, or other wondrous impossibilities are accepted as normal within an imagined world clearly separated from our own reality. The category includes *fairy tales, many *romances, and most *science fiction, along with various other kinds of *fantasy with 'other-worldly' settings, like J. R. R. Tolkien's *The Lord of the Rings* (1954–5). Modern theorists have distinguished marvellous tales from those of the *uncanny in terms of the explanations offered for strange events: in the marvellous, these are explained as magic, while in the uncanny they are given psychological causes.

**Marxist criticism** *See* p. 214.

**masculine ending** The ending of a metrical verse line on a stressed syllable, as in Emily Brontë's regular *iambic line:

<blockquote>And who can fight against despair?</blockquote>

Masculine endings are also common in *trochaic verse, where the final unstressed syllable expected in the regular pattern is frequently abandoned (*see* CATALECTIC). In French, a masculine line is any line not ending in mute *e*, *es*, or *ent*. A masculine *caesura is one that immediately follows a stressed syllable, usually in the middle of a line. *See also* METRE, STRESS.

**masculine rhyme** The commonest kind of rhyme, between single stressed syllables (e.g. de*lay*/*stay*) at the ends of verse lines. In contrast with *feminine rhyme, which adds further unstressed syllables after the rhyming stressed syllables, masculine rhyme matches only the final syllable with its equivalent in the paired line, as in Christina Rossetti's *couplet:

<blockquote>And all the rest forget,<br>But one remembers yet.</blockquote>

In French verse, the alternation of masculine and feminine rhymes became the norm from the 16th century onwards.

**masque** (**mask**) A spectacular kind of indoor performance combining poetic drama, music, dance, song, lavish costume, and costly stage effects, which was favoured by European royalty in the 16th and early 17th centuries, especially to celebrate royal weddings, birthdays and other special occasions. Members of the court would enter disguised, taking the parts of mythological persons alongside professional

## MARXIST CRITICISM

A tradition of literary and aesthetic interpretation and commentary
derived from the principles of Marxism ('historical materialism'),
and thus tending to view literature in the light of modes of
production (feudal, capitalist) and their property relations and class
struggles. Little in this tradition derives directly from the writings of
Karl Marx and his collaborator Friedrich Engels, who provided no
developed aesthetic theory, although they expressed doubts about
the value of propagandist fiction and thus discouraged the simple
judgement of literary works according to the degree of socialist
sentiment they express. In general, the claims of Marxist literary
analysis have been more compatible with *literary history (in which
the formative importance of economic factors in literary evolution
has commonly been accepted) than with evaluative *criticism itself.
Critical positions claiming to be Marxist arose later in the two
divergent currents of official Communist doctrine in the Soviet
Union and its satellite parties (1917–91) on the one hand, and of
'Western Marxism' on the other. Russian Communist literary policy
generated a short-lived ambition for the proletarianization of
literature and the rejection of the bourgeois inheritance, under the
name of *proletcult (memorably derided by Leon Trotsky in his
*Literature and Revolution*, 1924), and then a more conservative
doctrine of *socialist realism, which tended to impose a bland
official optimism upon writers while suppressing 'decadent'
alternatives along with independent critical positions such as those
of the *Russian Formalists and of the Bakhtin group (*see*
CARNIVALIZATION, DIALOGIC).

The more creative and ultimately more influential trends in
Marxist criticism emerged from various Western Marxist thinkers,
who tended to disagree on a range of questions including the
requirement upon writers to be 'committed' to the socialist cause
and the progressive or reactionary tendencies of *realism and
*modernism. Notable figures here include the Hungarian writer
Georg Lukács, who in *Studies in European Realism* (1950) and other
works upheld the value of 'bourgeois' realism as a basis for socialist
literature while attacking the allegedly apolitical pessimism of
modernist writing; the German poet-playwright Bertolt Brecht, who

argued to the contrary in defending modernist experiment as
potentially radical; and some writers associated with the *Frankfurt
School, notably Walter Benjamin, who interpreted the significance
of Brecht's *epic theatre and whose essay 'The Work of Art in the
Age of Mechanical Reproduction' (1935) is a widely admired classic
of Marxist reflection upon modern culture.

Western Marxist criticism underwent renewal and diversification
in the 1960s and 1970s, becoming more visible within academic
literary studies and interacting with a range of other critical schools
from *structuralism, *psychoanalytic criticism, *feminist criticism,
and *postcolonial theory to *deconstruction and *new historicism.
In this 'neo-Marxist' phase, the traditional Marxist metaphor of
economic causality in which a 'superstructure' of political and
cultural forms grew up from a 'base' of economic forces and
relations was either openly challenged (as it was by the British
socialist critic Raymond Williams, who inspired the school of
*cultural materialism) or quietly set aside in favour of explorations
of literature's relations with the specific cultural contradictions of
modern capitalist society. In English, the leading figures in this
phase have been the American theorist Fredric Jameson (in
*Marxism and Form* (1971), and later works) and the prolific
British essayist Terry Eagleton (in *Criticism and Ideology* (1976), *The
Ideology of the Aesthetic* (1990), and numerous other works).

**Further reading:** Terry Eagleton, *Marxism and Literary Criticism* (2nd edn,
2002); Terry Eagleton and Drew Milne (eds.), *Marxist Literary Theory* (1996).

(( )) SEE WEB LINKS

• Provides some early texts.

performers, and enact a simple *allegorical plot, concluding with the removal of masks, a dance joined by members of the audience, and a banquet. Shakespeare included a short masque scene in *The Tempest* (1611), and Milton's play *Comus* (1634) is loosely related to the masque; these are now the best-known examples, but at the courts of James I and Charles I the highest form of the masque proper was represented by the quarrelsome collaboration of Ben Jonson with the designer Inigo Jones from 1605 to 1631 in the hugely expensive *Oberon* (1611) and other works. The parliamentary Revolution of the 1640s brought this form of extravagance to an abrupt end.

**Further reading:** Lauren Shohet, *Reading Masques* (2010).

**(((⊕))) SEE WEB LINKS**

• Illustrated resource on masques at University of Victoria.

**matter of Britain** The *legends of King Arthur and his Knights of the Round Table, which form the subject-matter for a number of medieval *romances—usually known as *Arthurian romances. These are often distinguished from the romances dealing with the matter of France (i.e. legends of Charlemagne and his knights) or the matter of Rome (classical Roman legends or myths).

**maxim** A short and memorable statement of a general principle; thus an *aphorism or *apophthegm, especially one that imparts advice or guidance. The French writer La Rochefoucauld published his aphorisms as *Maximes* (1665), while Benjamin Franklin included several celebrated examples in his *Poor Richard's Almanack* (1733–58), including the maxim 'Three may keep a secret, if two of them are dead'. *Adjective*: **maximic**.

**measure** An older word for *metre. The term is also used to refer to any metrical unit such as a *foot, a *dipody, or a line.

**medievalism (mediaevalism)** Enthusiasm for or imitation of the arts and customs of Europe during the Middle Ages—that is, from about the 8th century to the 15th. In literature, this may manifest itself in the use of *archaisms, in the choice of medieval settings for *narrative works, or more broadly in endorsement of values associated with medieval societies (e.g. chivalry, religious faith, social hierarchy). Antiquarian interest in *ballads and other aspects of medieval art grew in the late 18th century, influencing the *Gothic novel and the strongly medievalist nostalgia of *Romanticism. Medievalism is a significant current in

19th-century literature from Walter Scott's novel *Ivanhoe* (1819) and Keats's poem 'The Eve of St Agnes' (1820) to the prose and verse *romances of William Morris. Important works of Victorian social criticism, notably Thomas Carlyle's *Past and Present* (1843) and John Ruskin's *The Stones of Venice* (1851–3), contrasted medieval social conditions favourably with those of the modern industrial city. A **medievalist** is usually a scholar studying some aspect of medieval history or culture.

**Further reading:** Michael Alexander, *Medievalism: The Middle Ages in Modern Literature* (2006).

**medium** (plural **-dia**) The material or the technical process employed in an art or a communication. In literature, the medium is language, although further distinctions are also made between the media of speech and print, between theatre and cinema, and between prose and poetry. A misleading implication in some uses of the term is that the meaning of a work already exists as a complete entity only requiring transmission through the medium of language; this notion is resisted by most modern theorists of literature.

**meiosis** [my-**oh**-sis] (plural **-oses**) The Greek term for understatement or 'belittling': a rhetorical *figure by which something is referred to in terms less important than it really deserves, as when Mercutio in *Romeo and Juliet* calls his mortal wound a 'scratch'. Usually the effect is one of *irony or *anticlimax, but it may be disparaging, as when a writer is called a scribbler. The favoured form of meiosis is *litotes, in which an affirmation is made indirectly by denying its opposite, e.g. *it was no mean feat*. *Adjective*: **meiotic**.

***Meistersinger*** (Mastersinger) A singing poet belonging to the musical guilds that flourished in the towns of southern Germany in the 15th and 16th centuries, claiming descent from the medieval *Minnesänger*. The *Meistersinger* were craftsmen (e.g. Hans Sachs, a cobbler) whose singing and poetic composition, both secular and religious, were governed by strict and secretive rules. Their form of composition for unaccompanied singing is known as ***Meistersang*** or ***Meistergesang***.

**melodrama** A popular form of sensational drama that flourished in the 19th-century theatre, surviving in different forms in modern cinema and television. The term, meaning 'song-drama' in Greek, was originally applied in the European theatre to scenes of mime or spoken dialogue accompanied by music. In early 19th-century London, many theatres were only permitted to produce musical entertainments, and from their simplified plays—some of them adapted from *Gothic novels—the modern sense of melodrama derives: an emotionally exaggerated conflict of pure maidenhood and scheming villainy in a plot full of suspense. Well-known examples are Douglas Jerrold's *Black-Ey'd Susan* (1829), the anonymous *Maria Marten* (*c*.1830), and *Sweeney Todd, the Demon Barber of Fleet Street* (1842); the Irish playwright Dion Boucicault wrote several melodramas from the 1850s onwards, notably *The Colleen Bawn* (1860). Similar plots and simplified characterization in fiction, as in Dickens, can also be described as melodramatic. *See also* DRAME, GRAND GUIGNOL.

**Further reading:** Elaine Hadley, *Melodramatic Tactics* (1995).

**memoir** A narrative recollection of the writer's earlier experiences, especially those involving unusual people, places, or events. A memoir is commonly distinguished from an *autobiography by its greater emphasis on other people or upon events such as war and travel experienced in common with others, and sometimes by its more *episodic structure, which does not need to be tied to the personal development of the narrator; however, the terms are often still confounded. Memoirs are supposed to be non-fictional, but the title has often been borrowed for a kind of fiction told as a *first-person narrative: *see* MEMOIR-NOVEL. A writer of memoirs is a **memoirist**. *See also* MISERY MEMOIR.

**memoir-novel** A kind of novel that pretends to be a true *autobiography or *memoir. It was an important form in the emergence of the modern novel during the 18th century, in such works as Daniel Defoe's *Moll Flanders* (1722) and John Cleland's *Memoirs of a Lady of Pleasure* (1748–9; usually known as *Fanny Hill*). A similar pseudo-autobiographical mode of *first-person narrative is found in very many later novels, but the pretence that the real author was only an 'editor' of a true account did not outlive the 18th century. *See also* AUTOBIOGRAFICTION.

**Menippean satire (Varronian satire)** A form of intellectually humorous work characterized by miscellaneous contents, displays of curious erudition, and comical discussions on philosophical topics. The name comes from the Greek Cynic philosopher Menippus (3rd century BCE), whose works are lost, but who was imitated by the Roman writer Varro (1st century BCE) among others. The Canadian critic Northrop Frye revived the term in *Anatomy of Criticism* (1957) while also introducing the overlapping term *anatomy after a famous example of Menippean satire, Robert Burton's *Anatomy of Melancholy* (1621). The best-known example of the form is Lewis Carroll's *Alice's Adventures in Wonderland* (1865); other examples include the novels of Thomas Love Peacock, and John Barth's *campus novel *Giles Goat-Boy* (1966). The humour in these works is more cheerfully intellectual and less aggressive than in those works which we would usually call *satires, although it holds up contemporary intellectual life to gentle ridicule.

**metacriticism** Criticism of *criticism; that is, the examination of the principles, methods, and terms of criticism either in general (as in critical theory) or in the study of particular critics or critical debates. The term usually implies a consideration of the principles underlying critical interpretation and judgement.

**metadrama (metatheatre)** Drama about drama, or any moment of self-consciousness by which a play draws attention to its own fictional status as a theatrical pretence. Normally, direct addresses to the audience in *prologues, *epilogues, and *inductions are metadramatic in that they refer to the play itself and acknowledge the theatrical situation; a similar effect may be achieved in *asides. In a more extended sense, the use of a play-within-the-play, as in *Hamlet*, allows a further metadramatic exploration of the nature of theatre, which is taken still further in plays *about* plays, such as Luigi Pirandello's *Sei personaggi in cerca d'autore* (*Six Characters in Search of an Author*, 1921). *See also* FOREGROUNDING, SELF-REFLEXIVE.

**metafiction** Fiction about fiction; or more especially a kind of fiction that openly comments on its own fictional status. In a weak sense, many modern novels about novelists having problems writing their novels may be called metafictional in so far as they discuss the nature of fiction; but the term is normally used for works that involve a significant degree of self-consciousness about themselves as fictions, in ways that go beyond occasional apologetic addresses to the reader. The most celebrated case is Sterne's *Tristram Shandy* (1760–67), which makes a continuous joke of its own digressive form. A notable modern example is John Fowles's *The French Lieutenant's Woman* (1969), in which Fowles interrupts the narrative to explain his procedures, and offers the reader alternative endings. Perhaps the finest of modern metafictions is Italo Calvino's *Se una notte d'inverno un viaggatore* (*If on a winter's night a traveler*, 1979), which begins 'You are about to begin reading Italo Calvino's new novel, *If on a winter's night a traveler*.' See also MISE-EN-ABYME, POSTMODERNISM, SELF-REFLEXIVE.

**Further reading:** Patricia Waugh, *Metafiction* (1984).

**metalanguage** Any use of language about language, as for instance in *glosses, definitions, or arguments about the usage or meaning of words. Linguistics sometimes describes itself as a metalanguage because it is a 'language' about language; and so on the same assumption *criticism is a metalanguage about literature. Some theorists of *structuralism have spoken of metalanguages as if they were clearly separate from or standing above the 'object-languages' they describe, but this claim is denied by *post-structuralism, which points out that linguistics, criticism, etc., are still within the same general language, albeit as specialized uses with their own terminologies. Thus there is in principle no absolute distinction between criticism and literature. Roman Jakobson in his listing of linguistic *functions describes the 'metalingual' (or **metalinguistic**) function as that by which speakers check that they understand one another. In a wider sense, literary works often have a metalinguistic aspect in which they highlight uses of language: a very clear case of this is Shaw's *Pygmalion* (1913). It is also possible to have a **meta-metalanguage**, i.e. a 'third-level' discourse such as an analysis of linguistics, or a work of *metacriticism.

**metalepsis** A term used in different senses in *rhetoric and *narratology. In rhetoric, the precise sense of metalepsis is uncertain, but it refers to various kinds of complex *figure or *trope that are figurative to the second or third degree; that is, they involve a figure that either refers us to yet another figure or requires a further imaginative leap to establish its reference, usually by a process of *metonymy. Extended *similes and *rhetorical questions sometimes show a **metaleptic** multiplication of figures. Thus Marlowe's famous lines

from *Dr Faustus* combine metaleptically a rhetorical question with
*synecdoche and *hyperbole:

> Was this the face that launched a thousand ships
> And burnt the topless towers of Ilium?

These same lines illustrate a slightly different sense of metalepsis as
a figure that brings together two distantly related facts (here, Helen's
beauty and the destruction of Troy), metonymically joining cause
and effect while jumping or compressing the intervening steps in the
causal chain. In narratology, metalepsis is a breaking of the boundaries
that separate distinct 'levels' of a narrative, usually between an
*embedded tale and its *frame story (*see* DIEGESIS). An example occurs
in Chaucer's *Merchant's Tale*, when a fictional character within the
tale told by the Merchant refers to the Wife of Bath, who should
be unknown to him since she exists on another level as one of the
pilgrims listening to the Merchant. Narrative metalepsis, sometimes
called 'frame-breaking', has become common in modern experimental
fiction.

**metaphor** The most important and widespread *figure of speech, in
which one thing, idea, or action is referred to by a word or expression
normally denoting another thing, idea, or action, so as to suggest some
common quality shared by the two. In metaphor, this resemblance
is assumed as an imaginary identity rather than directly stated as a
comparison: referring to a man as *that pig*, or saying *he is a pig* is
metaphorical, whereas *he is like a pig* is a *simile. Metaphors may also
appear as verbs (a talent may *blossom*) or as adjectives (a novice may be
*green*), or in longer *idiomatic phrases, e.g. *to throw the baby out with
the bath-water*. The use of metaphor to create new combinations of
ideas is a major feature of *poetry, although it is quite possible to write
poems without metaphors. Much of our everyday language is also made
up of metaphorical words and phrases that pass unnoticed as 'dead'
metaphors, like the *branch* of an organization. A **mixed metaphor**
is one in which the combination of qualities suggested is illogical or
ridiculous (*see also* CATACHRESIS), usually as a result of trying to apply
two metaphors to one thing: *those vipers stabbed us in the back*. Modern
analysis of metaphors and similes distinguishes the primary literal term
(called the '*tenor') from the secondary figurative term (the 'vehicle')
applied to it: in the metaphor *the road of life*, the tenor is life, and the
vehicle is the road.

**Further reading:** David Punter, *Metaphor* (2007).

**metaphysical poets** The name given to a diverse group of 17th-century English poets whose work is notable for its ingenious use of intellectual and theological concepts in surprising *conceits, strange *paradoxes, and far-fetched *imagery. The leading metaphysical poet was John Donne, whose colloquial, argumentative abruptness of rhythm and tone distinguishes his style from the *conventions of Elizabethan love-lyrics. Other poets to whom the label is applied include Andrew Marvell, Abraham Cowley, John Cleveland, and the predominantly religious poets George Herbert, Henry Vaughan, and Richard Crashaw. In the 20th century, T. S. Eliot and others revived their reputation, stressing their quality of *wit, in the sense of intellectual strenuousness and flexibility rather than smart humour. The term **metaphysical poetry** usually refers to the works of these poets, but it can sometimes denote any poetry that discusses **metaphysics**, that is, the philosophy of knowledge and existence.

**Further reading:** A. J. Smith, *Metaphysical Wit* (2006).

**metastasis** [met-**as**-tă-sis] (plural **–stases**) In rhetoric, a rapid transition from one point to the next, or a glossing over of some point as of too little importance to dwell upon (e.g. if it would be troublesome to the speaker's argument). *Adjective*: **metastatic**.

**metatheatre** *See* METADRAMA.

**metathesis** [met-**ath**-ĕ-sis] A transposition of sounds or letters, usually within a word or syllable. In etymology, it is invoked to explain changes of form, as in the case of the modern word *thrill*, which came from the older form *thyrl*; or *nostril*, which (from the same root) derives from Old English *nosthyrl*. A *Spoonerism is a special kind of metathesis that transposes sounds between words. *Adjective*: **metathetic**.

**meter** *See* METRE.

**metonymy** [met-**on**-ĭmi] A *figure of speech that replaces the name of one thing with the name of something else closely associated with it, e.g. *the bottle* for alcoholic drink, *the press* for journalism, *skirt* for woman, *Mozart* for Mozart's music, *the Oval Office* for the US presidency. A well-known metonymic saying is *the pen is mightier than the sword* (i.e. writing is more powerful than warfare). A word used in such metonymic expressions is sometimes called a **metonym**

[**met**-ŏnim]. An important kind of metonymy is *synecdoche, in which the name of a part is substituted for that of a whole (e.g. *hand* for worker), or vice versa. Modern literary theory has often used 'metonymy' in a wider sense, to designate the process of association by which metonymies are produced and understood: this involves establishing relationships of contiguity between two things, whereas *metaphor establishes relationships of similarity between them. The metonym/metaphor distinction has been associated with the contrast between *syntagm and *paradigm. *See also* ANTONOMASIA.

**metre (US meter)** *See* p. 224.

**metrics** Another word for *prosody, that is, the theory and practice of poetic *metre. A poet composing metrical verse, or a theorist of metre, may be called a **metrist** or **metrician**.

**Middle English** The term used by historians of the English language to denote a stage of its development intermediate between *Old English (or 'Anglo-Saxon') and modern English. In this historical scheme, Middle English is the language spoken and written between about 1100 and about 1500. In this period, English is influenced in many aspects of its vocabulary by a new French-speaking ruling class, and by a clergy that wrote mainly in Latin. Middle English grammar and syntax are clearly those inherited from the Germanic basis of Old English, although now shedding its inflections and distinctions of gender. Strong differentiation appears among dialects, of which the East Midlands variety proved to be the most important basis of modern English. The period is commonly subdivided into Early Middle English (approximately 1100–1300) and Later Middle English (1300–1500). In its literary manifestations, Early Middle English is the language of *The Owl and the Nightingale*, while Later Middle English is that of Langland, Chaucer, and Malory.

**Further reading:** R. D. Fulk, *An Introduction to Middle English* (2012).

(⊕) SEE WEB LINKS
• Labyrinth, an extensive medieval studies resource.

**middle generation** A term increasingly used since the 1980s to refer collectively to American poets who had been born in the first twenty years of the 20th century, and who made their reputations in its middle decades, 1940–60. Schematically, the middle-generation poets are regarded as intermediate between poets associated with *modernism

## METRE (US METER)

The pattern of measured sound-units recurring more or less regularly in lines of verse. Poetry may be composed according to one of four principal **metrical** systems: (i) in **quantitative metre**, used in Greek and Latin, the pattern is a sequence of long and short syllables counted in groups known as feet (*see* FOOT, QUANTITATIVE VERSE); (ii) in **syllabic metre**, as in French and Japanese, the pattern comprises a fixed number of syllables in the line (*see* SYLLABIC VERSE); (iii) in **accentual metre** (or 'strong-stress metre'), found in Old English and in later English popular verse, the pattern is a regular number of stressed syllables in the line or group of lines, regardless of the number of unstressed syllables (*see* ACCENTUAL VERSE); (iv) in **accentual-syllabic metre**, the pattern consists of a regular number of stressed syllables appropriately arranged within a fixed total number of syllables in the line (with permissible variations including *feminine endings), both stressed and unstressed syllables being counted (*see* ACCENTUAL-SYLLABIC VERSE).

The fourth system—accentual-syllabic metre—is the one found in most English verse in the literary tradition since Chaucer; some flexible uses of it incline towards the accentual system. However, the descriptive terms most commonly used to analyse it have, confusingly, been inherited from the vocabulary of the very different Greek and Latin quantitative system. Thus the various English metres are named after the classical feet that their groupings of stressed and unstressed syllables resemble, and the length of a metrical line is still often expressed in terms of the number of feet it contains: a *dimeter has two feet, a *trimeter three, a *tetrameter four, a *pentameter five, a *hexameter six, and a *heptameter seven. A simpler and often more accurate method of description is to refer to lines in either accentual or accentual-syllabic metre according to the number of stressed syllables: thus an English tetrameter is a 'four-stress line', a pentameter a 'five-stress line' (these being the commonest lines in English).

English accentual-syllabic metres fall into two groups, according to the way in which stressed (●) and unstressed (○) syllables alternate: in **duple metres**, stressed syllables alternate more or less regularly with single unstressed syllables, and so the line is traditionally described as a sequence of disyllabic (2-syllable) feet; while in **triple metres**, stressed syllables alternate with pairs of unstressed syllables, and the line is seen as a sequence of trisyllabic (3-syllable) feet.

Of the two duple metres, by far the more common in English is the **iambic metre**, in which the stressed syllables are for the most part perceived as following the unstressed syllables with which they alternate (○●○●○● etc.), although some variations on this pattern are accepted. In traditional analysis by feet, iambic verse is said to be composed predominantly of *iambs (○●). This iambic pentameter by John Dryden illustrates the metre:

> And doom'd to death, though fated not to die.

The other duple metre, used in English less frequently than the iambic, is **trochaic metre**, in which the iambic pattern is reversed so that the stressed syllables are felt to be preceding the unstressed syllables with which they alternate (●○●○●○ etc.); in terms of classical feet, trochaic verse is said to be made up predominantly of *trochees (●○). This trochaic tetrameter from Longfellow illustrates the metre:

> Dark behind it rose the forest

It is common, though, for poets using trochaic metre to begin and end the line on a stressed syllable (*see* CATALECTIC), as in Blake's line:

> Tyger, tyger, burning bright

In such cases it is hard to distinguish trochaic and iambic metres. The triple metres are far less common in English, although sometimes found. In **dactylic metre**, named after the *dactyl (●○○), the stressed syllables are felt to precede the intervening pairs of unstressed syllables:

> Cannon in front of them (Tennyson: dactylic dimeter)

In **anapaestic metre**, named after the *anapaest (○○●), the pattern is reversed:

> Of your fainting, dispirited race (Arnold: anapaestic trimeter)

Dactylic and anapaestic verse is not usually composed purely of dactyls and anapaests, however: other feet or additional syllables are frequently combined with or substituted for them.

All these patterns are open to different kinds of variation, of which the most common is traditionally called *substitution of one foot for another (but *see also* DEMOTION, PROMOTION); for the other feet sometimes mentioned in the context of substitution, *see* FOOT. Other variations include the addition or subtraction of syllables to alter the line's length. The theory and practice of metrical verse is known as *prosody or metrics, while the detailed analysis of the metrical pattern in lines of verse is called *scansion.

**Further reading:** Derek Attridge, *Poetic Rhythm: An Introduction* (1995); Martin J. Duffell, *A New History of English Metre* (2008).

(most of those having been born in the 1880s) and the later cohorts of the *New York school and the *Beat writers, mostly born in the 1920s. The poets most often identified as belonging to the middle generation are, by date of birth, Theodore Roethke (1908), Elizabeth Bishop (1911), Delmore Schwartz (1913), Robert Hayden (1913), Randall Jarrell (1914), John Berryman (1914), and Robert Lowell (1917).

**Miltonic sonnet**  *See* SONNET.

**mime**  In the modern sense, a dramatic performance or scene played with bodily movement and gesture and without words; thus a non-literary art. However, in ancient Greece and Rome the mime was a kind of crude *farce about domestic life, including dialogue as well as gesture, both often obscene. A performer in such a play could also be called a mime. *See also* DUMB SHOW, PANTOMIME.

**mimesis**  [my-**mees**-is]  The Greek word for imitation, a central term in aesthetic and literary theory since Aristotle. A literary work that is understood to be reproducing an external reality or any aspect of it is described as **mimetic**, while **mimetic criticism** is the kind of *criticism that assumes or insists that literary works reflect reality. *See also* DIEGESIS, REFLECTIONISM, *UT PICTURA POESIS*.

**Further reading:** Matthew Potolsky, *Mimesis* (2006).

**minimalism**  A literary or dramatic style or principle based on the extreme restriction of a work's contents to a bare minimum of necessary elements, normally within a short form, e.g. a *haiku, *epigram, brief dramatic *sketch, or *monologue. Minimalism is often characterized by bareness or starkness of vocabulary or of dramatic setting, and a reticence verging on or even becoming silence. The term has been borrowed from modern sculpture and painting, and applied especially to the later dramatic work of the Irish writer Samuel Beckett, whose 30-second play *Breath* (1969), for example, has no characters and no words. More loosely, the adjective **minimalist** may be applied to any strikingly abbreviated work, such as the shortest poems of *Imagism, or to the very short stories of Lydia Davis.

***Minnesänger***  [**min**-ĕ-zeng-er]  **(Minnesingers)**  The poets of *courtly love (*Minne*) who flourished in southern Germany in the late 12th and early 13th centuries, composing their love-lyrics to be sung at aristocratic courts, where several of the *Minnesänger* were themselves

noblemen. They are the German equivalents of the Provençal
*troubadours and French *trouvères*. Their form of love poetry is known
as **Minnesang**, a term sometimes extended to cover other *lyrics of this
period. Among the foremost Minnesingers were Dietmar von Aist,
Hartmann von Aue, and Walther von der Vogelweide.

**minstrel** A professional entertainer of late medieval Europe, either
itinerant or settled at a noble court. Minstrels of the 13th and 14th
centuries, the descendants of the *jongleurs*, sang and recited lyrics and
narrative poems including *chansons de geste* and *ballads. Their art,
sometimes called **minstrelsy**, declined with the advent of printing. They
are distinguished from the *troubadours, who were educated amateur
poets of higher social rank. In the USA, the **minstrel show** was a
19th-century form of entertainment with white performers in blackface
presenting stereotyped impressions of black American folk culture,
and playing banjos.

**miracle play** A kind of medieval religious play representing
non-scriptural legends of saints or of the Virgin Mary. The term is often
confusingly applied also to the *mystery plays, which form a distinct
body of drama based on biblical stories. Thanks to the book-burning
zeal of the English Reformation, no significant miracle plays survive in
English, but there is a French cycle of forty *Miracles de Notre-Dame*
probably dating from the 14th century.

***mise-en-abyme*** [meez on ab-**eem**] A term coined by the French
writer André Gide, supposedly from the language of heraldry, to refer
to an internal reduplication of a literary work or part of a work. Gide's
own novel *Les Faux-Monnayeurs* (*The Counterfeiters*, 1926) provides a
prominent example: its central character, Édouard, is a novelist working
on a novel called *Les Faux-Monnayeurs* which strongly resembles the
very novel in which he himself is a character. The 'Chinese box' effect
of *mise-en-abyme* often suggests an infinite regress, i.e. an endless
succession of internal duplications. It has become a favoured device in
*postmodernist fictions by Jorge Luis Borges, Italo Calvino, and others.
*See also* METAFICTION.

***mise en scène*** [meez ah$^{n}$ sen] The French term for the staging
or visual arrangement of a dramatic production, comprising scenery,
properties, costume, lighting, and human movement. The term is also
used in film-making for the staging of the action in front of the camera,

i.e. for the combination of setting, lighting, acting, and costume, as distinct from camerawork and editing.

**misery memoir** A kind of *memoir or *autobiography notable for its account of the narrator suffering and subsequently surviving extremely disturbing experiences, especially in childhood, whether of poverty, neglect, persecution, or physical and sexual abuse. It came to be recognized as a popular subgenre in the 1990s with the success of such works as Jung Chang's *Wild Swans* (1991), Dave Pelzer's *A Child Called "It"* (1995), and Frank McCourt's *Angela's Ashes* (1996). The first decade of the 21st century witnessed a publishing boom in what came to be called **misery lit**, large numbers of such books being sold through supermarkets. The commercial temptations of this boom attracted some authors whose extremely harrowing stories were exposed as fabrications or wild exaggerations.

**misprision** Misreading or misunderstanding. Harold Bloom, in his theory of the *anxiety of influence, uses the term to mean a kind of defensive distortion by which a poet creates a poem in reaction against another poet's powerful 'precursor' poem, and which is also necessarily involved in all readers' interpretations of poetry.

**mixed metaphor** *See* METAPHOR.

**mnemonic** [ni-**mon**-ik] Helpful in remembering something; or (as a noun) a form of words or letters that assists the memory, e.g. the rhyme beginning 'Thirty days hath September'. Rhyming verse is often employed for mnemonic purposes, and it is sometimes claimed that this was poetry's original function.

**mock epic** A poem employing the lofty style and the conventions of *epic poetry to describe a trivial or undignified series of events; thus a kind of *satire that mocks its subject by treating it in an inappropriately grandiose manner, usually at some length. Mock epics incidentally make fun of the elaborate conventions of epic poetry, including *invocations, battles, supernatural *machinery, *epic similes, and *formulaic descriptions (e.g. of funeral rites or of warriors arming for combat). The outstanding examples in English are Alexander Pope's *The Rape of the Lock* (1712–14) and *The Dunciad* (1728–43), while Boileau's *Le Lutrin* (1674–83) is an important French example. *Adjective*: **mock-epic** or *mock-heroic. *See also* BURLESQUE, IRONY, PARODY.

**mock-heroic** Written in an ironically grand style that is comically incongruous with the 'low' or trivial subject treated. This adjective is commonly applied to *mock epics, but serves also for works or parts of works using the same comic method in various forms other than that of the full-scale mock-epic poem: Swift's prose satire *The Battle of the Books* (1704) is an important case, as is Byron's intermittently mock-heroic poem *Don Juan* (1819–24). Shorter satirical poems employing fewer epic conventions, such as Ben Jonson's 'On the Famous Voyage' (1616) and Dryden's *MacFlecknoe* (1682), are probably better described as mock-heroic poems rather than mock epics, partly because they are not long enough to be divided into *cantos. Theatrical *burlesques of *heroic drama, such as Henry Fielding's *Tom Thumb* (1730) are also referred to as mock-heroic. *See also* HEROIC POETRY, PARODY, SATIRE.

**Further reading:** Ulrich Broich, *The Eighteenth-Century Mock-Heroic Poem* (1990).

**mode** An unspecific critical term usually designating a broad but identifiable kind of literary method, mood, or manner that is not tied exclusively to a particular *form or *genre. Examples are the *satiric mode, the *ironic, the *comic, the *pastoral, and the *didactic.

**modernism** A general term applied retrospectively to the wide range of experimental and *avant-garde* trends in the literature (and other arts) of the early 20th century, including *Symbolism, *Futurism, *Expressionism, *Imagism, *Vorticism, *Ultraismo*, *Dada, and *Surrealism, along with the innovations of unaffiliated writers. Modernist literature is characterized chiefly by a rejection of 19th-century traditions and of their consensus between author and reader: the conventions of *realism, for instance, were abandoned by Franz Kafka and other novelists, and by expressionist drama, while several poets rejected traditional *metres in favour of *free verse. Modernist writers tended to see themselves as an *avant-garde* disengaged from bourgeois values, and disturbed their readers by adopting complex and difficult new forms and styles. In fiction, the accepted continuity of chronological development was upset by Joseph Conrad, Marcel Proust, and William Faulkner, while James Joyce and Virginia Woolf attempted new ways of tracing the flow of characters' thoughts in their *stream-of-consciousness styles. In poetry, Ezra Pound and T. S. Eliot replaced the logical exposition of thoughts with *collages of fragmentary images and complex *allusions. Luigi Pirandello and Bertolt Brecht opened up the theatre to new forms of abstraction in place of realist and *naturalist representation.

Modernist writing is predominantly cosmopolitan, and often expresses a sense of urban cultural dislocation, along with an awareness of new anthropological and psychological theories. Its favoured techniques of juxtaposition and multiple *point of view challenge the reader to re-establish a coherence of meaning from fragmentary forms. In English, its major landmarks are Joyce's *Ulysses* and Eliot's *The Waste Land* (both 1922).

**Further reading:** Peter Childs, *Modernism* (2nd edn, 2007); Peter Nicholls, *Modernisms: An Introduction* (2nd edn, 2009).

(⊕) SEE WEB LINKS

• Modernism Lab: research resource at Yale.

**modernismo** A movement in Spanish-language poetry of the period from the 1880s to *c.*1916, inaugurated and named by the Nicaraguan poet Rubén Darío, whose many followers in Mexico, Cuba, Peru, and elsewhere in Latin America, as well as in Spain became known as **modernistas**. They were dedicated to formal experiment, rhythmic flexibility, and ideals of artistic purity, partly under the influence of the French *Parnassians and *Symbolists. It is preferable to avoid Anglicizing this term to '*modernism', since the latter term covers a much wider international range of work in prose as well as verse, extending into a slightly later period.

**monodrama** A play or dramatic scene in which only one character speaks; or a sequence of *dramatic monologues all spoken by the same single character. The second sense is rarely used, except of Tennyson's *Maud* (1855), to which the author attached the subtitle *A Monodrama* in 1875. In the first sense, some German playwrights of the late 18th century wrote monodramas that had musical accompaniment, notably J. C. Brandes's *Ariadne auf Naxos* (1774). Modern writers of monodramas include Samuel Beckett in *Krapp's Last Tape* (1958) and Alan Bennett, who has written several monodramas for television. *See also* MONOLOGUE.

**monody** An *elegy, *dirge, or *lament uttered by a single speaker, or presented as if to be spoken by a single speaker. In ancient Greek poetry, the term referred to an *ode sung by a single performer, as distinct from a choral ode. Milton applied the term to his elegy 'Lycidas' (1637), and Arnold used it in the subtitle of his 'Thyrsis' (1867). A composer or singer of monodies is a **monodist**. *Adjective*: **monodic**. *See also* THRENODY.

**monograph** A scientific or scholarly *treatise devoted to the sustained examination of a single clearly identified subject (originally a single species in natural history), as distinct from a general survey covering several related topics. This may be a short article, but is now usually understood to be a book-length work. The author of a monograph may be referred to as a **monographer** or **monographist**. *Adjective:* **monographic**.

**monologic (monological)** *See* DIALOGIC.

**monologue** An extended speech uttered by one speaker, either to others or as if alone. Significant varieties include the *dramatic monologue (a kind of poem in which the speaker is imagined to be addressing a silent audience), and the *soliloquy (in which the speaker is supposed to be 'overheard' while alone). Some modern plays in which only one character speaks, like Beckett's *Krapp's Last Tape* (1958), are known either as *monodramas or as monologues. In prose fiction, the *interior monologue is a representation of a character's unspoken thoughts, sometimes rendered in the style known as *stream of consciousness. The speaker of a monologue is sometimes called a **monologuist**.

**monometer** [mon-**om**-iter] A verse line consisting of only one *foot (or, in some classical Greek and Latin *metres, one *dipody, i.e. one linked pair of feet). Monometers are rarely used as the basis for whole poems, although Robert Herrick's 'Upon His Departure Hence' (1648) is one English example. *Adjective*: **monometric**.

**monorhyme** A poem or poetic passage in which every line ends on the same rhyme; found more commonly in Welsh, in medieval Latin, and in Arabic than in English. Christina Rossetti's poem 'Passing Away, Saith the World, Passing Away' (1862) is a notable English example.

**morality play** A kind of religious drama popular in England, Scotland, France, and elsewhere in Europe in the 15th and early 16th centuries. Morality plays are dramatized *allegories, in which personified virtues, vices, diseases, and temptations struggle for the soul of Man as he travels from birth to death. They instil a simple message of Christian salvation, but often include comic scenes, as in the lively obscenities of *Mankind* (*c.*1465). The earliest surviving example in English is the long *Castle of Perseverance* (*c.*1420), and the best-known is *Everyman* (*c.*1510). Most are anonymous, but *Magnyfycence* (*c.*1515) was written by John Skelton. Echoes of the morality plays can be found in Elizabethan drama, especially Marlowe's *Dr Faustus* and the character of Iago in Shakespeare's *Othello*, who resembles the sinister tempter known as the *Vice in morality plays. *See also* INTERLUDE, PSYCHOMACHY.

**morpheme** A linguistic term for a minimal unit of grammatical meaning in a language. Words are composed of one or more morphemes (e.g. *tables* = *table* + *s*). Prefixes, suffixes, plural endings etc. are called 'bound morphemes' because they do not occur on their own. *Adjective*: **morphemic**. *See also* INFLECTION.

**morphology** A branch of linguistics concerned with analysing the structure of words. The morphology of a given word is its structure or form.

**mosaic rhyme** *See* FEMININE RHYME, TRIPLE RHYME.

**motif** [moh-**teef**] A situation, incident, idea, image, or character-type that is found in many different literary works, folktales, or myths; or any element of a work that is elaborated into a more general *theme. The fever that purges away a character's false identity is a recurrent motif in Victorian fiction; and in European *lyric poetry the **ubi sunt* motif and the **carpe diem* motif are commonly found. Where an image, incident, or other element is repeated significantly within a single work, it is more commonly referred to as a *leitmotif. *See also* ARCHETYPE, STOCK CHARACTER, TOPOS.

**Movement, the** The term applied since 1954 to a loose group of English poets whose work subsequently appeared in the anthology *New Lines* (1956) edited by Robert Conquest. Apart from Conquest himself, the group included Kingsley Amis, Donald Davie, D. J. Enright, Thom Gunn, Elizabeth Jennings, Philip Larkin, and John Wain. Their common ground was limited to an avoidance of romantic postures in favour of ironic detachment, a reaction against the excesses of *modernism, and a cultivation of poetry as a disciplined craft. The central figures—Larkin and Amis (who both also wrote as novelists)—are associated with a defiantly provincial Englishness, for which the term 'movement' is singularly inappropriate, but others—notably Davie, Enright, and Gunn—had or later acquired a more international perspective.

**Further reading:** Blake Morrison, *The Movement* (1980).

**multi-accentuality** The ability of words and other linguistic signs to carry more than one meaning according to the contexts in which they are used. The concept was introduced in an important Russian critique of Saussure's abstract theory of *la *langue*: Valentin Voloshinov's *Marxism and the Philosophy of Language* (1929; sometimes alleged to have been written by Mikhail Bakhtin) accused Saussure of attributing fixed meanings to signs, when in actual practice the meaning of words is open to continual redefinition within the struggles between social classes and groups. In certain historical circumstances, particular words become objects of struggle between groups for whom they have different meanings: the meaning of *freedom* is constantly contested, while recent examples would include *terrorist*, among many others. *See also* DIALOGIC, POLYSEMY.

**muse** A source of inspiration to a poet or other writer, usually represented as a female deity, and conventionally called upon for assistance in a poet's *invocation. In ancient Greek religion, the muses were nine sister-goddesses, the daughters of Zeus and Mnemosyne (the goddess of memory), who presided over various arts and some branches of learning. Their cult was associated particularly with the Pierian Spring on Mount Olympus, with Mount Parnassus near Delphi, and with Mount Helicon in Boeotia. Their names and responsibilities are as follows: Calliope (*epic poetry); Clio (history); Erato (*lyric love poetry); Euterpe (flute music); Melpomene (*tragedy); Polyhymnia (*hymns); Terpsichore (choral dance and song); Thalia (*comedy); and Urania (astronomy). Later poets of the *Renaissance, however, often referred to the women praised in their love poems as muses who inspired their verse; and in modern *criticism the term has often been extended to any cause or principle underlying a writer's work.

**mystery play** A major form of popular medieval religious drama, representing a scene from the Old or New Testament. Mystery plays—also known as *pageants or as Corpus Christi plays—were

performed in many towns across Europe from the 13th century to the
16th (and later, in Catholic Spain and Bavaria). They seem to have
developed gradually from Latin *liturgical drama into civic occasions in
the local languages, usually enacted on Corpus Christi, a holy feast day
from 1311 onwards. Several English towns had *cycles of mystery plays,
in which wagons stopping at different points in the town were used as
stages for the various episodes, each presented by a trade guild (then
known as a 'mystery'). A full cycle, like the 48 plays enacted at York,
would represent the entire scheme of Christian cosmology from the
Creation to Doomsday. Other English cycles survive from Chester,
Wakefield, and the unidentified 'N-town'; the plays of the anonymous
'Wakefield Master', notably the *Second Shepherds' Play*, are the most
celebrated. *See also* MIRACLE PLAY, PASSION PLAY.

**SEE WEB LINKS**
• Luminarium archive of play texts and other materials.

**myth**  A kind of story or rudimentary *narrative sequence, normally
traditional and anonymous, through which a given culture ratifies
its social customs or accounts for the origins of human and natural
phenomena, usually in supernatural or boldly imaginative terms. The
term has a wide range of meanings, which can be divided roughly into
'rationalist' and 'romantic' versions: in the first, a myth is a false or
unreliable story or belief (*adjective*: **mythical**), while in the second,
'myth' is a superior intuitive mode of cosmic understanding (*adjective*:
**mythic**). In most literary contexts, the second kind of usage prevails,
and myths are regarded as fictional stories containing deeper truths,
expressing collective attitudes to fundamental matters of life, death,
divinity, and existence (sometimes deemed to be 'universal'). Myths are
usually distinguished from *legends in that they have less of an historical
basis, although they seem to have a similar mode of existence in oral
transmission, re-telling, literary adaptation, and *allusion. A **mythology**
is a body of related myths shared by members of a given people or
religion, or sometimes a system of myths evolved by an individual
writer, as in the 'personal mythologies' of William Blake and W. B. Yeats;
the term has sometimes also been used to denote the study of myths.
*Verb*: **mythicize** or **mythologize**. *See also* ARCHETYPE, MYTH CRITICISM,
MYTHOPOEIA.

**Further reading:** Laurence Coupe, *Myth* (2nd edn, 2008).

**myth criticism** A kind of literary interpretation that regards literary works as expressions or embodiments of recurrent mythic patterns and structures, or of 'timeless' *archetypes. Myth criticism, which flourished in the 1950s and 1960s, is less interested in the specific qualities of a given work than in those features of its *narrative structure or *symbolism that seem to connect it to ancient myths and religions. An important precedent for many myth-critical studies was J. G. Frazer's speculative anthropological work *The Golden Bough* (1890–1915), which proposed a cycle of death and rebirth found in fertility cults as the common basis for several mythologies. The most influential modern myth critic, Northrop Frye, translated this hypothesis into a universal scheme of literary history in his *Anatomy of Criticism* (1957), in which the major narrative *genres are related to the seasonal cycle. Other leading myth critics have included Gaston Bachelard, Richard Chase, and Leslie Fiedler. More recently, myth criticism has been widely dismissed as a form of *reductionism that neglects cultural and historical differences as well as the specific properties of literary works.

**mythopoeia** [mith-oh-**pee**-ă] (**mythopoesis**) [mith-ŏ-poh-**ees**-is]  The making of myths, either collectively in the *folklore and religion of a given (usually pre-literate) culture, or individually by a writer who elaborates a personal system of spiritual principles as in the writings of William Blake. The term is often used in a loose sense to describe any kind of writing that either draws upon older myths or resembles myths in subject-matter or imaginative scope. *Adjective*: **mythopoeic** or **mythopoetic**.

**mythos**  *See* PLOT.

**narratee** The imagined person whom the *narrator is assumed to be addressing in a given *narrative. The narratee is a notional figure within the 'space' of the *text itself, and is thus not to be confused either with the real reader or with the *implied reader (who is addressed by the *implied author at a separate 'level'). Narratees are often hard to identify clearly, since they are not usually described or characterized explicitly. In some works, though, they appear as minor characters, especially in a *frame story (e.g. the Wedding Guest in Coleridge's 'The Rime of the Ancient Mariner'), and in some they even function as narrators as well: Lockwood, the narratee of Nelly's *embedded narratives in *Wuthering Heights*, is the narrator of the story as a whole.

**narration** The process of relating a sequence of events; or another term for a *narrative. In the first sense, narration is often distinguished from other kinds of writing (*dialogue, description, commentary) which may be included in a narrative; it is also distinguished from the events recounted, i.e. from the *story, and from the narrative itself. *Verb*: **narrate**.

**narrative** [na-ră-tiv] A telling of some true or fictitious event or connected sequence of events, recounted by a *narrator to a *narratee (although there may be more than one of each). Narratives are to be distinguished from descriptions of qualities, states, or situations, and also from dramatic enactments of events (although a dramatic work may also include narrative speeches). A narrative will consist of a set of events (the *story) recounted in a process of narration (or *discourse), in which the events are selected and arranged in a particular order (the *plot). The category of narratives includes both the shortest accounts of events (e.g. *the cat sat on the mat*, or a brief news item) and the longest historical or biographical works, diaries, travelogues, etc., as well as novels, ballads, epics, short stories, and other fictional forms. In the study of fiction, it is usual to divide novels and shorter stories into *first-person narratives and *third-person narratives. As an adjective, 'narrative' means 'characterized by or relating to story-telling': thus **narrative technique** is the method of telling stories, and **narrative poetry** is the class of poems (including ballads, epics, and verse romances) that tell stories, as distinct from dramatic and *lyric poetry. Some theorists of *narratology have attempted to isolate the quality or set of properties that distinguishes narrative from non-narrative writings: this is called **narrativity**.

**Further reading:** Michael J. Toolan, *Narrative* (2nd edn, 2001).

**narratology** A term used since 1969 to denote the branch of literary study devoted to the analysis of *narratives, and more specifically of forms of narration and varieties of *narrator. Narratology as a modern theory is associated chiefly with European *structuralism, although older studies of narrative forms and devices, as far back as Aristotle's *Poetics* (4th century BCE) can also be regarded as narratological works. Modern narratology may be dated from Vladimir Propp's *Morphology of the Folktale* (1928), with its theory of narrative *functions.

**Further reading:** Mieke Bal, *Narratology* (3rd edn, 2009).

**(((⊕))) SEE WEB LINKS**

• Living Handbook of Narratology: reference resource at Hamburg University, offering full articles on key concepts.

**narrator** [nă-**ray**-ter] One who tells, or is assumed to be telling, the story in a given *narrative. In modern analysis of fictional narratives, the narrator is the imagined 'voice' transmitting the story, and is distinguished both from the real author (who may have written other tales with very different narrators) and from the *implied author (who does not recount the story, but is inferred as the authority responsible for selecting it and inventing a narrator for it). Narrators vary according to their degree of participation in the story: in *first-person narratives they are involved either as witnesses or as participants in the events of the story, whereas in *third-person narratives they stand outside those events; an *omniscient narrator stands outside the events but has special privileges such as access to characters' unspoken thoughts, and knowledge of events happening simultaneously in different places. Narrators also differ in the degree of their overtness: some are given noticeable characteristics and personalities (as in first-person narratives and in some third-person narratives; *see* INTRUSIVE NARRATOR), whereas 'covert' narrators are identified by no more than a 'voice' (as in most third-person narratives). Further distinctions are made between reliable narrators, whose accounts of events we are obliged to trust, and *unreliable narrators, whose accounts may be partial, ill-informed, or otherwise misleading: most third-person narrators are reliable, but some first-person narrators are unreliable. In a dramatic work, a narrator is a performer who recounts directly to the audience a summary of events preceding or during a scene or act. *See also* POINT OF VIEW.

**naturalism** A more deliberate kind of *realism in novels, stories, and plays, usually involving a view of human beings as passive victims of natural forces and social environment. As a literary movement, naturalism was initiated in France by Jules and Edmond Goncourt with their novel *Germinie Lacerteux* (1865), but it came to be led by Émile Zola, who claimed a 'scientific' status for his studies of impoverished characters miserably subjected to hunger, sexual obsession, and hereditary defects in *Thérèse Raquin* (1867), *Germinal* (1885), and many other novels. Naturalist fiction aspired to a sociological objectivity, offering detailed and fully researched investigations into unexplored corners of modern society—railways in Zola's *La Bête humaine* (1890), the department store in his *Au Bonheur des dames* (1883)—while enlivening this with a new sexual sensationalism. Other novelists and storytellers associated with naturalism include Alphonse Daudet and Guy de Maupassant in France, Theodore Dreiser and Frank Norris in the United States, and George Moore and George Gissing in England; the most significant work of naturalism in English being Dreiser's *Sister Carrie* (1900). In the theatre, Henrik Ibsen's play *Ghosts* (1881), with its stress on heredity, encouraged an important tradition of dramatic naturalism led by August Strindberg, Gerhart Hauptmann, and Maxim Gorky; in a somewhat looser sense, the realistic plays of Anton Chekhov are sometimes grouped with the naturalist phase of European drama at the turn of the century. The term **naturalistic** in drama usually has a broader application, denoting a very detailed illusion of real life on the stage, especially in speech, costume, and sets. *See also* VERISIMILITUDE, *VERISMO*.

**Further reading:** David Baguley, *Naturalist Fiction* (1990).

**negative capability** The phrase used by the English poet John Keats to describe the quality of selfless receptivity necessary to a true poet. In a letter to his brothers (December 1817), he writes at once it struck me, what quality went to form a Man of Achievement especially in Literature & which Shakespeare possessed so enormously—I mean *Negative Capability*, that is when man is capable of being in uncertainties, Mysteries, doubts, without any irritable reaching after fact & reason.

He goes on to criticize Coleridge for not being 'content with half knowledge'; and in later letters complains of the 'egotistical' and philosophical bias of Wordsworth's poetry. By negative capability, then, Keats seems to have meant a poetic capacity to efface one's own mental identity by immersing it sympathetically and spontaneously within the subject described, as Shakespeare was thought to have done.

**négritude** [nay-gri-tood] The slogan (literally 'negro-ness') of a cultural movement launched by black students in Paris in 1932, subsequently influencing many black writers, especially in the French-speaking world. The movement aimed to reassert traditional African cultural values against the French colonial policy of assimilating blacks into white culture. Its two most important figures were the Senegalese poet and politician Léopold Sédar Senghor and the Martiniquan poet and politician Aimé Césaire, and its literary masterpiece is Césaire's *Cahier d'un retour au pays natal* (1938). Senghor defined *négritude* very broadly as 'the sum total of the values of the civilization of the African world,' understood in terms of 'intuitive reason' and 'cosmic rhythm'. The influential journal *Présence Africaine*, founded in 1947, promoted this ideal. A later, more politically radical generation of black writers, however, questioned the movement's limited aims: as Wole Soyinka wrote, 'the tiger does not proclaim his tigritude—he pounces'.

**Further reading:** Lilyan Kesteloot, *Black Writers in French: A Literary History of Négritude* (1991).

**nemesis** [nem-ĭ-sis] (plural **-eses**) Retribution or punishment for wrongdoing; or the agent carrying out such punishment, often personified as Nemesis, a minor Greek goddess responsible for executing the vengeance of the gods against erring humans. The term is applied especially to the retribution meted out to the *protagonist of a *tragedy for his or her insolence or *hubris. *See also* POETIC JUSTICE.

**neoclassicism** The literary principle according to which the writing and *criticism of poetry and drama were to be guided by rules and precedents derived from the best ancient Greek and Roman authors;

a codified form of *classicism that dominated French literature in the 17th and 18th centuries, with a significant influence on English writing, especially from c.1660 to c.1780. In a more general sense, often employed in contrast with *Romanticism, the term has also been used to describe the characteristic world-view or value-system of this 'Age of Reason', denoting a preference for rationality, clarity, restraint, order, and *decorum, and for general truths rather than particular insights. In its more immediately literary sense as a habitual deference to Greek and Roman models in literary theory and practice, neoclassicism emerged from the rediscovery of Aristotle's *Poetics* (4th century BCE) by Italian scholars in the 16th century, notably by J. C. Scaliger, whose dogmatic interpretation of the dramatic *unities in his *Poetica* (1561) profoundly affected the course of French drama. Along with Aristotle's theory of poetry as imitation and his classification of *genres, the principles of the Roman poet Horace as expounded in his *Ars Poetica* (c.20 BCE) dominated the **neoclassical** or **neoclassic** view of literature: these included the principle of decorum by which the style must suit the subject-matter, and the belief that art must both delight and instruct. The central assumption of neoclassicism was that the ancient authors had already attained perfection, so that the modern author's chief task was to imitate them—the imitation of Nature and the imitation of the ancients amounting to the same thing. Accordingly, the approved genres of classical literature—*epic, *tragedy, *comedy, *elegy, *ode, *epistle, *eclogue, *epigram, *fable, and *satire—were adopted as the favoured forms in this period. The most influential summary of neoclassical doctrine is Boileau's verse treatise *L'Art poétique* (1674); its equivalent in English is Alexander Pope's *Essay on Criticism* (1711). In England, neoclassicism reached its height in the *Augustan Age, when its general view of the world was presented memorably in Pope's *Essay on Man* (1733–4). Some modern critics refer to the period 1660–1780 in England as the 'Neoclassical period', but as an inclusive label this is misleading in that one very important development in this period—the emergence of the *novel—falls outside the realm of neoclassicism, there being no acknowledged classical model for the new form.

**Further reading:** Craig A. Kallendorf (ed.), *A Companion to the Classical Tradition* (2007).

**neologism** [ni-**ol**-ŏ-jizm]  A word or phrase newly invented or newly introduced into a language. *Verb*: **neologize**. *See also* COINAGE, NONCE WORD, PORTMANTEAU WORD.

**Neoplatonism** A philosophical and religious system that both rivalled and influenced Christianity from the 3rd to the 6th century, and was derived from the work of the Greek philosopher Plato (427–347 BCE) along with elements of oriental mysticism. The founder of Neoplatonism was Plotinus (205–270 CE), who constructed an elaborate hierarchy of spiritual levels through which the individual soul could ascend from physical existence to merge with the One. Interest in Neoplatonic philosophy, often associated with magic and demonology, was revived in the *Renaissance. *See also* PLATONISM.

**neo-realism** Any revival of *realism in fiction, especially in novels and stories describing the lives of the poor in a contemporary setting. The term is associated especially with the dominant trend of Italian fiction in the 1940s and 1950s, led by Cesare Pavese, Alberto Moravia, and Elio Vittorini, and with the parallel movement in Italian cinema of the same period, led by Roberto Rossellini and Vittorio de Sica. *See also* VERISMO.

**neuronovel (syndrome novel)** A term coined by the journalist-critic Marco Roth in a 2009 magazine article, 'The Rise of the Neuronovel', to describe a number of recent British and American novels in which leading characters are affected and largely defined by neurological disorders. The principal cases are Ian McEwan's *Enduring Love* (1997), in which one character suffers from de Clérambault's syndrome; Jonathan Lethem's *Motherless Brooklyn* (1999), in which the narrator has Tourette's syndrome; Mark Haddon's *The Curious Incident of the Dog in the Night-Time* (2001), told by an autistic narrator; McEwan's *Saturday* (2005), featuring a neurosurgeon who recognizes another character's hostile manner as symptomatic of Huntingdon's chorea; and Richard Powers's *The Echo Maker* (2006), about a case of Capgras syndrome. Jonathan Franzen's family novel *The Corrections* (2001), in which the father has Parkinsonism, is sometimes referred to as another of these 'syndrome' novels.

Although such afflictions as amnesia and multiple-personality disorder had been used before as plot devices in popular thrillers, and Martin Amis's *Yellow Dog* (2003) likewise transforms its protagonist's personality by means of a brain injury, the neuronovel draws more directly on neuroscientific ideas of cognition. Unlike the novel of ideas, in which questions of cognition and consciousness may arise in discussion (as they do, for example, in David Lodge's *campus novel *Thinks . . . *(2002)), the neuronovel incorporates elements of neuroscientific knowledge into its constructions of character and sometimes its narrative perspective. The phenomenon appears to arise from the growing prestige and intellectual resonance of cognitive science since the 1980s, which entered the literary world through such works as neurologist Oliver Sacks's *The Man Who Mistook His Wife for a Hat* (1985).

**Further reading:** T. J. Lustig and James Peacock (eds), *Diseases and Disorders in Contemporary Fiction: The Syndrome Syndrome* (2013).

**New Apocalypse** A short-lived literary movement that emerged in Britain between 1938 and 1943, announced by the appearance of an anthology of essays, poems, and stories, *The New Apocalypse*, in 1939. Dylan Thomas, who was not an active member of the Apocalypse group, contributed one poem and one story (each of which had already appeared elsewhere), but the dominant figures were J. F. Hendry, Henry Treece, Dorian Cooke, and Norman McCaig (later known as MacCaig). Hendry's Introduction declared that Apocalyptic writing was concerned with 'the collapse of social forms and the emergence of new and more organic ones. . . . it occurs where expression breaks through the structure of language to become more organic', and expressed the hope of replacing the bankrupt systems of contemporary politics, philosophy, and even science with a new conception of 'the wholeness of man'. The Apocalypse writers saw themselves as continuing the aims of *surrealism in cultivating the power of the unconscious mind, and its poetry is often violently mythological. Two further anthologies appeared, *The White Horseman* (1941) and *The Crown and the Sickle* (1943), but the group was dispersed by war service and eventually blended into the larger current of 1940s writing that became known as the 'New Romanticism', in which Thomas was the most prominent figure.

**Further reading:** A. T. Tolley, *The Poetry of the Forties* (1985).

**New Comedy** The name given to the kind of *comedy that superseded the *Old Comedy of Aristophanes in Athens from the late 4th century BCE, providing the basis for later Roman comedy and eventually for the comic theatre of Molière and Shakespeare. Preceded by a phase of 'middle comedy' (of which almost nothing has survived), New Comedy abandoned topical *satire in favour of fictional plots based on contemporary life: these portrayed the tribulations of young lovers caught up among *stock characters such as the miserly father and the boastful soldier. The *chorus was reduced to a musical interlude. The chief exponent of New Comedy was Menander, of whose many works only one complete play, *Dyskolos (The Bad-Tempered Man,* 317 BCE), survives, along with several fragments. Greek New Comedy was further adapted and developed in Rome by Plautus and Terence in the early 2nd century BCE. *See also* ROMANTIC COMEDY.

**New Criticism** A movement in American literary *criticism from the 1930s to the 1960s, concentrating on the verbal complexities and ambiguities of short poems considered as self-sufficient objects without attention to their origins or effects. The name comes from John Crowe Ransom's book *The New Criticism* (1941), in which he surveyed the theories developed in England by T. S. Eliot, I. A. Richards, and William Empson, together with the work of the American critic Yvor Winters. Ransom called for a more 'objective' criticism focusing on the intrinsic qualities of a work rather than on its biographical or historical context; and his students Cleanth Brooks and Robert Penn Warren had already provided a very influential model of such an approach in their college textbook *Understanding Poetry* (1938), which helped to make New Criticism the academic orthodoxy for the next twenty years. Other critics grouped under this heading, despite their differences, include Allen Tate, R. P. Blackmur, W. K. Wimsatt Jr, and Kenneth Burke. Influenced by T. S. Eliot's view of poetry's *autotelic status, and by the detailed *semantic analyses of I. A. Richards in *Practical Criticism* (1929) and Empson in *Seven Types of Ambiguity* (1930), the American New Critics repudiated 'extrinsic' criteria for understanding poems, dismissing them under such names as the *affective fallacy and the *intentional fallacy. Moreover, they sought to overcome the traditional distinction between *form and *content: for them, a poem was ideally an 'organic unity' in which tensions were brought to equilibrium. Their favoured terms of analysis—*irony, *paradox, *imagery, *metaphor, and *symbol—tended to neglect questions of *genre, and were not successfully transferred to the study of dramatic and *narrative works. Many later critics—often unsympathetic to the New Critics' Southern religious conservatism—accused them of cutting literature off from history, but their impact has in some ways been irreversible, especially in replacing biographical source-study with text-centred approaches. The outstanding works of New Criticism are Brooks's *The Well-Wrought Urn* (1947) and Wimsatt's *The Verbal Icon* (1954).

**New Formalism (Neoformalism)** A movement in American poetry of the 1980s and 1990s that returned, after the prolonged dominance of *free verse, to traditional *metres, *stanza forms, *rhyme, logical syntax, and comprehensible narrative or discursive exposition. There were a number of distinguished 'old' formalist poets writing at that time, including Anthony Hecht, Howard Nemerov, Richard Wilbur, and Donald Justice (of whom the last three contributed to the inaugural issue of the Neoformalist magazine *The Formalist* in 1990); but the label was applied to recently emerging poets who had been born after 1940, especially to Timothy Steele, Dana Goia, Gjertrud Schnackenberg, Mark Jarman, Brad Leithauser, Marilyn Hacker, and Vikram Seth, most of whom published notable collections in the mid-1980s. The movement's origins may be traced to the launch in 1980 by Jarman and Robert McDowell of *The Reaper*, a magazine dedicated to formal verse and *narrative verse (the movement overlaps with a revival of narrative verse sometimes called the 'New Narrative'). There followed two significant anthologies, *Strong Measures: Contemporary American Poetry in Traditional Forms* (ed. P. Dacey and D. Jauss, 1986) and *The Direction of Poetry* (ed. R. Richman, 1988), along with some critical defences of the Neoformalist position, most notably Goia's essay 'Notes on the New Formalism' (1987), in which he declares 'the bankruptcy of the *confessional mode', and Steele's book *Missing Measures: Modern Poetry and the Revolt Against Meter* (1990), which regrets the wrong turn taken by *modernism. An important later anthology is *Rebel Angels: 25 Poets of the New Formalism* (ed. M. Jarman and D. Mason, 1996).

**Further reading:** Robert McPhillips, *The New Formalism* (2005).

**new historicism** A term applied to a trend in American academic literary studies in the 1980s that emphasized the historical nature of literary texts and at the same time (in contrast with older *historicisms) the 'textual' nature of history. As part of a wider reaction against purely formal or linguistic critical approaches such as the *New Criticism and *deconstruction, the new historicists, led by Stephen Greenblatt, drew new connections between literary and non-literary texts, breaking down the familiar distinctions between a text and its historical 'background' as conceived in established historical forms of criticism. Inspired by Michel Foucault's concepts of *discourse and power, they attempted to show how literary works are implicated in the power-relations of their time, not as secondary 'reflections' of any coherent world-view but as active participants in the continual remaking of meanings. New historicism is less a system of interpretation than a set of shared assumptions about the relationship between literature and history, and an essayistic style that often develops general reflections from a startling historical or anthropological anecdote. Greenblatt's books *Renaissance Self-Fashioning* (1980) and *Shakespearean Negotiations* (1988) are the exemplary models. Other scholars of *Early Modern ('Renaissance') culture associated with him include Jonathan Goldberg, Stephen Orgel, Lisa Jardine, and Louis Montrose. The term has been applied to similar developments in the study of *Romanticism, such as the work of Jerome McGann and Marjorie Levinson. A major concern of new historicism, following Foucault, is the cultural process by which subversion or dissent is ultimately contained by 'power'.

**Further reading:** John Brannigan, *New Historicism and Cultural Materialism* (1998).

**New Humanism** The slogan of a small but influential group of American critics in the 1920s and 1930s, led by Irving Babbitt and Paul Elmer More, and including among its champions Norman Foerster and (for a short period before defecting to an incompatible position) Stuart P. Sherman. It derived its concept of humanism and many of its literary principles from the critical writings of Matthew Arnold, upholding an ethical doctrine of self-restraint in place of formal religious doctrine and opposing the excessive individualism of the *Romantic tradition in the name of *classical order and harmony. It was especially hostile to the Romantic cult of nature, and tended to blame the nationalism exhibited in the First World War upon Romantic forms of irrationalism. Its principal joint publication was a book of essays, *Humanism and America* (1930) edited by Foerster, who in the same year published his own book, *Towards Standards*; but its positions can be seen to have developed from earlier writings including some of More's essays in his long sequence of *Shelburne Essays* (11 vols, 1904–21) and Babbitt's books *Rousseau and Romanticism* (1919) and *Democracy and Leadership* (1924). Among its more sceptical followers was T. S. Eliot, who had studied under Babbitt and sympathized with his anti-Romantic principles but came to regard the New Humanism as incoherent because lacking in secure religious foundations.

**Further reading:** Thomas R. Nevin, *Irving Babbitt* (1984).

**New Journalism** The name given to two distinct developments in modern journalism, the first in Britain in the 1880s, the second in the United States in the 1960s and 1970s. The original New Journalism involved a successful attempt to make news more appealing to readers, both in content and presentation, with stronger emphasis on 'human interest' angles and interviews in more concise articles, the columns of print being broken up by cross-heads and illustrations. This new style was pioneered by W. T. Stead at the *Pall Mall Gazette* from 1886 and T. P. O'Connor at *The Star* (from 1888), and became the norm in the early 20th century.

Of more direct literary interest, the later American movement involved a new blend of fictional presentation with journalistic research and reportage. The first important example, which provoked controversy about its techniques and credibility (was it fiction, '*faction', 'non-fiction novel' or highly subjective feature story?), was Truman Capote's *In Cold Blood* (1966), an account of a murder case in Kansas, presented in novelistic form but based on journalistic research and interviews. Other major examples in the late 1960s were Hunter S. Thompson's *Hell's Angels* (1967, about motorbike gangs), Tom Wolfe's *The Electric Kool-Aid Acid Test* (1968, about the drug subcultures of California), and Norman Mailer's *Armies of the Night* (1968, about protests against the Vietnam War). Wolfe's anthology-cum-*manifesto, *The New Journalism* (1973), justified its imaginative methods on the grounds that the objectivity of orthodox journalism was illusory; and he continued the tradition in *The Right Stuff* (1979, about the world of astronauts) and other works. Thompson's unusual blend of fact and fiction, which he called 'gonzo journalism', is characterized by sequences of unbelievable drug consumption and grotesque hallucination, notably in *Fear and Loathing in Las Vegas* (1971), a novel in which the journalist narrator fails to cover a motorbike race and a legal convention on narcotics because he and his attorney are deranged by their superhuman intake of illegal substances. Among other important examples are Michael Herr's *Dispatches* (1977), a widely admired account of the strange unreality of the Vietnam War, and the essays of Joan Didion in *Slouching Towards Bethlehem* (1968) and *The White Album* (1979), both partly about Californian subcultures. A central implication of this movement was that American actuality in the age of Vietnam and the Watergate scandal had become far stranger than fiction, and required the artistic resources of the novelist to capture its enormities.

**Further reading:** Marc Weingarten, *Who's Afraid of Tom Wolfe?* (2005).

**New Woman writing** A body of fiction and drama concerning the 'New Woman', a type of self-assertive younger woman much discussed in the British press in the 1890s and the early *Edwardian period as the focus for public debates about marriage and women's rights. The term was coined in an article in March 1894 by the feminist novelist Sarah Grand, and reappeared as the title of an anti-feminist satirical play *The New Woman*, by Sidney Grundy in September of that year, after which it stuck in the public mind as the term for independent-minded women seeking emancipation (or in unsympathetic eyes for misguided and 'unwomanly' women). As popularly caricatured, the New Woman was a hopelessly idealistic creature attempting to reverse accepted gender roles by taking the sexual initiative with men, smoking cigarettes, and immodestly riding bicycles. In literary works, however, she is more often a tragic victim of marriage laws, tied to a syphilitic or drunken husband. New Woman writing is usually seen as commencing in 1893 with the appearance of the short-story collection *Keynotes* by 'George Egerton' (Chavelita Dunne) and of Grand's novel *The Heavenly Twins*. These works were followed by Mona Caird's *Daughters of Danaus* (1894), by Grant Allen's scandalous novel about an extramarital affair, *The Woman Who Did* (1895), by Thomas Hardy's *Jude the Obscure* (1895), and by many other fictions by women and men about loveless marriages and runaway wives. New Woman figures appeared in dramatic works too, as in Arthur Wing Pinero's *The Notorious Mrs Ebbsmith* (1895) and Bernard Shaw's *Mrs Warren's Profession* (published 1893, performed 1902). By the time of H. G. Wells's novel *Ann Veronica* and St John Hankin's play *The Last of the De Mullins* (both 1909), the self-possessed heroines of these works were familiar enough not to be 'new'.

**Further reading:** Sally Ledger, *The New Woman* (1997).

**New York Intellectuals** The collective title given to an important group of American literary and cultural critics active in the period from the late 1930s to the 1960s, and associated with the periodical *Partisan Review*. The group was inspired by the example of the older critic Edmund Wilson, whose critical outlook in *The Triple Thinkers* (1938) and other works synthesized a semi-Marxist view of culture with sympathy for the achievements of literary *modernism and some interest in the implications of Freudian psychoanalysis. This combination of liberal-leftist (and emphatically anti-Stalinist) politics with concern for literature in its social and psychological contexts became characteristic of the group. The principal figures in its early phase were Lionel Trilling, Philip Rahv, Delmore Schwartz, Alfred Kazin, Richard Chase, Diana Trilling, Mary McCarthy, and Dwight McDonald; they were joined at later stages by Irving Howe, Richard Poirier, Elizabeth Hardwick, Leslie Fiedler, and Susan Sontag, among others. Of these, Schwartz, McCarthy, and Hardwick are better known for their creative than for their critical works. Several of the *Partisan Review* critics made important contributions to the understanding of the American literary tradition in particular, as in Kazin's *On Native Grounds* (1942), Rahv's essay 'Paleface and Redskin' (1949), Chase's *The American Novel and its Tradition* (1957), and Fiedler's *Love and Death in the American Novel* (1960). Major representative works of the group include Trilling's *The Liberal Imagination* (1951) and Rahv's *The Myth and the Powerhouse* (1965).

**Further reading:** Alexander Bloom, *Prodigal Sons: The New York Intellectuals and their World* (1986).

**New York school** Originally a term of art criticism applied in the 1950s and after to the group of abstract expressionist painters working in New York, including Mark Rothko and Jackson Pollock; but the term was reapplied, at first by John Bernard Myers in a 1961 magazine article, to a group of contemporary poets active in the same city. The principal poets of the group were Frank O'Hara (1926–66), John Ashbery (b. 1927), Kenneth Koch (1925–2002), and James Schuyler (1922–91); others who came to be grouped with them included Ted Berrigan, Barbara Guest, and Harry Mathews. The transposition of the group term from painting to poetry is appropriate, since one of the common characteristics of these poets was an involvement with the world of visual arts: Ashbery was for many years an art critic by profession, and both O'Hara and Schuyler worked at the Museum of Modern Art. An interest in aesthetic problems posed by visual art is often evident in their poems, notably in Ashbery's major long poem 'Self-Portrait in a Convex Mirror' (1975). As a distinctive group, they distanced themselves from what they felt to be the solemnity of their predecessors, especially T. S. Eliot and Robert Lowell, by cultivating tones of nonchalant colloquial informality and by showing appreciation of American popular cultural forms of music and cinema. Their work shows a variety of *modernist influences, particularly that of literary *surrealism.

**Further reading:** Geoff Ward, *Statutes of Liberty: The New York School of Poets* (2nd edn, 2001).

**Newgate novel** A term applied to certain popular English novels of the 1830s that are based on legends of 18th-century highwaymen and other notorious criminals as recorded in the *Newgate Calendar* (*c*.1773). Edward Bulwer's *Paul Clifford* (1830) and *Eugene Aram* (1832), along with W. H. Ainsworth's *Rookwood* (1834) and *Jack Sheppard* (1840), were the principal examples, and all came under fierce attack from critics, including W. M. Thackeray, who accused them of encouraging crime. Dickens's *Oliver Twist* (1838) shares many features of Newgate fiction, but by stressing the squalor and misery of the criminal world it managed to escape the censure meted out to Ainsworth and Bulwer.

**nō (noh)** A traditional form of Japanese drama characterized by highly ritualized chant and gesture, and its use of masked actors. Combining music, dance, and speech in prose and verse, the *nō* play derives from religious rituals, and is performed by an all-male cast, originally for an aristocratic audience. More than 200 such plays survive from as early as the 14th century, mostly on religious and mythological subjects. English translations appeared in the early 20th century, influencing the work of Ezra Pound, W. B. Yeats, and Bertolt Brecht.

**noir** A term derived from French critical usage, both literary and cinematic, and applied in English to a kind of crime novel or *thriller characterized less by rational investigation (as in the classic *detective story) than by violence, treachery, and moral confusion. In French usage, *film noir* is a period style of 1940s and 1950s American movie thriller commonly adapted from *hard-boiled detective fiction (as in the film versions of *The Big Sleep*, *The Maltese Falcon*, and others) and distinguished cinematically by the use of menacing shadows and camera angles, while the *roman noir* (a term once applied to *Gothic novels) is broadly equivalent to the thriller. Although noir fiction derives in important ways from the hard-boiled school of detective writing and overlaps with it at some points (especially in the case of James M. Cain's work), it can be distinguished from most detective stories and from other kinds of thriller by its powerful tendency to dissolve orderly distinctions between the roles of criminal and hero: thus in Cain's *Double Indemnity* (1936) and *The Postman Always Rings Twice* (1934), the protagonists are lured into murder by sexual obsession. In noir fiction generally, rational detachment is overwhelmed by criminal temptation and bewildered by multiple deceptions, and the reader is commonly invited to adopt the point of view of a murderer or of an accessory to serious crime. Leading practitioners include Jim Thompson (e.g. *The Killer Inside Me*, 1952), Patricia Highsmith (in *The Talented Mr Ripley*, 1955, and its sequels), and James Ellroy (e.g. *The Black Dahlia*, 1987).

**Further reading:** Lee Horsley, *The Noir Thriller* (2001).

**nom de plume**  A pen-name, i.e. a pseudonym under which a writer's work is published, as Marian Evans's novels appeared under the name of 'George Eliot'.

**nonce word**  A word invented to be used for a single specific occasion; or an old word of which only one occurrence has been found. *See also* COINAGE, NEOLOGISM, PORTMANTEAU WORD.

**nonsense verse**  A kind of humorous poetry that amuses by deliberately using strange non-existent words and illogical ideas. Its masters in English are Edward Lear and Lewis Carroll, followed by G. K. Chesterton and Ogden Nash. Classics of the genre are Lear's 'The Owl and the Pussy-Cat' (1871) and his *limericks, along with the songs in Carroll's *Through the Looking-Glass* (1871), including 'The Walrus and the Carpenter' and the celebrated 'Jabberwocky'. *See also* DOGGEREL, JINGLE, LIGHT VERSE.

**nouveau roman, le**  [noo-voh roh-**mah**$^n$]  The French term ('new novel') applied since the mid-1950s to experimental novels by a group of French writers who rejected many of the traditional elements of novel-writing, such as the sequential *plot and the analysis of characters' motives. The leading light of this group was Alain Robbe-Grillet, whose essays on the novel in *Pour un nouveau roman* (1963) argue for a neutral registering of sensations and things rather than an interpretation of events or a study of characters: these principles were put into practice most famously in his *anti-novel *La Jalousie* (1957). Other notable *nouveaux romans* include Nathalie Sarraute's *Le Planétarium* (1959) and Michel Butor's *La Modification* (1957); Sarraute's *Tropismes* (1938) is often cited as the first *nouveau roman*.

**Further reading:** Ann Jefferson, *The Nouveau Roman and the Poetics of Fiction* (1980).

**nouvelle**  *See* NOVELLA.

**NOVEL**

Nearly always an extended fictional prose *narrative, although some novels are very short, some are non-fictional, some have been written in verse, and some do not even tell a story. Such exceptions help to indicate that the novel as a literary *genre is itself exceptional: it disregards the constraints that govern other literary forms, and acknowledges no obligatory structure, style, or subject-matter. Thriving on this openness and flexibility, the novel has become the most important literary genre of the modern age, superseding the *epic, the *romance, and other narrative forms. Novels can be distinguished from *short stories and *novellas by their greater length, which permits fuller, subtler development of characters and themes. (Confusingly, it is a shorter form of tale, the Italian *novella*, that gives the novel its name in English.) There is no established minimum length for a novel, but it is normally at least long enough to justify its publication in an independent volume, unlike the short story. The novel differs from the prose romance in that a greater degree of *realism is expected of it, and that it tends to describe a recognizable secular social world, often in a sceptical and prosaic manner inappropriate to the marvels of romance. The novel has frequently incorporated the structures and languages of non-fictional prose forms (history, autobiography, journalism, travel writing), even to the point where the non-fictional element outweighs the fictional. It is normally expected of a novel that it should have at least one character, and preferably several characters shown in processes of change and social relationship; a *plot, or some arrangement of narrated events, is another normal requirement. Special *subgenres of the novel have grown up around particular kinds of character (the *Künstlerroman*, the spy novel), setting (the *historical novel, the *campus novel), and plot (the detective novel); while other kinds of novel are distinguished either by their structure (the *epistolary novel, the *picaresque novel) or by special emphases on character (the *Bildungsroman*) or ideas (the *roman à thèse*).

Although some ancient prose narratives like Petronius' *Satyricon* (1st century CE) can be called novels, and although some significant forerunners of the novel—including François Rabelais's *Gargantua*

(1534)—appeared in the 16th century, it is the publication in Spain of the first part of Miguel de Cervantes's *Don Quixote de la Mancha* in 1605 that is most widely accepted as announcing the arrival of the true novel. In France the inaugural landmark was Madame de Lafayette's *La Princesse de Clèves* (1678), while in England Daniel Defoe is regarded as the founder of the English novel with his *Robinson Crusoe* (1719) and *Moll Flanders* (1722). The novel achieved its predominance in the 19th century, when Charles Dickens and other writers found a huge audience through serial publication, and when the conventions of realism were consolidated. In the 20th century a division became more pronounced between the popular forms of novel and the various experiments of *modernism and *postmodernism—from the *stream of consciousness to the *anti-novel; but repeated reports of the 'death of the novel' have been greatly exaggerated. *Adjective*: **novelistic**. *See also* FICTION.

**Further reading:** Jeremy Hawthorn, *Studying the Novel* (6th edn, 2010); David Lodge, *The Art of Fiction* (1992).

**novelette** A trivial or cheaply sensational novel or *romance; or (in a neutral sense, especially in the USA) a short novel or extended short story, i.e. a *novella. The adjective **novelettish** carries the unfavourable connotations of the first sense.

**novella** [nŏ-**vel**-ă] A fictional tale in prose, intermediate in length and complexity between a *short story and a *novel, and usually concentrating on a single event or chain of events, with a surprising turning point. Joseph Conrad's 'Heart of Darkness' (1902) is a fine example; Henry James and D. H. Lawrence also favoured the novella form. The term comes from the Italian word *novella* ('novelty'; plural *novelle*), which was applied to the much shorter stories found in Boccaccio's *Decameron* (1349–53), until it was borrowed at the end of the 18th century by Goethe and other writers in Germany, where the novella (German, *Novelle*) in its modern sense became established as an important literary *genre. In France it is known as the *nouvelle*. *See also* CONTE, NOVELETTE.

***Novelle*** [no-**vel**-ĕ] (plural -*ellen*) The German term for a fictional prose tale that concentrates on a single event or situation, usually with a surprising conclusion. The term, adopted from the Italian (*see* NOVELLA), was introduced in 1795 by J. W. von Goethe. The outstanding German tradition of *Novellen* includes works by Tieck, Kleist, and Thomas Mann, most of which conform (in terms of length) to the English sense of 'novella'.

**numbers** A term—now obsolete—formerly applied to poetry in general, by association with the counting of feet or syllables in regular verse *metres.

**nursery rhyme** A traditional verse or set of verses chanted to infants by adults as an initiation into rhyme and verbal rhythm. Most are hundreds of years old, and derive from songs, proverbs, riddles, *ballads, street cries, and other kinds of composition originally intended for adults, which have become almost meaningless outside their original contexts. Their exact origins are often obscure, although a few more recent examples are by known authors: 'Mary had a little lamb' was written by Sarah Josepha Hale in 1830. *See also* JINGLE, NONSENSE VERSE.

**obiter dicta** The Latin phrase ('things said in passing') sometimes used to refer to the table-talk or incidental remarks made by a writer or other person, of the kind recalled in biographies.

**objective correlative** An external equivalent for an internal state of mind; thus any object, scene, event, or situation that may be said to stand for or evoke a given mood or emotion, as opposed to a direct subjective expression of it. The phrase was given its vogue in modern criticism by T. S. Eliot in the rather tangled argument of his essay 'Hamlet and His Problems' (1919), in which he asserts that Shakespeare's *Hamlet* is an 'artistic failure' because Hamlet's emotion does not match the 'facts' of the play's action. The term is symptomatic of Eliot's preference—similar to that of *Imagism—for precise and definite poetic images evoking particular emotions, rather than the effusion of vague yearnings which Eliot and Ezra Pound criticized as a fault of 19th-century poetry.

**Objectivism** The doctrine of a small group of American poets in the 1930s led by William Carlos Williams and Louis Zukofsky, and including among its followers George Oppen, Carl Rakosi, and Charles Reznikoff. It derived most of its principles from those of *Imagism, such as precise evocation rather than subjective effusion, and it expressed admiration for the work of Ezra Pound, T. S. Eliot, Wallace Stevens, and other *modernist forerunners. An Objectivist movement was announced in 1931 with a special Objectivist issue of the Chicago magazine *Poetry* guest-edited by Zukofsky, in which he declared sincerity and 'objectification' to be the essential requirements of a poem. There followed in 1932 *An 'Objectivists' Anthology* edited again by Zukofsky, and in 1933 the foundation by Oppen of the Objectivist Press in New York City, which published Williams's *Collected Poems 1921–31* (1933) and Oppen's own volume, *Discrete Series* (1934). The intended movement then petered out as Oppen took up Communist activism and abandoned poetry for the next 28 years. Although Williams and Zukofsky continued to exert an influence by example upon later poets, the Objectivist label quickly fell into disuse.

**Further reading:** Peter Nicholls, *George Oppen and the Fate of Modernism* (2007).

**occasional verse** Poetry written for or prompted by a special occasion, e.g. a wedding, funeral, anniversary, birth, military or sporting victory, or scientific achievement. Poetic forms especially associated with occasional verse are the *epithalamion, the *elegy, and the *ode. Occasional verse may be serious, like Andrew Marvell's 'An Horation Ode upon Cromwell's Return from Ireland' (1650) and Walt Whitman's 'Passage to India' (1871), or light, like William Cowper's 'On the Death of Mrs Throckmorton's Bullfinch' (1789). Significant modern examples of occasional verse in English are W. B. Yeats's 'Easter, 1916', and W. H. Auden's 'September 1, 1939', 'August 1968', and 'Moon Landing'.

**occupatio** A rhetorical device (also known under the Greek name *paralipsis*) by which a speaker emphasizes something by pretending to pass over it: 'I will not mention the time when . . .' The device was favoured by Chaucer, who uses it frequently in his *Canterbury Tales*.

**octameter** [ok-**tamm**-ĕt-er] A metrical verse line of eight feet (*see* FOOT), or in most English verse a line of eight stresses. In English, **octametric** lines are rare on account of their unwieldy length, the best-known example of their use being in Edgar A. Poe's poem 'The Raven' (1845).

**octastich** *See* OCTAVE.

**octave (octet)** A group of eight verse lines forming the first part of a *sonnet (in its Italian or Petrarchan form); or a *stanza of eight lines. In the first and most frequently used sense, an octave usually rhymes *abbaabba*. In the second sense, it may also be called an **octastich**. The Spanish stanza form known as *octavas reales* is the equivalent of *ottava rima*. *See also* HUITAIN, OTTAVA RIMA, TRIOLET.

**octavo** [ok-**tay**-voh] A book size resulting from folding a printer's sheet of paper three times to make eight leaves (i.e. sixteen pages): thus a size smaller than *quarto but bigger than *duodecimo.

**octosyllabic** [ok-toh-sĭ-**lab**-ik]  Having eight syllables to the line.
Octosyllabic verse in English is usually written in the form of iambic
or trochaic *tetrameters. It appears in various forms including the *In
Memoriam* stanza, but is most commonly found in *couplets, both in
light *Hudibrastic verse and in more serious works such as
Wordsworth's poem beginning

> She was a phantom of delight
> When first she gleamed upon my sight

In medieval French poetry, octosyllabic couplets were used in *lais,
*fabliaux, and other kinds of poem.

**ode**  An elaborately formal *lyric poem, often in the form of a lengthy
ceremonious address to a person or abstract entity, always serious and
elevated in tone. There are two different classical models: in Greek, the
*epinicion or **choral ode** of Pindar devoted to public praise of athletes
(5th century BCE), and Horace's more privately reflective odes in Latin
(c.23–13BCE). Pindar composed his odes for performance by a *chorus,
using lines of varying length in a complex three-part structure of
*strophe, *antistrophe, and *epode corresponding to the chorus's
dancing movements (*see* PINDARIC), whereas Horace wrote literary odes
in regular *stanzas. Close English imitations of Pindar, such as Thomas
Gray's 'The Progress of Poesy' (1754), are rare, but a looser **irregular
ode** with varying lengths of strophes was introduced by Abraham
Cowley's 'Pindarique Odes' (1656) and followed by John Dryden,
William Collins, William Wordsworth (in 'Ode: Intimations of
Immortality' (1807)), and S. T. Coleridge, among others; this irregular
form of ode is sometimes called the **Cowleyan ode**. Odes in which the
same form of stanza is repeated regularly (*see* HOMOSTROPHIC) are
called **Horatian odes**: in English, these include the celebrated odes of
John Keats, notably 'Ode on a Grecian Urn' and 'Ode to a Nightingale'
(both 1820). *Adjective*: **odic.**

**Further reading:** Carol Maddison, *Apollo and the Nine: A History of the Ode*
(1960).

**OED**  The abbreviation widely used for the *Oxford English Dictionary*,
the most comprehensive dictionary of the English language, which has
been published under that title since 1933 (it was formerly the *New
English Dictionary on Historical Principles*, abbreviated as *NED* and
appearing in instalments from 1884). Apart from its sheer size, defining

414,825 words in twelve large volumes in its first full edition (1928), the significance of this work and of widespread references to it lies in its provision of 1.8 million quotations illustrating the first recorded written use of each word (subject, in many cases, to further discoveries) and later changes of usage or meaning. References are sometimes found to its Supplements, the first of these being issued in 1933, followed by a major four-volume replacement (1972–86); but these were subsequently incorporated into the enormous second edition of the *OED* published in twenty volumes in 1989 (defining 615,100 words with over 2.4 million quotations) and then in CD-ROM and online editions. This is commonly abbreviated as *OED2*. A third edition is in progress.

**Further reading:** Simon Winchester, *The Meaning of Everything* (2003).

**oeuvre** [ervr] The French word for a work, often used to refer instead to the total body of works produced by a given writer. A *chef d'oeuvre* is a given writer's principal work or masterpiece. *See also* CANON, CORPUS.

**off-Broadway** A New York theatrical term applied since the 1950s to dramatic productions staged in cheaper venues (mostly found in Greenwich Village and the Lower East Side) away from the main commercial theatres located on Broadway. An off-Broadway production was usually associated with the literary or at least relatively uncommercial kind of drama, but when it enjoyed increasing commercial success, the more experimental 'fringe' drama of the 1960s distanced itself from that taint by advertising itself as **off-off-Broadway** theatre.

**Old Comedy** The kind of *comedy produced in Athens during the 5th century BCE, before the emergence of the *New Comedy. Old Comedy is distinguished by its festive, farcical mood, by its *lampooning of living persons in topical *satire, and by its prominent use of a *chorus in grotesque masks and costumes. Its leading exponent, and the only one whose plays have survived, was Aristophanes, author of *The Clouds* (423 BCE) and *The Frogs* (405 BCE).

**Old English** The early form of the English language spoken and written between the 5th and the 12th centuries. Popularly known as 'Anglo-Saxon', a usage repudiated by most historians of the language, it evolved from a range of related Germanic dialects spoken by Angles, Saxons, and Jutes settling from northern Europe from the 5th century, further influenced by the arrival in northern and eastern England of Scandinavian settlers in the 9th and 10th centuries. In its written form, found from the late 6th century, it employed a slightly reduced and adapted version of the Roman alphabet. It is the language used in the *Anglo-Saxon Chronicle* commissioned by King Alfred in 890 and updated until the 12th century, of the great prose writer Aelfric (late 10th century), and of the epic poem *Beowulf*, which is thought to have been composed in the 8th century. Following the Norman Conquest of 1066 and its establishment of a French-speaking ruling order, the language evolved into a new form that is now called *Middle English.

**Further reading:** Peter S. Baker, *An Introduction to Old English*, 3rd edn (2012).

((**⊕**)) SEE WEB LINKS

• Woruldhord: Old English and Anglo-Saxon resource at University of Oxford.

**omniscient narrator** [om-**nish**-ĕnt] An 'all-knowing' kind of *narrator very commonly found in works of fiction written as *third-person narratives. The omniscient narrator has a full knowledge of the story's events and of the motives and unspoken thoughts of the various characters. He or she will also be capable of describing events happening simultaneously in different places—a capacity not normally available to the limited *point of view of *first-person narratives. *See also* INTRUSIVE NARRATOR.

**Onegin stanza** A *stanza comprising 14 lines of iambic *tetrameter, employing a complex rhyme-scheme adapted from that of the English *sonnet, incorporating three different forms of *quatrain followed by a couplet, in the sequence *ababccddeffegg*, with the *a, c,* and *e* rhymes always feminine and the others masculine. The stanza was invented by the Russian poet Alexander Pushkin and exhibited at length in his verse-novel *Eugene Onegin* (1833). The most notable revival of the stanza in English is in Vikram Seth's verse-novel *The Golden Gate* (1986).

**onomatopoeia** [on-ŏ-mat-ŏ-**pee**-ă] The use of words that seem to imitate the sounds they refer to (whack, fizz, crackle, hiss); or any combination of words in which the sound gives the impression of echoing the sense. This *figure of speech is often found in poetry, sometimes in prose. It relies more on conventional associations between verbal and non-verbal sounds than on the direct duplication of one by the other. *Adjective*: **onomatopoeic**.

**op. cit.** Abbreviated form of *opere citato* (Latin, 'in the work cited'), a formula employed in scholarly footnotes and endnotes when referring to a quotation from a work of which the title has already been specified, this reference usually being preceded by the name of the work's author. *See also* IBID., LOC. CIT.

**open form** A term popularized by the American poet Charles Olson, a leader of the *Black Mountain school of modern poetry, to indicate his preferred principle of verse composition, which should not follow regular structures of line and stanza but should reflect the energies and spontaneous processes of the poet's encounter with the subject, and in particular the natural intervals of breathing. The result in terms of the poem's layout and typography is commonly a spatial dispersal of lines and *strophes, even of words and syllables, across the page. His major statement of these principles, the essay 'Projective Verse' (1950) summarized Olson's own practice, that of his poetic mentors Ezra Pound and William Carlos Williams, and that of his co-thinker Robert Creeley, as 'Projectivism', although it is the term 'open form' that has been more widely adopted.

**opuscule** Any composition on a small scale, such as a *short story, an *epigram, *haiku, or one-act play.

**oral tradition** The passing on from one generation (and/or locality) to another of songs, chants, proverbs, and other verbal compositions within and between non-literate cultures; or the accumulated stock of works thus transmitted by word of mouth. *Ballads, *folktales, and other works emerging from an oral tradition will often be found in several different versions, because each performance is a fresh improvisation based around a 'core' of narrative incidents and *formulaic phrases. The state of dependence on the spoken word in oral cultures is known as **orality**.

**oratory** [o-rǎ-tri] The art of public speaking; or the exercise of this art in **orations**—formal speeches for public occasions. A literary style resembling public speech and its formal devices may be called **oratorical**. *See also* RHETORIC.

**orature** A *portmanteau term coined by the Kenyan novelist and playwright Ngugi wa Thiong'o to denote imaginative works of the *oral tradition usually referred to as 'oral literature'. The point of the coinage is to avoid suggesting that oral compositions belong to a lesser or derivative category.

**organic form**  A concept that likens literary works to living organisms forming themselves by a process of 'natural' growth. The doctrine of organic form, promoted in the early 19th century by S. T. Coleridge and subsequently favoured by American *New Criticism, argues that in an artistic work the whole is more than the mere sum of its component parts, and that *form and *content fuse indivisibly in an 'organic unity'. It rejects as 'mechanical' the *neoclassical concept of conformity to rules, along with the related assumption that form or style is an 'ornament' to a pre-existing content. It tends to be hostile to conceptions of *genre and *convention, as it is to the practice of *paraphrase. Carried to a dogmatic conclusion, its emphasis on unity condemns any literary analysis as a destructive abstraction; this attitude is sometimes referred to as **organicism**.

**Ossianism**  The craze for Celtic *folklore and *myth that was prompted by the appearance of two *epic poems, *Fingal* (1762) and *Temora* (1763), supposedly composed by Ossian (i.e. Oisin, the legendary 3rd-century Gaelic warrior and *bard, son of Finn or Fingal) and 'translated' by James Macpherson, a Scottish schoolteacher. The supposed discovery of an ancient northern epic had a great imaginative impact in Europe after the translation of 'Ossian' into German (1768–9) and French (1777): Goethe, Herder, and Napoleon Bonaparte were among the leading Ossianic enthusiasts. Even after 1805, when investigators found the epics to be forgeries concocted around some genuine Gaelic folklore, Macpherson's vision of the misty and melancholy Celtic world lived on in the Romantic imagination. *See also* ROMANTICISM, PREROMANTICISM.

**Further reading:** Fiona J. Stafford, *The Sublime Savage* (1988).

*ostranenie*  *See* DEFAMILIARIZATION.

*ottava rima*  [ot-**ahv**-ă-**ree**-mă]  A form of verse *stanza consisting of eight lines rhyming *abababcc*, usually employed for *narrative verse but sometimes used in *lyric poems. In its original Italian form ('eighth rhyme'), pioneered by Boccaccio in the 14th century and perfected by Ariosto in the 16th, it used *hendecasyllables; but the English version uses iambic *pentameters. It was introduced into English by Thomas

Wyatt in the 16th century, and later used by Byron in *Don Juan* (1819–24) as well as by Keats, Shelley, and Yeats.

**Oulipian** Belonging to or characteristic of the French experimental writers' group calling itself OULIPO or OuLiPo (Ouvroir de Littérature Potentielle) in the 1960s and thereafter. The group's founders in 1960 included the lapsed *surrealist writer Raymond Queneau and the mathematician François Le Lionnais, and they were joined by Jacques Roubaud (from 1966), Georges Perec (from 1967), and others, including some foreign members, notably the Italian author Italo Calvino (from 1973) and the American Harry Mathews, both then resident in Paris. The group's central purpose was to explore the literary possibilities of artificial constraints and mathematical combinations, for instance in the use of *lipograms such as Perec's novel *La Disparition* (1969), or in Queneau's extraordinary sonnet sequence *Cent mille milliards de poèmes* (1961), in which the lines could be recombined in an enormous number of possible permutations. Among the other major works of Oulipian experiment is Perec's novel *Vie mode d'emploi* (1978; translated as *Life: A User's Manual*). The group's most important collective work was *La littérature potentielle* (1973). For an introductory anthology in English, consult Warren F. Motte (ed. and trans.), *Oulipo: A Primer of Potential Literature* (1986).

**SEE WEB LINKS**
• OULIPO: official site of the group, in French.

**oxymoron** [oksi-**mor**-on] (plural **-mora**) A *figure of speech that combines two usually contradictory terms in a compressed *paradox, as in the word *bittersweet* or the phrase *living death*. **Oxymoronic** phrases, like Milton's 'darkness visible', were especially cultivated in 16th- and 17th-century poetry. Shakespeare has his Romeo utter several in one speech:

> Why then, O brawling love, O loving hate,
> O anything of nothing first create;
> O heavy lightness, serious vanity,
> Misshapen chaos of well-seeming forms,
> Feather of lead, bright smoke, cold fire, sick health,
> Still-waking sleep, that is not what it is!

**paean** [**pee**-ăn] **(pean)** A song or chant of triumphant rejoicing usually after a military victory. Originally choral hymns of thanksgiving to the Greek god Apollo, paeans were later extended to other gods and to military leaders.

**paeon** [**pee**-on] A Greek metrical unit (*foot) consisting of one long syllable and three short syllables, usually in that order (– ⏑ ⏑ ⏑, known as the 'first paeon' from the position of the long syllable). Named after its use in *paeans, it occurs in some classical Greek comedy. In English, the paeon combines one stressed syllable with three unstressed syllables; but the foot is rarely found outside the poetry of Gerard Manley Hopkins, who used the second (○●○○) and third (○○●○) paeons in combination with other feet in his 'The Windhover' and other poems. *Adjective*: **paeonic**.

**pageant** A wagon used as a mobile stage on which were performed *mystery plays and related dramas in the Middle Ages. The term is sometimes also applied to a play performed on such a movable stage, usually a mystery play. In a later sense, a pageant is a public procession displaying *tableaux and costumes appropriate to the commemoration of some historical event or tradition, sometimes involving short dramatic scenes.

**palaeography** [pal-i-**og**-răfi] The study and deciphering of old manuscripts.

**palimpsest** A manuscript written on a surface from which an earlier text has been partly or wholly erased. Palimpsests were common in the Middle Ages before paper became available, because of the high cost of parchment and vellum. In a figurative sense, the term is sometimes applied to a literary work that has more than one 'layer' or level of meaning. *Adjective*: **palimpsestic**.

**palindrome** A word (like *deed, eye,* or *tenet*) that remains the same if read backwards; or a sentence or verse in which the order of letters is the same reading backwards or forwards, disregarding punctuation and spaces between words: *Madam, I'm Adam. Adjective*: **palindromic**.

**palinode** A poem or song retracting some earlier statement by the poet. A notable example in English is Chaucer's *The Legend of Good Women*, written to recant his earlier defamation of women in *Troilus and Criseyde*.

**panegyric** [pan-ĕ-**ji**-rik] A public speech or written composition devoted to the prolonged, effusive praise of some person, group of people, or public body (e.g. a government or army). This branch of *rhetoric was particularly cultivated in ancient Greece and Rome. A composer or speaker of a panegyric is known as a **panegyrist**. *Verb*: **panegyrize**. *See also* ENCOMIUM, ÉLOGE.

**pantomime** Now a theatrical entertainment for children, based on a *fairy tale but including songs, dances, topical jokes, and the playing of the hero's part by a woman. In ancient Rome, however, a pantomime was a play on a mythological subject, in which a single performer mimed all the parts while a *chorus sang the story. The term is sometimes also used as a *synonym for *mime or *dumb show. *Adjective*: **pantomimic**.

**p**

**pantoum (*pantun*)** A verse form of Malay origin, employing *quatrains rhyming *abab* and repetition of whole lines so that the second and fourth lines of each stanza are repeated as the first and third lines of the next, and in the final quatrain the poem's first line appears as the final line, its third line as the second. Unlike the *villanelle and the *triolet, which use similar kinds of repetition, it has no fixed number of lines. The form, originally known as the *pantun*, was discovered and domesticated by French poets in the 19th century, including Victor Hugo and Charles Baudelaire, under the spelling 'pantoum', which has become standard in English. A modern example in English is Marilyn Hacker's twenty-stanza 'Pantoum' (1980).

**parable** A brief tale intended to be understood as an *allegory illustrating some lesson or moral. The forty parables attributed to Jesus of Nazareth in Christian literature have had a lasting influence upon the Western tradition of *didactic allegory. A modern instance is Wilfred Owen's poem 'The Parable of the Old Man and the Young' (1920), which adapts a biblical story to the 1914–18 war; a longer prose parable is John Steinbeck's *The Pearl* (1948). *Adjective*: **parabolic**. *See also* FABLE.

**paradigm** [pa-ră-dym]  In the general sense, a pattern or model in which some quality or relation is illustrated in its purest form; but in the terminology of *structuralism, a set of linguistic or other units that can be substituted for each other in the same position within a sequence or structure. A paradigm in this sense may be constituted by all words sharing the same grammatical function, since the substitution of one for another does not disturb the *syntax of a sentence. Linguists often refer to the **paradigmatic** [pa-ră-dig-**mat**-ik] dimension of language as the 'vertical axis' of selection, whereas the syntagmatic dimension governing the combination of linguistic units is the 'horizontal axis' (*see* SYNTAGM). Thus any *sign has two kinds of relation to other signs: a paradigmatic relation to signs of the same class (which are absent in any given utterance), and a syntagmatic relation to signs present in the same sequence.

**paradox**  A statement or expression so surprisingly self-contradictory as to provoke us into seeking another sense or context in which it would be true (although some paradoxes cannot be resolved into truths, remaining flatly self-contradictory, e.g. *Everything I say is a lie*). Wordsworth's line 'The Child is father of the Man' and Shakespeare's 'the truest poetry is the most feigning' are notable literary examples. Ancient theorists of *rhetoric described paradox as a *figure of speech, but 20th-century critics have given it a higher importance as a mode of understanding by which poetry challenges our habits of thought. Paradox was cultivated especially by poets of the 17th century, often in the verbally compressed form of *oxymoron. It is also found in the prose *epigram; and is pervasive in the literature of Christianity, a notoriously paradoxical religion. In a wider sense, the term may also be applied to a person or situation characterized by striking contradictions. A person who utters paradoxes is a **paradoxer**.

**paralipsis** (**paralepsis; paraleipsis**)  A rhetorical figure in which the speaker or writer draws attention to some important matter by pretending to pass over it, as in the everyday expression 'not to mention . . .'. It is also known under its Latin name, *occupatio*.

**paraliterature** The category of written works relegated to the margins of recognized *literature and often dismissed as subliterary despite evident resemblances to the respectable literature of the recognized *canon. Paraliterature thus includes many modern forms of popular fiction and drama: children's adventure stories, most *detective and spy *thrillers, most *science fiction and *fantasy writing, *pornography and women's *romances, along with much television and radio drama.

**parallelism** The arrangement of similarly constructed clauses, sentences, or verse lines in a pairing or other sequence suggesting some correspondence between them. The effect of parallelism is usually one of balanced arrangement achieved through repetition of the same syntactic forms (*see* SYNTAX). In classical *rhetoric, this device is called parison or isocolon. These lines from Shakespeare's *Richard II* show parallelism:

> I'll give my jewels for a set of beads,
> My gorgeous palace for a hermitage,
> My gay apparel for an almsman's gown,
> My figured goblets for a dish of wood . . .

Parallelism is an important device of 18th-century English prose, as in Edward Gibbon's sentence from his *Memoirs* (1796): 'I was neither elated by the ambition of fame, nor depressed by the apprehension of contempt.' Where the elements arranged in parallel are sharply opposed, the effect is one of *antithesis. In a more extended sense, the term is applied to correspondences between larger elements of dramatic or narrative works, such as the relation of *subplot to main *plot in a play.

**paraphrase** A restatement of a text's meaning in different words, usually in order to clarify the sense of the original. Paraphrase involves the separation or abstraction of *content from *form, and so has been resisted strongly by *New Criticism and other schools of modern critical opinion: Cleanth Brooks in *The Well-Wrought Urn* (1947) issued a notable denunciation of the 'heresy of paraphrase', i.e. the idea that a poem is **paraphrasable**. This is a necessary theoretical warning, since the particular form and *diction of a poem (or other work) give it meanings that are not reducible to simple statements and that do not survive the substitution of *synonyms; but the practice of paraphrase can help to establish this very fact, and is an analytic procedure too useful to be outlawed. *Adjective*: **paraphrastic**.

**pararhyme** A rhyming effect produced by 'rich' *consonance (*see* RIME RICHE*) without assonance: thus the consonantal sounds before and after the stressed vowels of a rhyming pair are matched while the vowel sounds are not, e.g. *love/leave*. This unusual variety of *half-rhyme is found in various traditions of poetry, especially in Welsh, but in English it was re-invented in 1917 by Wilfred Owen for some of his war poems, notably 'Strange Meeting' (1918). The term was coined by Edmund Blunden in the introduction to his edition of *The Poems of Wilfred Owen* (1931). Owen himself in private correspondence had referred to this form of rhyming as 'my vowel-rhyme stunt', apparently forgetting that its basis is consonantal, not vocalic.

**paratactic** Marked by the juxtaposition of clauses or sentences, without the use of connecting words: *I'll go; you stay here.* A paratactic style has the effect of abruptness, because the relationship between one statement and the next is not made explicit. This passage from H. D. Thoreau's *Walden* (1854) displays **parataxis** in the lack of obvious connection between sentences:

> I think that we may safely trust a good deal more than we do. We may waive just so much care of ourselves as we honestly bestow elsewhere. Nature is as well adapted to our weakness as our strength. The incessant anxiety and strain of some is a well nigh incurable form of disease.

The opposite, explicitly connected style is called *hypotactic.
*See also* ASYNDETON, POLYSYNDETON.

**paratext** A textual item that serves some supplementary function in relation to a principal text that it describes, introduces, justifies, or explains. There are several kinds of paratext, including *prefaces, introductions, *forewords, afterwords, *glosses, *blurbs, footnotes, and appendices. *Adjective*: **paratextual**. *See also* APPARATUS.

**parison** *See* PARALLELISM.

**Parnassians (*Parnassiens*)** A group of French poets who set a new standard of formal precision in *lyric poetry from the 1860s to the 1890s, partly in reaction against the emotional extravagance of *Romanticism. Adopting Leconte de Lisle as their leader, they followed Théophile Gautier's principle of *art for art's sake, sometimes championing the virtues of impersonality and of traditional verse forms. Their work appeared in the anthology *Le Parnasse contemporain* (1866), which was followed by two further collections with the same title in 1871 and 1876. The leading figures in the group included José-Maria de Hérédia—whose sonnets in *Les Trophées* (1893) constitute the foremost achievement of Parnassianism—along with R.-F.-A. Sully-Prudhomme, Catulle Mendès, Léon Dierx, and François Coppée. Their name refers to Mount Parnassus, a site associated with the Greek *muses.

**Further reading:** Robert T. Denommé, *The French Parnassian Poets* (1972).

**parody** A mocking imitation of the *style of a literary work or works, ridiculing the stylistic habits of an author or school by exaggerated mimicry. Parody is related to *burlesque in its application of serious styles to ridiculous subjects, to *satire in its punishment of eccentricities, and even to *criticism in its analysis of style. The Greek dramatist Aristophanes parodied the styles of Aeschylus and Euripides in *The Frogs* (405 BCE), while Cervantes parodied *chivalric romances in *Don Quixote* (1605). In English, two of the leading parodists are Henry Fielding and James Joyce. Poets in the 19th century, especially William Wordsworth and Robert Browning, suffered numerous parodies of their works. *Adjective*: **parodic**. *See also* MOCK-HEROIC, TRAVESTY.

**Further reading:** Simon Dentith, *Parody* (2000).

***parole*** *See* LANGUE.

**p**

**paronomasia** [pa-rŏ-noh-**may**-ziă] Punning; the term used in ancient *rhetoric to refer to any play on the sounds of words. *Adjective*: **paronomastic**. *See* ANTANACLASIS, PUN.

***passim*** A Latin word meaning 'widely scattered', used in scholarly notes with the sense 'throughout', to indicate that the word or expression referred to occurs so often in a given text that references to specific instances are needless.

**passion play** A religious play representing the trials, crucifixion, and resurrection of Jesus of Nazareth. Performances of such plays are recorded in various parts of Europe from the early 13th century onwards, in Latin and in the *vernaculars. Some formed part of the cycles of *mystery plays, others were performed separately, usually on Good Friday. The most famous example today is the *Oberammergauer Passionsspiel* still performed by the villagers of Oberammergau in

Bavaria at ten-year intervals; this custom originated in a vow made during an outbreak of plague in 1633.

**passus** (plural **passus**) A section of a longer poem or story, especially a medieval work such as William Langland's *Piers Plowman*. The term is borrowed from the Latin word for a 'step'. *See also* CANTO.

**pastiche** [pas-**teesh**] A literary work composed from elements borrowed either from various other writers or from a particular earlier author. The term can be used in a derogatory sense to indicate lack of originality, or more neutrally to refer to works that involve a deliberate and playfully imitative tribute to other writers. Pastiche differs from *parody in using imitation as a form of flattery rather than mockery, and from *plagiarism in its lack of deceptive intent. A well-known modern example is John Fowles's novel *The French Lieutenant's Woman* (1969), which is partly a pastiche of the great Victorian novelists. The frequent resort to pastiche has been cited as a characteristic feature of *postmodernism. A writer of pastiches is sometimes called a **pasticheur**. *Verb*: **pastiche**.

**Further reading:** Richard Dyer, *Pastiche* (2007).

**pastoral** A highly conventional mode of writing that celebrates the innocent life of shepherds and shepherdesses in poems, plays, and prose *romances. Pastoral literature describes the loves and sorrows of musical shepherds, usually in an idealized Golden Age of rustic innocence and idleness; paradoxically, it is an elaborately artificial cult of simplicity and virtuous frugality. The pastoral tradition in Western literature originated with the Greek *idylls of Theocritus (3rd century BCE), who wrote for an urban readership in Alexandria about shepherds in his native Sicily. His most influential follower, the Roman poet Virgil, wrote *eclogues (42–37 BCE) set in the imagined tranquillity of *Arcadia. In the 3rd century CE, the prose romance *Daphnis and Chloe* by Longus continued the tradition. An important revival of pastoral writing in the 16th century was led by Italian dramatists including Torquato Tasso and Battista Guarini, while long prose romances also appeared in other languages, notably Sir Philip Sidney's *Arcadia* (1590) and Honoré d'Urfé's *L'Astrée* (1607–27).

English pastorals were written in several forms, from the eclogues of Edmund Spenser's *The Shephearde's Calender* (1579) and the comedy of Shakespeare's *As You Like It* (c.1599) to *lyrics like Marlowe's 'The

Passionate Sheepeard to his Love' (1600). A significant form within this tradition is the pastoral *elegy, in which the mourner and the mourned are represented as shepherds in decoratively mythological surroundings: the outstanding English example is John Milton's 'Lycidas' (1637). While most forms of pastoral literature died out during the 18th century, Milton's influence secured for the pastoral elegy a longer life: P. B. Shelley's 'Adonais' (1821) and Matthew Arnold's 'Thyrsis' (1867) are both elegiac imitations of 'Lycidas'. By the late 18th century, pastoral poetry had been overshadowed by the related but distinct fashions for *georgics and *topographical poetry, and it came to be superseded by the more realistic poetry of country life written by George Crabbe, William Wordsworth, and John Clare.

**Further reading:** Terry Gifford, *Pastoral* (1999).

**pastourelle** A short *narrative poem in which a knight relates his encounter with a humble shepherdess whom he attempts (with or without success) to seduce in the course of their amusing *dialogue. Such poems were fashionable in France, Italy, and Germany in the 13th century.

**pathetic fallacy** The poetic convention whereby natural phenomena which cannot feel as humans do are described as if they could: thus rain-clouds may 'weep', or flowers may be 'joyful' in sympathy with the poet's (or imagined speaker's) mood. The pathetic fallacy normally involves the use of some *metaphor which falls short of full-scale *personification in its treatment of the natural world. The rather odd term was coined by the influential Victorian art critic John Ruskin in the third volume of his *Modern Painters* (1856). Ruskin's strict views about the accurate representation of nature led him to distinguish great poets like Shakespeare, who use the device sparingly, from lesser poets like Wordsworth and Shelley, whose habitual use of it becomes 'morbid'. Later critics, however, employ the term in a neutral sense. *See also* APOSTROPHE, POETIC LICENCE.

**pathos** [**pay**-thoss] The emotionally moving quality or power of a literary work or of particular passages within it, appealing especially to our feelings of sorrow, pity, and compassionate sympathy. *Adjective*: **pathetic**.

**patronage** The provision of financial or other material assistance
to a writer by a wealthy person or public institution, in return for
entertainment, prestige, or homage. Dr Johnson defined a patron as
'a wretch who supports with insolence, and is paid with flattery'. The
system of patronage has had several varieties, from the accommodation
of a poet in a royal household to the payment of a single fee for a
flattering dedication. Its importance declined sharply in the 18th century
with the appearance of a publishing market, but patronage continues
in some modern forms such as business sponsorship of dramatic
performances, or government subsidies to the arts.

**pattern poetry** Verse that is arranged in an unusual shape on the
page so as to suggest some object or movement matching the ideas or
mood of the words. Pattern poems were known in Greece in the 4th
century BCE. A well-known English example is George Herbert's 'Easter
Wings' (1633); later poets who have used this form in English include
e. e. cummings and Dylan Thomas. Since the 1950s, pattern poetry has
often been referred to as *concrete poetry or as visual poetry.

**Further reading:** Willard Bohn, *Reading Visual Poetry* (2010).

(((())) SEE WEB LINKS

• Bibliography and links for pattern and concrete poetry.

**penny dreadful** The name given in the Victorian age to a kind of
cheaply produced book containing bloodthirsty narratives of crime,
sometimes merely *plagiarisms from *Gothic novels. In the later 19th
century the term was extended to include tamer adventure stories for
boys in cheap formats.

**pentameter** [pen-**tamm**-ĕt-er] A metrical verse line having five main
*stresses, traditionally described as a line of five 'feet' (*see* FOOT). In
English poetry since Chaucer, the pentameter—almost always an
*iambic line normally of 10 syllables—has had a special status as the
standard line in many important forms including *blank verse, the
*heroic couplet, *ottava rima*, *rhyme royal, and the *sonnet. In its pure
iambic form, the pentameter shows a regular alternation of stressed
and unstressed syllables, as in this line by Percy Bysshe Shelley:

> If Winter comes, can Spring be far behind?

There are, however, several permissible variations in the placing of
stresses, which help to avoid the monotony of such regular alternation
(*see* DEMOTION, PROMOTION, INVERSION); and the pentameter may be

lengthened from 10 syllables to 11 by a *feminine ending. In classical Greek and Latin poetry, the second line of the elegiac *distich, commonly but inaccurately referred to as a 'pentameter' is in fact composed of two half-lines of two and a half feet each, with *dactyls or *spondees in the first half and dactyls in the second.

**Further reading:** Peter Groves, *Strange Music: Metre in the English Heroic Line* (1998).

**pentastich** (**pen**-tă-stik) A *stanza or poem of five lines, more often known as a *quintain, quintet, or *cinquain. Examples include the *limerick, the Spanish *lira* and *quintilla*, and the Japanese *tanka.

**performative** A kind of utterance that performs with language the deed to which it refers (e.g. *I promise to come*), instead of describing some state of affairs. The term was coined by the philosopher J. L. Austin in *How to Do Things with Words* (1962) as part of his *speech act theory. Austin distinguishes 'constative' utterances, which state that something is or is not the case, from performatives, which are verbal actions rather than true or false statements; however, he goes on to argue that constatives are also implicitly performative, in that they perform the act of asserting something. The concept has been adapted in *Queer theory and related discussions of gender, notably by Judith Butler, who has argued that a person's gender is continually and variably performed rather than given as a fact. *See also* ILLOCUTIONARY ACT.

**Further reading:** James Loxley, *Performativity* (2006).

**periodical** A magazine published at regular intervals, usually weekly, fortnightly, monthly, or quarterly.

**periodic sentence** A long sentence in which the completion of the *syntax and sense is delayed until the end, usually after a sequence of balanced subordinate clauses. The effect is a kind of suspense, as the reader's attention is propelled forward to the end, as in this sentence from Ann Radcliffe's *Romance of the Forest* (1791), describing the heroine's response to an unwelcome sexual advance:

> While he was declaring the ardour of his passion in such terms, as but too often make vehemence pass for sincerity, Adeline, to whom this declaration, if honourable, was distressing, and if dishonourable, was shocking, interrupted him and thanked him for the offer of a distinction, which, with a modest, but determined air, she said she must refuse.

*See also* HYPOTACTIC, LATINATE.

**peripeteia** [pe-ri-pĕ-**tee**-ă] (**peripety** [pe-**rip**-ĕti]) A sudden reversal of a character's circumstances and fortunes, usually involving the downfall of the *protagonist in a *tragedy, and often coinciding with the 'recognition' or *anagnorisis. In a *comedy, however, the peripeteia abruptly restores the prosperity of the main character(s). *See also* COUP DE THÉÂTRE.

**periphrasis** [pe-**rif**-ră-sis] (plural -**ases**) A roundabout way of referring to something by means of several words instead of naming it directly in a single word or phrase. Commonly known as *circumlocution, periphrasis is often used in euphemisms like *passed away* for 'died', but can have a more emphatic effect in poetry, as in the use of *kennings. It was especially cultivated by 18th-century poets whose principle of *decorum discouraged them from using commonplace words: thus fish were called *the finny tribe*, and in Robert Blair's poem 'The Grave' (1743) a telescope is *the sight-invigorating tube*. The 17th-century French fashion for *préciosité* cultivated periphrasis to excess. *Adjective*: **periphrastic**. *See also* ANTONOMASIA, LITOTES, POETIC DICTION.

**perlocutionary act** A term used in *speech act theory to designate an utterance that has an effect upon the actions, thoughts, or feelings of the listener, e.g. convincing, alarming, insulting, boring. The perlocutionary effect of an utterance may differ from the intended effect of the speaker's *illocutionary act. *See also* AFFECTIVE.

**peroration** [pe-rŏ-**ray**-shŭn] The conclusion of a formal speech (or written argument), in which the previous points are summed up in a forceful appeal to the audience; or any formal and impassioned speech, in its entirety. *Verb*: **perorate**. *Adjective*: **perorational** or **perorative**. *See also* EPILOGUE.

**persona** [per-**soh**-nă] (plural -**onae**) The assumed identity or fictional 'I' (literally a 'mask') assumed by a writer in a literary work; thus the speaker in a *lyric poem, or the *narrator in a fictional narrative. In a *dramatic monologue, the speaker is evidently not the real author but an invented or historical character. Many modern critics, though, insist further that the speaker in any poem should be referred to as the persona, to avoid the unreliable assumption that we are listening to the true voice of the poet. One reason for this is that a given poet may write different poems in which the speakers are of distinct kinds: another is that our identification of the speaking voice with that of the real poet would confuse imaginative composition with autobiography. Some theorists of narrative fiction have preferred to distinguish between the narrator and the persona, making the persona equivalent to the *implied author.

**personification** A *figure of speech by which animals, abstract ideas, or inanimate things are referred to as if they were human, as in Sir Philip Sidney's line:

> Invention, Nature's child, fled stepdame Study's blows

This figure or *trope, known in Greek as *prosopopoeia*, is common in most ages of poetry, and particularly in the 18th century. It has a special function as the basis of *allegory. In drama, the term is sometimes applied to the impersonation of non-human things and ideas by human actors. *Verb*: **personify**. *See also* PATHETIC FALLACY.

**Petrarchan** [pet-**rar**-kăn] Characteristic of, or derived from, the work of the major Italian poet Petrarch (Francesco Petrarca, 1304–74), especially his *sonnets and other love *lyrics in Italian. The **Petrarchan sonnet**, also known as the Italian sonnet, is divided into an *octave rhyming *abbaabba* and a *sestet normally rhyming *cdecde*, and thus avoids the final *couplet found in the English or 'Shakespearean' sonnet. The **Petrarchan conceit** is an exaggerated comparison or striking *oxymoron of the kind found in sonnets written under Petrarch's influence: common varieties are the comparison of a lady's eyes with the sun, and the description of love in terms of its pleasurable pains. The widespread imitation of Petrarch's love poetry in Europe, reaching its height in the 16th century, is known as **Petrarchism**. This important imitative tradition is marked by the increasingly conventional presentation of *courtly love, in which the despairing poet speaks in fanciful and paradoxical terms of his torments as the worshipper of a disdainful mistress. A notable Petrarchan *convention is the *blazon or catalogue of the lady's physical beauties: coral lips, pearly teeth, alabaster neck, etc. Petrarchism is evident in French poets of the *Pléiade* and in the English sonneteers from Wyatt to Shakespeare.

**Further reading:** Gordon Braden, *Petrarchan Love and the Continental Renaissance* (1998).

**phenomenology** A philosophical movement based on the investigation of 'phenomena' (i.e. things as apprehended by consciousness) rather than on the existence of anything outside of human consciousness. Phenomenology was founded in the early years of the 20th century by the German philosopher Edmund Husserl, who hoped to return philosophy to concrete experience and to reveal the essential structures of consciousness. In an amended form, Husserl's phenomenology was developed by his student Martin Heidegger, and became an important influence on *existentialism and the modern tradition of *hermeneutics. Its impact on literary studies is most evident in the work of the *Geneva school on authors' characteristic modes of awareness; but other kinds of phenomenological criticism—such as that of the Polish theorist Roman Ingarden—place more emphasis on the reader's consciousness of literary works. In this sense, phenomenology has prepared the ground for *reception theory.

**Further reading:** Robert R. Magliola, *Phenomenology and Literature* (1977).

**philistine** A person devoted narrow-mindedly to material prosperity at the expense of intellectual and artistic awareness; or (as an adjective) ignorantly uninterested in culture and ideas. This sense of the term comes from the insulting label *Philister* applied by German students to their non-academic neighbours in university towns, likening them to the enemies of the chosen people in the Hebrew scriptures; it was given wide currency in English by the poet and critic Matthew Arnold in his book *Culture and Anarchy* (1869), which attacks the **philistinism** of the British middle class. Arnold usually applied the term 'the Philistines' to the prosperous bourgeoisie, especially to its nonconformist Liberal representatives.

**philology** A field of scholarly study that investigates languages and their literatures, especially in their historical evolution. It covers a wide range of scholarly endeavour, from the decipherment of ancient scripts and *textual criticism to the interpretation of literary texts; but since the emergence of *linguistics as a distinct and professedly scientific discipline in the early 20th century, 'philology' has tended to refer to the 19th-century tradition of historical and comparative linguistic studies. Its older and broader meaning survives in the names of some university departments and academic journals. A researcher in this scholarly field is a **philologist**.

**philosophes** [feel-o-zof] The French word ('philosophers') applied
especially to the sceptical thinkers of the 18th-century *Enlightenment
in France, who subjected the established institutions and beliefs of their
time to rational criticism. The foremost *philosophes* included Voltaire,
Montesquieu, Helvétius, and the **Encyclopédistes* led by Diderot,
d'Alembert and d'Holbach. Their sceptical undermining of religious
dogma and political injustice is often regarded as a factor contributing to
the downfall of the *ancien régime* in the French Revolution.

**phoneme** [foh-neem] A minimal unit of potentially meaningful
sound within a given language's system of recognized sound
distinctions. Each phoneme in a language acquires its identity by
contrast with other phonemes, for which it cannot be substituted
without potentially altering the meaning of a word: our recognition of a
difference between the words *level* and *revel* indicates a phonemic
distinction in English between /l/ and /r/. (It is usual for phonemic
symbols to be printed between oblique strokes in this fashion.)
However, the actual *phonetic* difference between the two /l/ sounds in
most pronunciations of the word *level* is disregarded by speakers of
English, who treat them as 'allophones' (i.e. phonetic variations) of the
same phoneme. Each language divides up the infinite number of
possible sounds into a fairly small number of distinct phonemes, in ways
which do not always match the distinctions observed in other languages
(/l/ and /r/ are not distinguished in Chinese, for example). The concept
of the phoneme has great significance for *structuralism, because it
suggests that meanings are dependent on an abstract system of
differences. The branch of linguistics that analyses the sound systems of
languages is known as **phonemics**. *See also* GRAPHEME, MORPHEME,
PHONOLOGY.

**phonetics** [fŏ-net-iks] The science devoted to the physical analysis of
the sounds of human speech, including their production, transmission,
and perception. A pure science connected to acoustics and anatomy,
phonetics is concerned with the accurate description of speech sounds
as sounds, rather than with the way languages divide sounds up into
meaningful units (this being the domain of *phonology). A person
practising the science of phonetics is a **phonetician**.

**phonocentrism** The term employed in *deconstruction to refer to
an alleged bias in Western thinking about language, whereby writing

is regarded suspiciously as an untrustworthy parasite upon the authenticity of speech. According to Jacques Derrida in his book *De la grammatologie* (1967), the preference for speech—whose truth seems to be guaranteed by the presence of the speaker—is still upheld even in the modern linguistic theories of Ferdinand de Saussure (*see* SIGN), despite Saussure's demonstration that language is a system of abstract differences. Derrida's argument equates 'writing' with difference, and speech with illusory presence; he can thus claim that speech actually relies upon a prior 'writing'—that is, upon that system of differences which produces meanings in a language. Phonocentrism is one important aspect of a more general attachment to stability of meanings, which Derrida calls *logocentrism.

**phonology** [fŏ-**nol**-ŏji] The branch of linguistics concerned with the analysis of sound-systems as they function in languages (rather than with physical sounds as such, as in *phonetics). The term is sometimes also applied to the sound-system itself, in a given language: the 'phonology of English' is the system of distinctions and rules governing the speech of this language. The founding concept of phonology is that of the *phoneme.

**Phosphorists (*fosforister, fosforisterna*)** A group of Swedish poets and critics based at Uppsala in the early 19th century, so named after their journal *Phosphoros* (1810–13), which absorbed and promoted the new influences of German *Romanticism. The group's dominant figure, as editor of the journal, was the poet Per Daniel Amadeus Atterbom, founder both of the pro-Romantic *Auroraförbundet* ('Aurora League', 1807) and of the larger Romantic tradition in Swedish poetry. Since the late 19th-century spelling reforms that abolished *ph* in Swedish, this group has been referred to as the *fosforisterna*, the name of their journal being retrospectively corrected to *Fosforos*.

**picaresque novel** [pik-ă-**resk**] In the strict sense, a *novel with a **picaroon** (Spanish, *picaró*: a rogue or scoundrel) as its hero or heroine, usually recounting his or her escapades in a *first-person narrative marked by its *episodic structure and realistic low-life descriptions. The picaroon is often a quick-witted servant who takes up with a succession of employers. The true Spanish picaresque novel is represented by the anonymous *Lazarillo de Tormes* (1554) and by Mateo Alemán's more widely influential *Guzmán de Alfarache* (1599–1604); its imitators

include Johann Grimmelhausen's *Simplicissimus* (1669) in German,
Alain-René Lesage's *Gil Blas* (1715–35) in French, and Daniel Defoe's
*Moll Flanders* (1722) in English. In the looser sense now more frequently
used, the term is applied to *narratives that do not have a picaroon as
their central character, but are loosely structured as a sequence of
episodes united only by the presence of the central character, who
is often involved in a long journey: Cervantes's *Don Quixote* (1605),
Henry Fielding's *Tom Jones* (1749), and Mark Twain's *Adventures of
Huckleberry Finn* (1884) are examples of novels that are referred to as
being wholly or partly picaresque in this sense, while Byron's narrative
poem *Don Juan* (1819–24) is a rare case of a picaresque story in verse.

**Further reading:** Walter L. Reed, *An Exemplary History of the Novel* (1981).

**Pindaric** [pin-**da**-rik] Characteristic of or derived from the work of the
Greek poet Pindar (Pindaros, 518–438 BCE), a writer of public choral
*odes. The **Pindaric ode** has an unfixed number of *stanzas arranged in
groups of three, in which a *strophe and *antistrophe sharing the same
length and complex metrical pattern are followed by an *epode of
differing length and pattern. This triadic arrangement matches the
movements of the *chorus that would have performed Pindar's works on
public occasions. In English, two rare examples of 'regular' odes
conforming to this Pindaric model are Thomas Gray's 'The Progress
of Poesy' and 'The Bard' (both 1747). More common, though, is the
'irregular' or 'Cowleyan' ode comprising a number of strophes that do
not correspond in length or in the arrangement of their lines: Abraham
Cowley's 'Pindarique Odes' (1656) began this kind of departure from
strict Pindaric precedent. A more clearly distinct tradition in the
composition of odes is represented by the *Horatian ode, which employs
a regularly repeated stanza form.

**pirated** Published without the author's permission by some other
person who thereby steals part of the author's potential income from a
written work. Literary piracy was often a problem for writers before the
enforcement of international copyright agreements in the late 19th
century.

**plagiarism** [**play**-jä-rizm] The theft of ideas (such as the plots of
narrative or dramatic works) or of written passages or works, where
these are passed off as one's own work without acknowledgement of
their true origin; or a piece of writing thus stolen. Plagiarism is not

always easily separable from imitation, adaptation, or *pastiche, but is usually distinguished by its dishonest intention. A person practising this form of literary theft is a **plagiarist**. The older term **plagiary** was applied both to plagiarisms and to plagiarists. *Verb*: **plagiarize**.

**Platonism** [**play**-tŏn-izm] The doctrines of the Greek philosopher Plato (Platon, 427–347 BCE), especially the idealist belief that the perceptible world is an illusory shadow of some higher realm of transcendent Ideas or Forms. Despite Plato's hostility to poets as misleading imitators of worldly illusions, **Platonic** ideas have repeatedly been adopted in Western literature: in the *Renaissance his view of physical beauty as an outward sign of spiritual perfection was prevalent in love poetry, while in the age of *Romanticism his idealist philosophy was absorbed by many poets, notably Percy Bysshe Shelley. The **Cambridge Platonists** were a group of theologians associated with Cambridge University in the mid-17th century, who sought to reconcile the Anglican faith with human Reason while promoting religious tolerance; their leading writers were Henry More and Ralph Cudworth. *See also* NEOPLATONISM.

***Pléiade, la*** [play-ahd] The name given to an important group of 16th-century French poets founded in 1549 and led by Pierre de Ronsard. The name, taken from the constellation of seven stars known in English as the Pleiades, had formerly been applied to a group of Greek *Alexandrian poets; Ronsard himself adopted it for his group in 1556. The group of seven comprised Ronsard, Joachim du Bellay, Pontus de Tyard, Jean-Antoine de Baïf, Etienne Jodelle, Remy Belleau, and either Jacques Peletier or Jean Dorat (according to differing lists). Devoted students and translators of the Greek and Latin classics, the poets of the *Pléiade* were nevertheless strongly committed to developing the French language as a medium for major poetry, in emulation of the Italian poets whom they also admired. Rejecting the popular traditions and forms of medieval verse, they transformed French poetry by establishing the *alexandrine as the major verse line, and by introducing the *ode and the *sonnet into the language. Their most important manifestos are Du Bellay's *Deffence et illustration de la langue francoyse* (1549) and Ronsard's Preface to his *Odes* (1550). The same name is now used by the distinguished Paris publisher Gallimard for its prestigious series of edited works by French and other Francophone writers:

a modern author whose works appear in a Pléiade edition is deemed to have been elevated to the *canon.

**Further reading:** Grahame D. Castor, *Pléiade Poetics* (1964).

**pleonasm** [plee-ŏn-azm] The use of unnecessary additional words; or a phrase in which such needless repetition occurs, e.g. *the main protagonist* or *at this moment in time*. *Adjective*: **pleonastic**.

**ploce** [ploh-kay] **(ploche)** A very common *figure of speech that consists in a delayed repetition of the same word or words: 'the truth, the whole truth, and nothing but the truth'. By contrast with *epizeuxis (immediate repetition), it interposes some other words between the recurrences of the terms emphasized. *See also* EPANALEPSIS.

**plot** The pattern of events and situations in a narrative or dramatic work, as selected and arranged both to emphasize relationships—usually of cause and effect—between incidents and to elicit a particular kind of interest in the reader or audience, such as surprise or suspense. Although in a loose sense the term commonly refers to that sequence of chief events which can be summarized from a story or play, modern criticism often makes a stricter distinction between the plot of a work and its *story: the plot is the selected version of events as presented to the reader or audience in a certain order and duration, whereas the story is the full sequence of events as we imagine them to have taken place in their 'natural' order and duration. The story, then, is the hypothetical 'raw material' of events which we reconstruct from the finished product of the plot. The critical discussion of plots originates in Aristotle's *Poetics* (4th century BCE), in which his term *mythos* corresponds roughly with our 'plot'. Aristotle saw plot as more than just the arrangement of incidents: he assigned to plot the most important function in a drama, as a governing principle of development and coherence to which other elements (including character) must be subordinated. He insisted that a plot should have a beginning, a middle, and an end, and that its events should form a coherent whole. Plots vary in form from the fully integrated or 'tightly knit' to the loosely *episodic. In general, though, most plots will trace some process of change in which characters are caught up in a developing conflict that is finally resolved. *See also* INTRIGUE, SUBPLOT.

**plurisignation** *See* AMBIGUITY.

**poetaster** [**poh**-ĕt-as-ter] A writer of verse who does not deserve to be called a poet, despite his or her pretensions; an inferior poet lacking in ability. Trivial or worthless verse may sometimes be called **poetastery**.

***poète maudit*** [poh-**et** moh-dee] A French phrase for an 'accursed' poet, usually a brilliant but self-destructive writer misunderstood by an indifferent society. The name for this romantic stereotype comes from the title of Paul Verlaine's collection of essays on Mallarmé, Rimbaud, and other French poets, *Les Poètes maudits* (1884).

**poetic diction** In the most general sense, the choice of words and *figures in poetry. The term is more often used, however, to refer to that specialized language which is peculiar to poetry in that it employs words and figures not normally found in common speech or prose. Some elements of poetic diction, such as *kennings, compound *epithets, contracted and elided forms (*yon*, *o'er*, etc.), and *archaisms, occur widely in earlier periods of poetry, as do poetic figures such as *apostrophe; but the most elaborate system of poetic diction in English is found among poets of the 18th century, when the principle of *decorum required the use of *periphrasis to avoid naming 'common' things: thus Pope refers to a pair of scissors as 'the glitt'ring Forfex'. Poetic diction in the 18th century is also marked by *Latinate vocabulary, conventional epithets and archaisms, and frequent use of *personification; it was rejected as 'gaudy and inane phraseology' by William Wordsworth, whose Preface to the second edition (1800) of *Lyrical Ballads* argues for a plainer diction closer to 'the real language of men'. *See also* POETICISM.

**Further reading:** Emerson R. Marks, *Taming the Chaos: English Poetic Diction Theory since the Renaissance* (1998).

**poetic drama** The category of plays written wholly or mainly in verse. This includes most *tragedies and other serious plays from the earliest times to the 19th century, along with most *comedy up to the late 17th century. Strictly speaking, the term is not identical with dramatic poetry (*see* DRAMA), which also includes verse compositions not suited for the stage, such as *closet dramas.

**poetic justice** The morally reassuring allocation of happy and unhappy fates to the virtuous and the vicious characters respectively, usually at the end of a *narrative or dramatic work. The term was coined by the critic Thomas Rymer in his *The Tragedies of the Last Age Consider'd* (1678) with reference to Elizabethan *poetic drama: such justice is 'poetic', then, in the sense that it occurs more often in the fictional plots of plays than in real life. As Miss Prism explains in Oscar Wilde's *The Importance of Being Earnest*, 'The good ended happily, and the bad unhappily. That is what Fiction means.' In a slightly different but commonly used sense, the term may also refer to a strikingly appropriate reward or punishment, usually a 'fitting retribution' by which a villain is ruined by some process of his own making. *See also* NEMESIS.

**poetic licence** (US **license**) The imaginative and linguistic freedom granted to poets, allowing them to depart from normal prose standards of factual accuracy, *syntax, grammar, or pronunciation where this may produce a more satisfying imaginative or metrical effect. Depending upon prevailing aesthetic conventions, this may permit the use of *elision or of syntactic *inversion to fit the *metre of a line, of *eye rhyme or *broken rhyme to fit a *rhyme scheme, of unusual *diction, of illogical *figures (e.g. *catachresis, *hyperbole), or of other imaginative 'liberties' ranging from *personification and the *pathetic fallacy to inaccuracies of chronology (*anachronism), geography, or natural science.

**poeticism** [poh-**et**-is-izm] A word or phrase that survives only within a tradition of *poetic diction, usually an *archaism like *of yore* or a conventional *syncope such as *o'er*.

**poetics** [poh-**et**-iks] The general principles of *poetry or of *literature in general, or the theoretical study of these principles. As a body of theory, poetics is concerned with the distinctive features of poetry (or literature as a whole), with its languages, forms, *genres, and modes of composition. A theorist of poetry or literature may be called a **poetician**. *See also* AESTHETICS, CRITICISM.

**poetry** Language sung, chanted, spoken, or written according to some pattern of recurrence that emphasizes the relationships between words on the basis of sound as well as sense: this pattern is almost always a rhythm or *metre, which may be supplemented by *rhyme or *alliteration or both. The demands of verbal patterning usually make poetry a more condensed medium than *prose or everyday speech, often involving variations in *syntax, the use of special words and phrases (*poetic diction) peculiar to poets, and a more frequent and more elaborate use of *figures of speech, principally *metaphor and *simile. All cultures have their poetry, using it for various purposes from sacred ritual to obscene insult, but it is generally employed in those utterances and writings that call for heightened intensity of emotion, dignity of expression, or subtlety of meditation. Poetry is valued for combining pleasures of sound with freshness of ideas, whether these be solemn or comical. Some critics make an evaluative distinction between poetry, which is elevated or inspired, and *verse, which is merely clever or mechanical. The three major categories of poetry are *narrative, dramatic, and *lyric, the last being the most extensive.

**Further reading:** Jeffrey Wainwright, *Poetry: The Basics* (2004).

(⊕) SEE WEB LINKS

• Academy of American Poets: extensive guide to poets and poems.

**point of view** The position or vantage-point from which the events of a story seem to be observed and presented to us. The chief distinction usually made between points of view is that between *third-person narratives and *first-person narratives. A third-person *narrator may be *omniscient, and therefore show an unrestricted knowledge of the story's events from outside or 'above' them; but another kind of third-person narrator may confine our knowledge of events to whatever is observed by a single character or small group of characters, this method being known as 'limited point of view' (*see* FOCALIZATION). A first-person narrator's point of view will normally be restricted to his or her partial knowledge and experience, and therefore will not give us access to other characters' hidden thoughts. Many modern authors have also used 'multiple point of view', in which we are shown the events from the positions of two or more different characters.

**polemic** [pŏ-**lemm**-ik] A thorough written attack on some opinion or policy, usually within a theological or political dispute, sometimes also in philosophy or *criticism. Notable **polemicists** in English are John Milton, whose *Areopagitica* (1644) attacks censorship, and H. D. Thoreau, whose 'Slavery in Massachusetts' (1854) berates upholders of the Fugitive Slave Law. *Adjective*: **polemical**.

**police procedural** *See* DETECTIVE STORY.

**polyphonic** [poli-**fon**-ik] Literally 'many-voiced', a term found in the writings of the Russian literary theorist Mikhail Bakhtin, where it is equivalent to *dialogic. Thus a polyphonic novel is one in which several different voices or points of view interact on more or less equal terms. The term **polyphonic prose** has been applied to a kind of *free verse printed as if it were prose and showing similarities to the *prose poem, as in Amy Lowell's *Can Grande's Castle* (1918). *Noun*: **polyphony**.

**polyptoton** A *figure of speech in which a partial repetition arises from the use in close proximity of two related words having different forms, e.g. singular and plural forms of the same word. An example is found at the close of this couplet by Byron:

> A little while she strove, and much repented,
> And whispering 'I will ne'er consent'—consented.

**polysemy** [poli-**see**-mi] A linguistic term for a word's capacity to carry two or more distinct meanings, e.g. *grave*: 'serious' or 'tomb' (*see also* HOMONYM). In some modern linguistic and literary theory, it is argued that all *signs are polysemic, and the term has been extended to larger units including entire literary works. *See also* AMBIGUITY, MULTI-ACCENTUALITY.

**polysyndeton** [poli-**sin**-dĕ-ton] A rhetorical term for the repeated use of conjunctions to link together a succession of words, clauses, or sentences, as in Keats's *Endymion* (1818):

> And soon it lightly dipped, and rose, and sank,
> And dipped again...

Polysyndeton is the opposite of *asyndeton. *Adjective*: **polysyndetic**.

**pornography** A kind of fictional writing composed so as to arouse sexual excitement in its readers, usually by the repeated and explicit description of sexual acts in abstraction from their emotional and other interpersonal contexts; also visual images having the same purpose. The distinction between pornography and literary *erotica is open to continued debate, but it is commonly accepted that eroticism treats sexuality within some fuller human and imaginative context, whereas pornographic writing tends to be narrowly functional and often physiologically improbable. Further confusion arises from the questionable assimilation of the term into the distinct legal concept of *obscenity*, which usually governs the public mention or display of

specific acts, organs, words, and supposed 'perversions'. Several
works of serious literary merit, including Radclyffe Hall's *The Well of
Loneliness* (1928) and James Joyce's *Ulysses* (1922), have been legally
condemned as obscene although they do not fit most definitions of
pornography. The term's etymology is of little help: it is a rather bogus
19th-century coinage combining Greek words to mean 'writing about
prostitutes'.

**portmanteau word** A word concocted by fusing two different words
together into one: a common example is *brunch,* from 'breakfast' and
'lunch'; other modern colloquial cases are *motel* and *guesstimate*.
The term was coined by Lewis Carroll in *Through the Looking-Glass*
(1871), where he invents the word *slithy* from 'lithe' and 'slimy'; the
portmanteau referred to is a kind of suitcase composed of two halves.
The most extended literary use of portmanteau words is found in
James Joyce's novel *Finnegans Wake* (1939). *See also* COINAGE,
NEOLOGISM, NONCE WORD, PUN.

**postcolonial literature** A category devised to replace and expand
upon what was once in Britain called Commonwealth Literature. As a
label, it thus covers a very wide range of writings from countries that
were once colonies or dependencies of the European powers. There has
been much debate about the scope of the term: should predominantly
white ex-colonies like Ireland, Canada, and Australia be included? why
are the United States exempted both from the accepted list of former
colonies and from the category of colonizing powers? In practice,
the term is applied most often to writings from Africa, the Indian
sub-continent, the Caribbean, and other regions whose histories during
the 20th century were marked by colonialism, anti-colonial movements,
and subsequent transitions to post-Independence society. Critical
attention to this large body of work in academic contexts is often
influenced by a distinct school of **postcolonial theory** which developed
in the 1980s and 1990s, under the influence of Edward W. Said's
landmark study *Orientalism* (1978). Postcolonial theory considers vexed
cultural-political questions of national and ethnic identity, 'otherness',
race, imperialism, and language, during and after the colonial periods. It
draws upon *post-structuralist theories such as those of *deconstruction
in order to unravel the complex relations between imperial 'centre' and
colonial 'periphery', often in ways that have been criticized for being

excessively abstruse. The principal luminaries of postcolonial theory after Said have been Gayatri C. Spivak and Homi K. Bhabha.

**Further reading:** A. Loomba, *Colonialism/Postcolonialism* (1998); Bart Moore-Gilbert, *Postcolonial Theory* (1997).

**(⊕) SEE WEB LINKS**

• Postcolonial Web: general resource for postcolonial literature and theory at National University of Singapore.

## postmodernism *See* p. 288.

## post-structuralism
A school of thought that emerged partly from within French *structuralism in the 1960s, reacting against structuralist pretensions to scientific objectivity and comprehensiveness. The term covers the philosophical *deconstruction practised by Jacques Derrida and his followers, along with the later works of the critic Roland Barthes, the psychoanalytic theories of Jacques Lacan and Julia Kristeva, the historical critiques of Michel Foucault, and the cultural-political writings of Jean-François Lyotard and Gilles Deleuze. These thinkers emphasized the instability of meanings and of intellectual categories (including that of the human 'subject'), and sought to undermine any theoretical system that claimed to have universal validity—such claims being denounced as 'totalitarian'. They set out to dissolve the fixed *binary oppositions of structuralist thought, including that between language and *metalanguage—and thus between literature and criticism. Instead they favoured a non-hierarchical plurality or 'free play' of meanings, stressing the *indeterminacy of texts. Although waning in French intellectual life by the end of the 1970s, post-structuralism's delayed influence upon literary and cultural theory in the English-speaking world has persisted.

**Further reading:** Catherine Belsey, *Poststructuralism: A Very Short Introduction* (2002).

## pot-boiler
A derogatory term for a work written solely or mainly to earn money.

## poulter's measure
An English poetic *metre composed of alternate lines of 12 and 14 syllables (iambic *hexameters and *heptameters), usually in rhyming *couplets, as shown in these lines by the Earl of Surrey, a 16th-century poet:

> Then comes a sudden fear, that riveth all my rest,
> Lest absence cause forgetfulness to sink within her breast.

Although popular in the 16th century, the metre was rarely used thereafter. It seems to be related to *short measure and to the *limerick, despite differences in *rhyme scheme. Its name comes from the poulterer's former custom of providing eggs in 'dozens' of twelve and fourteen. *See also* FOURTEENER.

**practical criticism** In the general sense, the kind of *criticism that analyses specific literary works, either as a deliberate application of a previously elaborated theory or as a supposedly non-theoretical investigation. More specifically, the term is applied to an academic procedure devised by the critic I. A. Richards at Cambridge University in the 1920s and illustrated in his book *Practical Criticism* (1929). In this exercise, students are asked to analyse a short poem without any information about its authorship, date, or circumstances of composition, thus forcing them to attend to the 'words on the page' rather than refer to biographical and historical contexts. This discipline, enthusiastically adopted by the *Cambridge school, became a standard model of rigorous criticism in British universities, and its style of '*close reading' influenced the *New Criticism in America. *See also* EXPLICATION.

**Prague School** The name commonly given to the Prague Linguistic Circle, a group of linguistic and literary theorists based at Charles University, Prague, from 1926 to 1948, of whom the most influential was Roman Jakobson, who had arrived from Moscow bringing the principles of *Russian Formalism, which were to be further developed in Prague. Other important figures were Jan Mukařovský, who developed the theory of *foregrounding, René Wellek, later a leading *New Critic in America, and the literary historian Felix Vodička. The Prague School was a major influence on the development of *structuralism.

**Further reading:** F. W. Galan, *Historic Structures: The Prague School Project, 1928–1946* (1985).

**préciosité, la** A cult of refined language and manners that established itself in French high society of the mid-17th century, led by the *salon of Catherine de Vivonne, Marquise de Rambouillet from about 1618 to 1650. The *précieuses* devised elegant expressions to remedy what they felt to be the indelicacies of French speech; many of these are recorded in A. B. de Somaize's *Dictionnaire des précieuses* (1660). This sometimes excessive fashion for *periphrasis was satirized by Molière in his one-act

## POSTMODERNISM

A disputed term that occupied much late 20th-century debate about culture from the early 1980s. In its simplest and least satisfactory sense it refers generally to the phase of 20th-century Western culture that succeeded the reign of high *modernism, thus indicating the products of the age of mass television since the mid-1950s. More often, though, it is applied to a cultural condition prevailing in the advanced capitalist societies since the 1960s, characterized by a superabundance of disconnected images and styles—most noticeably in television, advertising, commercial design, and pop video. In this sense, promoted by Jean Baudrillard and other commentators, **postmodernity** is said to be a culture of fragmentary sensations, eclectic nostalgia, disposable simulacra, and promiscuous superficiality, in which the traditionally valued qualities of depth, coherence, meaning, originality, and authenticity are evacuated or dissolved amid the random swirl of empty signals.

As applied to literature and other arts, the term is notoriously ambiguous, implying either that modernism has been superseded or that it has continued into a new phase. Postmodernism may be seen as a continuation of modernism's alienated mood and disorienting techniques and at the same time as an abandonment of its determined quest for artistic coherence in a fragmented world: in very crude terms, where a modernist artist or writer would try to wrest a meaning from the world through myth, symbol, or formal complexity, the postmodernist greets the *absurd or meaningless confusion of contemporary existence with a certain numbed or flippant indifference, favouring self-consciously 'depthless' works of *fabulation, *pastiche, *bricolage, or *aleatory disconnection. The term cannot usefully serve as an inclusive description of all literature since the 1950s or 1960s, but is applied selectively to those works that display most evidently the moods and formal disconnections described above. In poetry, it has been applied most often to the work of the *New York school and to *Language poetry; in drama mainly to the 'absurdist' tradition; but is used more widely in reference to fiction, notably to the novels (or *anti-novels) and stories of Thomas Pynchon, Kurt Vonnegut, Italo Calvino, Vladimir Nabokov, William S. Burroughs, Angela Carter, Salman Rushdie,

Peter Ackroyd, Julian Barnes, Jeanette Winterson, and many of their followers. Some of their works, like Pynchon's *Gravity's Rainbow* (1973) and Nabokov's *Ada* (1969), employ devices reminiscent of *science fiction, playing with contradictory orders of reality or the irruption of the fabulous into the secular world.

Opinion is still divided, however, on the value of the term and of the phenomenon it purports to describe. Those who most often use it tend to welcome 'the postmodern' as a liberation from the hierarchy of 'high' and 'low' cultures; while sceptics regard the term as a symptom of irresponsible academic euphoria about the glitter of consumerist capitalism and its moral vacuity. *See also* POST-STRUCTURALISM.

**Further reading:** Brian McHale, *Postmodernist Fiction* (1987); Ian Gregson, *Postmodern Literature* (2004).

comedy *Les Précieuses ridicules* (1659). The English term **preciosity** has a less specific sense, referring to any kind of affectation.

**précis** [**pray**-see] A short summary of the essential points of some longer text. *See also* ABRIDGEMENT, PARAPHRASE.

**Pre-Raphaelites** A group of English artists and writers of the Victorian period, associated directly or indirectly with the self-styled Pre-Raphaelite Brotherhood of young artists founded in 1848 by Dante Gabriel Rossetti, John Everett Millais, and William Holman Hunt. The PRB (as it is usually abbreviated) rebelled against the conventional academic styles of painting modelled upon Raphael (1483–1520), seeking a freshness and simplicity found in earlier artists, along with a closer fidelity to Nature. The organized Brotherhood itself lasted only a few years, but **Pre-Raphaelitism** as a broader current survived in the paintings of Edward Burne-Jones, the designs of William Morris, and the art criticism of John Ruskin, as well as in the poetry of Christina Rossetti, D. G. Rossetti, Morris, and A. C. Swinburne—the last three being dubbed 'The Fleshly School of Poetry' in a hostile review by Robert Buchanan (*Contemporary Review*, 1871). Pre-Raphaelite poetry is often characterized by dreamy *medievalism, mixing religiosity and sensuousness, notably in D. G. Rossetti's 'The Blessed Damozel' (1850), Morris's *The Defence of Guenevere* (1858), and Swinburne's *Poems and Ballads* (1866).

**((⊕)) SEE WEB LINKS**
• Site of the Pre-Raphaelite Society.

**preromanticism** A general term applied by modern literary historians to a number of developments in late 18th-century culture that are thought to have prepared the ground for *Romanticism in its full sense. In various ways, these are all departures from the orderly framework of *neoclassicism and its authorized *genres. The most important constituents of preromanticism are the *Sturm und Drang* phase of German literature; the *primitivism of Jean-Jacques Rousseau and of *Ossianism; the cult of *sensibility in the *sentimental novel; the taste for the *sublime and the picturesque in landscape; the sensationalism of the early *Gothic novels; the melancholy of English *graveyard poetry; and the revival of interest in old *ballads and *romances. These developments seem to have helped to give a new importance to subjective and spontaneous individual feeling.

**Further reading:** Marshall Brown, *Preromanticism* (1991).

**prescriptive** Seeking to lay down rules and instructions. Prescriptive
*criticism formulates the norms according to which literary works
ought to be written, whereas descriptive criticism tries to account for
the ways in which they actually have been written. In discussions
of language, **prescriptivism** is the attitude that tries to impose an
unchanging standard of 'correct' usage in language, especially in
grammar; it is rejected as a misconceived dogma by most modern
linguists.

**primitivism** A preference for the supposedly free and contented
existence found in a 'primitive' way of life as opposed to the artificialities
of urban civilization. Often connected with a nostalgia for a lost Eden
or Golden Age (as in much *pastoral literature), primitivism is found in
the literature of many periods, but it had a particular prominence in
18th-century Europe and 19th-century America, contributing to the
values of *Romanticism. The most influential primitivist, Jean-Jacques
Rousseau, argued in his *Discours sur l'origine de l'inégalité* (1755) and
other writings that the freedom and dignity of the 'noble savage' had
become stifled by the constraints of civilized society. The popularity
of the supposedly ancient epic poems of 'Ossian' (*see* OSSIANISM)
encouraged this view, which was given a new form by William
Wordsworth in his exaltation of rural simplicity, and by several
American writers including James Fenimore Cooper, H. D. Thoreau,
and Herman Melville in the mid-19th century. Later, D. H. Lawrence
maintained a strongly primitivist stance against industrial society and
its crushing of individual spontaneity.

**Further reading:** Michael Bell, *Primitivism* (1972).

**problem play** Usually a play dealing with a particular social problem
in a realistic manner designed to change public opinion; also called a
thesis play. Significant examples are Henrik Ibsen's *A Doll's House*
(1879), on women's subordination in marriage, and Bernard Shaw's *Mrs
Warren's Profession* (1902) on prostitution. In studies of Shakespeare,
however, the term has been used since the 1890s to designate a group
of his plays written in the first years of the 17th century: the 'dark
comedies' *Measure for Measure* and *All's Well That Ends Well*, and the
*tragicomedy *Troilus and Cressida*. Critics have often been disturbed by

the sombre and cynical mood of these plays, which seems to clash oddly with their comic conventions. *See also* DISCUSSION PLAY.

**proem** A preface or introduction to a work. *Adjective*: **proemial.**

**Projectivism** The poetic doctrine of Charles Olson and of his followers in the *Black Mountain group of American poets, declared in his essay 'Projective Verse' (1950). *See* OPEN FORM.

**prolepsis** (plural **-epses**) The Greek word for 'anticipation', used in three senses: **1.** In a speech, the trick of answering an opponent's objections before they are even made. **2.** As a *figure of speech, the application of an *epithet or description before it actually becomes applicable, e.g. the wounded Hamlet's exclamation 'I am dead, Horatio'. **3.** In narrative works, a 'flashforward' by which a future event is related as an interruption to the 'present' time of the narration. A well-known example of this occurs in the thirteenth chapter of Aldous Huxley's novel *Brave New World* (1932): Lenina is distracted by Henry Foster from her task of inoculating bottled human embryos against sleeping-sickness, and the narrator observes, before returning to Lenina's conversation with Henry, that the first fatal case of the disease would occur twenty-two years later (as the result of her inattention, we assume). In this third sense, prolepsis is an *anachrony which is the opposite of 'flashback' or *analepsis. *Adjective*: **proleptic.**

**proletcult** An abbreviation for 'proletarian culture' (Russian, *proletarskaya kul'tura*), the slogan and title adopted by a movement of cultural revolution and popular education in the Soviet Union, launched in 1917 by A. A. Bogdanov. It claimed to be initiating a new working-class culture uncontaminated by the bourgeois artistic heritage, and it promoted the publication of works by proletarian writers.

**prologue** [**proh**-log] An introductory section of a play, speech, or other literary work. The term is also sometimes applied to the performer who makes an introductory speech in a play.

**promotion** The use of an unstressed syllable to realize the rhythmic 'beat' in a position normally occupied within a metrical verse line by a stressed syllable (*see* METRE). This common device of metrical variation in English verse occurs where an unstressed syllable appears between two other unstressed syllables, or between an unstressed syllable and a line-break. In Keats's line:

His soul shall taste the sadness of her might.

the syllable *of* has been promoted to a 'beat' position between two other unstressed syllables; this does not mean, though, that it should be heavily stressed in reading aloud. Where promotion occurs on the last syllable of an *iambic line, it sometimes produces a *weak ending. *See also* DEMOTION.

**prompt-book** An official copy of the script of a play, held by the theatre's prompter in order to remind performers of their entrances and, if forgotten, their lines. Before the practice of prompting was adopted in the English theatre, which seems to have been in the eighteenth century, an official copy of the script was held by the theatre's 'bookkeeper' for other purposes: under conditions of censorship, this copy contained the censor's licence, and from it the actors' parts were copied. In theatrical jargon, this copy is often known simply as the Book, sometimes as the play-book.

**propagandism** The tendency to compose literary works chiefly to serve the purpose of propaganda, that is, writing to persuade people to support a particular religious or political cause. Propagandist writing is thus a kind of *didactic literature directed toward changing or confirming readers' and audiences' allegiances. Although the concept of propaganda derives from Christian evangelizing traditions, this term is usually applied to socialist literature of the 20th century taking forms such as *agitprop, *socialist realism, or the *epic theatre of Brecht.

**props** The usual abbreviation for stage 'properties', i.e. those objects that are necessary to the action of a dramatic work (other than scenery, costumes, and fixed furnishings): weapons, documents, cigarettes, items of food and drink, etc.

**proscenium arch** [prŏ-**seen**-iŭm] The structure separating the main acting area from the auditorium in most Western theatres of the 19th and early 20th centuries. It usually forms a rectangular 'picture frame', the 'picture' being revealed by opening a curtain. Its associated dramatic *conventions often involve the illusion of looking into a room through an invisible 'fourth wall'.

**prose** The form of written language that is not organized according to the formal patterns of *verse; although it will have some sort of rhythm and some devices of repetition and balance, these are not governed by a regularly sustained formal arrangement, the significant unit being the sentence rather than the line. Some uses of the term include spoken language as well, but it is usually more helpful to maintain a distinction at least between written prose and everyday speech, if not formal *oratory. Prose has as its minimum requirement some degree of continuous coherence beyond that of a mere list. The adjectives **prosaic** and **prosy** have a derogatory meaning of dullness and ordinarinesss; the neutral adjective is simply 'prose', as in 'prose writings'.

**prose poem** A short composition employing the rhythmic *cadences and other devices of *free verse (such as poetic *imagery and *figures) but printed wholly or partly in the format of prose, i.e. with a right-hand margin instead of regular line-breaks. This *genre emerged in France during the 19th century, notably in Charles Baudelaire's *Spleen de Paris* (1869) and Arthur Rimbaud's *Les Illuminations* (1886); a significant English sequence of prose poems is Geoffrey Hill's *Mercian Hymns* (1971). A prose poem is a self-contained work usually similar to a *lyric, whereas **poetic prose** may occur intermittently within a longer prose work.

**prosody** [**pros**-ŏdi] The systematic study of *versification, covering the principles of *metre, *rhythm, *rhyme, and *stanza forms; or a particular system of versification. In linguistics, the term is applied to patterns of *stress and *intonation in ordinary speech. Prosody in the literary sense is also known as *metrics. *Adjective*: **prosodic**. *See also* SCANSION.

**prosopopoeia** [pros-ŏ-pŏ-**pee**-ă] The Greek rhetorical term for a *trope consisting either of the *personification of some non-human being or idea, or of the representation of an imaginary, dead, or absent person as alive and capable of speech and hearing, as in an *apostrophe. *Adjective*: **prosopopoeial**.

**protagonist** [proh-**tag**-ŏn-ist] The chief character in a play or story, who may also be opposed by an *antagonist. Originally, in ancient Greek theatre, the protagonist was the principal actor in a drama. The phrase 'main protagonist' often found in popular usage is a *pleonasm. The word is also often misused to mean 'advocate', 'proponent', or 'champion'. *See also* HERO.

**prothalamion** [proh-thă-**lam**-iŏn]  A marriage-poem. The term, invented by Edmund Spenser for the title of his poem celebrating the weddings of Katherine and Elizabeth Somerset in 1596, is derived from *epithalamion, literally meaning 'before the bridal chamber'.

**proverb**  A short popular saying of unknown authorship, expressing some general truth or superstition: 'Too many cooks spoil the broth.' Proverbs are found in most cultures, and are often very ancient. The Hebrew scriptures include a book of Proverbs. Many poets—notably Chaucer—incorporate proverbs into their works, and others imitate their condensed form of expression: William Blake's 'Proverbs of Hell' in *The Marriage of Heaven and Hell* (1793) are, strictly speaking, *aphorisms, since they originate from a known author. *Adjective*: **proverbial**.

**psalm**  A sacred song or *hymn. The term usually refers to the Hebrew verses in the biblical book of Psalms, traditionally (but unreliably) attributed to King David. These psalms, notably in the English translation attributed to Miles Coverdale and found in the *Book of Common Prayer*, have had an important place in Christian worship, in English religious poetry, and in the development of *free verse. The art of singing psalms is called **psalmody**, while a collection of psalms is known as a **psalter**. *Adjective*: **psalmic** or **psalmodic**.

**pseudepigrapha** [soo-dĕ-**pig**-ră-fă]  The collective term for spurious or inauthentic writings, usually those falsely attributed to persons other than their true authors. *Adjective*: **pseudepigraphic**. *See also* APOCRYPHA.

**pseudo-statement**  A term invented by the British critic I. A. Richards in *Science and Poetry* (1926) in an attempt to distinguish the special kind of 'truth' provided by poetry and fiction: whereas scientific or ordinary 'referential' language makes statements that are either true or false, poetry's 'emotive' language gives us pseudo-statements, i.e. utterances that are not subject to factual verification but which are valuable in 'organizing our attitudes'. The term proved to be controversial, partly because it was misunderstood to mean 'falsehood', and partly because it implied that poetry can have no cognitive status; but the idea itself is traditional: Sir Philip Sidney's *Apology for Poetry* (1595) argued that the poet 'nothing affirms, and therefore never lieth'. A somewhat similar distinction is involved in the later concept of the *performative.

## PSYCHOANALYTIC CRITICISM

A tradition of modern literary interpretation employing methods derived from psychoanalysis, whether in its orthodox forms based on the works of Sigmund Freud or in various heretical versions. This tradition is almost exclusively interpretative, showing little interest or competence in evaluation. It originates in the method of dream-analysis exhibited in Freud's *The Interpretation of Dreams* (1900) and in similar analyses of jokes, slips of the tongue, and neurotic symptoms in his later writings. Here Freud argues that a dream is the disguised expression of a wish; and he outlines his dynamic theory of 'drives' coming from the Unconscious and meeting repression from the mind's censoring functions, which force it to seek indirect expression in *symbols and in condensed or displaced images resembling, as some commentators observe, the rhetorical forms of *metaphor, *metonymy, and other *tropes. In tandem with this theory, Freud also outlined a narrative model of child development explaining how the unreasonable demands of the infant are subdued to the requirements of civilization: the infant boy who desires undisputed possession of his mother wishes therefore to dispose of his father, but is coaxed into deferment of gratification until he can assume the father's powers. This resolution of the Oedipus Complex is a victory for civilization, but splits the mind into the competing realms of the Id ('It'), Ego, and Superego or conscience. As for girls, Freud conceded defeat in the face of the 'dark continent' of feminine psychology.

The application of these theories to literary interpretation is as old as psychoanalysis itself: Freud drew heavily upon myth and literature, paying tribute to the poets and playwrights who had understood the workings of the Unconscious long before he reformulated them. His model of the Oedipus Complex itself may be understood as a commentary on Sophocles' play *Oedipus the King*, and he used it to suggest an answer to the enigma of Shakespeare's *Hamlet* (later elaborated by his British disciple Ernest Jones), namely that the Prince feels unable to avenge his father's murder because his uncle Claudius has done what he himself unconsciously desired: kill the father to possess the mother. This interpretation typifies the way in which Freudian reading treats a text like a dream, which has a manifest content that disguises a latent content at a deeper level. Objectors protest that such an approach disregards the conscious element in literary composition and strips away the linguistic texture of a work (Shakespeare's dramatic poetry, in this case) to disclose something supposedly more authentic behind it.

Freud also attempted to psychoanalyse long-dead artists and writers including Leonardo da Vinci and E. T. A. Hoffman, thus founding the tradition of *psychobiography in which characteristics of an author's work are traced to imputed neuroses or other pathologies. In doing so he contravened his own strictures, which permit analysis only of patients who willingly make themselves available to answer an analyst's questions, which dead authors and fictional characters (who have no real past to discuss) cannot do. Psychoanalysis of authors and of characters is questionable in analytic terms, and many writers have found it objectionable in literary terms too: even critics who were sympathetic to Freud, such as Lionel Trilling and his associates in the *New York Intellectual circle saw a danger of reducing art to symptoms of neuroses. There remains an alternative field of psychoanalytic investigation, necessarily speculative, which is the understanding of readers' fascination with certain kinds of narrative or drama. Here Freudian answers can be given in terms of the overcoming of fears, as with horror stories, or of the resolution of conflicting desires, as in *romance or *comedy.

There are many versions of psychoanalytic criticism that follow authorities other than Freud, principally C. G. Jung in the case of *archetypal or *myth criticism, Melanie Klein or Julia Kristeva (*see* ABJECTION) in some versions of *feminist criticism, and the complex theories of Jacques Lacan in the *post-structuralist tradition. Lacan's work, widely influential since the 1970s, has offered some interpreters a way of understanding literary works in terms of their quest for an imaginary wholeness that is lost upon our entry into the linguistic realm of differences and distinctions (*see* SYMBOLIC). Other unauthorized critical approaches draw upon aspects of Freud's model selectively, as in Harold Bloom's Oedipal theory of the poetic *anxiety of influence.

**Further reading:** Elizabeth Wright, *Psychoanalytic Criticism* (2nd edn, 1998).

**psychobiography** A kind of *biography that seeks to explain the character and behaviour of its subject according to a psychological theory of human development, usually one derived from Freudian psychoanalysis. The links that Freud made in several of his case histories between disturbing events in an individual's childhood and neurotic symptoms in later life offered an explanatory model that some biographers adopted under his influence, among the earliest of these being Lytton Strachey, whose book *Elizabeth and Essex* (1928) offered to explain the political conduct of Queen Elizabeth I as the result of an early deformation of her sexuality. Freud himself wrote a psychobiographical essay on Leonardo da Vinci (1910), and among his immediate disciples Marie Bonaparte wrote a full-length study of Edgar Allan Poe (1935) that arrives at a clinical diagnosis of his writings as symptoms of necrophilic sadism. More sophisticated exercises in psychobiography appeared in the United States in the 1950s and 1960s, notably Leon Edel's five-volume life of Henry James (1953–72) and Erik Erikson's *Young Man Luther* (1968). Since then, a more sceptical intellectual climate has led biographers to be cautious about the dangers of *reductionism in this approach. For a series of introductory accounts, consult William Todd Schultz (ed.), *Handbook of Psychobiography* (2005).

**psychomachy** [sy-**kom**-ăki] A battle for the soul. The term comes from the Latin poem *Psychomachia* (*c.*400 CE) by Prudentius, describing a battle between virtues and vices for the soul of Man. This depiction of moral conflict had an important influence on medieval *allegory, especially in the *morality plays. Later echoes of medieval psychomachy can be found in Shakespeare's 144th sonnet and in Tennyson's poem 'The Two Voices' (1842).

**pulp fiction** A colloquial American term for cheaply produced books and magazines of the early 20th century containing popular kinds of fiction ranging from westerns and *detective stories to *romances and *science fiction. The name comes from the cheap kind of paper upon which they were printed, and is often abbreviated simply to 'pulp', as in 'pulp writer', 'pulp magazine', etc. *See also* DIME NOVEL, NOVELETTE, PARALITERATURE.

**pun** An expression that achieves emphasis or humour by contriving an *ambiguity, two distinct meanings being suggested either by the same word (*see* POLYSEMY) or by two similar-sounding words (*see* HOMOPHONE). In the terminology of *rhetoric, punning is regarded as a *figure of speech, and known as *paronomasia. *See also* ANTANACLASIS, *DOUBLE ENTENDRE*, EQUIVOQUE.

**purple patch** An over-written passage in which the writer has strained too hard to achieve an impressive effect, by elaborate *figures or other means. The phrase (Latin, *purpureus pannus*) was first used by the Roman poet Horace in his *Ars Poetica* (*c*.20 BCE) to denote an irrelevant and excessively ornate passage; the sense of irrelevance is normally absent in modern usage, although such passages are usually incongruous. By extension, 'purple prose' is lavishly figurative, rhythmic, or otherwise overwrought. *See also* BOMBAST, FUSTIAN.

**pyrrhic** A hypothetical metrical unit sometimes invoked in traditional *scansion: it consists of two unstressed syllables (or, in *quantitative verse, two short syllables), and is rather questionably referred to as a *foot. It has been called upon in many attempts to clear up problems of traditional scansion by feet, as a device of *substitution. Some modern systems of scansion, however, have abolished it by considering pairs of unstressed syllables in terms of *promotion and other concepts. *See also* METRE.

**pythiambics** Verses in uneven couplets in which dactylic *hexameters alternate with iambic lines either of *dimeter or *trimeter length. Some of Horace's *Epodes* employ this kind of couplet.

p

**quantitative verse** Verse in which the *metre is based on the principle of **quantity** (i.e. the duration of a syllable's sound), and in which the basic metrical unit, the *foot, is composed of syllables classified either as 'long' or as 'short'. This metrical system is found in Greek and Latin, as well as in Arabic and some other languages, but does not apply to English verse, which uses patterns of stress rather than quantitatively measured syllables and feet. Some unfruitful attempts were, however, made in the 16th and 17th centuries to write quantitative verse in English.

**quarto** A size of book or page that results from folding a standard printer's sheet twice, forming four leaves (i.e. eight pages). Many of Shakespeare's plays first appeared in quarto editions, most of these being textually unreliable. For other book sizes, *see* DUODECIMO, FOLIO, OCTAVO.

((●)) SEE WEB LINKS
• British Library collection of Shakespeare Quartos viewed in facsimile.

**quatrain** A verse *stanza of four lines, rhymed or (less often) unrhymed. The quatrain is the most commonly used stanza in English and most modern European languages. Most *ballads and many *hymns are composed in quatrains in which the second and fourth lines rhyme (*abcb* or *abab*); the 'heroic quatrain' of iambic *pentameters also rhymes *abab*. A different *rhyme scheme (*abba*) is used in the *In Memoriam* stanza and some other forms. The rhyming four-line groups that make up the first eight or twelve lines of a *sonnet are also known as quatrains.

**Queer theory** A body of academic writings that has since the early 1990s attempted to redefine and de-stabilize categories of sexuality in the light of *post-structuralist theory, and especially under the influence of Michel Foucault's *La Volonté de savoir* (1976). Rooted in the lesbian and gay activism of the 1970s but now more sceptical about inherited conceptions of 'gay' and 'lesbian' as simple or given 'identities', certain gay and lesbian intellectuals and activists adopted the more controversial but also more inclusive label 'queer' to cover a range of sexual orientations and sub-cultures. Queer theory stresses the historical variability, fluidity, and provisional or 'performed' nature of sexualities (*see* PERFORMATIVE), notably in the writings of Judith Butler, whose book *Gender Trouble* (1990) is a key text of this school. The pursuit of these concerns in the reading of literary texts is more often associated with the work of Eve Kosofsky Sedgwick, whose *Between Men* (1985) and *Epistemology of the Closet* (1990) investigate the paradoxes of 'homosocial' male bonding and homophobia in English fiction.

**Further reading:** Annamarie Jogose, *Queer Theory* (1996).

**quintain (quintet)** A verse *stanza of five lines. It appears in various forms, from the English *limerick and Spanish *lira* and *quintilla* to the Japanese *tanka. *See also* PENTASTICH.

***quintilla*** [kin-**tee**-yă]  A Spanish stanza of five *octosyllabic lines using only two rhymes, in which no three consecutive lines are to rhyme: the usual rhyme scheme is *abaab*, but *abbab*, *aabab*, and other permutations are found. The form flourished in the 15th century, and is related to the four-line *redondilla*. A *quintilla real*, however, is a stanza of five *hendacasyllabic lines.

q

**raisonneur**  A character in a play who appears to act as a mouthpiece for the opinions of the play's author, usually displaying a superior or more detached view of the action than the other characters.

**readerly**  *See* LISIBLE.

**reader-response criticism**  A general term for those kinds of modern *criticism and literary theory that focus on the responses of readers to literary works, rather than on the works themselves considered as self-contained entities. It is not a single agreed theory so much as a shared concern with a set of problems involving the extent and nature of readers' contribution to the meanings of literary works, approached from various positions including those of *structuralism (*see* COMPETENCE), psychoanalysis, *phenomenology, and *hermeneutics. The common factor is a shift from the description of *texts in terms of their inherent properties to a discussion of the production of meanings within the reading process. Important contributions to this debate include Wolfgang Iser's *The Act of Reading* (1978), which sees readers as 'actualizing' texts by filling in their 'gaps' or *indeterminacies of meaning, and Stanley Fish's *Is There a Text in this Class?* (1980), which gives the reader an even more active role as the text's true producer. A somewhat distinct line of historical investigation is represented by the *reception theory of Hans Robert Jauss.
**Further reading:** Elizabeth Freund, *The Return of the Reader* (1987).

**realism**  A mode of writing that gives the impression of recording or 'reflecting' faithfully an actual way of life. The term refers, sometimes confusingly, both to a literary method based on detailed accuracy of description (i.e. *verisimilitude) and to a more general attitude that rejects idealization, escapism, and other extravagant qualities of *romance in favour of recognizing soberly the actual problems of life. Modern criticism frequently insists that realism is not a direct or

simple reproduction of reality (a 'slice of life') but a system of
*conventions producing a lifelike illusion of some 'real' world outside
the text, by processes of selection, exclusion, description, and manners
of addressing the reader. In its methods and attitudes, realism may be
found as an element in many kinds of writing prior to the 19th century
(e.g. in Chaucer or Defoe, in their different ways); but as a dominant
literary trend it is associated chiefly with the 19th-century novel of
middle- or lower-class life, in which the problems of ordinary people in
unremarkable circumstances are rendered with close attention to the
details of physical setting and to the complexities of social life.

The outstanding works of realism in 19th-century fiction include
Honoré de Balzac's *Illusions perdues* (1837–43), Gustave Flaubert's
*Madame Bovary* (1857), and George Eliot's *Middlemarch* (1871–2); and
in early 20th-century fiction Arnold Bennett's *The Old Wives' Tale* (1908)
and Edith Wharton's *The House of Mirth* (1905). In France, a
self-consciously realist school announced itself in 1857 with the
publication of Champfleury's *Le Réalisme*, but the term normally refers
to the general convention rather than to this barely significant group. In
the work of some novelists, realism passes over into the movement of
*naturalism, in which sociological investigation and determinist views
of human behaviour predominate. Realism also established itself as
an important tradition in the theatre in the late 19th and early 20th
centuries, in the work of Henrik Ibsen, Bernard Shaw, and others; and
it remains a standard convention of film and television drama. Despite
the radical attempts of *modernism to displace the realist emphasis
on external reality (notably in the movements of *expressionism and
*surrealism), realism survived as a major current within 20th-century
fiction, sometimes under the label of *neo-realism.

**Further reading:** Pam Morris, *Realism* (2003).

**recension** A version of a literary work arrived at by a process of
*revision or *textual criticism; or the process of reconstructing the
most reliable readings from variant versions of a text. *See also* EDITION.

**reception theory** A branch of modern literary studies concerned
with the ways in which literary works are received by readers.
The term has sometimes been used to refer to *reader-response
criticism in general, but it is associated more particularly with the
'reception-aesthetics' (German, *Rezeptionsästhetik*) outlined in 1970 by

the German literary historian Hans Robert Jauss. Drawing on philosophical *hermeneutics, Jauss argued that literary works are received against an existing *horizon of expectations consisting of readers' current knowledge and presuppositions about literature, and that the meanings of works change as such horizons shift. Unlike most varieties of reader-response theory, then, reception theory is interested more in historical changes affecting the reading public than in the solitary reader.

**recessive accent** A *stress placed on the first syllable of a two-syllable word that is normally pronounced with the stress on its second syllable. This sometimes occurs in English verse when such a word is followed by a stressed syllable: for the sake of conformity to the *metre, the stress is shifted to the initial position, as in John Donne's line

But éxtreme sense hath made them desperate

The recessive accent is thus a specific type of 'wrenched accent' (*see* ACCENT).

***récit*** [ray-see] The French word for an 'account' or *narrative of events. As used in modern French *narratology, the term refers to the actual narrative *text itself, as opposed both to the *story and to its *narration.

**recognition** *See* ANAGNORISIS.

**recto** The front side of a printed sheet; thus the right-hand (and odd-numbered) page in a book, as opposed to the verso, which is the left-hand, even-numbered page on the other side.

**redaction** The editing or revising of a work for publication; or a new (sometimes shortened) *edition of a work. An editor is sometimes called a **redactor**. *Verb*: **redact**.

***redondilla*** [re-don-**dee**-yä] A Spanish stanza of four *octosyllabic lines usually rhyming *abab*. It was widely used in verse drama of the 16th and 17th centuries.

**reductionism** The tendency to explain away the complexities of a literary work as the products of a single, much simpler cause. A **reductive** interpretation of a work reduces or 'collapses' its actual complexity into a reassuring simplicity, seeing it as the direct expression of some originating element such as a personal motive, a psychological defect, a national or social identity, or a mythic *archetype.

**referent** That to which a linguistic expression refers. Usually this means some thing, process, or state of affairs in the world outside language. The Saussurean theory of the *sign, however, regards external reality as an unnecessary complication, preferring to replace the notion of the referent with the purely conceptual notion of the *signified. A distinction has sometimes been made in modern criticism between the **referential** language of factual information and the 'emotive' language of poetry (*see* PSEUDO-STATEMENT).

**reflectionism** A term sometimes used to refer to the common assumption that literary works reflect (or, in the well-worn *metaphor, 'hold a mirror up to') a pre-existing reality. This view is often challenged in modern literary theory, on the grounds that it denies the active nature of language and of the writer's transforming work. *See also* MIMESIS, REALISM.

**refrain** A line, group of lines, or part of a line repeated at regular or irregular intervals in a poem, usually at the end of each *stanza. It may recur in exactly the same form, or may be subject to slight variations (*see* INCREMENTAL REPETITION). It may form part of a stanza, as in the *ballade or *villanelle; or it may appear separately, as in many songs and *ballads, in which case it may be called a *burden, and, if intended for group singing, a *chorus. *See also* REPETEND.

**register** A term used in *stylistics to refer to a variety of language used in specified kinds of social situation, e.g. familial, legal, military: thus a formal register differs from an informal one, usually in vocabulary, pronunciation, and (if written) punctuation.

**Renaissance (Renascence)** The 'rebirth' of literature, art, and learning that progressively transformed European culture from the mid-14th century in Italy to the mid-17th century in England, strongly influenced by the rediscovery of classical Greek and Latin literature, and accelerated by the development of printing. The Renaissance is commonly held to mark the close of the Middle Ages and the beginning of the modern Western world, although the problems of dating this process have caused much debate: the existence of a significant renaissance of European learning in the 12th century is now accepted, while the 18th-century *Enlightenment is a direct continuation of the Renaissance's intellectual tendencies. However, the term normally refers to the combined intellectual and artistic transformations of the 15th and 16th centuries, including the emergence of *humanism, Protestant individualism, Copernican astronomy, and the discovery of America.

In literary terms, the Renaissance may be seen as a new tradition running from Petrarch and Boccaccio in Italy to Jonson and Milton in England, embracing the work of the French *Pléiade* and of Sidney, Spenser, and Shakespeare; it is marked by a new self-confidence in *vernacular literatures, a flourishing of *lyric poetry, and a revival of such classical forms as *epic and *pastoral literature. Use of the term in this sense has since the late 20th century been discouraged in academic history and literary study in favour of the more neutral term '*early modern'. The term 'Renaissance' has also been extended to various periods at which literature has flourished remarkably in specific places, without any suggestion of rebirth: for examples, *see* AMERICAN RENAISSANCE, HARLEM RENAISSANCE, IRISH LITERARY RENAISSANCE, SCOTTISH RENAISSANCE.

**Further reading:** Jerry Brotton, *The Renaissance* (2006).

((⊕)) SEE WEB LINKS
• Luminarium: extensive study resource for the period.

**repartee** [rep-ar-**tee**] A rapid and witty response in conversation, especially one that turns an insult back on its originator; or a succession of such replies in a *dialogue between characters (usually in a drama). The term may also be applied to a person's talent for making witty replies.

**repertory (rep)** A system of theatrical production in which a resident company performs different plays succeeding each other at short intervals, commonly weekly or fortnightly. A theatre company that uses this system is called a repertory company, and the repertory is also the name for the current list (or **repertoire**) of plays that it can produce at short notice. The term, originally meaning 'catalogue', was first applied in this sense in the 1890s, although a similar system had been employed in the theatre long before then, as with Shakespeare's company, the Lord Chamberlain's Men (later the King's Men) and the 19th-century troupes known as stock companies. A strong revival of their principles, referred to as the **Repertory Movement**, was launched by the wealthy patroness Annie Horniman, leading to the establishment of the Manchester Repertory Theatre in 1907, the Liverpool Playhouse

(1911), the Birmingham Repertory Theatre (1913), and others in many English provincial cities. The dominant London practice in modern times has been the long run of a single play performed by a temporary cast that disbands when the run concludes, but the Royal Shakespeare Company and the National Theatre have used the repertory system.

**repetend** [rep-eĕt-end]  A word, phrase, or line that recurs in a poem. As distinct from a *refrain, a repetend is repeated only partially or only at irregular intervals.

**Restoration comedy**  A kind of English *comedy, usually in the form of the *comedy of manners, that flourished during the Restoration period in England (i.e. from the Restoration of the Stuart monarchy in 1660 to about 1700), when actresses were first employed on the London stage. Appealing to a fairly narrow audience of aristocrats in the recently reopened theatres, Restoration comedy relied upon sophisticated *repartee and a knowledge of the exclusive code of manners in high society, the plots being based on the complex *intrigues of the marriage-market. The characters can often be divided between the young aristocrats who can understand and manipulate the rules of the social game, and the middle-class upstarts who wish to be thought fashionable and witty but expose their ignorance in a series of blunders. The frequently cynical approach to marriage and sexual infidelity in Restoration comedy invited accusations of immorality. Significant examples are George Etherege's *The Man of Mode* (1676), William Wycherley's *The Country Wife* (1675), and William Congreve's *The Way of the World* (1700).

**Further reading:** Edward Burns, *Restoration Comedy* (1987).

(((🌐))) SEE WEB LINKS

• Restoration Comedy project at University of Seville, catalogues plays and performances.

**revenge tragedy**  A kind of *tragedy popular in England from the 1590s to the 1630s, following the success of Thomas Kyd's sensational play *The Spanish Tragedy* (c.1589). Its action is typically centred upon a leading character's attempt to avenge the murder of a loved one, sometimes at the prompting of the victim's ghost; it involves complex intrigues and disguises, and usually some exploration of the morality of revenge. Drawing partly on precedents in *Senecan tragedy, the English revenge tragedy is far more bloodthirsty in its explicit presentation of premeditated violence, and so the more gruesome examples such as

Shakespeare's *Titus Andronicus* are sometimes called 'tragedies of blood'. Notable examples of plays that are fully or partly within the revenge tradition are Christopher Marlowe's *The Jew of Malta*, Cyril Tourneur's *The Revenger's Tragedy*, John Webster's *The Duchess of Malfi*, and John Ford's *'Tis Pity She's a Whore*. A more famous play drawing on the revenge *conventions is Shakespeare's *Hamlet*.

**Further reading:** John Kerrigan, *Revenge Tragedy* (1996).

***reverdie*** A kind of medieval French dancing song celebrating the arrival of spring. The term is sometimes extended to include any poem or poetic passage that welcomes spring's return.

**reversal** *See* PERIPETEIA.

**revision** The process of amending an earlier version (published or unpublished) of a work; or the newly amended text thus produced. *Adjective*: **revisionary** or **revisional**. *Verb*: **revise**.

**revisionist** Dedicated to the overturning of an established interpretation or widely shared assumption, especially in the contexts of politics and the study of history. The term is increasingly found in debates within *literary history.

**revue** A theatrical entertainment consisting of a series of songs, dances, and comic *sketches. It is often devoted to topical *satire, although another kind of revue concentrates on spectacular costumes and dancing. *See also* BURLESQUE.

***Rezeptionsästhetik*** *See* RECEPTION THEORY.

**rhapsody** In the modern sense, a work or passage expressing ecstatic or uncontrolled emotion, often in a loosely structured fashion. In ancient Greece, a rhapsody was a selection of *epic poetry sung by a **rhapsode** or **rhapsodist**—literally a 'stitcher' who combined memorized passages with his own improvisations, although this kind of *minstrel was later required chiefly to recite Homer's *Iliad* and *Odyssey* in their established versions. *Adjective*: **rhapsodic**. *Verb*: **rhapsodize**.

**rhetoric** [ret-er-ik] The deliberate exploitation of eloquence for the most persuasive effect in public speaking or in writing. It was cultivated as an important art and science in antiquity, and was an essential element of medieval university education, involving the elaborate categorizing of *figures of speech together with the arts of memory, arrangement, and oratorical delivery. The emphasis on sincerity in the culture of *Romanticism helped to discredit rhetoric, so that the usual modern sense of the term implies empty and ineffectual grandness in public speech. Modern critics sometimes refer to the rhetorical dimension of a literary work, meaning those aspects of the work that persuade or otherwise guide the responses of readers. A practitioner or theorist of rhetoric is called a **rhetorician**.

**Further reading:** Jennifer Richards, *Rhetoric* (2007).

(🌐) SEE WEB LINKS

- Silva Rhetoricae (The Forest of Rhetoric): extensive reference source for rhetorical theory and figures.

**rhetorical figure** *See* FIGURE.

**rhetorical question** A question asked for the sake of persuasive effect rather than as a genuine request for information, the speaker implying that the answer is too obvious to require a reply, as in Milton's line

> For what can war but endless war still breed?

**rhyme** The identity of sound between syllables or paired groups of syllables, usually at the ends of verse lines; also a poem employing this device. Normally the last stressed vowel in the line and all sounds following it make up the rhyming element: this may be a monosyllable (*love*/ab*ove*—known as '*masculine rhyme'), or two syllables (wh*ether*/tog*ether*—known as '*feminine rhyme' or 'double rhyme'), or even three syllables (*glamorous/amorous*—known as '*triple rhyme'). Where a rhyming element in a feminine or triple rhyme uses more than one word (*famous*/sh*ame us*), this is known as a 'mosaic rhyme'. The rhyming pairs illustrated so far are all examples of 'full rhyme' (also called 'perfect rhyme' or 'true rhyme'); departures from this norm take four main forms: (i) *rime riche*, in which the consonants preceding the rhyming elements are also identical, even if the spellings and meanings of the words differ (*made/maid*); (ii) *eye rhyme, in which the spellings of the rhyming elements match, but the sounds do not (l*ove*/pr*ove*); (iii) *half-rhyme or 'slant rhyme', where the vowel sounds do not match (l*ove*/h*ave*); (iv) *pararhyme, i.e. half-rhyme with additional rich *consonance (*love/leave*).

Half-rhyme is known by several other names: 'imperfect rhyme', 'near rhyme', etc. Although rhyme is most often used at the ends of verse lines, *internal rhyme between syllables within the same line is also found (*see also* CROSSED RHYME, LEONINE RHYME). Rhyme is not essential to poetry: many languages rarely use it, and in English it finally replaced *alliteration as the usual patterning device of verse only in the late 14th century. A writer of rhyming verse may sometimes be referred to disparagingly as a **rhymester** or **rhymer**.

**Further reading:** Donald Wesling, *The Chances of Rhyme* (1980).

**rhyme royal** A *stanza form consisting of seven 5-stress lines (iambic *pentameters) rhyming *ababbcc*, first used by Chaucer and thus also known as the Chaucerian stanza. Following Chaucer's use of rhyme royal in his *Troilus and Criseyde, The Parlement of Fowles*, and some of the *Canterbury Tales*, it continued to be an important form of English verse in the 15th and 16th centuries, being used by Dunbar, Henryson, Spenser, and Shakespeare (in his *Lucrece*, 1594); W. H. Auden's 'Letter to Lord Byron' (1937) is the most notable modern revival of the form. The name of this stanza seems to come from its use in *The Kingis Quair* (*c*.1424), a poem uncertainly attributed to King James I of Scotland.

**rhyme scheme** The pattern in which the rhymed line-endings are arranged in a poem or *stanza. This may be expressed as a sequence of recurrences in which each line ending on the same rhyme is given the same alphabetic symbol: thus the rhyme scheme of a *limerick is given the notation *aabba*. Rhyme schemes may follow a fixed pattern, as in the *sonnet and several other forms, or they may be arranged freely according to the poet's requirements. The simplest rhyme schemes are those of rhyming *couplets (*aabbcc*, etc.) and of the common *quatrain forms (*abab, abcb, abba*), while those of *ottava rima*, *rhyme royal, the *Spenserian stanza, and the French *fixed forms are far more intricate.

**rhythm** The pattern of sounds perceived as the recurrence of equivalent 'beats' at more or less equal intervals. In most English poetry, an underlying rhythm (commonly a sequence of four or five beats) is manifested in a metrical pattern (*see* METRE)—a sequence of measured beats and 'offbeats' arranged in verse lines and governing the alternation of stressed and unstressed syllables. While metre involves the recurrence of measured sound units, rhythm is a less clearly structured principle: one can refer to the unmeasured rhythms of everyday speech, or of *prose, and to the rhythms or *cadences of non-metrical verse (i.e. *free verse). *See also* FALLING RHYTHM, RISING RHYTHM, SPRUNG RHYTHM.

**riddle** A puzzlingly indirect description of some thing, person, or idea, framed in such a way as to challenge the reader to identify it. Riddles, usually in verse, are found as a popular literary form in most cultures and periods. An important Old English collection is preserved in the 10th-century Exeter Book.

*rime riche* [reem reesh] A kind of *rhyme (also called 'identical rhyme') in which the rhyming elements include matching consonants before the stressed vowel sounds. Often this means the rhyming of two words with the same sound and sometimes the same spelling but different meanings, e.g. *seen/scene*. The term also covers word-endings where the consonant preceding the stressed vowel sound is the same: com*pare*/des*pair*. An even more excessive kind of rhyme is *rime très riche*, in which not only the preceding consonant but also the vowel sound before that remains the same: *allowed/aloud*. Usually avoided in English, *rimes riches* are found far more often in French verse. The normal kind of English rhyme, in which the rhyming element begins only with the stressed vowel sound nearest to the end of the line, is referred to in French as *rime suffisante*. *See also* PARARHYME.

**rising rhythm** A rhythmic effect often found in metrical verse in which the unstressed syllables are perceived as being linked with the succeeding stressed syllables rather than with those preceding them. In terms of classical *prosody, lines composed of *iambs or *anapaests may show this rising rhythm, although this is not inevitable. Rising rhythm in English verse is far more common than its opposite, *falling rhythm.

*rispetto* (plural *-etti*) An alternative name, especially in Tuscany, for the Italian verse form more widely known as the *strambotto*.

**rococo** [rŏ-**koh**-koh] An 18th-century style of architecture and furnishing characterized by elaborately playful decoration, and regarded by stern classical purists as 'effeminate' or tastelessly pretty. As applied to literature, the term is unhelpfully vague, but usually suggests a cheerful lightness and intimacy of tone, and an elegant playfulness:

Pope's *The Rape of the Lock* (1712–14) and Sterne's *Tristram Shandy* (1759–67) have been cited as English examples.

**rodomontade** [rod-ŏ-mon-**tayd**] A blusteringly boastful speech, or any arrogantly inflated manner of speaking or writing. *See also* BOMBAST.

*rogatio* A rhetorical *figure in which a question is posed and then answered by the same speaker or writer, as in Mr Chadband's speeches in Charles Dickens's *Bleak House*: 'What is peace? Is it war? No. Is it strife? No.' *See also* RHETORICAL QUESTION.

*roman à clef* [**roh**-mah$^n$ a klay] The French term ('novel with a key') for a kind of novel in which the well-informed reader will recognize identifiable persons from real life thinly disguised as fictional characters. A significant English example is Thomas Love Peacock's satirical novel *Nightmare Abbey* (1818), in which 'Mr Flosky' is clearly the poet Samuel Taylor Coleridge, 'Mr Cypress' is Lord Byron, and 'Scythrop' is Percy Bysshe Shelley. Very many novels based upon their authors' own lives are to some degree *romans à clef*.

*roman à thèse* [**roh**-mah$^n$ a tez] The French term for a 'thesis novel', that is, a *didactic novel that puts forward an argument or proposes a solution to some problem of politics, morality, or philosophy. The most celebrated example in English is Harriet Beecher Stowe's *Uncle Tom's Cabin* (1852), which powerfully urged the abolition of slavery. A more philosophical kind of thesis novel is Jean-Paul Sartre's *La Nausée* (1938), which embodies many of the principles of his *existentialism. *See also* PROPAGANDISM, THESIS.

*roman à tiroirs* [**roh**-mah$^n$ a tee-rwah] The French term for an *episodic novel, such as Alain-René Lesage's *Gil Blas* (1715–35)—a *tiroir* being a drawer in a desk or chest. *See also* PICARESQUE NOVEL.

**romance** A fictional story in verse or prose that relates improbable adventures of idealized characters in some remote or enchanted setting; or, more generally, a tendency in fiction opposite to that of *realism. The term now embraces many forms of fiction from the *Gothic novel and the popular escapist love story (also known popularly as romances) to the 'scientific romances' of H. G. Wells, but it usually refers to the tales of King Arthur's knights written in the late Middle Ages by Chrétien de Troyes (in verse), Sir Thomas Malory (in prose), and many others (*see* ARTHURIAN LITERATURE, CHIVALRIC ROMANCE). Medieval romance is distinguished from *epic by its concentration on *courtly love rather than warlike heroism. Long, elaborate romances were written during the *Renaissance, including Ludovico Ariosto's *Orlando Furioso* (1532), Edmund Spenser's *The Faerie Queene* (1590–96), and Sir Philip Sidney's prose romance *Arcadia* (1590), but Cervantes's *parody of romances in *Don Quixote* (1605) helped to undermine this tradition. Later prose romances differ from novels in their preference for *allegory and psychological exploration rather than realistic social observation, especially in American works like Nathaniel Hawthorne's *The Blithedale Romance* (1852). Several modern literary *genres, from *science fiction to the *detective story, can be regarded as variants of the romance (*see also* FANTASY, MARVELLOUS). In modern criticism of Shakespeare, the term is also applied to four of his last plays—*Pericles*, *Cymbeline*, *The Winter's Tale*, and *The Tempest*—which are distinguished by their daring use of magical illusion and improbable reunions.

The **Romance languages** are those languages originating in southern Europe that are derived from Latin: the most important of these are Spanish, French, Italian, and Portuguese. In Spanish literature, the term has a special sense, the *romance* [ro-**mahn**-thay] being a *ballad composed in *octosyllabic lines.

**Further reading:** Barbara Fuchs, *Romance* (2004).

***romancero*** [roh-man-**their**-oh] The Spanish term, derived from *romance* ('ballad'), both for a collection of ballads and for balladry; also applied to the corpus of Spanish ballads as a whole.

***roman-feuilleton*** A serialized novel: *see* FEUILLETON.

***roman-fleuve*** [**roh**-mah$^n$ flerv] A continuous sequence of novels through which are traced the fortunes of the same character or group of characters; literally a 'river-novel' that flows through from one book to the next. The most celebrated example is Marcel Proust's seven-novel sequence *A la recherche du temps perdu* (1913–27). In English, significant examples are Anthony Trollope's five Barsetshire novels (1855–67), Anthony Powell's *A Dance to the Music of Time* (twelve novels, 1951–75), and Doris Lessing's *Children of Violence* sequence (five novels, 1952–69). *See also* CYCLE, SAGA.

**romantic comedy** A general term for *comedies that deal mainly with the follies and misunderstandings of young lovers, in a light-hearted and happily concluded manner which usually avoids serious *satire. The best-known examples are Shakespeare's comedies of the late 1590s, *A Midsummer Night's Dream*, *Twelfth Night*, and *As You Like It* being the most purely romantic, while *Much Ado About Nothing* approaches the *comedy of manners and *The Merchant of Venice* is closer to *tragicomedy. The romantic comedy has become a recognized genre of popular film, in which context it is now sometimes abbreviated as **romcom**. *See also* NEW COMEDY.

**romantic irony** A kind of literary self-consciousness in which an author signals his or her freedom from the limits of a given work by puncturing its fictional illusion and exposing its process of composition as a matter of authorial whim. This is often a kind of protective self-mockery involving a playful attitude towards the conventions of the (normally narrative) genre. Byron's narrative poem *Don Juan* (1819–24) is a sustained exercise in romantic irony, as is Laurence Sterne's novel *Tristram Shandy* (1759–67), but the effect may also be found in Chaucer and many other authors of different periods.

**Further reading:** Anne K. Mellor, *English Romantic Irony* (1980).

**romanticism** *See* p. 316.

**rondeau** A medieval French verse form also used by some late 19th-century poets in English. It normally consists of 13 *octosyllabic lines, grouped in *stanzas of five, three, and five lines. The whole poem uses only two rhymes, and the first word or phrase of the first line recurs twice as a *refrain after the second and third stanzas. The standard *rhyme scheme (with the unrhymed refrain indicated as *R*) is *aabba aabR aabbaR*. Variant forms of the rondeau include those using 10-syllable lines and those having only 12 lines, but in all cases the refrain and the restriction to two rhymes are retained. An even more complicated form is the *rondeau redoublé*, a 24-line poem also using only two rhymes in its six *quatrains, with each line of the first stanza recurring in turn as the final line of the following stanzas until the poem's opening phrase recurs after the last line. *See also* RONDEL, ROUNDEL.

**rondel** A medieval French verse form related to the *triolet and the *rondeau. In its usual modern form, it is a 13-line poem using only two rhymes in its three *stanzas. It employs a two-line *refrain which opens

## ROMANTICISM

A sweeping but indispensable modern term applied to the profound shift in Western attitudes to art and human creativity that dominated much of European culture in the first half of the 19th century, and that has shaped most subsequent developments in literature—even those reacting against it. In its most coherent early form, as it emerged in the 1790s in Germany and Britain, and in the 1820s in France and elsewhere, it is known as the **Romantic Movement** or **Romantic Revival**. Its chief emphasis was upon freedom of individual self-expression: sincerity, spontaneity, and originality became the new standards in literature, replacing the decorous imitation of classical models favoured by 18th-century *neoclassicism. Rejecting the ordered rationality of the *Enlightenment as mechanical, impersonal, and artificial, the **Romantics** turned to the emotional directness of personal experience and to the boundlessness of individual imagination and aspiration. Increasingly independent of the declining system of aristocratic patronage, they saw themselves as free spirits expressing their own imaginative truths; several found admirers ready to hero-worship the artist as a genius or prophet. The restrained balance valued in 18th-century culture was abandoned in favour of emotional intensity, often taken to extremes of rapture, nostalgia (for childhood or the past), horror, melancholy, or sentimentality. Some—but not all—Romantic writers cultivated the appeal of the exotic, the bizarre, or the macabre; almost all showed a new interest in the irrational realms of dream and delirium or of folk superstition and legend. The creative imagination occupied the centre of Romantic views of art, which replaced the 'mechanical' rules of conventional form with an 'organic' principle of natural growth and free development.

The emergence of Romanticism has been attributed to several developments in late 18th-century culture (*see* PREROMANTICISM), including a strong antiquarian interest in *ballads and medieval *romances (from which Romanticism takes its name). The immediate inspiration for the first self-declared Romantics—the German group including the Schlegel brothers and Novalis—was the transcendental philosophy of Kant and Fichte, which stressed the creative power of the mind and allowed nature to be seen as a responsive mirror of the soul. This new German thinking spread via S. T. Coleridge to Britain and via Mme de Staël to France, eventually shaping American *Transcendentalism. English Romanticism had emerged independently with William Blake's then little-known anti-Enlightenment writings of the 1790s and with the landmark of William Wordsworth's 1800 Preface to *Lyrical Ballads*. In a second wave after the Napoleonic wars, Romanticism established itself in France and across Europe; by the 1830s the movement extended from Pushkin in Russia to Poe in the USA. Romanticism drew some of its energies from the associated revolutionary movements of democracy and nationalism, although the 'classical' culture of the French Revolution actually delayed the arrival of French Romanticism, and a strong element of conservative nostalgia is also evident in many Romantic writers.

The literary rebellion of Wordsworth in England and Victor Hugo in France declared an end to the artificiality of older *conventions, breaking up the 18th-century system of distinct *genres and of *poetic diction. *Lyric poetry underwent a major revival led by Wordsworth, Keats, Shelley, Pushkin, Leopardi, Heine, and others; *narrative verse took on a new subjective dimension in the work of Wordsworth and Byron, but the theatre tended towards the sensationalism of *melodrama. In fiction, Hoffmann and Poe pioneered the tale of terror in the wake of the *Gothic novel, while the *historical novels of Walter Scott, Alessandro Manzoni, Victor Hugo, and James Fenimore Cooper combined bold action with nostalgic sentiment. A new wave of women novelists led by Mary Shelley, George Sand, and the Brontë sisters broke the imposed restraints of modesty in works of powerful imaginative force. The astonishing personality of Byron provided Alfred de Musset, Mikhail Lermontov, and other admirers throughout Europe with a model of the Romantic poet as tormented outcast. The growing international cult of Shakespeare also reflected the Romantic hero-worship which, in the writings of Thomas Carlyle and R. W. Emerson, became a 'heroic' view of history as the product of forceful personalities like Napoleon.

Although challenged in the second half of the 19th century by the rise of *realism and *naturalism, Romanticism has in some ways maintained a constant presence in Western literature, providing the basis for several schools and movements from the *Pre-Raphaelites and *Symbolists to *expressionism and *Surrealism. In a broader sense, the term 'romantic' may be applied to works and authors of other periods, by explicit or implicit comparison with a 'classical' standard: thus Shakespeare is more romantic than Molière or Ben Jonson, both because he disregards the structural models of Greek drama and because he exploits freely the supernatural elements of folk legend; and in a different way, W. B. Yeats and D. H. Lawrence are more romantic than W. H. Auden and E. M. Forster, because they assert the absolute primacy of their personal visions, rejecting common norms of objectivity.

**Further reading:** Aidan Day, *Romanticism* (2nd edn, 2011).

（(∰)) SEE WEB LINKS

• Romantic Circles: extensive scholarly resource based at University of Maryland.

the poem and recurs at lines 7 and 8, the first line (or, in a 14-line variant, both opening lines) also completing the poem. The *rhyme scheme—with the repeated lines given in capitals—is thus *ABba abAB abbaA(B)*. There is no fixed *metre. This form was adopted by some poets in England in the late 19th century, including Austin Dobson and W. E. Henley.

**roundel** An English version of the *rondeau, devised by A. C. Swinburne for his collection *A Century of Roundels* (1883). It is a poem of eleven lines using only two rhymes in its three *stanzas of 4, 3, and 4 lines. Lines 4 and 11 are formed by the repetition of the poem's opening word or phrase as a *refrain, which may be rhymed with lines 2, 5, 7, and 9. The rhyme scheme (with the refrain represented as *R*) is thus *abaR bab abaR*, or, with a rhyming refrain, *abaB bab abaB*. The term was at one time a *synonym for a rondeau or *rondel.

**roundelay** A short dancing song with a *refrain. The term covers the *rondeau, the *rondel, and various simpler forms, but commonly refers to such works as they are set to music.

***rubáiyát*** A sequence or collection of Arabic or Persian *quatrains. The term is most often associated with *The Rubáiyát of Omar Khayyám* (1859), a free English translation by Edward Fitzgerald of the 12th-century Persian poet's quatrains.

**rune** A letter belonging to an old Germanic alphabet thought to have been used from the 2nd century CE, which is found in inscriptions on stones, coins, etc. The **runic** alphabet came to be associated with magical powers, and so the term has sometimes been used to refer to any inscription, sign, or written message having magical properties or secret power.

**Russian Formalism** A school of literary theory and analysis that emerged in Russia around 1915, devoting itself to the study of *literariness, i.e. the sum of 'devices' that distinguish literary language from ordinary language. In reaction against the vagueness of previous literary theories, it attempted a scientific description of literature (especially poetry) as a special use of language with observable features. This meant deliberately disregarding the contents of literary works, and thus inviting strong disapproval from Marxist critics, for whom *formalism was a term of reproach. With the consolidation of Stalin's dictatorship around 1929, Formalism was silenced as a heresy in the Soviet Union, and its centre of research migrated to the *Prague School in the 1930s. Along with 'literariness', the most important concept of the school was that of *defamiliarization: instead of seeing literature as a 'reflection' of the world, Victor Shklovsky and his Formalist followers saw it as a linguistic dislocation, or a 'making strange'. In the period of Czech Formalism, Jan Mukařovský further refined this notion in terms of *foregrounding. In their studies of *narrative, the Formalists also clarified the distinction between *plot (*sjuzet*) and *story (*fabula*). Apart from Shklovsky and his associate Boris Eikhenbaum, the most prominent of the Russian Formalists was Roman Jakobson, who was active both in Moscow and in Prague before introducing Formalist theories to the United States (*see* FUNCTION). A somewhat distinct Russian group is the 'Bakhtin school' comprising Mikhail Bakhtin, Pavlev Medvedev, and Valentin Voloshinov; these theorists combined elements of Formalism and Marxism in their accounts of verbal *multi-accentuality and of the *dialogic text. Rediscovered in the West in the 1960s, the work of the Russian Formalists has had an important influence on *structuralist theories of literature, and on some of the more recent varieties of Marxist literary criticism.

**Further reading:** Peter Steiner, *Russian Formalism* (1984).

r

**saga** The Norse name for various kinds of prose tales composed in medieval Scandinavia and Iceland and written down from the 12th century to the 14th. These usually tell of heroic leaders—early Norse kings or 13th-century bishops—or of the heroic settlers of Iceland in the 9th and 10th centuries; others, like the *Vǫlsunga saga*, relate earlier legends. The emphasis on feuds and family histories in some famous sagas like *Njáls saga* has led to the term's application in English to any long family story spanning two or more generations: this may take the form of a lengthy novel like D. H. Lawrence's *The Rainbow* (1915) or of a novel-sequence (*see* ROMAN-FLEUVE) such as John Galsworthy's *The Forsyte Saga* (1922).

**salon** A French cultural institution consisting of a weekly social gathering at the private house of an aristocratic lady, at which social, artistic, and scientific questions are discussed. From the early 17th century to the early 19th, several important literary and philosophical salons provided a social base for French writers. The term can also refer to an exhibition of paintings by living artists, so that in a second literary sense the title *Salon* has been given to an essay on contemporary art and related matters: Diderot in the 18th century and Baudelaire in the 19th both wrote important *Salons*. In this capacity they may be referred to as *salonniers*, i.e. art critics. *See also* CÉNACLE.

**samizdat** A Russian word meaning 'self-publishing', applied since the 1960s to a clandestine mode of publication by which 'dissident' writings and other banned works were secretly circulated during the late Soviet period, usually in typed carbon copies or photocopies. Novels by Alexander Solzhenitsyn and articles by Andrei Sakharov were among the important *samizdat* works of the 1960s and 1970s.

**Sapphics** *Lyric verses written in a Greek *metre named after Sappho, the legendary woman poet of Lesbos (7th/6th century BCE). Sapphic verse uses *stanzas of four lines, the first three having eleven syllables, the last having five. In the first three lines, the sequence of five metrical feet is: *trochee; trochee or *spondee; *dactyl; trochee; trochee or spondee. In the fourth line, a dactyl is followed by a trochee or a spondee. The metre was used frequently in Latin by Horace, but it is difficult to adapt to the stress-patterns of English. Sidney, Swinburne, and Pound are among the poets who have attempted English Sapphics.

**satire** A mode of writing that exposes the failings of individuals, institutions, or societies to ridicule and scorn. Satire is often an incidental element in literary works that may not be wholly satirical, especially in *comedy. Its tone may vary from tolerant amusement, as in the verse satires of the Roman poet Horace, to bitter indignation, as in the verse of Juvenal and the prose of Jonathan Swift (*see* JUVENALIAN). Various forms of literature may be satirical, from the plays of Ben Jonson or of Molière and the poetry of Chaucer or Byron to the prose writings of Rabelais and Voltaire. The models of Roman satire, especially the verse satires of Horace and Juvenal, inspired some important imitations by Boileau, Pope, and Johnson in the greatest period of satire—the 17th and 18th centuries—when writers could appeal to a shared sense of normal conduct from which vice and folly were seen to stray. In this classical tradition, an important form is 'formal' or 'direct' satire, in which the writer directly addresses the reader (or recipient of a verse letter) with satiric comment. The alternative form of 'indirect' satire usually found in plays and novels allows us to draw our own conclusions from the actions of the characters, as for example in the novels of Evelyn Waugh or Chinua Achebe. *See also* LAMPOON.

**Further reading:** Ruben Quintero (ed.), *A Companion to Satire* (2006).

**S**

**satyr play (satyric drama)** A humorous performance presented in Athenian dramatic contests, following a *trilogy of tragedies. The satyr play had a *chorus of satyrs (men with horses' tails and ears), and its action was a *burlesque of some mythical story appropriate to the fore-going tragedies, involving obscene language and gestures. Although fragments of satyr plays by Aeschylus and Sophocles have been found, the only complete example to have survived is the *Cyclops* (*c*.412 BCE) of Euripides. Tony Harrison's *The Trackers of Oxyrhynchus* (1988) is a modern satyr play adapted from the fragmentary *Ichneutae* of Sophocles.

**scansion** The analysis of poetic *metre in verse lines, by displaying
*stresses, pauses, and rhyme patterns with conventional visual symbols.
The simplest system, known as graphic scansion, marks stressed
syllables (' or − or •), unstressed syllables (ˣ or ‿ or ○), divisions
between metrical units or 'feet' (*see* FOOT) (|), and major pauses or
*caesuras (‖) in a verse line, determining whether its metre is, for
example, *iambic or *dactylic, and how many feet make up the line. In
Greek and Latin *quantitative verse, the symbols − and ‿ indicate long
and short syllables respectively. Scansion also analyses the *rhyme
scheme in a poem or *stanza, giving alphabetical symbols to the rhymes:
*abcb* or *abab* in most *quatrains, *aabba* in *limericks, for instance. The
verb **scan** is applied not only to the activity of analysing metre, but also
to the lines analysed: of a line with an irregular or inconsistent metrical
pattern it is said that it does not scan. *See also* DIACRITIC, PROSODY.

**scatology** The study of excrement, e.g. in medicine or palaeontology.
In the literary sense it means repeated reference to excrement and
related matters, as in the coarse humour of François Rabelais or
Jonathan Swift, whose works have passages of a scatological nature.

**scenario** [sin-**ar**-i-oh] A brief outline of the *plot, characters, and
scene-changes of a play; or the script of a film. In the cinematic sense, a
scenario is usually more detailed, whereas the theatrical scenarios of the
*commedia dell' arte* were 'skeleton' summaries used as the basis for
improvisations. A writer of scenarios, usually for the cinema, is
sometimes called a **scenarist**.

**scene** In a drama, a subdivision of an *act or of a play not divided into
acts. A scene normally represents actions happening in one place at one
time, and is marked off from the next scene by a curtain, a black-out, or a
brief emptying of the stage. In the study of *narrative works, 'scene' is
also the name given to a 'dramatic' method of narration that presents
events at roughly the same pace as that at which they are supposed to be
occurring, i.e. usually in detail and with substantial use of *dialogue. In
this sense the scenic narrative method is contrasted with 'summary', in
which the duration of the story's events is compressed into a brief
account. *Adjective*: **scenic**.

***scène à faire*** [sen a fair] A French term for the kind of *scene within a
drama towards which the preceding action seems inevitably to tend,

such as the crucial encounter between hero and villain. It usually provides an emotional *climax. The term is sometimes rendered in English as 'obligatory scene'. *See also* ANAGNORISIS, CATASTROPHE, CRISIS, DÉNOUEMENT, WELL-MADE PLAY.

**Schauerroman** [show-er-roh-man] (plural -*mane*)  The German term for a *Gothic novel or similar horror story, literally a 'shudder-novel'.

**scheme**  A term once used for a rhetorical *figure (or figure of speech), usually one that departs from the normal order or sound of words but does not extended their meanings as a *trope does. Some rhetoricians, however, have used the term to cover tropes as well.

**scholasticism**  The methods and doctrines of the leading academic philosophers and theologians of the late Middle Ages in Europe. The **schoolmen** of the 12th, 13th, and 14th centuries attempted to reconcile Christian theology with the Greek philosophy of Aristotle. The leading figures of scholasticism included Peter Abelard, Albertus Magnus, Duns Scotus, and above all Thomas Aquinas, whose *Summa Theologica* (mid-13th century) is the most ambitious of scholastic works; his followers are called Thomists. During the *Renaissance, the deductive logic of scholasticism was superseded by the inductive methods of modern science, while its theological concerns were challenged by the emergence of *humanism.

**school drama**  *See* ACADEMIC DRAMA.

**science fiction**  A popular modern branch of prose fiction that explores the probable consequences of some improbable or impossible transformation of the basic conditions of human (or intelligent non-human) existence. This transformation need not be brought about by a technological invention, but may involve some mutation of known biological or physical reality, e.g. time travel, extraterrestrial invasion, ecological catastrophe. Science fiction is a form of literary *fantasy or *romance that often draws upon earlier kinds of *utopian and *apocalyptic writing. The term itself was first given general currency by Hugo Gernsback, editor of the American magazine *Amazing Stories* from 1926 onwards, and it is usually abbreviated to **SF** or **sci-fi**; before this, such works were called 'scientific romances' by H. G. Wells and others. Several early precedents have been claimed for the genre—notably Mary

Shelley's *Frankenstein* (1818)—but true modern science fiction begins
with Jules Verne's *Voyage au centre de la terre* (1864) and H. G. Wells's
*The Time Machine* (1895). Once uniformly dismissed as *pulp fiction,
SF gained greater respect during the 1950s, as writers like Isaac Asimov,
Ray Bradbury, and Arthur C. Clarke expanded its range. SF has also
had an important influence on *postmodernist fiction by writers not
devoted to this *genre alone: Thomas Pynchon, Kurt Vonnegut, Doris
Lessing, and Italo Calvino are significant examples.

**Further reading:** Roger Luckhurst, *Science Fiction* (2005).

(((⊕))) SEE WEB LINKS

• Science Fiction and Fantasy Research Database at Texas A&M.

## Scottish Chaucerians
The name given to a group of 15th- and
16th-century Scottish poets who wrote under the influence of Geoffrey
Chaucer (or of his follower John Lydgate), often using his seven-line
*rhyme royal stanza. The most important poets of this group were
Robert Henryson, whose *Testament of Cresseid* continues and
reinterprets the story of Chaucer's *Troilus and Criseyde*, and William
Dunbar, whose *Lament for the Makaris* briefly pays tribute to Chaucer.
Other figures are Gavin Douglas, Sir David Lyndsay, and (if his
authorship of *The Kingis Quair* be accepted) King James I of Scotland.
The term unfortunately diverts attention from the genuinely original
character of these poets, and is thus not much favoured in Scotland.

## Scottish Renaissance
A term applied to the notable revival of
literary innovation in Scotland, and by émigré Scottish writers
elsewhere, in the 1920s and 1930s. Before becoming recognized as an
achievement, the Scottish Renaissance was first projected as a goal,
partly in emulation of the *Irish Literary Renaissance and in response
to European *modernism, in critical articles of the early 1920s by
Christopher M. Grieve, who subsequently wrote under the pen-name
Hugh MacDiarmid. His long poem *A Drunk Man Looks at the Thistle*
(1926) is the first major work of this movement. At this time MacDiarmid
wrote in a newly devised literary dialect known as 'synthetic Scots' or
'Lallans', blending Lowlands speech with *diction derived from
etymological dictionaries; this he later abandoned, while other Scottish
poets of this period, notably Edwin Muir, preferred standard English. In
prose fiction, the term is applied to the early novels of Neil M. Gunn and
Nan Shepherd, but the outstanding work is Lewis Grassic Gibbon's
novel trilogy *A Scots Quair* (1932–4). Accounts of modern Scottish

S

literature usually apply the term principally to these nationally self-conscious works by MacDiarmid and his associates (some of whom also helped to revive political nationalism at this time), and sometimes include writings by Naomi Mitchison, A. J. Cronin, and others. Some popular Scottish-born writers of the time—Arthur Conan Doyle, J. M. Barrie, John Buchan—are usually not counted as participants in the Renaissance.

**Further reading:** Margery Palmer McCulloch, *Scottish Modernism and its Contexts 1918–1959* (2009).

**screenplay** The script of a film, comprising *dialogue (and/or *narration) with instructions for sets and camera positions.

*scriptible* [scrip-teebl] A term used by the French critic Roland Barthes in his book *S/Z* (1970), and usually translated as 'writerly'. In contrast with the easily readable or 'readerly' text (*texte *lisible*), the writerly text does not have a single 'closed' meaning; instead, it obliges each reader to produce his or her own meanings from its fragmentary or contradictory hints. Ideally—and the concept is very much a theoretical ideal rather than a description—the writerly text is challengingly 'open', giving the reader an active role as co-writer, rather than as passive consumer. The nearest actual equivalents of this ideal would seem to be the more difficult works of *modernism and *postmodernism. *See also* INDETERMINACY, *JOUISSANCE*.

*Secentismo* A general and commonly disparaging Italian term for the various kinds of elaborately artificial styles cultivated in the literature of the 17th century (the *Seicento*), more commonly known as *baroque styles, including *Marinism and *concettismo*.

*seguidilla* [seg-i-**dee**-yă] A Spanish verse form consisting of a *quatrain of alternate long and short lines, the first and third lines of six or seven syllables, the second and fourth of five or six syllables. The rhyme scheme is *abab*, but in some variants the first and third lines are unrhymed. An extended version known as the *seguidilla compuesta* adds a three-line refrain (*estribillo*) to form a seven-line stanza. The form was derived from *folk songs by poets of the 16th century, and was employed by many Spanish poets from Lope de Vega to Federico García Lorca.

**self-reflexive** A term applied to literary works that openly reflect upon their own processes of artful composition. Such self-referentiality is frequently found in modern works of fiction that repeatedly refer to their own fictional status (*see* METAFICTION). The *narrator in such works, and in their earlier equivalents such as Sterne's *Tristram Shandy* (1759–67), is sometimes called a 'self-conscious narrator'. Self-reflexivity may also be found often in poetry. *See also* MISE-EN-ABYME, ROMANTIC IRONY.

**semantics** The philosophical or linguistic study of meanings in language. The semantic aspect of any expression is its meaning as opposed to its form.

**seme** An elementary unit of meaning, usually a defining feature or characteristic of something. A basic description of a person as, e.g., 'white, male, grey-haired, clean-shaven' is a listing of semes. Some *structuralist studies of fiction have analysed fictional characters in terms of the presence or absence of given semes. *Adjective*: **semic**.

**semiology** *See* SEMIOTICS.

**semiotic, the** A term used by Julia Kristeva in *La Révolution du langage poétique* (1974) to designate the flow of pre-linguistic rhythms or 'pulsions' that is broken up by the child's entry into the *Symbolic order of language. The unconscious energies of the semiotic are repressed and marginalized by patriarchal logic and rationality, but they may still disrupt the Symbolic order, transgressing its rigid categories (including those of identity and sexual difference). In Kristeva's psychoanalytic theory, the semiotic is associated with the mother's body, but she detects the anarchic energies of the semiotic in the writings of both female and male authors, especially those of the *Symbolist and *modernist *avant-garde*.

**semiotics (semiology)** The systematic study of *signs, or, more precisely, of the production of meanings from sign-*systems*, linguistic or non-linguistic. As a distinct tradition of inquiry into human communications, semiotics was founded by the American philosopher C. S. Peirce (1839–1914) and separately by the Swiss linguist Ferdinand de Saussure (1857–1913), who proposed that linguistics would form one part of a more general science of signs: 'semiology'. Peirce's term 'semiotics' is usually preferred in English, although Saussure's principles and concepts—especially the distinctions between *signifier and *signified and between *langue* and *parole*—have been more influential as the basis of *structuralism and its approach to literature. Semiotics is concerned not with the relations between signs and things but with the interrelationships between signs themselves, within their structured systems or *codes of signification (*see* PARADIGM, SYNTAGM). The semiotic approach to literary works stresses the production of literary meanings from shared *conventions and codes; but the scope of semiotics goes beyond spoken or written language to other kinds of communicative systems such as cinema, advertising, clothing, gesture, and cuisine. A practitioner of semiotics is a **semiotician**. The term **semiosis** is sometimes used to refer to the process of signifying.

**Further reading:** Winfried Nöth, *Handbook of Semiotics* (1990).

(((●))) SEE WEB LINKS
• University of Colorado site with clearly arranged links.

**Senecan tragedy** A form of *tragedy developed by the Roman philosopher-poet Lucius Annaeus Seneca (*c*.4 BCE–65 CE) in his nine plays based on Greek drama (especially that of Euripides), and further adapted by playwrights of the Italian, French, and English *Renaissance. Seneca's plays were almost certainly *closet dramas intended for recitation rather than stage performance. Composed in five acts with intervening *choruses, they employ long rhetorical speeches, with important actions being recounted by messengers. Their bloodthirsty *plots, including ghosts and horrible crimes, appealed to the popular English dramatists of the late 16th century, who presented such horrors on stage in their *revenge tragedies. These were preceded by a purer form of English Senecan tragedy, notably in Thomas Norton and Thomas Sackville's *Gorboduc* (1561), the first English tragedy. The conventional five-act structure of Renaissance drama owes its origin to the influence of Seneca.

**sensation novel** A kind of *novel that flourished in Britain in the 1860s, exploiting the element of suspense in stories of crime and mystery. The most successful examples are Wilkie Collins's *The Woman in White* (1860), Mary Elizabeth Braddon's *Lady Audley's Secret* (1862), and J. Sheridan Le Fanu's *Uncle Silas* (1864). The sensation novel has been seen as an early kind of *thriller in that it exposes dark secrets and conspiracies, but is distinguished from the classic *detective story by its lack of a central detective figure.

**Further reading:** Lyn Pykett, *The Sensation Novel* (1994).

**sensibility** An important 18th-century term designating a kind of sensitivity or responsiveness that is both aesthetic and moral, showing a capacity to feel both for others' sorrows and for beauty. The term is also used in a different sense in modern *criticism, the sensibility of a given writer being his or her characteristic way of responding—intellectually and emotionally—to experience (*see also* DISSOCIATION OF SENSIBILITY). Its major significance, though, is as a concept or mood of 18th-century culture. In terms of moral philosophy, it signalled a reaction against Thomas Hobbes's view of human behaviour as essentially selfish: the 3rd Earl of Shaftesbury and other 18th-century thinkers argued that human beings have an innate 'benevolence' or sympathy for others. In literature, the quality of sensibility was explored and displayed in the 'novel of sensibility' (*see* SENTIMENTAL NOVEL), in *sentimental comedy, in *graveyard poetry, and in the poems of William Cowper among others. The cult of sensibility is also apparent in late 18th-century *primitivism and in the new interest in the *sublime. At its self-indulgent extremes—later criticized by Jane Austen in *Sense and Sensibility* (1811)—it is called sentimentalism. It was one of the cultural trends that gave rise to *Romanticism (*see* PREROMANTICISM).

**Further reading:** Janet Todd, *Sensibility: An Introduction* (1986).

⊕ SEE WEB LINKS
• The Dictionary of Sensibility: project at University of Virginia.

***sententia*** (plural **-*tiae***) A Latin term for an *aphorism or *maxim. Its English adjective, **sententious**, usually has a pejorative sense, referring to a style or statement that is condescending or self-important in giving advice; but it may be used neutrally to mean 'aphoristic'.

**sentimental comedy** A kind of *comedy that achieved some popularity with respectable middle-class audiences in the 18th century. In contrast with the aristocratic cynicism of English *Restoration comedy, it showed virtue rewarded by domestic bliss; its plots, usually involving unbelievably good middle-class couples, emphasized *pathos rather than humour. Pioneered by Richard Steele in *The Funeral* (1701) and more fully in *The Conscious Lovers* (1722), it flourished in mid-century with the French **comédie larmoyante* ('tearful play') and in such plays as Hugh Kelly's *False Delicacy* (1768). The pious moralizing of this tradition, which survived into 19th-century *melodrama, was opposed in the 1770s by Sheridan and Goldsmith, who attempted a partial return to the *comedy of manners.

**sentimental novel (novel of sentiment; novel of sensibility)** An emotionally extravagant *novel of a kind that became popular in Europe in the late 18th century. Partly inspired by the emotional power of Samuel Richardson's *Pamela, or Virtue Rewarded* (1740), the sentimental novels of the 1760s and 1770s exhibit the close connections between virtue and sensibility, in repeatedly tearful scenes; a character's feeling for the beauties of nature and for the griefs of others is taken as a sign of a pure heart. An excessively sentimental example is Henry Mackenzie's *The Man of Feeling* (1771), but Oliver Goldsmith's *The Vicar of Wakefield* (1766) and Laurence Sterne's *A Sentimental Journey* (1768) are more ironic. In Europe, the most important sentimental novels were J.-J. Rousseau's *La Nouvelle Héloïse* (1761) and J. W. von Goethe's *The Sorrows of Young Werther* (1774; *see* WERTHERISM). The fashion lingered on in the early *Gothic novels of Ann Radcliffe in the 1790s.

**Further reading:** R. F. Brissenden, *Virtue in Distress* (1974).

**septenary** A verse line of seven feet (*see* FOOT) or of seven metrical stresses, more commonly known as a *heptameter.

**septet** A *stanza of seven lines, such as the English *rhyme royal stanza.

**serialized** Published in successive instalments, either in a newspaper or magazine, or independently in cheaply bound pamphlet form. Serialization of literary works, especially novels, was a major feature of magazine and newspaper culture from the early 19th century to the early 20th. Alexander Pushkin's verse novel *Eugene Onegin*, for example, first appeared serially in magazines from 1825 to 1831 before becoming available as a book in 1833. Many of Charles Dickens's novels were first issued in monthly parts, usually containing three chapters apiece. An author of serialized works is a **serialist**.

**Further reading:** Graham Law, *Serializing Fiction in the Victorian Press* (2000).

**sestet** A group of six verse lines forming the second part of a *sonnet (in its Italian or Petrarchan form), following the opening *octave. More rarely, the term may refer to a *stanza of six lines (also called a sexain,

sextain, or sextet), such as the *Burns stanza or the stanza used in a
*sestina.

**sestina** [ses-**tee**-nă]  A poem of six 6-line *stanzas and a 3-line *envoi*,
linked by an intricate pattern of repeated line-endings. The most
elaborate of the medieval French *fixed forms, it uses only six end-words
(normally unrhymed), repeating them in a different order in each
stanza so that the ending of the last line in each stanza recurs as the
ending of the first line in the next. The *envoi* uses all six words, three
of them as line-endings. The established pattern of repetition for the
six stanzas is as follows: 1-ABCDEF, 2-FAEBDC, 3-CFDABE, 4-ECBFAD,
5-DEACFB, 6-BDFECA. The form was introduced into English by
Sir Philip Sidney in his *Arcadia* (1590). Modern examples include
W. H. Auden's 'Paysage Moralisé' (1933) and John Ashbery's 'The
Painter' (1970). Even more remarkable as a technical feat is A. C.
Swinburne's 'The Complaint of Lisa' (1878), a rhyming double sestina
with twelve 12-line stanzas and a 6-line *envoi*.

**sex'n'shopping novel**  A kind of popular *romance marketed to
women, flourishing as a distinctive commercial *genre in the 1980s. Its
charactcristic features include shamelessly explicit descriptions of
expensive clothes, jewellery, cars, perfumes, and other accessories of thc
very rich, naming actual brands; a few graphic accounts of sexual
encounters are usually thrown in, providing a flimsy excuse for the more
delirious excitements of the shopping and dressing-up scenes. The
founding work of this tradition was Judith Krantz's *Scruples* (1978),
which inspired numerous imitations. The formula was revived, with a
flavouring of light bondage, in E. L. James's *Fifty Shades of Grey* (2011)
and its sequels. The term originally used by book-trade insiders for such
fiction was **Shopping and Fucking**, sometimes discrectly abbreviated
to **S&F**.

**Shakespearean sonnet**  *See* SONNET.

**Shavian** [**shay**-vi-ăn]  Belonging to or characteristic of the work of the
Irish playwright and controversialist Bernard Shaw (1856–1950). *See also*
IBSENITE; DISCUSSION PLAY.

**short measure (short metre)**  A form of verse *quatrain often used in
*hymns. A variant of *common metre, it has four *stresses in its third
line, but only three stresses in the other three, the metre usually being

*iambic. The *rhyme scheme is usually *abcb*, or, as in this cheerful example from the children's hymn-writer Isaac Watts, *abab*:

> There is a dreadful Hell,
> And everlasting pains;
> There sinners must with devils dwell
> In darkness, fire, and chains.

The form has some similarity to *poulter's measure.

**short story** A fictional prose tale of no specified length, but too short to be published as a volume on its own, as *novellas sometimes and *novels usually are. A short story will normally concentrate on a single event with only one or two characters, more economically than a novel's sustained exploration of social background. There are similar fictional forms of greater antiquity—*fables, *lais, *folktales, *parables, and the French *conte*—but the short story as we know it flourished in the magazines of the 19th and early 20th centuries, especially in the USA, which has a particularly strong tradition.

**Further reading:** Adrian Hunter, *The Cambridge Introduction to the Short Story in English* (2007).

**sibilance** The marked recurrence of the 'hissing' sounds known as sibilants (usually spelt *s*, *sh*, *zh*, *c*). The effect, also known as sigmatism after the Greek letter *sigma*, is often exploited in poetry, as in Longfellow's lines

> Ships that pass in the night, and speak each other in passing;
> Only a signal shown and a distant voice in the darkness

*See also* ALLITERATION.

**sigmatism** *See* SIBILANCE.

**sign** A basic element of communication, either linguistic (e.g. a written character or a word) or non-linguistic (e.g. a picture, or article of dress); or anything that can be construed as having a meaning. According to the influential theory of the Swiss linguist Ferdinand de Saussure, every sign has two inseparable aspects: the *signifier, which is the materially perceptible component such as a sound or written mark, and the *signified, which is the conceptual meaning. In a linguistic sign, according to Saussure, the relationship between signifier and signified is 'unmotivated' or *arbitrary; that is, it is based purely on social convention rather than on natural necessity: there is nothing about a horse which demands that it be called 'horse', since the French call the same thing *un cheval*. Saussure's theory deliberately leaves out the *referent or real external object referred to by a sign. The alternative theory of the American philosopher C. S. Peirce has more room for referents and for 'motivated' signs. Peirce calls the unmotivated sign a *symbol, while identifying two further kinds of sign: the *icon, which resembles its referent (e.g. a photograph), and the *index, which is caused by its referent (e.g. a medical symptom). *Verb*: **signify**. *See also* SEMIOTICS.

**signified** The conceptual component of a *sign, as distinct from its material form, the *signifier. The signified, also known in French as the *signifié*, is the idea conventionally indicated by the signifier, rather than the actual external object or *referent (if any).

**signifier** The concretely perceptible component of a *sign, as distinct from its conceptual meaning (the *signified). In language, this may be a meaningful sound, or a written mark such as a letter or sequence of letters making up a word. The term often appears in its French form, *significant*.

***sijo*** [**shee**-joh] The principal verse-form of Korean lyric poetry in a tradition traced at least as far back as the 14th century. Originally composed to be sung, the *sijo*, like its younger and shorter cousin the Japanese *haiku, is a three-line *syllabic form, although with longer lines, each divisible into four syllable-groups. The first two lines contain 14 or 15 syllables each, depending on permissible variation in the third syllable-group, while the stricter pattern of the 15-syllable final line follows a syllable-count of 3, 5, 4, and 3. The first half of this final line is expected to provide a surprising 'twist' in sound or sense. Original English-language *sijo* by Larry Gross and others emerged in the specialist journal *Sijo West* (1995–9). Because each line comes in two halves or *hemistichs, it has become customary for English-language *sijo*, whether original or translated, to be presented as six lines, each of 7 or 8 syllables.

**Further reading:** Richard Rutt (ed.), *The Bamboo Grove: An Introduction to Sijo* (1998).

**silver-fork novel** A kind of *novel that was popular in Britain from the 1820s to the 1840s, and was marked by concentration upon the fashionable etiquette and manners of high society. The term was used mockingly by critics of the time, and has been applied to works by Theodore Hook, Catherine Gore, Frances Trollope, Lady Caroline Lamb, Benjamin Disraeli, and Susan Ferrier.

**Further reading:** Alison Adburgham, *Silver Fork Society* (1983).

**simile** [**sim**-ĭ-li] An explicit comparison between two different things, actions, or feelings, using the words 'as' or 'like', as in Wordsworth's line:

> I wandered lonely as a cloud

A very common *figure of speech in both prose and verse, simile is more tentative and decorative than *metaphor. A lengthy and more elaborate kind of simile, used as a digression in a narrative work, is the *epic simile.

**sjuzet** [syuu-zhet] (*suzet; syuzhet*) The term used in *Russian Formalism to denote the *plot of a narrative work, as opposed to the events of its *story (called the *fabula*). The *sjuzet* is the finished arrangement of narrated events as they are presented to the reader, rather than the sequence of such events as reconstructed in their 'true' sequence and duration.

**skald** (**scald**) An Old Norse word for a poet, usually applied to a Norwegian or Icelandic court poet or *bard of the period from the 9th century to the 13th. Skaldic verse is marked by its elaborate patterns of *metre, rhyme, and *alliteration, and by its use of *kennings.

**skaz** A Russian term, derived from *skazat* ('to tell'), for a kind of *folktale in which an episode of rustic life is recounted in the first person and in colloquial style. The term is now used more generally in studies of fictional prose for the exploitation of colloquial speech in first-person narratives, especially where the *narrator's language is marked by non-literary or indecorous features such as slang and dialect terms, expletives, *solecisms, *malapropisms, hesitations, and other indications that the narrative is to be understood as being 'spoken' rather than written down. In English, the prominent use of *skaz* in prose fiction begins with Mark Twain's *Adventures of Huckleberry Finn* (1884), in which the story is told by an uneducated fourteen-year-old boy. Another notable instance, in which again a teenage boy narrates, is J. D. Salinger's *The Catcher in the Rye* (1951). Older narrators can be used in similar ways to create the *skaz* effect, though: James Kelman's

*How Late it Was, How Late* (1994) gives us a story told by a
hard-drinking Glaswegian ex-convict, in a 'spoken' style notable for its
repetitive use of expletives. *See also* IDIOLECT.

**Skeltonics** Verses written in the manner favoured by John Skelton
(*c.*1460–1529), whose lively satirical poems use irregular short lines of
two or three *stresses, and often extend the same rhyme over several
consecutive lines. A similar effect of vivid colloquial word-play is often
found in modern *dub poetry.

**sketch** A short composition, dramatic, narrative, or descriptive. In
the theatre, a sketch is a brief, self-contained dramatic scene, usually
comic. As a kind of prose narrative, a sketch is more modest than a
*short story, showing less development in *plot or *characterization.
The term is also applied to brief descriptions of people (the 'character
sketch') or places, as in the non-fictional components of Charles
Dickens's *Sketches by Boz* (1836).

**slant rhyme** *See* HALF-RHYME.

**slave narrative** A written account by an escaped or freed slave of his
or her experiences of slavery. A special American form of autobiography,
the slave narrative appeared as an important kind of abolitionist
literature in the period preceding the Civil War. The outstanding
example is the *Narrative of the Life of Frederick Douglass* (1845).

**socialist realism** A slogan adopted by the Soviet cultural authorities
in 1934 to summarize the requirements of Stalinist dogma in literature:
the established techniques of 19th-century *realism were to be used
to represent the struggle for socialism in a positive, optimistic light,
while the allegedly 'decadent' techniques of *modernism were to be
avoided as bourgeois deviations. The approved model was Maxim
Gorky's novel *The Mother* (1907). A few outstanding novels have
conformed to this official prescription, including Mikhail Sholokhov's
*Virgin Soil Upturned* (1932) and Lewis Grassic Gibbon's *Grey Granite*
(1934), but the doctrine acted chiefly to stifle imaginative experiment,
and has been rejected as such by many leading socialist writers, notably
Bertolt Brecht. *See also* PROLETCULT, PROPAGANDISM.

**sociology of literature** A branch of literary study that examines the
relationships between literary works and their social contexts, including
patterns of literacy, kinds of audience, modes of publication and

dramatic presentation, and the social class positions of authors and readers. Originating in 19th-century France with works by Mme de Staël and Hippolyte Taine, the sociology of literature was revived in the English-speaking world with the appearance of such studies as Raymond Williams's *The Long Revolution* (1961), and is most often associated with Marxist approaches to cultural analysis.

**Socratic** [sŏ-**krat**-ik] Pertaining to the Greek philosopher Socrates (469–399 BCE). His manner of feigning ignorance in order to expose the self-contradictions of his interlocutors through cross-examination is known as Socratic irony. His method of seeking the truth by such processes of question-and-answer is illustrated in the Socratic *Dialogues* of his follower, Plato.

**solecism** [**sol**-ĭ-sizm] A grammatical error; or, more loosely, any mistake that exposes the perpetrator's ignorance. *Adjective*: **solecistic**.

**soliloquy** [sŏl-**il**-ŏ-kwi] A dramatic speech uttered by one character speaking aloud while alone on the stage (or while under the impression of being alone). The **soliloquist** thus reveals his or her inner thoughts and feelings to the audience, either in supposed self-communion or in a consciously direct address. Soliloquies often appear in plays from the age of Shakespeare, notably in his *Hamlet* and *Macbeth*. A poem supposedly uttered by a solitary speaker, like Robert Browning's 'Soliloquy of the Spanish Cloister' (1842), may also be called a soliloquy. Soliloquy is a form of *monologue, but a monologue is not a soliloquy if (as in the *dramatic monologue) the speaker is not alone. *Verb*: **soliloquize**.

**sonnet** *See* p. 338.

**soubrette** The *stock character of the heroine's maidservant in French comedy of the 17th and 18th centuries. The soubrette usually protests against the delusions of her master, ingeniously scheming on behalf of her young mistress. The character of Dorine in Molière's *Le Tartuffe* (1664) is a model for the type, which originated in the *commedia dell' arte*.

**Spasmodic School** A title applied mockingly by the Scottish poet and critic W. E. Aytoun in 1854 to a group of poets who had lately achieved some popularity in Britain: P. J. Bailey, Sydney Dobell, Alexander Smith, and others. Their work is marked by extravagant attempts to represent emotional turmoil, sometimes in a manner derived from Byron. Dobell's dramatic poem *Balder* (1853) includes the notorious line:

Ah! Ah! Ah! Ah! Ah! Ah! Ah! Ah! Ah! Ah!

The term has sometimes been extended to the comparable emotional intensities of Tennyson's *Maud* (1855), and of some poems by Elizabeth Barrett Browning.

**speech act theory** A modern philosophical approach to language, which has challenged the long-standing assumption of philosophers that human utterances consist exclusively of true or false statements about the world. Initiated by the English philosopher J. L. Austin in lectures published posthumously as *How to Do Things with Words* (1962), speech act theory begins with the distinction between 'constative' utterances (which report truly or falsely on some external state of affairs) and *performatives (which are verbal actions in themselves—such as promising—rather than true or false statements). Further analysis reveals that a single utterance may comprise three distinct kinds of speech act: in addition to its simple 'locutionary' status as a grammatical utterance, it will have an *illocutionary force (i.e. an active function such as threatening, affirming, or reassuring), and probably a *perlocutionary force (an effect on the listener or reader). After Austin's death in 1960, speech act theory was developed further by J. R. Searle in *Speech Acts* (1969) and other works, and applied to problems of literary analysis by Mary Louise Pratt in *Toward a Speech Act Theory of Literary Discourse* (1977).

**Spenserian stanza** An English poetic *stanza of nine *iambic lines, the first eight being *pentameters while the ninth is a longer line known either as an iambic hexameter or as an *alexandrine. The rhyme scheme is *ababbcbcc*. The stanza is named after Edmund Spenser, who invented it—probably on the basis of the *ottava rima* stanza—for his long allegorical *romance *The Faerie Queene* (1590–96). It was revived successfully by the younger English Romantic poets of the early 19th century: Byron used it for *Childe Harold's Pilgrimage* (1812, 1816), Keats for 'The Eve of St Agnes' (1820), and Shelley for *The Revolt of Islam* (1818) and *Adonais* (1821). For the Spenserian sonnet, *see* SONNET.

**spondee** A metrical unit (*foot) consisting of two *stressed syllables (or, in *quantitative verse, two long syllables). Spondees occur regularly

## SONNET

A short *lyric poem, usually comprising fourteen rhyming lines of equal length: iambic *pentameters in English, *alexandrines in French, *hendecasyllables in Italian. The *rhyme schemes of the sonnet follow two basic patterns. **1.** The Italian sonnet (also called the *Petrarchan sonnet after the most influential of the Italian sonneteers) comprises an 8-line 'octave' of two *quatrains, rhymed *abbaabba*, followed by a 6-line 'sestet' usually rhymed *cdecde* or *cdcdcd*. The transition from octave to sestet usually coincides with a 'turn' (Italian, *volta*) in the argument or mood of the poem. In a variant form used by the English poet John Milton, however, the 'turn' is delayed to a later position around the tenth line. Some later poets—notably William Wordsworth—have employed this feature of the 'Miltonic sonnet' while relaxing the rhyme scheme of the octave to *abbaacca*. The Italian pattern has remained the most widely used in English and other languages. **2.** The English sonnet (also called the Shakespearean sonnet after its foremost practitioner) comprises three quatrains and a final couplet, rhyming *ababcdcdefefgg*. An important variant of this is the Spenserian sonnet (introduced by the Elizabethan poet Edmund Spenser), which links the three quatrains by rhyme, in the sequence *ababbabccdcdee*. In either form, the 'turn' comes with the final couplet, which may sometimes achieve the neatness of an *epigram.

Originating in Italy, the sonnet was established by Petrarch in the 14th century as a major form of love poetry, and came to be adopted in Spain, France, and England in the 16th century, and in Germany in the 17th. The standard subject-matter of early sonnets was the torments of sexual love (usually within a *courtly love convention), but in the 17th century John Donne extended the sonnet's scope to religion, while Milton extended it to politics. Although largely neglected in the 18th century, the sonnet was revived in the 19th by Wordsworth, Keats, and Baudelaire, and is still widely used. Some poets have written connected series of sonnets, known as sonnet sequences or sonnet cycles: of these, the outstanding English examples are Sir Philip Sidney's *Astrophel and Stella* (1591), Spenser's *Amoretti* (1595), and Shakespeare's *Sonnets* (1609); later examples include Elizabeth Barrett Browning's *Sonnets from the Portuguese* (1850) and W. H. Auden's 'In Time of War' (1939). A group of sonnets formally linked by repeated lines is known as a *crown of sonnets. Irregular variations on the sonnet form have included the 12-line sonnet sometimes used by Elizabethan poets, G. M. Hopkins's *curtal sonnets of 10½ lines, and the 16-line sonnets of George Meredith's sequence *Modern Love* (1862).

**Further reading:** Michael R. G. Spiller, *The Development of the Sonnet* (1992); Stephen Burt and David Mikics, *The Art of the Sonnet* (2010); A. D. Cousins and Peter Howarth (eds), *The Cambridge Companion to the Sonnet* (2011).

(⊕) SEE WEB LINKS

• Sonnet Central: archive of sonnets with historical notes and links.

in several Greek and Latin metres, and as substitutes for other feet, as in the dactylic *hexameter; but in English the spondee is an occasional device of metrical variation. The normal alternation of stressed and unstressed syllables in English speech makes it virtually impossible to compose a complete line of true spondees. Some English compound words like *childbirth* are **spondaic**, although even these do not have exactly equal stresses. The occurrence of adjacent stressed syllables in English verse may be accounted for more convincingly in terms of *demotion, rather than in the doubtfully applicable terms of classical quantitative feet.

**Spoonerism** A phrase in which the initial consonants of two words have been exchanged, creating an amusing new expression. It takes its name from the Revd W. A. Spooner (1844–1930), Warden of New College, Oxford. His reputed utterances, like the accusation that a student had 'hissed my mystery lectures', appear to have been inadvertent slips, but Spoonerisms may also be used for deliberately humorous effect: W. H. Auden referred dismissively to Keats and Shelley as 'Sheets and Kelly', while a feminist theatre group toured Britain in the 1970s under the name Cunning Stunts. *See also* METATHESIS.

**sprung rhythm** The term used by the English poet Gerard Manley Hopkins (1844–89) to describe his peculiar metrical system, based on the *accentual verse of nursery rhymes and on medieval *alliterative metres. It counts the number of strong stresses in a line, regardless of the number of unstressed syllables, and permits the juxtaposition of stressed syllables more frequently than normal English *duple or *triple metre (*see* METRE). Hopkins saw his metre as having four kinds of *foot, each beginning with a stressed syllable: the stressed monosyllable (●), the *trochee (●○), the *dactyl (●○○), and the first *paeon (●○○○); additional unstressed syllables or 'outrides' were also permitted. Hopkins's aim was to make use of the energies of everyday speech, and his sprung rhythm may be regarded as a kind of *free verse based partly on accentual metres.

**squib** Another word for a *lampoon: a short satirical attack upon a person, work, or institution.

**stanza** A group of verse lines forming a section of a poem and sharing the same structure as all or some of the other sections of the same poem, in terms of the lengths of its lines, its *metre, and usually its *rhyme scheme. In printed poems, stanzas are separated by spaces. Stanzas are often loosely referred to as 'verses', but this usage causes serious confusion and is best avoided, since a verse is, strictly speaking, a single line. Although some writers regard the *couplet and the *tercet as kinds of stanza, the term is most often applied to groups of four lines or more, the four-line *quatrain being by far the most common, in the *ballad metre and various other forms. Among the longer and more complex kinds of stanza used in English are the *Burns stanza, *ottava rima*, *rhyme royal, and the *Spenserian stanza; but there are many others with no special names. The *fixed forms derived from medieval French verse have their own intricate kinds of stanza. Poems that are divided regularly into stanzas are **stanzaic**, whereas poems that form a continuous sequence of lines of the same length are referred to as being *stichic or composed in *block form. In many poems which are divided up irregularly (usually those written in *blank verse, *heroic couplets, or *free verse), the sections are sometimes called *verse paragraphs, but in the irregular form of the *ode, these unmatched subdivisions are usually called stanzas or *strophes.

**stave** Another word for a *stanza, especially in a song.

**stichic** [**stik**-ik] Composed as a continuous sequence of verse lines of the same length and *metre, and thus not divided into *stanzas. Poems written in *blank verse or in *heroic couplets are usually stichic; if divided up at all, their uneven subdivisions are called *verse paragraphs.

**stichomythia** [stik-oh-**mith**-iă] A form of dramatic *dialogue in which two disputing characters answer each other rapidly in alternating single lines, with one character's replies balancing (and often partially repeating) the other's utterances. This kind of verbal duel or 'cut and thrust' dialogue was practised more in ancient Greek and Roman tragedy than in later drama, although a notable English example occurs in the dialogue between Richard and Elizabeth in Shakespeare's *Richard III* (Act IV, scene iv). *See also* HEMISTICH, REPARTEE.

*stilnovisti* The collective term for the poetic pioneers and partisans of the Italian *dolce stil novo* in the late 13th century and early 14th. These were Guido Cavalcanti (1260?–1300), Dante Alighieri (1265–1321), and Cino da Pistoia (*c*.1270–1337).

**stock character** A stereotyped character easily recognized by readers or audiences from recurrent appearances in literary or folk tradition, usually within a specific *genre such as comedy or fairy tale. Common examples include the absent-minded professor, the country bumpkin, the damsel in distress, the old miser, the whore with a heart of gold, the bragging soldier, the villain of *melodrama, the wicked stepmother, the jealous husband, and the *soubrette. Similarly recognizable incidents or plot-elements which recur in fiction and drama are known as **stock situations**: these include the mistaken identity, the 'eternal triangle', the discovery of the birthmark, the last-minute rescue, the dying man's confession, and love at first sight. *See also* ARCHETYPE, CONVENTION, TYPE.

**stock response** A routinely insensitive reaction to a literary work or to some element of it. A stock response perceives in a work only those meanings that are already familiar from a reader's or audience's previous experience, failing to recognize fresh or unfamiliar meanings. Writers may deliberately exploit stock responses (e.g. our sympathy for the hero or heroine), but often fall victim to them when attempting to reach beyond readers' habitual expectations.

**story** In the everyday sense, any *narrative or tale recounting a series of events. In modern *narratology, however, the term refers more specifically to the sequence of imagined events that we reconstruct from the actual arrangement of a narrative (or dramatic) *plot. In this modern distinction between story and plot, derived from *Russian Formalism and its opposed terms *fabula* and *sjuzet*, the story is the full sequence of events as we assume them to have occurred in their likely order, duration, and frequency, while the plot is a particular selection and (re-)ordering of these. Thus the story is the abstractly conceived 'raw material' of events which we reconstruct from the finished arrangement of the plot: it includes events preceding and otherwise omitted from the perceived action, and its sequence will differ from that of the plot if the action begins *in medias res* or otherwise involves an *anachrony. As an abstraction, the story can be translated into other languages and media (e.g. film) more successfully than the style of the *narration could be.

***strambotto*** (plural *-otti*) A short Italian poem meant to be set to music, and usually taking the form of eight rhymed *hendecasyllabic

lines (*see* ENDECASYLLABO), although some are of six lines. In the most
common form, known as the Sicilian octave (*ottava siciliana*), the rhyme
scheme is *ababababab*, but there are others including the Tuscan octave
(*ottava toscana*) with the scheme *ababbcc*. This kind of octave is
sometimes divided into two *quatrains. An alternative name for it,
principally in Tuscany, is the *rispetto*. It was used widely in the 15th and
16th centuries.

**stream of consciousness** The continuous flow of
sense-perceptions, thoughts, feelings, and memories in the human
mind; or a literary method of representing such a blending of mental
processes in fictional characters, usually in an unpunctuated or
disjointed form of *interior monologue. The term is often used as a
synonym for interior monologue, but they can also be distinguished, in
two ways. In the first (psychological) sense, the stream of consciousness
is the subject-matter while interior monologue is the technique for
presenting it; thus Marcel Proust's novel *A la recherche du temps perdu*
(1913–27) is *about* the stream of consciousness, especially the
connection between sense-impressions and memory, but it does not
actually use interior monologue. In the second (literary) sense, stream of
consciousness is a special style of interior monologue: while an interior
monologue always presents a character's thoughts 'directly', without the
apparent intervention of a summarizing and selecting narrator, it does
not necessarily mingle them with impressions and perceptions, nor does
it necessarily violate the norms of grammar, syntax, and logic; but the
stream-of-consciousness technique also does one or both of these
things. An important device of *modernist fiction and its later imitators,
the technique was pioneered by Dorothy Richardson in *Pilgrimage*
(1915–35) and by James Joyce in *Ulysses* (1922), and further developed
by Virginia Woolf in *Mrs Dalloway* (1925) and William Faulkner in *The
Sound and the Fury* (1928).

**stress** The relative emphasis given in pronunciation to a syllable, in
loudness, pitch, or duration (or some combination of these). The term is
usually interchangeable with *accent, although some theorists of
*prosody reserve it only for the emphasis occurring according to a
metrical pattern (*see* METRE). In English verse, the metre of a line is
determined by the number of stresses in a sequence composed of
stressed and unstressed syllables (also referred to as strongly stressed
and weakly stressed syllables). In *quantitative verse, on the other hand,

the metrical pattern is made up of syllables measured by their duration rather than by stress.

**strong-stress metre**  Another term for the metre of *accentual verse, in which only the stressed syllables are counted while the unstressed syllables may vary in number. The term thus encompasses the Old Germanic *alliterative metre, various kinds of popular English metre, and G. M. Hopkins's *sprung rhythm.

**strophe** [stroh-fi]  A *stanza, or any less regular subdivision of a poem, such as a *verse paragraph. In a special sense, the term is applied to the opening section (and every third succeeding section) of a Greek choral *ode. In the *Pindaric ode, sometimes imitated in English, the strophe is followed by an *antistrophe having the same number of lines and the same complex metrical arrangement; this is then followed by an *epode of differing length and structure, and the triadic pattern may then be repeated a number of times. In choral odes, the *chorus would dance in one direction while chanting the strophe, then back again during the antistrophe, standing still for the epode. *Adjective*: **strophic**.

**structuralism**  A mid 20th-century intellectual movement that analysed cultural phenomena according to principles derived from linguistics, emphasizing the systematic interrelationships among the elements of any human activity, and thus the abstract *codes and *conventions governing the social production of meanings. Building on the linguistic concept of the *phoneme—a unit of meaningful sound defined purely by its differences from other phonemes rather than by any inherent features—structuralism argued that the elements composing any cultural phenomenon (from cooking to drama) are similarly 'relational': that is, they have meaning only by virtue of their contrasts with other elements of the system, especially in *binary oppositions of paired opposites. Their meanings can be established not by referring each element to any supposed equivalent in natural reality, but only by analysing its function within a self-contained cultural code. Accordingly, structuralist analysis sought the underlying system or *langue* that governs individual utterances or instances. In formulating the laws by which elements of such a system are combined, it distinguished between sets of interchangeable units (*paradigms) and sequences of such units in combination (*syntagms), thereby outlining a basic '*syntax' of human culture.

Structuralism and its 'science of signs' (*see* SEMIOTICS) were derived chiefly from the linguistic theories of Ferdinand de Saussure (1857–1913), and partly from *Russian Formalism and the related *narratology of Vladimir Propp's *Morphology of the Folktale* (1928). It flourished in France in the 1960s, following the widely discussed applications of structural analysis to mythology by the anthropologist Claude Lévi-Strauss. In the study of literary works, structuralism was distinguished by its rejection of those traditional notions according to which literature 'expresses' an author's meaning or 'reflects' reality. Instead, the '*text' was seen as an objective structure activating various codes and conventions which are independent of author, reader, and external reality. Structuralist criticism was less interested in interpreting what literary works mean than in explaining *how* they can mean what they mean; that is, in showing what implicit rules and conventions are operating in a given work. The structuralist tradition has been particularly strong in narratology, from Propp's analysis of narrative *functions to Greimas's theory of *actants. The French critic Roland Barthes was an outstanding practitioner of structuralist literary analysis notably in his book *S/Z* (1970)—and is famed for his witty analyses of wrestling, striptease, and other phenomena in *Mythologies* (1957): some of his later writings, however, show a shift to *post-structuralism, in which the over-confident 'scientific' pretensions of structuralism are abandoned.

**Further reading:** John Sturrock, *Structuralism* (2nd edn, 2002).

**Sturm und Drang** [shtoorm uunt drang] The name—'Storm and Stress'—given to a short-lived but important movement in German literature of the 1770s. An early precursor of *Romanticism, it was passionately individualistic and rebellious, maintaining a hostile attitude to French *neoclassicism and the associated rationalism of the *Enlightenment. The term is taken from the title of a play by F. M. Klinger (1776), but the leaders of the movement were J. G. Herder and J. W. von Goethe. Herder, inspired by the *primitivism of J.-J. Rousseau, encouraged the cult of *Ossianism and praised the 'natural' qualities of Shakespeare and of folk song. Goethe's play *Götz von Berlichingen* (1773), a Shakespearean *chronicle play about a leader in the 16th-century peasants' revolt, is the major dramatic work of the *Sturm und Drang* period, while his *sentimental novel of hopeless love and suicide, *The Sorrows of Young Werther* (1774), is its most significant novel. A belated product of the movement is Friedrich Schiller's play *Die Räuber* (1781), which influenced the later development of *melodrama.

**Further reading:** Alan C. Leidner, *The Impatient Muse: Germany and the Sturm und Drang* (1994).

**style** Any specific way of using language, which is characteristic of an author, school, period, or *genre. Particular styles may be defined by their *diction, *syntax, *imagery, *rhythm, and use of *figures, or by any other linguistic feature. Different categories of style have been named after particular authors (e.g. Ciceronian), periods (e.g. Augustan), and professions (e.g. journalistic), while in the *Renaissance a scheme of three stylistic 'levels' was adopted, distinguishing the high or 'grand' style from the middle or 'mean' style and the low or 'base' style. The principle of *decorum held that certain subjects required particular levels of style, so that an *epic should be written in the grand style whereas *satires should be composed in the base style. Since the literary revolution of *Romanticism, however, this hierarchy has been replaced by the notion of style as an expression of individual personality. *Adjective*: **stylistic**.

**stylistics** A branch of modern linguistics devoted to the detailed analysis of literary *style, or of the linguistic choices made by speakers and writers in non-literary contexts.

**Further reading:** Mick Short, *Exploring the Language of Poems, Plays and Prose* (1996).

**subgenre** [**sub**-*zh*ah$^n$r] Any category of literary works that forms a specific class within a larger *genre: thus the *pastoral elegy may be regarded as a subgenre of *elegy, which is in turn a subgenre of *lyric poetry.

**sublime, the** A quality of awesome grandeur in art or nature, which some 18th-century writers distinguished from the merely beautiful. An anonymous Greek critical treatise of the 1st century CE, *Peri hypsous* ('On the Sublime', mistakenly attributed to the 3rd-century rhetorician Longinus), provided the basis for the 18th-century interest in sublimity, after Boileau's French translation in 1672. 'Longinus' refers to the sublime as a loftiness of thought and feeling in literature, and associates it with terrifyingly impressive natural phenomena such as mountains,

volcanoes, storms, and the sea. These associations were revived in
Edmund Burke's influential *Philosophical Enquiry into the Origin of our
Ideas of the Sublime and Beautiful* (1757), which argues that the sublime
is characterized by obscurity, vastness, and power, while the beautiful is
light, smooth, and delicate. The 18th-century enthusiasm for the
sublime in landscape and the visual arts was one of the developments
that undermined the restraints of *neoclassicism and thus prepared the
way for *Romanticism. Interest in the sublime has more recently
become a feature of the discourses of *postmodernism, especially under
the influence of the French philosopher Jean-François Lyotard.

**Further reading:** Philip Shaw, *The Sublime* (2005).

**subplot** A secondary sequence of actions in a dramatic or narrative
work, usually involving characters of lesser importance (and often of
lower social status). The subplot may be related to the main plot as a
parallel or contrast, or it may be more or less separate from it. Subplots
are especially common in Elizabethan and Jacobean drama, a famous
example being that of Gloucester and his sons in Shakespeare's *King
Lear*; but they are also found in long novels such as those of Dickens.

**substitution** A term used in traditional *prosody to denote the use of
one kind of *foot in place of the foot normally required by the metrical
pattern of a verse line. In English verse, the kind of substitution most
commonly referred to by prosodists is the replacement of the first *iamb
in an iambic line by a *trochee; this 'initial trochaic *inversion', as it is
called, appears in Tennyson's line:

> Far on the ringing plains of windy Troy.

The substitution of an *anapaest for an iamb, or of a *dactyl for a
trochee, is called trisyllabic substitution, since it increases the number of
syllables from two to three. The feet known as the *spondee (●●) and the
*pyrrhic (○○) are sometimes invoked as substitute feet where stressed or
unstressed syllables occur in pairs. Thus Keats's line

> O for a beaker full of the warm South

shows, in addition to its initial trochaic inversion, a metrical variation
at the end, which would be described in traditional prosody as the
substitution of a pyrrhic and a spondee for the final two iambs. Some
more modern theories of versification, however, have rejected the
concept of the foot and along with it that of substitution, accounting for
such metrical variations in terms of *demotion, *promotion, and the

'pairing' of stressed and unstressed syllables. In this view, the ending of Keats's line illustrates a permissible variation in English iambic verse, whereby the occurrence of two stressed syllables together can be compensated (in certain positions) by the pairing of two unstressed syllables. In Greek and Latin *quantitative verse, some kinds of substitution are governed by the principle of 'equivalence' whereby one long syllable is equal to two short syllables, so that under certain conditions a spondee, for example, can stand in for a dactyl.

**subtext** Any meaning or set of meanings which is implied rather than explicitly stated in a literary work, especially in a play. Modern plays such as those of Harold Pinter, in which the meaning of the action is sometimes suggested more by silences and pauses than by dialogue alone, are often discussed in terms of their hidden subtexts.

*succès d'estime* [suuk-sed est-eem] A high reputation enjoyed by a work on the basis of critics' favourable judgements; thus a critical success rather than a merely commercial one. Another kind of reputation for which the French have a phrase is the *succès de scandale*: a success based on notoriety, when a work becomes famous because of some public excitement or outrage not directly arising from its actual merits. Some works have both kinds of success: Vladimir Nabokov's novel *Lolita* (1956) enjoyed a *succès de scandale* based on its notorious paedophilic subject-matter, but still ranks as a *succès d'estime* on the strength of its widely admired use of English prose.

**Surrealism** An anti-rational movement of imaginative liberation in European (mainly French and Spanish) art and literature in the 1920s and 1930s, launched by André Breton in his *Manifeste du Surréalisme* (1924) after his break from the *Dada group in 1922. The term *surréaliste* had been used by the French poet Guillaume Apollinaire in 1917 to indicate an attempt to reach beyond the limits of the 'real'. Surrealism seeks to break down the boundaries between rationality and irrationality, exploring the resources and revolutionary energies of dreams, hallucinations, and sexual desire. Influenced both by the *Symbolists and by Sigmund Freud's theories of the unconscious, the surrealists experimented with *automatic writing and with the free association of random images brought together in surprising juxtaposition. Although surrealist painting is better known, a significant tradition of surrealist poetry established itself in France, in the work of

Breton, Paul Éluard, Louis Aragon, and Benjamin Péret. Although dissolved as a coherent movement by the end of the 1930s, its tradition has survived in many forms of post-war experimental writing, from the theatre of the *absurd to the songs of Bob Dylan and the poetry of the *New York school. The adjectives **surreal** and **surrealistic** are often used in a loose sense to refer to any bizarre imaginative effect.

**Further reading:** David Hopkins, *Dada and Surrealism* (2004).

(((⊕))) **SEE WEB LINKS**

• Surrealism Centre: Tate Gallery, with Essex and Manchester Universities.

**syllabic verse** [si-**lab**-ik] **(syllabics)** Verse in which the lines are measured according to the number of syllables they contain, regardless of the number of *stresses. This syllabic principle operates in the poetry of the Romance languages (French, Italian, Spanish, etc.) and of Chinese and Japanese; but in English, purely syllabic verse occurs only in an experimental modern tradition launched by Robert Bridges in 1921 and exhibited notably in his *Testament of Beauty* (1929); this was taken up later in some poems by Marianne Moore, W. H. Auden, and Thom Gunn, among others. Otherwise the *haiku derived from Japanese principles is the only widely recognized syllabic form in English. The conventions of European syllabic verse give us the names of certain standard lines: the *hendecasyllable is important in Italian verse, as the 12-syllable *alexandrine is in French, while *octosyllabic verse is very common in many languages including English (where it is composed in four-stress lines). *See also* METRE.

**syllepsis** A construction in which one word (usually a verb or preposition) is applied to two other words or phrases, either ungrammatically or in two differing senses. In the first case, the verb or preposition agrees grammatically with only one of the two elements which it governs, e.g. 'He works his work, I mine' (Tennyson). In the second case, the word also appears only once but is applied twice in differing senses (often an abstract sense and a concrete sense), as in Pope's *The Rape of the Lock*:

> Here, thou, great Anna! whom three realms obey
> Dost sometimes counsel take—and sometimes tea.

A more far-fetched instance occurs in Dickens's *Pickwick Papers* when it is said of a character that she 'went home in a flood of tears and a sedan chair'. There is usually a kind of *pun involved in this kind of syllepsis, as in Anthony Hecht's poem 'The Feast of Stephen' (1977), which refers to 'the flush | Of health and toilets'. The term is frequently used interchangeably with *zeugma, attempts to distinguish the two terms having foundered in confusion: some rhetoricians place the ungrammatical form under the heading of syllepsis while others allot it to zeugma. It seems preferable to keep zeugma as the more inclusive term for syntactic 'yoking' and to reserve syllepsis for its ungrammatical or punning varieties. *Adjective*: **sylleptic**.

**syllogism** [sil-ŏ-jizm] A form of logical argument that derives a conclusion from two propositions ('premisses') sharing a common term, usually in this form: all $x$ are $y$ (major premiss); $z$ is $x$ (minor premiss); therefore $z$ is $y$ (conclusion). For example: all poets are alcoholics; Jane is a poet; therefore Jane is an alcoholic. In this deductive logic, the conclusion is of course reliable only if both premisses are true. Syllogistic reasoning was cultivated in medieval *scholasticism, and is sometimes found in Chaucer and Shakespeare. *Verb*: **syllogize**.

**symbol** In the simplest sense, anything that stands for or represents something else beyond it—usually an idea conventionally associated with it. Objects like flags and crosses can function symbolically; and words are also symbols. In the *semiotics of C. S. Peirce, the term denotes a kind of *sign that has no natural or resembling connection with its referent, only a conventional one: this is the case with words. In literary usage, however, a symbol is a specially evocative kind of image (*see* IMAGERY); that is, a word or phrase referring to a concrete object, scene, or action which also has some further significance associated with it: roses, mountains, birds, and voyages have all been used as common literary symbols. A symbol differs from a *metaphor in that its application is left open as an unstated suggestion: thus in the sentence *She was a tower of strength*, the metaphor ties a concrete image (the 'vehicle': tower) to an identifiable abstract quality (the *tenor: strength). Similarly, in the systematically extended metaphoric parallels of *allegory, the images represent specific meanings: at the beginning of Langland's allegorical poem *Piers Plowman* (*c*.1380), the tower seen by the dreamer is clearly identified with the quality of Truth, and it has no independent status apart from this function. But the symbolic tower in Robert Browning's poem '"Childe Roland to the Dark Tower Came"' (1855), or that in W. B. Yeats's collection of poems *The Tower* (1928), remains mysteriously indeterminate in its possible meanings. It is therefore usually too simple to say that a literary symbol 'stands for' some idea as if it were just a convenient substitute for a fixed meaning; it is usually a substantial image in its own right, around which further significances may gather according to differing interpretations. The term **symbolism** refers to the use of symbols, or to a set of related symbols; however, it is also the name given to an important movement in late 19th-century and early 20th-century poetry: for this sense, *see* SYMBOLISTS. One of the important features of *Romanticism and succeeding phases of Western literature was a much more pronounced reliance upon enigmatic symbolism in both poetry and prose fiction, sometimes involving obscure private codes of meaning, as in the poetry of Blake or Yeats. A well-known early example of this is the albatross in Coleridge's 'The Rime of the Ancient Mariner' (1798). Many novelists— notably Herman Melville and D. H. Lawrence—have used symbolic methods: in Melville's *Moby-Dick* (1851) the White Whale (and indeed almost every object and character in the book) becomes a focus for many different suggested meanings. Melville's extravagant symbolism was encouraged partly by the importance which American *Transcendentalism gave to symbolic interpretation of the world. *Verb*: **symbolize**. *See also* MOTIF.

**Symbolic, the** A term used by the French psychoanalyst Jacques Lacan and by the literary theorist Julia Kristeva to designate the objective order (sometimes called the Symbolic Order) of language, law, morality, religion, and all social existence, which is held to constitute the identity of any human subject who enters it. Drawing on Freud's theory of the Oedipus Complex and on the *structuralist anthropology of Claude Lévi-Strauss, Lacan developed an opposition between the 'Imaginary' state enjoyed by the infant who has no distinct sense of a self opposed to the world, and the Symbolic Order in which the child then becomes a separate subject within human culture. The Symbolic is the realm of distinctions and differences—between self and others, subject and object—and of absence or 'lack', since in it we are exiled from the completeness of the Imaginary, and can return to it only in fantasized identifications. The infant's entry into the Symbolic is associated with the 'splitting' of the subject by language, which allots distinct 'subject-positions' ('I' and 'you') for us to occupy in turn. In Kristeva's literary theory, the Symbolic is opposed to the

S

disruptive energies of the *semiotic, which have their source in
the Imaginary state.

**Symbolists** An important group of French poets who, between the
1870s and the 1890s, founded the modern tradition in Western poetry.
The leading Symbolists—Paul Verlaine, Arthur Rimbaud, and Stephane
Mallarmé—wrote in reaction against *realism and *naturalism, and
against the objectivity and technical conservatism of the *Parnassians.
Among the minor Symbolist poets were Jules Laforgue and Tristan
Corbière. The Symbolists aimed for a poetry of suggestion rather than of
direct statement, evoking subjective moods through the use of private
*symbols, while avoiding the description of external reality or the
expression of opinion. They wanted to bring poetry closer to music,
believing that sound had mysterious affinities with other senses (*see*
SYNAESTHESIA). Among their influential innovations were *free
verse and the *prose poem. Their chief inspiration was the work of
the poet Charles Baudelaire (1821–67), especially his theory of the
'correspondences' between physical and spiritual realms and between
the different senses; Baudelaire had also promoted Edgar Allan Poe's
doctrine of 'pure' poetry, which the Symbolists attempted to put
into practice.

As a self-conscious movement, French symbolism declared itself
under that name only in 1886, forming part of the so-called *decadence
of that period. It appeared in drama too, notably in the works of the
Belgian playwright Maurice Maeterlinck in the 1890s; and some of its
concerns were reflected in novels by J.-K. Huysmans and Édouard
Dujardin. The influence of symbolism on European and American
literature of the early 20th century was extensive: Paul Valéry in French,
Rainer Maria Rilke in German, and W. B. Yeats in English carried the
tradition into the 20th century, and hardly any major figure of
*modernism was unaffected by it. *See also* HERMETICISM,
IMPRESSIONISM, *POÈTE MAUDIT*.

**Further reading:** Charles Chadwick, *Symbolism* (1971).

**synaeresis** [sin-**eer**-ĭsis] **(syneresis)** A form of contraction or *elision
in which two adjacent vowel sounds are run together into a single
*diphthong or vowel: thus 'the effect' becomes *th'effect*, and 'seëst'
becomes *seest*. The device is used in poetry for the sake of conformity to
the *metre, especially in *syllabic and accentual-syllabic verse. A

distinction is sometimes made between synaeresis, which creates diphthongs, and **sinizesis**, which creates simple vowels. *See also* DIAERESIS, SYNCOPE.

**synaesthesia** [sin-ĕs-**thee**-ziă] A blending or confusion of different kinds of sense-impression, in which one type of sensation is referred to in terms more appropriate to another. Common synaesthetic expressions include the descriptions of colours as 'loud' or 'warm', and of sounds as 'smooth'. This effect was cultivated consciously by the French *Symbolists, but is often found in earlier poetry, notably in Keats. *See also* CATACHRESIS.

**synchronic** [sin-**kron**-ik] Concerned only with the state of something at a given time, rather than with its historical development. In modern linguistics, the synchronic study of language as it is has generally been preferred to the *diachronic study of changes in language that dominated the concerns of 19th-century *philology. *Noun*: **synchrony**.

**syncope** [**sink**-ŏ-pi] A kind of verbal contraction by which a letter or syllable is omitted from within a word (rather than from the beginning or end of the word, as in *elision). Obvious cases are *heav'n* for 'heaven' and *o'er* for 'over'; but the term also covers the omission of sounds without indication in the spelling (e.g. the word *extraordinary*, commonly pronounced as four or five syllables instead of six). The device is especially common in *syllabic and accentual-syllabic verse, where it keeps the word within the metrical scheme. *Adjective*: **syncopal** or **syncopic**.

**synecdoche** [si-**nek**-dŏki] A common *figure of speech (or *trope) by which something is referred to indirectly, either by naming only some part or constituent of it (e.g. *hands* for manual labourers) or—less often—by naming some more comprehensive entity of which it is a part (e.g. *the law* for a police officer). Usually regarded as a special kind of *metonymy, synecdoche occurs frequently in political journalism (e.g. *Moscow* for the Russian government) and sports commentary (e.g. *Liverpool* for one of that city's football teams), but also has literary uses like Dickens's habitual play with bodily parts: the character of Mrs Merdle in *Little Dorrit* is referred to as 'the Bosom'. *Adjective*: **synecdochic**.

**synizesis** *See* SYNAERESIS.

**synonym** A word that has the same—or virtually the same—meaning as another word, and so can substitute for it in certain contexts. This identity of meaning is called **synonymy**. *Adjective*: **synonymous**.

**synopsis** A brief summary or précis of a work's *plot or argument. *Adjective*: **synoptic**.

**syntagm** [**sin**-tam] (**syntagma** [sin-**tag**-mǎ]) A linguistic term designating any combination of units (usually words or *phonemes) which are arranged in a significant sequence. A sentence is a syntagm of words. Language is said to have two distinct dimensions: the **syntagmatic** or 'horizontal' axis of combination in which sequences of words are formed by combining them in a recognized order, and the *paradigmatic or 'vertical' axis of selection, from which particular words are chosen to fill given functions within the sequence. The syntagmatic dimension is therefore the 'linear' aspect of language. *See also* SYNTAX.

**syntax** The way in which words and clauses are ordered and connected so as to form sentences; or the set of grammatical rules governing such word-order. Syntax is a major determinant of literary *style: while simple English sentences usually have the structure 'subject-verb-object' (e.g. *Jane strangled the cat*), poets often distort this syntax through *inversion, while prose writers can exploit elaborate **syntactic** structures such as the *periodic sentence.

*syuzhet* *See* SJUZET.

**tableau** [tab-loh] (plural **-leaux** or **-leaus**) A 'picture' formed by living persons caught in static attitudes. Tableaux were sometimes used at the ends of *acts in 19th-century *melodrama and *farce. The parlour-game of *tableaux vivants* ('living pictures'), in which living people adopt the postures of characters in a famous painting, was also a popular diversion in the 19th century, and is sometimes found in modern *pageants. In a story or poem, a description of some group of people in more or less static postures is sometimes called a tableau.

**Tagelied** *See* AUBADE.

**tail-rhyme stanza** A *stanza that combines longer lines with two or more short lines or 'tails'. Several English verse *romances of the late Middle Ages use a twelve-line stanza rhyming *aabccbddbeeb* or *aabaabccbddb*, with the lines ending in the *b*-rhyme having three stresses, the other lines having four. Chaucer's *parody, the *Tale of Sir Thopas*, uses a six-line version of this, rhyming *aabaab* in some stanzas, *aabccb* in others. Tail-rhyme is also known as caudate rhyme (the tail being a '*cauda' or 'coda'), and in French as *rime couée*.

**tall tale** (tall story) A humorously exaggerated story of impossible feats. Several tall stories attributed to the German Baron Münchhausen appeared in the 1780s, but the form flourished in the *oral tradition of the American frontier in the 19th century, several tall tales being published by Mark Twain, George Washington Harris, and others.

**tanka** A traditional form of Japanese *lyric poem consisting of 31 syllables arranged in lines of 5, 7, 5, 7, and 7 syllables. It has had fewer Western imitators than the *haiku.

**tenor** The subject to which a metaphorical expression is applied. In a *metaphor like *the ship of state*, the state is the tenor, while the metaphorical term *ship* is called the 'vehicle'. This distinction between tenor and vehicle was formulated by the critic I. A. Richards in *The*

*Philosophy of Rhetoric* (1936), where he argues that the total meaning of a metaphor is the product of a complex interaction between them.

**tercet** [ter-**set** or **ter**-sit]  A unit of three verse lines, usually rhyming either with each other or with neighbouring lines. The three-line *stanzas of *terza rima and of the *villanelle are known as tercets. The *sestet of an Italian *sonnet is composed of two tercets. *See also* TRIPLET.

*terza rima* [**ter**-tsǎ **ree**-mǎ]  A verse form consisting of a sequence of interlinked *tercets rhyming *aba bcb cdc ded*, etc. Thus the second line of each tercet provides the rhyme for the first and third lines of the next; the sequence closes with one line (or in a few cases, two lines) rhyming with the middle line of the last tercet: *yzy z(z)*. The form was invented by Dante Alighieri for his *Divina Commedia* (*c*.1320), using the Italian *hendecasyllabic line. It has been adopted by several poets in English *pentameters, notably by P. B. Shelley in his 'Ode to the West Wind' (1820).

**tetralogy** [tet-**ral**-ŏji]  A group of four connected plays or novels. Ancient Greek dramatic festivals presented tetralogies comprising three related tragedies and a *satyr play. Shakespeare's major *history plays fall into two tetralogies, the first comprising the three parts of *Henry VI* and *Richard III*, the second comprising *Richard II*, *Henry IV* Parts 1 and 2, and *Henry V*. Lawrence Durrell's *Alexandria Quartet* (1957–60) is a tetralogy of novels.

**tetrameter** [tet-**ram**-ĕt-er]  A verse line of four feet (*see* FOOT). In English verse, this means a line of four *stresses, usually *iambic or *trochaic—a very common form.

**text**  The actual wording of a written work, as distinct from a reader's (or theatrical director's) interpretation of its *story, *theme, *subtext, etc.; or a specific work chosen as the object of analysis. *Adjective*: **textual**.

**textual criticism**  A branch of literary scholarship that attempts to establish the most accurate version of a written work by comparing all existing manuscript and/or printed versions so as to reconstruct from them the author's intention, eliminating copyists' and printers' errors and any corrupt *interpolations. *See also* BIBLIOGRAPHY, HIGHER CRITICISM, REDACTION.

**textuality** The condition of being textual, or in other words of 'writtenness'. The term is a favoured one in the discourses of *post-structuralism, which insist that there is no escape from text into a pre-textual or extra-textual realm of pure things or events. For example, a central slogan of the critical tendency known as the *new historicism is 'the historicity of texts, the textuality of history', by which it is suggested that all texts arise from specific historical conditions, and that history is not a set of events outside language but a body of writings in which events and their causes are 'constructed' textually. The post-structuralist insistence that everything is textual, often applied to the human body and less often to the rest of the natural world, is sometimes referred to by opponents as **textualism**.

**texture** A term used in some modern criticism (especially in *New Criticism) to designate those 'concrete' properties of a literary work that cannot be subjected to *paraphrase, as distinct from its paraphrasable 'structure' or abstract argument. The term is applied especially to the particular pattern of sounds used in a poem: its *assonance, *consonance, *alliteration, *euphony, and related effects. Often, though, the term also covers *diction, *imagery, *metre, and *rhyme.

**theatre in the round** A form of theatrical presentation in which the audience is placed around a central acting area or stage, as in a circus or boxing match.

**theatre of cruelty** A term introduced by the French actor Antonin Artaud in a series of manifestos in the 1930s, collected as *Le Théâtre et son double* (1938). It refers to his projected revolution in *drama, whereby the rational 'theatre of psychology' was to be replaced by a more physical and primitive rite intended to shock the audience into an awareness of life's cruelty and violence. The idea, derived partly from *Surrealism, was that the audience should undergo a *catharsis through being possessed by a 'plague' or epidemic of irrational responses. Artaud's own attempts to put this theory into dramatic practice failed, and he was locked up for some time as a lunatic. Some later dramatists, though, have developed these principles more successfully: a celebrated instance was Peter Brook's production in 1964 of Peter Weiss's *Marat/Sade*.

**theatre of the absurd** *See* ABSURD.

**theme** A salient abstract idea that emerges from a literary work's treatment of its subject-matter; or a topic recurring in a number of literary works. While the subject of a work is described concretely in terms of its action (e.g. 'the adventures of a newcomer in the big city'), its theme or themes will be described in more abstract terms (e.g. love, war, revenge, betrayal, fate, etc.). The theme of a work may be announced explicitly, but more often it emerges indirectly through the recurrence of *motifs. *Adjective*: **thematic**.

**Theory** A shorthand term used since the 1970s in this capitalized form to refer to a miscellaneous body of intellectual approaches that had increasingly become interlinked and mutually reinforcing in their repudiation of *humanist (and specifically 'liberal-humanist') traditions in literary study, history, *aesthetics, and philosophy. Included under the heading of 'Theory' were fairly long-established currents of thought such as psychoanalysis (*see* PSYCHOANALYTIC CRITICISM), some versions of Marxism (*see* MARXIST CRITICISM), and the recently rediscovered *Russian Formalism; along with these were counted more recent developments affecting Parisian intellectual life and deriving from *structuralism in linguistics and anthropology: the psychoanalytic theories of Jacques Lacan and Julia Kristeva, the 'structural' Marxism of Louis Althusser, the structuralist poetics of Roman Jakobson (*see* FUNCTION), and the work of various *post-structuralist thinkers including Roland Barthes, Jacques Derrida (*see* DECONSTRUCTION), and Michel Foucault. Also included as late developments were the *Yale school of deconstructive criticism, the various kinds of *reader-response criticism, and the emergent schools of *postcolonial theory and *new historicism.

In the cases of psychoanalysis, Marxism, Russian Formalism, and structuralism, a shared distinctive feature was their claim to 'scientific' understanding of psychology, history, poetry, and culture as a whole, which justified their variously elaborate conceptual systems and specialized terminologies, just as it struck practitioners of more traditional literary criticism (and history, philosophy, etc.) as alarmingly alien or misguided, especially in its relegation of the conscious human agent to a 'subject' subordinate to linguistic codes. The rise of the post-structuralist tendency had the severely complicating effect of challenging the scientific pretensions of the older Theoretical schools, but it further provoked the 'humanist' camp by appearing to undermine central concepts of truth and reason. One result was the outbreak of the so-called 'Theory Wars' in Western intellectual life from the late 1970s through the 1980s which seemed to pit partisans of the new thinking against guardians of humanistic orthodoxy—although in fact many opponents of Theory were radicals, e.g. those feminists who dismissed it as self-important 'male theory' and the Marxist historian E. P. Thompson in his polemic *The Poverty of Theory* (1978). The excitements and controversies of Theory had to some extent exhausted themselves by the end of the 1980s, although their impact is still widely felt in what is now often said to be a post-theoretical phase.

Such a broadly applied and unspecified term necessarily has its problems. 'Theory' is not the same thing as literary theory or even cultural theory, because it extends into realms of psychology, philosophy, linguistics, and history. It cannot amount to a theory 'of' anything in particular, because it is many theories of almost everything, several of these being incompatible with one another.

**Further reading:** Peter Barry, *Beginning Theory* (2nd edn, 2002); Thomas Docherty, *After Theory* (1997); Terry Eagleton, *After Theory* (2003).

**thesis** An argument or proposition, which may be opposed by an *antithesis; or a scholarly essay defending some proposition, usually a dissertation submitted for an academic degree. The thesis of a literary work is its abstract doctrinal content, that is, a proposition for which it argues. For 'thesis novel', *see* ROMAN À THÈSE; for 'thesis play', *see* PROBLEM PLAY.

**third-person narrative** A *narrative or mode of storytelling in which the *narrator is not a character within the events related, but stands 'outside' those events. In a third-person narrative, all characters within the story are therefore referred to as 'he', 'she', or 'they'; but this does not, of course, prevent the narrator from using the first person 'I' or 'we' in commentary on the events and their meaning. Third-person narrators are often *omniscient or 'all-knowing' about the events of the story, but they may sometimes appear to be restricted in their knowledge of these events. Third-person narrative is by far the most common form of storytelling. *See also* POINT OF VIEW.

**threnody** A *dirge or lament for the dead. A writer or speaker of threnodies is a **threnodist**. *Adjective*: **threnodic** or **threnodial**. *See also* ELEGY, MONODY.

**thriller**  A kind of popular novel in which a protagonist endangered by a criminal or otherwise sinister conspiracy is followed through heroic adventures made up of flight, pursuit, capture, and escape. Although the genre has always been relatively loosely defined, it may still be distinguished from the *detective story in that its interest in criminal activity concentrates on imminent dangers and evasive actions rather than on retrospective analysis or investigation, its atmosphere being more anxious and frenetic than that of detective fiction. The first significant novel of this kind was William Godwin's *Things as They Are, or the Adventures of Caleb Williams* (1794, better known simply as *Caleb Williams*), in which the hero is pursued by his former employer's agents after discovering an unnamed secret. Similar emphases on dark secrets and menacing intrigues are found in the *sensation novels of the 1860s, but the modern thriller as an identifiable popular genre emerged from the early years of the 20th century, at which time John Buchan's books, notably *The Thirty-Nine Steps* (1915), set the standard to be followed, while Sax Rohmer in *The Mystery of Dr Fu Manchu* (1913) and its sequels showed the depths of inane xenophobia to which the genre could sink. A major subgenre is the **spy thriller**, practised by Buchan and others, further popularized by Ian Fleming in his James Bond novels (1953–63), and later raised to significant literary distinction by John Le Carré in *The Spy Who Came in From the Cold* (1963) and other works. The *noir thriller is less clearly differentiated, but commonly leads the reader into identification with a criminal, as in several novels by Patricia Highsmith.

**Further reading:** Jerry Palmer, *Thrillers* (1978).

**tone**  A very vague critical term usually designating the mood or atmosphere of a work, although in some more restricted uses it refers to the author's attitude to the reader (e.g. formal, intimate, pompous) or to the subject-matter (e.g. ironic, light, solemn, satiric, sentimental). *Adjective*: **tonal**. *See also* VOICE.

**topographical poetry**  Poetry devoted to the description of specific places, usually with additional meditative passages. Following John Denham's poem 'Cooper's Hill' (1642), topographical poetry became a significant genre of English verse throughout the 18th century, culminating in the poems of Wordsworth, notably his 'Lines Composed a few miles above Tintern Abbey, on revisiting the banks of the Wye

during a tour. July 13, 1798' (usually called 'Tintern Abbey'). This kind
of poetry is sometimes called loco-descriptive verse.

**topos** [top-oss] (plural **topoi**) An older term for a *motif commonly
found in literary works, or for a stock device of *rhetoric.

**touchstone** A short quotation from a recognized poetic masterpiece,
employed as a standard of instant comparison for judging the value
of other works. The term was used by the English poet and critic
Matthew Arnold in his essay 'The Study of Poetry' (1880), in which he
recommends certain lines of Homer, Dante, Shakespeare, and Milton
as touchstones for testing 'the presence or absence of high poetic
quality' in samples chosen from other poets. Arnold's claim that this
procedure is 'objective' has not been accepted by many modern critics.
Literally, a touchstone is a hard stone of the kind once used for testing
the quality of gold or silver. *See also* CRITERION.

**tract** A short pamphlet or essay presenting some religious
(or political) argument or doctrine.

**tradition** Any body of works, styles, conventions, or beliefs which
are represented as having been 'handed down' from the past to the
present. In practice, this means a specific selection of works arranged
according to a certain interpretation of the past, usually made in
order to lend authority to present critical arguments. Thus T. S. Eliot
re-invented the tradition of English poetry by aligning it with the work
of John Donne rather than John Milton; while F. R. Leavis in *The Great
Tradition* (1948) excluded several major novelists from 'the' tradition
of English fiction. A special sense of the adjective **traditional** applies
in reference to old poems and songs, especially *folk songs: it indicates
that their authorship is not known.

**tragedy** A serious play (or, by extension, a novel) representing the
disastrous downfall of a central character, the *protagonist. In some
ancient Greek tragedies such as the *Eumenides* of Aeschylus, a happy
ending was possible, provided that the subject was mythological and
the treatment dignified, but the more usual conclusion, involving the
protagonist's death, has become the defining feature in later uses of the
term. From the works of the Greek tragedians Aeschylus, Euripides,
and Sophocles, the philosopher Aristotle arrived at the most influential
definition of tragedy in his *Poetics* (4th century BCE): the imitation of

an action that is serious and complete, achieving a *catharsis ('purification') through incidents arousing pity and terror. Aristotle also observed that the protagonist is led into a fatal calamity by a *hamartia ('error') which often takes the form of *hubris (excessive pride leading to divine retribution or *nemesis). The tragic effect usually depends on our awareness of admirable qualities—manifest or potential—in the protagonist, which are wasted terribly in the fated disaster. The most painfully tragic plays, like Shakespeare's *King Lear*, display a disproportion in scale between the protagonist's initial error and the overwhelming destruction with which it is punished. English tragedy of Shakespeare's time was not based directly on Greek examples, but drew instead upon the more rhetorical Roman precedent of *Senecan tragedy (*see also* REVENGE TRAGEDY). Shakespearean tragedy thus shows an 'irregular' construction in the variety of its scenes and characters, whereas classical French tragedy of the 17th century is modelled more closely on Aristotle's observations, notably in its observance of the *unities of time, place, and action.

Until the beginning of the 18th century, tragedies were written in verse, and usually dealt with the fortunes of royal families or other political leaders. Modern tragic drama, however, normally combines the socially inferior protagonist of *domestic tragedy with the use of prose, as in the plays of Henrik Ibsen and Arthur Miller. Some novels, like Thomas Hardy's *The Mayor of Casterbridge* (1886) and Malcolm Lowry's *Under the Volcano* (1947), and some novellas like Edith Wharton's *Ethan Frome* (1911) can be described as tragedies, since they describe the downfall of a central character.

**Further reading:** Adrian Poole, *Tragedy: A Very Short Introduction* (2005).

**tragedy of blood** *See* REVENGE TRAGEDY.

**tragic flaw** A term used by some modern critics to denote what they interpret as the defect of character that brings about the protagonist's downfall in a *tragedy: Othello's jealousy is a famous example. The idea of the tragic flaw involves a narrowing and personalizing of the broader Greek concept of *hamartia ('error' or 'failure'). *See also* HUBRIS.

**tragic irony** *See* IRONY.

**tragicomedy** A play that combines elements of tragedy and comedy, either by providing a happy ending to a potentially tragic story or by

some more complex blending of serious and light moods. In its broadest
sense, the term may be applied to almost any kind of drama that does
not conform strictly to comic or tragic conventions—from the medieval
*mystery play to the *epic theatre of Brecht—but it is associated more
specifically with a dramatic tradition that emerged from Italy in the 16th
century, notably in Battista Guarini's *pastoral play *Il Pastor Fido* (1583).
Guarini mixed 'high' and 'low' characters who had usually been kept
apart in the separate genres, and he aimed for a 'middle' style between
the tragic and the comic. The English playwrights Francis Beaumont
and John Fletcher followed his example in their *Philaster* (*c*.1609),
creating a new fashion for dramatic 'romances' that turned threatening
situations into improbably happy conclusions through surprising
reversals of fortune. This kind of tragicomedy appears to have
influenced Shakespeare's later plays, including *The Winter's Tale* and
*Cymbeline*, although the tragicomic pattern of sudden release from
deadly danger had appeared before in his *Measure for Measure* and
*The Merchant of Venice*. Shakespeare's *Troilus and Cressida* is also
known as a tragicomedy for different reasons, primarily the lack of any
other term to describe it (*see* PROBLEM PLAY). The conventions of *poetic
justice came to be associated with later kinds of tragicomedy, including
the French **drame* and the English *heroic drama. In modern dramatic
criticism, the term has come to be attached to the theatre of the *absurd:
Samuel Beckett applied it to his own play *En attendant Godot* (1952),
while the plays of Harold Pinter are often seen as tragicomic. *See also*
BLACK COMEDY, COMIC RELIEF.

**Further reading:** Verna A. Foster, *The Name and Nature of Tragicomedy* (2004).

## transcendental signified *See* LOGOCENTRISM.

## Transcendentalism
An idealist philosophical tendency among
writers in and around Boston in the mid-19th century. Growing out of
Christian Unitarianism in the 1830s under the influence of German and
British *Romanticism, Transcendentalism affirmed Kant's principle
of intuitive knowledge not derived from the senses, while rejecting
organized religion for an extremely individualistic celebration of the
divinity in each human being. The leading Transcendentalist Ralph
Waldo Emerson issued what was virtually the movement's manifesto
in his essay *Nature* (1836), which presents natural phenomena as
symbols of higher spiritual truths. The nonconformist individualism

of the Transcendentalists is expressed in Emerson's essay 'Self-Reliance' (1841) and in Henry David Thoreau's *Walden* (1854)—a kind of autobiographical sermon against modern materialism. Others involved in the Transcendental Club in the late 1830s and with its magazine *The Dial* (1840–44) included Amos Bronson Alcott, Margaret Fuller, and William Ellery Channing. The Transcendentalists' manner of interpreting nature in symbolic terms had a profound influence on American literature of this period, notably in the works of Nathaniel Hawthorne, Herman Melville, and Walt Whitman. *See also* AMERICAN RENAISSANCE.

**Further reading:** George Hochfield (ed.), *Selected Writings of the American Transcendentalists* (2nd edn, 2004).

((⊕)) SEE WEB LINKS
• American Transcendentalism Web at Texas A & M.

**transferred epithet** *See* EPITHET, HYPALLAGE.

**trauma theory** A body of 20th-century psychological research into the effects upon people of various traumatic events (assault, rape, war, famine, incarceration, etc.), leading to the official recognition in the 1980s of Post-Traumatic Stress Disorder. Concepts developed from that work have since the 1990s been taken up and developed as an interdisciplinary field of study involving literature, psychology, history, and philosophy, with a concentration upon questions of memory, forgetting, and *narrative. The impact of trauma theory on literary studies was felt from the publication of essays by various critics in *Trauma: Explorations in Memory* (ed. Cathy Caruth, 1995) and of Caruth's own study, *Unclaimed Experience* (1996). Since then, a number of specialized critical writings have applied trauma theory to the memoirs of Holocaust survivors and war veterans, and to topics such as sexual violence in women's fiction.

**Further reading:** Anne Whitehead, *Trauma Fiction* (2004).

**travelogue** An account of one's travels: a book, article, or film recording places visited and people encountered. The literary variety is more often known simply as the travel book.

**travesty** A mockingly undignified or trivializing treatment of a dignified subject, usually as a kind of *parody. Travesty may be distinguished from the *mock epic and other kinds of *burlesque in that it treats a solemn subject frivolously, while they treat frivolous subjects with mock solemnity. Cervantes's *Don Quixote* (1605) is a travesty of chivalric *romances, and James Joyce's *Ulysses* (1922) is partly a travesty of Homer's *Odyssey*. *Verb*: **travesty**.

**treatise** [tree-tiz]  A written work devoted to the systematic examination of a particular subject, usually philosophical or scientific.

**trilogy**  A group of three connected plays or novels. Ancient Greek tragedies were presented at Athenian festivals in groups of three, but the *Oresteia* of Aeschylus is the only such trilogy to have survived. Shakespeare's *Henry VI* is a later dramatic example. There are several examples in modern prose fiction, including Samuel Beckett's trilogy of novels, *Molloy* (1950), *Malone Meurt* (*Malone Dies*, 1951), and *L'Innommable* (*The Unnameable*, 1952).

**trimeter** [trim-ĕt-er]  A verse line of three feet (*see* FOOT). In English verse, this means a line of three *stresses.

**triolet**  A poem of eight lines using only two rhymes, the first two lines being repeated as the final two lines, the first line also recurring as the fourth. The rhyme scheme—with repeated lines given in capitals—is *ABaAabAB*. The triolet is one of the medieval French *fixed forms, and may be considered as a simplified form of the *rondel. A few English poets, including Austin Dobson and W. E. Henley, revived it in the late 19th century.

**triple metre**  A term covering poetic *metres based on a *foot of three syllables (a **triple foot**), as opposed to the much more common *duple metre in which the predominant foot has two syllables. English verse in triple metres thus displays a more or less regular alternation of single stressed syllables with pairs of unstressed syllables, the feet being described traditionally as *anapaests or *dactyls.

**triple rhyme**  A rhyme on three syllables, the first stressed and the others unstressed: *beautiful/dutiful*. Triple rhymes are used chiefly for comic purposes in *light verse, as in Edward Lear's *limerick beginning

> There was an old man of Thermopylae
> Who never did anything properly.

Byron's *Don Juan* has some ludicrous examples. *See also* RHYME.

**triplet** A sequence of three verse lines sharing the same *rhyme, sometimes appearing as a variation among the *heroic couplets of Dryden and some 18th-century poets: or any group or *stanza of three lines. Triplets occurring among heroic couplets are sometimes indicated by a brace, as in Pope's *Essay on Criticism* (1711):

> Musick resembles Poetry, in each
> Are nameless Graces which no Methods teach, ⎫
> And which a Master-Hand alone can reach. ⎭

The three-line units used in *terza rima* and those composing the *sestet of an Italian sonnet are more often referred to as *tercets.

**trochee** [troh-ki] A metrical unit (*foot) of verse, having one stressed syllable followed by one unstressed syllable, as in the word 'tender' (or, in Greek and Latin *quantitative verse, one long syllable followed by one short syllable). Lines of verse made up predominantly of trochees are referred to as **trochaic verse** or **trochaics**. Regular trochaic lines are quite rare in English, Longfellow's *Song of Hiawatha* (1855) being a celebrated example of their extended use:

> Ye whose hearts are fresh and simple

Far more common in English is the truncated or *catalectic line that drops the final unstressed syllable, as in Emily Brontë's lines:

> Long neglect has worn away
> Half the sweet enchanting smile.

Since the trochee is often found as a variation at the beginning of *iambic lines (*see* SUBSTITUTION), this sort of trochaic line beginning and ending with a stressed syllable can be difficult to distinguish from iambic verse.

**trope** A *figure of speech, especially one that uses words in senses beyond their *literal meanings. The theory of *rhetoric has involved several disputed attempts to clarify the distinction between tropes (or 'figures of thought') and *schemes (or 'figures of speech'). The most generally agreed distinction in modern theory is that tropes change the meanings of words, by a 'turn' of sense, whereas schemes merely rearrange their normal order. The major figures that are agreed upon as being tropes are *metaphor, *simile, *metonymy, *synecdoche, *irony, *personification, and *hyperbole; *litotes and *periphrasis are also sometimes called tropes. The figurative sense of a word is sometimes called its **tropological** sense, tropology being the study of tropes—and especially of the spiritual meanings concealed behind the literal meanings of religious scriptures (*see* TYPOLOGY). In a second sense, the term was applied in the Middle Ages to certain additional passages introduced into church services. The most important of these, the *quem quaeritis* trope in the Easter Introit, is thought to have been the origin of *liturgical drama. *Adjective*: **tropical**.

**troubadour**  A poet of southern France (or sometimes northern Italy) writing in Provençal in the late Middle Ages. The troubadours, mostly aristocratic poets rather than wandering *minstrels or *jongleurs*, flourished in the period 1100–1350, composing elaborate *lyrics of *courtly love which had an extensive influence on Western poetry and culture. Among the best known are Guillaume d'Aquitaine, Arnaut Daniel, and Betran de Born. Their favoured poetic forms included the *aubade, the *chanson*, and the *pastourelle*. From the late 12th century onwards they found imitators in northern France (the *trouvères*) and in Germany (the *Minnesänger*).

**Further reading:** Simon Gaunt and Sarah Kay (eds), *The Troubadours: An Introduction* (1999).

**trouvère** [troo-**vair**]  A poet of northern France in the late Middle Ages. The *trouvères* flourished in the late 12th and early 13th centuries, and were in many respects the followers of the Provençal *troubadours, although their repertoire extended beyond love *lyrics into *narrative verse, especially the *chanson de geste* and the verse *romance. The term covers some of the professional entertainers known as *jongleurs*, but applies mainly to poets of higher rank. The most important was Chrétien de Troyes, who established the Arthurian romance of *courtly love with his *Lancelot* (*c*.1170); other notable *trouvères* include Conon de Béthune, Thibaud de Champagne, and Blondel de Nesle—who, according to legend, discovered the imprisoned Richard the Lionheart by singing under his window.

**truncation**  The shortening of a metrical verse line by omitting a syllable or syllables (usually unstressed) from the full complement expected in the regular metrical pattern. This may occur at the beginning of the line (acephalexis: *see* ACEPHALOUS) or, more usually, at the end (catalexis: *see* CATALECTIC). In English verse, truncation is most often found in trochaic verse (*see* TROCHEE), where the final unstressed syllable is commonly not employed.

**turn** The English term for an abrupt change in the mood or argument of a poem, especially in a *sonnet (*see* VOLTA); also an older word for a *trope.

**two-hander** A play written for only two speaking parts, such as Samuel Beckett's *Happy Days* (1961).

**type** A fictional character who stands as a representative of some identifiable class or group of people. Although some uses of the term equate it with the stereotyped *stock character of literary and folk *tradition, other uses distinguish between this 'two-dimensional' stock character and the more individualized type: in the work of the Hungarian Marxist critic Georg Lukács, 'typicality' is a quality combining uniquely individualized with historically representative features. Lukács found this typicality in the characters of early 19th-century *realist novels like those of Balzac; similarly, the realist fiction of George Eliot and Henry James is inhabited by such types, who are certainly not mere stock characters. In two other senses, the term is used in reference to literary *forms as a synonym for *genre, and in reference to religious *allegory as another word for emblem or *symbol (*see* TYPOLOGY).

**typography** The arrangement of printed words on the page. Typographical factors—most obviously the lack of a right-hand margin in most verse, and the spaces between *stanzas—have some influence on readers' understanding of literary works. The exploitation of typography for special effects is found in *pattern poetry and modern *concrete poetry, and in some experimental prose works like those of the Scottish novelist Alasdair Gray.

**typology** A system of interpretation applied by early Christian theologians to the Hebrew scriptures (the 'Old Testament'), by which certain events, images, and personages of pre-Christian *legend could be understood as prophetic 'types' or 'figures' foreshadowing the life of Christ. Typology—literally the study of types—is thus a method of re-reading the Old Testament anachronistically in terms of the New Testament, so that Adam, Isaac, Jonah, and other characters are pre-figurings of Christ, the Tree of Knowledge in Eden is a type of the

Cross, and so on. By the 13th century an elaborate system of *allegory had been constructed, dividing the sense of anything in the Old Testament into four levels of meaning: the literal, the allegorical (referring to the New Testament or the Christian Church), the moral or tropological (referring to the fate of the individual soul), and the *anagogical (referring to universal history and *eschatology). In the standard illustration of this scheme, Jerusalem is literally a city, allegorically the Church, tropologically the soul of the believer, and anagogically the heavenly City of God. Typological allegory is an important element in many literary works of medieval Christianity, including Dante's *Divina Commedia* (*c*.1320), and in some later sermons and religious verse.

**ubi sunt** [uubi suunt] A Latin phrase ('where are . . . ?') often used in medieval Latin poems on the transitoriness of life and beauty, usually as an opening line or *refrain referring to the dead who are listed in the poem. The phrase serves as the name for a common *motif in medieval (and some later) poetry, Latin and *vernacular, in which the speaker asks what has become of various heroes and beautiful ladies. The most celebrated example of the motif is François Villon's 'Ballade des dames du temps jadis' (*c.*1460), with its refrain:

> Mais ou sont les neiges d'antan?

In D. G. Rossetti's translation, this is rendered 'But where are the snows of yesteryear?'

**Ultraísmo** The doctrine of an *avant-garde group of Spanish poets in the early 1920s, led by Guillermo de Torre. The Grupo Ultra was founded in 1919, issued its *Manifesto vertical ultraísta* in the following year, and produced a short-lived magazine, *Ultra* (1920–21). Under the influence of the French poet Stéphane Mallarmé, the Ultraists rejected all previous poetic traditions, and aimed for the creation of a purified poetry liberated from formal, logical, or narrative structures and from human emotional substance (love poetry was firmly repudiated). The Argentine writer Jorge Luis Borges was briefly associated with the group while in Madrid (1919–21), and proclaimed its principles on his return to Buenos Aires, but he later distanced himself from Ultraism and from his early poetry of the 1920s. Ultraism also had the effect of provoking the philosopher Ortega y Gasset into writing *La deshumanización del arte* (1925), his consideration of the problems of experimental modern art movements.

**uncanny, the** A kind of disturbing strangeness evoked in some kinds of horror story and related fiction. In Tzvetan Todorov's theory of the *fantastic, the uncanny is an effect produced by stories in which the incredible events can be explained as the products of the *narrator's or *protagonist's dream, hallucination, or delusion. A clear case of this is Edgar Allan Poe's tale 'The Tell-Tale Heart' (1843), in which the narrator is clearly suffering from paranoid delusions. In tales of the *marvellous, on the other hand, no such psychological explanation is offered, and strange events are taken to be truly supernatural. In *psychoanalytic criticism, the term carries further significance from the influence of Sigmund Freud's article *Das Unheimliche* ('The "Uncanny"', 1919), in which he proposes that the apparently strange is a disguised representation of what is in fact familiar.

**Further reading:** Nicholas Royle, *The Uncanny* (2002).

**undecidable**  *See* APORIA, INDETERMINACY.

**unexpurgated**  Not subjected to cuts arising from censorship or fear of censorship. An expurgated *edition of a written work is one from which controversial, especially sexual or allegedly blasphemous, passages have been omitted. A favoured marketing device of paperback publishers in the 1950s and 1960s was to proclaim on the covers of books (by D. H. Lawrence, Henry Miller, Giovanni Boccaccio, Emile Zola, and others whose books were rumoured to be sexually explicit) that their editions were 'Complete and Unexpurgated', thus reassuring the buyer that the sexually exciting episodes, if there actually had been any, had been left in.

**unities, the**  Principles of dramatic structure proposed by critics and dramatists of the 16th and 17th centuries, claiming the authority of Aristotle's *Poetics* (4th century BCE). The three unities were the unity of time, the unity of place, and the unity of action. In fact Aristotle in his discussion of *tragedy insists only on unity of action, mentioning unity of time in passing, and says nothing about place. Italian and French critics of the 16th century attempted to codify his views into rules, but with little effect on dramatic practice until Jean Mairet's *Sophonisbe* (1634), the first French tragedy to observe the unities. As formulated by Mairet and later by Boileau in *L'Art poétique* (1674), the unities required that any serious play should have a unified action, without the distractions of a *subplot, representing events of a single day (24 hours, or 12, or ideally the same time as the duration of the performance itself) within a single setting—which could include different parts of the same city. The tragedies of Pierre Corneille—apart from his controversial play *Le Cid* (1637)—and those of Jean Racine were the outstanding examples of this

mode of dramatic composition. In England, however the French rules
never established themselves in dramatic practice, although they
were much debated by critics. The influence of Shakespeare is usually
believed to be the reason for this resistance: apart from *The Tempest* and
*The Two Gentlemen of Verona*, all of his plays violate the unities. The
rise of *Romanticism involved a rebellion against *neoclassicism and its
rules, including the unities; the example of Shakespeare was again
invoked to support freely structured drama.

**university wits** The name given by some modern literary historians
to a group of English poets and playwrights who established themselves
in London in the 1580s and 1590s after attending university at either
Oxford or Cambridge. The most important member of the group was
Christopher Marlowe, whose powerful *blank-verse plays prepared the
way for Shakespeare. Others included George Peele, Robert Greene,
Thomas Nashe, John Lyly, and Thomas Lodge. There seems to have
been some rivalry between this group and the newcomers Shakespeare
and Jonson, who did not have university educations.

**univocal** [yoo-ni-**voh**-kǎl]  Having only one meaning; unmistakable in
sense. The term **univocality** is sometimes employed in contrast with the
*ambiguity of literary works; for other contrasting terms, *see* POLYSEMY,
MULTI-ACCENTUALITY.

**unreliable narrator**  A *narrator whose account of events appears to
be faulty, misleadingly biased, or otherwise distorted, so that it departs
from the 'true' understanding of events shared between the reader and
the *implied author. The discrepancy between the unreliable narrator's
view of events and the view that readers suspect to be more accurate
creates a sense of *irony. The term does not necessarily mean that such a
narrator is morally untrustworthy or a habitual liar (although this may
be true in some cases), since the category also includes harmlessly
naïve, 'fallible', or ill-informed narrators. A classic case is Huck in Mark
Twain's *Adventures of Huckleberry Finn* (1884): this fourteen-year-old
narrator does not understand the full significance of the events he is
relating and commenting on. Other kinds of unreliable narrator seem to
be falsifying their accounts from motives of vanity or malice. In either
case, the reader is offered the pleasure of picking up 'clues' in the
narrative that betray the true state of affairs. This kind of *first-person
narrative is particularly favoured in 20th-century fiction: a virtuoso

u

display of its use is William Faulkner's *The Sound and the Fury* (1929), which employs three unreliable narrators—an imbecile, a suicidal student, and an irritable racist bigot. *See also* POINT OF VIEW.

**Urtext** The German term for an original version of a text, usually applied to a version that is lost and so has to be reconstructed by *textual criticism. Some scholars believe that Shakespeare's *Hamlet* is based on an earlier play that has not survived even in name; this hypothetical work is referred to as the *Ur-Hamlet*.

**ut pictura poesis** [uut pik-**too**-ră poh-**ees**-is] A phrase used by the Roman poet Horace in his *Ars Poetica* (*c*.20 BCE), meaning 'as painting is, so is poetry'. The phrase has come to stand for the principle of similarity between the two arts, an idea shared by many writers and artists of different periods and found in common metaphors of literary 'depiction' or 'portrayal'. It held an important place in aesthetic debates of the late *Renaissance and in the theories of *neoclassicism, but was subjected to an important *critique by the German dramatist and critic G. E. Lessing in his essay *Laokoon* (1766). The relationship between the two 'sister arts' is usually said to lie in their imitation of nature (*see* MIMESIS).

**utopia** An imagined form of ideal or superior (usually communistic) human society; or a written work of *fiction or philosophical speculation describing such a society. Utopias may be distinguished from mythological Golden Ages or religious paradises in that they are the products of human (i.e. political) arrangement for human benefit. The word was coined by Sir Thomas More in his Latin work *Utopia* (1516), as a pun on two Greek words, *eutopos* ('good place') and *outopos* ('no place'). More's account of an ideal commonwealth was followed by several others including Francis Bacon's *New Atlantis* (1627); later examples include Edward Bellamy's *Looking Backward* (1888), and William Morris's *dream vision of socialism in *News from Nowhere* (1890). Utopian fiction has often been used as the basis of *satire on contemporary life, as in Samuel Butler's *Erewhon* (1872); it is also closely related to some kinds of *science fiction. For the inverted or undesirable equivalent of a utopia, the term *dystopia is often used, as it is for works describing such a 'bad place'.

u

**variorum edition** Originally an *edition of an author's works (or of a single work) containing explanatory notes by various commentators and editors. In recent usage, however, the term has come to mean an edition that includes all the variant readings from manuscript and other versions. Many modern variorum editions answer both descriptions.

**Varronian satire** *See* MENIPPEAN SATIRE.

**vatic** Inspired by powers of prophecy, or relating to a divinely inspired poet or *bard, such a poet being called in Latin a *vates*.

**vaudeville** A form of variety show popular in the USA in the late 19th and early 20th centuries, and more respectable than the American *burlesque show. In Britain, this form of entertainment with various songs, dances, sketches, acrobatics, ventriloquisms, and other 'acts' is more often called music hall. In 18th- and 19th-century France, however, vaudeville was a more coherent form of light-hearted comedy interspersed with satirical songs; it evolved into the comic opera.

**vehicle** *See* TENOR.

***Verfremdungseffekt*** *See* ALIENATION EFFECT.

**verisimilitude** The semblance of truth or reality in literary works; or the literary principle that requires a consistent illusion of truth to life. The term covers both the exclusion of improbabilities (as in *realism and *naturalism) and the careful disguising of improbabilities in non-realistic works. As a critical principle, it originates in Aristotle's concept of *mimesis or imitation of nature. It was invoked by French critics (as *vraisemblance*) to enforce the dramatic *unities in the 17th and 18th centuries, on the grounds that changes of scene or time would break the illusion of truth to life for the audience. *Adjective*: **verisimilar.**

***verismo*** [ve-**riz**-moh] An Italian form of *naturalism, best exemplified by the novels and stories written in the 1880s by the Sicilian writer

Giovanni Verga; these document the harsh lives of the Sicilian poor. Another notable **verist** of this period is the short-story writer Federico de Roberto. *Verismo*, through Verga's story *Cavalleria rusticana*, had a significant influence on Italian opera (notably on Puccini), and later upon the emergence of *neo-realism. In English, the term **verism** is sometimes applied to *realism as a critical doctrine. *Adjective*: **veristic**.

**vernacular** [ver-**nak**-yŭ-ler] The local language or *dialect of common speech; or (as an adjective) written in such a local language or dialect. The term distinguishes living languages from dead or priestly languages (e.g. French or English rather than Latin or Greek), the languages of the colonized from those of the colonists (e.g. Middle English rather than French; Welsh or Bengali rather than English), or the use of dialect rather than 'standard' forms of the same language; but in a looser sense it may refer to the use of a colloquial rather than a formal style.

***vers de société*** [vaird sos-yay-tay] The French term ('society verse') for a kind of *light verse which deals with the frivolous concerns of upper-class social life, usually in a harmlessly playful vein of *satire and with some technical elegance. Some of Alexander Pope's minor poems fall into this category, while the modern master of *vers de société* in English is John Betjeman.

***vers libre*** [vair leebr] *See* FREE VERSE.

**verse** 1. *Poetry, as distinct from *prose. The term is usually more neutral than 'poetry', indicating that the technical requirements of *rhythm and *metre are present, while poetic merit may or may not be. It is almost always reserved for metrical compositions, the looser non-metrical category of *free verse being a special case. 2. A line of poetry; or, in common usage, a *stanza, especially of a hymn or song. Strictly, the term should refer to a line rather than a stanza, although the battle to retain this distinction seems to have been lost. Even so, to avoid confusion it is preferable to call a line a line and a stanza a stanza. 3. A poem.

**verse form** A general term for any given arrangement of metrical verse lines into a poem, sequence of *stanzas, or *stichic form, along with its *rhyme scheme (if any). The range of possible verse forms thus includes stichic poems of indeterminate length, either unrhymed (e.g.

*blank verse) or rhymed (e.g. as *couplets or in *terza rima); poems of specified length and metre in rhyme (e.g. *sonnet, *limerick) or unrhymed (e.g. *haiku); sequences of particular stanzas (e.g. *quatrains, *ottava rima); and *fixed forms such as the *sestina or *villanelle.

**verse paragraph** A group of verse lines forming a subdivision of a poem, the length of this unit being determined by the development of the sense rather than by a formal *stanza pattern. Long *narrative poems in *blank verse or *heroic couplets are often divided into paragraphs of uneven lengths, the breaks being indicated either by indentation (as in prose) or by spaces. Some shorter poems like Matthew Arnold's 'Dover Beach' are also composed in irregular verse paragraphs rather than stanzas. The subdivisions of *free verse are necessarily non-stanzaic and are therefore also usually called verse paragraphs. Some critics have claimed that a stanza or even a complete short poem like a *sonnet should be considered as a verse paragraph, but this usage loses the valuable distinction between the terms. See also STICHIC, STROPHE.

**versification** The techniques, principles, and practice of composing *verse, especially in its technical aspects of *metre, *rhyme, and *stanza form; or the conversion of a prose passage or work into metrical verse form. Verb: **versify**. See also PROSODY.

**verso** The back of a printed sheet; thus the left-hand (and even-numbered) page in a book, as opposed to the recto, which is the right-hand, odd-numbered page on the other side.

**verso piano** In Italian versification, a 'plain' line of verse that conforms to the regularly expected number of syllables by closing with a single unstressed syllable after the stress on the penultimate syllable. Thus in the standard Italian *hendecasyllabic line (endecasyllabo), the stressed tenth syllable is followed by one unstressed syllable. A line at the end of which a further unstressed syllable appears is called a verso sdrucciolo.

**verso tronco** In Italian versification, a 'truncated' line of verse that concludes with a stressed syllable and not with the normally expected further unstressed syllable. The tronco version of the Italian *hendecasyllabic line is thus in fact a line of only ten syllables, although still regarded as a legitimate endecasyllabo. See also CATALECTIC.

**Vice, the** A *stock character in medieval *morality plays; he is a cynical kind of fool in the service of the Devil, and tries to tempt others in a comical but often sinister manner. The Vice is believed to be the ancestor of some later dramatic villains like Shakespeare's Iago, and of some more comic characters like his Falstaff.

**Victorian** Belonging to the period of British history, and that of the British Empire, between the accession of Queen Victoria in 1837 and her death in January 1901. This being a very long reign, the period is sometimes subdivided by historians into early (1837–c.1860), middle (c.1860–c.1880), and late phases. In literature, the chronology is complicated by the usually agreed completion of the previous 'Romantic' period at either 1830 with the death of George IV or at 1832 with the Great Reform Act and the death of Walter Scott: this would leave all or most of William IV's reign (1830–37), during which Alfred Tennyson and Robert Browning began their literary careers, lost to literary history, but for the common expedient of treating it—and the earliest works of those poets—as 'Victorian'. The literary achievements of the period, aside from Tennyson's and Browning's work, belong mostly to the realm of prose, as with the novels of Dickens, Thackeray, the Brontë sisters, Elizabeth Gaskell, George Eliot, and Thomas Hardy, and the non-fictional writings of Thomas Carlyle, John Ruskin, and Matthew Arnold. The drama of the period is undistinguished, until a notable revival in the 1890s. Special literary developments in the Victorian age include the emergence of *Pre-Raphaelitism, *Spasmodic poetry, *nonsense verse, the *detective story, the *ghost story, the *sensation novel, the boys' *adventure story, the linked cults of *Aestheticism and *decadence, and *New Woman writing.

The term 'Victorian' was not used within the period itself, but gained currency from about 1918, the year in which Lytton Strachey's disrespectful biographical essays were published as *Eminent Victorians*. In a largely anti-Victorian climate of opinion during much of the 20th century, the term acquired a range of derogatory connotations arising from caricatured presentations of 'the Victorians' as blindly imperialistic, self-satisfied, humourlessly religiose, hypocritically sentimental, and above all sexually repressed. The serious appreciation of Victorian literature and culture has struggled against such perceptions. A scholar devoted to the study of this period is a **Victorianist**.

**Further reading:** Alexandra Warwick and Martin Willis, *The Victorian Literature Handbook* (2008).

(((⊕))) SEE WEB LINKS
• Victorian Web: extensive web resource for Victorian studies.

**vignette** [vin-yet] Any brief composition or self-contained passage, usually a descriptive prose *sketch, *essay, or *short story. The term also refers to a kind of decorative design sometimes found at the beginning or end of a chapter in a book; these were often based on vine-leaves.

**villain** The principal evil character in a play or story. The villain is usually the *antagonist opposed to the *hero (and/or heroine), but in some cases he may be the *protagonist, as in Shakespeare's *Richard III*. The villains of English Elizabethan and *Jacobean drama, especially in *revenge tragedy, appear to be descended from the devils and the *Vice in earlier *morality plays. A more simplified villainous *stock character appears in 19th-century *melodrama, usually as a bewhiskered seducer. *See also* MACHIAVEL.

**villanelle** A poem composed of an uneven number (usually five) of *tercets rhyming *aba*, with a final *quatrain rhyming *abaa*. In this French *fixed form, the first and third lines of the opening tercet are repeated alternately as the third lines of the succeeding tercets, and together as the final couplet of the quatrain. Representing these repeated lines in capitals, with the second of them given in italic, the rhyme scheme may be displayed thus: Ab*A* abA ab*A* abA ab*A* abA*A*. The form was established in France in the 16th century, and used chiefly for *pastoral songs. In English, it was used for light **vers de société* by some minor poets of the late 19th century; but it has been adopted for more serious use by W. H. Auden, William Empson, and Derek Mahon. The best-known villanelle in English, however, is Dylan Thomas's 'Do Not Go Gentle into That Good Night' (1951).

**virelay** [vi-rě-lay] **(*virelai*)** A form of *lyric poem or song found in medieval France, but hardly ever in English. It has various forms, usually employing short lines and only two rhymes. In some a *refrain is used, while in others a pattern of interlinked rhymes connects the *stanzas, with the final rhyme of each stanza providing the main rhyme of the next.

**voice** A rather vague metaphorical term by which some critics refer to distinctive features of a written work in terms of spoken utterance. The voice of a literary work is then the specific group of characteristics displayed by the *narrator or poetic 'speaker' (or, in some uses, the actual author behind them), assessed in terms of *tone, *style, or personality. Distinctions between various kinds of narrative voice tend to be distinctions between kinds of narrator in terms of how they address the reader (rather than in terms of their perception of events, as in the distinct concept of *point of view). Likewise in non-narrative poems, distinctions can be made between the personal voice of a private lyric and the assumed voice (the *persona) of a *dramatic monologue.

***volta (volte)*** The Italian term for the 'turn' in the argument or mood of a *sonnet, occurring (in the Italian form of sonnet) between the octave and the sestet, i.e. at the 9th line. In the Miltonic variant of the Italian pattern, though, the *volta* comes later, about the 10th line; while in the Shakespearean or English form of the sonnet—which does not observe the octave/sestet division—it usually comes with the final couplet, i.e. at the 13th line.

**Vorticism** A short-lived artistic movement that announced itself in London in 1914. It was led by the painter and writer Wyndham Lewis, and attracted the support of the sculptors Jacob Epstein and Henri Gaudier-Brzeska. Its literary significance is negligible except in that Ezra Pound regarded it as an advance upon his previous phase of *Imagism. The Vorticist manifestos that appeared in the two issues of Lewis's magazine *Blast* (1914–15) celebrated the dynamic energies of the machine age while accusing *Futurism of having romanticized the machine. Vorticism called for an end to all sentimentality, and for a new abstraction that would, paradoxically, be both dynamic and static. For Pound the 'vortex' was the concentrated energy of the *avant-garde*, which was to blast away the complacency of the established culture. Vorticism was thus one of the minor currents of *modernism.

***vraisemblance*** [vray-som-blah[n]s] The French word for the artistic illusion of truth, usually known in English as *verisimilitude. *Adjective*: ***vraisemblable***.

**vulgate** A commonly used version of a work; or the common form of a language (i.e. *vernacular prose). In *textual criticism, the vulgate is the version of a text most commonly used, as distinct from its most accurate version. The **Vulgate** is a version of the Bible in Latin, translated mainly by St Jerome in the late 14th century, and later adapted as the authorized Catholic text. The **Vulgate Cycle** of *chivalric romances is a group of 13th-century French prose works dealing with King Arthur and his knights; it includes the accounts of the quest for the Holy Grail and of Arthur's death upon which Thomas Malory based his *Le Morte Darthur* (1485).

V

**weak ending** The *promotion of a normally unstressed monosyllable (usually a conjunction, preposition, or auxiliary verb) to the position usually occupied by a stressed syllable at the end of an *iambic line, causing a wrenched *accent. In this quotation from Shakespeare's *Antony and Cleopatra*, both line-endings are weak:

> Friends, be gone. You shall
> Have letters from me to some friends that will
> Sweep your way for you.

The weak ending may be distinguished from the *feminine ending in that it places the unstressed syllable in a stress position (the 10th syllable in an iambic *pentameter) rather than adding an extra 11th syllable. *See also* ENJAMBMENT.

**well-made play** Now a rather unfavourable term for a play that is neatly efficient in the construction of its plot but superficial in ideas and characterization. In 19th-century France, the term (*pièce bien faite*) at first had a more positive sense, denoting the carefully constructed suspense in comedies and *melodramas by Eugène Scribe (1791–1861) and his follower Victorien Sardou (1831–1908). As this tradition was displaced by the more serious concerns of dramatic *naturalism, the term acquired its dismissive sense, especially in the critical writings of Bernard Shaw.

**Further reading:** John Russell Taylor, *The Decline and Fall of the Well-Made Play* (1967).

***Weltanschauung*** [velt-an-show-uung] The German term for a 'world-view', that is, either the 'philosophy of life' adopted by a particular person or the more general outlook shared by people in a given period.

**Weltliteratur** 'World literature', a term coined by Goethe to suggest the capacity of literature to transcend national and linguistic boundaries. *See also* COMPARATIVE LITERATURE.

**Weltschmerz** [velt-shmairts] The German word for world-weariness (literally 'world-ache'), a vague kind of melancholy often associated with Romantic poetry.

**Wertherism** [ver-ter-izm] A fashion for morbid and self-indulgent melancholy or *\*Weltschmerz* provoked by J. W. von Goethe's *\*sentimental novel Die Lieden des jungen Werthers (The Sorrows of Young Werther*, 1774), in which the hero commits suicide because of his hopeless love for a young married woman. The novel was a sensation throughout Europe: Napoleon read it several times, and young men copied Werther's distinctive costume of yellow breeches with a blue coat. More alarmingly, one young woman drowned herself with a copy of the novel in her pocket, and several other youthful suicides were blamed on this craze.

**West End** In theatrical parlance, the area of central London in and around Shaftesbury Avenue where the major commercial theatres have been concentrated since the 19th century. It has become associated with polished but generally 'lighter' kinds of dramatic entertainment (musicals, \*farces, etc.) by contrast with the higher literary drama offered at theatres located in less fashionable districts—such as the Old Vic or the National Theatre, both south of the Thames.

**wit** A much-debated term with a number of meanings ranging from the general notion of 'intelligence' through the more specific 'ingenuity' or 'quickness of mind' to the narrower modern idea of amusing verbal cleverness. In its literary uses, the term has gone through a number of shifts: it was associated in the \*Renaissance with intellectual keenness and a capacity of 'invention' by which writers could discover surprisingly appropriate \*figures and \*conceits, by perceiving resemblances between apparently dissimilar things. It took on an additional sense of elegant arrangement in the 17th and 18th centuries, as in Pope's famous definition of true wit in his *Essay on Criticism* (1711):

> What oft was Thought, but ne'er so well Exprest.

However, the advent of *Romanticism with its cult of *imagination and genius tended to relegate wit, along with *fancy and ingenuity, to an inferior position, transferring its older positive senses to the imaginative faculty. The usual modern sense of wit, then, is one of light cleverness and skill in *repartee or the composition of amusing *epigrams. In 20th-century criticism, an attempt to restore a stronger sense of wit was mounted by T. S. Eliot in his discussions of the *metaphysical poets: he praised the wit of Andrew Marvell as a kind of 'tough reasonableness', while other critics have seen wit as a kind of disposition towards *irony. The important point to note is that earlier uses of the term included the positive sense of imaginative capacity, which has since become rather detached from the weaker modern notion of what is witty.

**wrenched accent**  *See* ACCENT.

**writerly**  *See* SCRIPTIBLE.

W

**Yale school** A group of literary theorists and critics associated in the 1970s and 1980s with Yale University, formerly a bastion of the \*New Criticism in literary theory. The five identified members of the group were notable for their promotion of the then controversial project of \*deconstruction. Their partly misleading self-identification as a 'school' arose from the publication in 1979 of *Deconstruction and Criticism*, a volume that was taken as a kind of manifesto or showcase: it contained essays by Harold Bloom (Professor of Humanities at Yale), Paul de Man (Chair of Yale's Department of Comparative Literature), Jacques Derrida (who held a part-time Visiting Professorship at Yale), Geoffrey H. Hartman (Professor of English and Comparative Literature at Yale), and J. Hillis Miller (Professor of English at Yale). Hartman's preface to the volume, though, distanced his own and Bloom's positions from those of the more fully committed deconstructionist styles of de Man, Derrida, and Miller. De Man's death four years later, along with Bloom's increasing intellectual distance from deconstructive approaches to literature, had the effect of breaking up this group identity.

**Further reading:** Vincent B. Leitch, *Deconstructive Criticism* (1983).

**Zeitgeist** [tsyt-gyst] The German word for 'time-spirit', more often translated as 'spirit of the age'. It usually refers to the prevailing mood or attitude of a given period.

**zeugma** [zewg-mä] A *figure of speech by which one word refers to two others in the same sentence. Literally a 'yoking', zeugma may be achieved by a verb or preposition with two objects, as in the final line of Shakespeare's 128th sonnet:

> Give them thy fingers, me thy lips to kiss.

Or it may employ a verb with two subjects, as in the opening of his 55th sonnet:

> Not marble nor the gilded monuments
> Of princes shall outlive this powerful rhyme.

However, the term is frequently used as a synonym for *syllepsis—a special kind of zeugma in which the yoking term agrees grammatically with only one of the terms to which it is applied, or refers to each in a different sense. In the confusion surrounding these two terms, some rhetoricians have reserved 'zeugma' for the ungrammatical sense of syllepsis. *Adjective*: **zeugmatic**.

# Further Reference

Many terms lying beyond the scope of this dictionary are found explained in other reference works, which are listed below by category.

## General

William Harmon, *A Handbook to Literature* (12th edn, 2011) offers wide coverage, and includes lists of Nobel and Pulitzer prizewinners.

## Literary and Cultural Theory

A careful historical investigation into general terms such as *creative* and *culture* is conducted in Raymond Williams, *Keywords* (1976). Among the many reference books on modern Theory, the most substantial is Michael Groden, Martin Kreiswirth, and Imre Szeman (eds), *Literary Theory and Criticism: The Johns Hopkins Guide* (2012), which offers lengthy essays on theorists and schools internationally, with substantial bibliographies. Others in this category are Michael Payne, *A Dictionary of Cultural and Critical Theory* (2nd edn, 2010), David Macey, *The Penguin Dictionary of Critical Theory* (2nd edn, 2002), and Ian Buchanan, *A Dictionary of Critical Theory* (2010). Confining itself to terms rather than theorists is Jeremy Hawthorn, *A Glossary of Contemporary Literary Theory* (4th edn, 2000).

## Poetry

The most substantial work in this sphere is Roland Greene and Stephen Cushman (eds), *The Princeton Encyclopedia of Poetry and Poetics* (4th edn, 2012). Some terms not found in that work are covered in either Jack Myers and Don Charles Wukasch, *Dictionary of Poetic Terms* (2003) or Lewis Turco, *The Book of Forms: A Handbook of Poetics* (3rd edn, 2000).

## Drama and Shakespeare

The fullest coverage of dramatic concepts is found in a work translated from the French: Patrice Pavis, *Dictionary of the Theatre: Terms, Concepts, and Analysis* (1998). For Shakespearian terminology, see Michael Dobson and Stanley Wells (eds), *The Oxford Companion to Shakespeare* (2001).

## Rhetoric

A convenient guide is Richard A. Lanham, *A Handlist of Rhetorical Terms* (2nd edn, 1991). Many terms are explained more fully in the *Princeton Encyclopedia* (see above under Poetry).

## Narrative

The vocabulary of modern narrative theory is explained in Gerald Prince, *A Dictionary of Narratology* (2nd edn, 2003).

## Biography and Autobiography

The terminology of this field is covered in Donald J. Winslow, *Life-Writing: A Glossary of Terms in Biography, Autobiography, and Related Forms* (1995), and in Margareta Jolly (ed.), *Encyclopedia of Life Writing* (2002).

## Linguistics

The standard guide to linguistic terms is David Crystal, *A Dictionary of Linguistics and Phonetics* (6th edn, 2008). Often more suitable to literary purposes is Katie Wales, *A Dictionary of Stylistics* (3rd edn, 2011).

# Oxford Quick Reference

**The Concise Oxford Companion to English Literature**
Dinah Birch and Katy Hooper

Based on the best-selling *Oxford Companion to English Literature*, this is an indispensable guide to all aspects of English literature.

Review of the parent volume:
'the foremost work of reference in its field'

*Literary Review*

**A Dictionary of Shakespeare**
Stanley Wells

Compiled by one of the best-known international authorities on the playwright's works, this dictionary offers up-to-date information on all aspects of Shakespeare, both in his own time and in later ages.

**The Oxford Dictionary of Literary Terms**
Chris Baldick

A best-selling dictionary, covering all aspects of literature, this is an essential reference work for students of literature in any language.

**A Dictionary of Critical Theory**
Ian Buchanan

The invaluable multidisciplinary guide to theory, covering movements, theories, and events.

'an excellent gateway into critical theory'

*Literature and Theology*

# Oxford Quick Reference

**The Concise Oxford Dictionary of English Etymology**
T. F. Hoad

A wealth of information about our language and its history, this reference source provides over 17,000 entries on word origins.

'A model of its kind'

*Daily Telegraph*

**New Oxford Rhyming Dictionary**

From writing poems to writing birthday cards, and from composing advertising slogans to music lyrics, this dictionary has what every writer (or budding writer) needs. It contains rhymes for over 45,000 words, including proper names, place names, and foreign terms used in English.

'All wordsmiths are bound to enjoy feeling indebted (fetid, minareted, rosetted ...)'

Julia Donaldson (author of *The Gruffalo*)

**The Oxford Dictionary of Slang**
John Ayto

Containing over 10,000 words and phrases, this is the ideal reference for those interested in the more quirky and unofficial words used in the English language.

'hours of happy browsing for language lovers'

*Observer*

# Oxford Quick Reference

**A Dictionary of Marketing**
Charles Doyle

Covers traditional marketing techniques and theories alongside the latest concepts in over 2,000 clear and authoritative entries.

'Flick to any page [for] a lecture's worth of well thought through information'

*Dan Germain, Head of Creative, innocent ltd*

**A Dictionary of Media and Communication**
Daniel Chandler and Rod Munday

Provides over 2,200 authoritative entries on terms used in media and communication, from concepts and theories to technical terms, across subject areas that include advertising, digital culture, journalism, new media, radio studies, and telecommunications.

'a wonderful volume that is much more than a simple dictionary'
*Professor Joshua Meyrowitz, University of New Hampshire*

**A Dictionary of Film Studies**
Annette Kuhn and Guy Westwell

Features terms covering all aspects of film studies in 500 detailed entries, from theory and history to technical terms and practices.

**A Dictionary of Journalism**
Tony Harcup

Covers terminology relating to the practice, business, and technology of journalism, as well as its concepts and theories, organizations and institutions, publications, and key events.

# Oxford Quick Reference

**Concise Medical Dictionary**

Over 12,000 clear entries covering all the major medical and surgical specialities make this one of our best-selling dictionaries.

'"No home should be without one" certainly applies to this splendid medical dictionary'

*Journal of the Institute of Health Education*

'An extraordinary bargain'                                              *New Scientist*

**A Dictionary of Nursing**

Comprehensive coverage of the ever-expanding vocabulary of the nursing professions. Features over 10,000 entries written by medical and nursing specialists.

**A Dictionary of Dentistry**
Robert Ireland

Over 4,000 succinct and authoritative entries define all the important terms used in dentistry today. This is the ideal reference for all members of the dental team.

**A Dictionary of Forensic Science**
Suzanne Bell

In over 1,300 entries, this new dictionary covers the key concepts within Forensic Science and is a must-have for students and practitioners of forensic science.

# Oxford Quick Reference

**The Oxford Dictionary of Dance**
Debra Craine and Judith Mackrell

Over 2,600 entries on everything from hip-hop to classical ballet, covering dancers, dance styles, choreographers and composers, techniques, companies, and productions.

'A must-have volume ... impressively thorough'

Margaret Reynolds, *The Times*


**The Oxford Guide to Plays**
Michael Patterson

Covers 1,000 of the most important, best-known, and most popular plays of world theatre.

'Superb synopses ... Superbly formatted ... Fascinating and accessible style'

*THES*


**The Oxford Dictionary of Music**
Michael & Joyce Kennedy & Tim Rutherford-Johnson

The most comprehensive, authoritative, and up-to-date dictionary of music available in paperback.

'clearly the best around ... the dictionary that everyone should have'

*Literary Review*

# Oxford Quick Reference

**A Dictionary of the Bible**
W. R. F. Browning

In over 2,000 entries, this authoritative dictionary provides clear and concise information about the important people, places, themes, and doctrines of the Bible.

**The Oxford Dictionary of Saints**
David Farmer

From the famous to the obscure, over 1,400 saints are covered in this acclaimed dictionary.

'an essential reference work'                                        *Daily Telegraph*

**The Concise Oxford Dictionary of the Christian Church**
E. A. Livingstone

This indispensable guide contains over 5,000 entries and provides full coverage of theology, denominations, the church calendar, and the Bible.

'opens up the whole of Christian history, now with a wider vision than ever'                          Robert Runcie, former Archbishop of Canterbury

**The Oxford Dictionary of Popes**
J. N. D. Kelly and M. J. Walsh

Spans almost 2,000 years of papal history: from St Peter to Pope Benedict XVI.

'well-researched, extremely well written, and a delightful exercise in its own right'                                      *Church Times*

# Oxford Quick Reference

### A Dictionary of Chemistry

Over 4,700 entries covering all aspects of chemistry, including physical chemistry and biochemistry.

'It should be in every classroom and library ... the reader is drawn inevitably from one entry to the next merely to satisfy curiosity.'

School Science Review

### A Dictionary of Physics

Ranging from crystal defects to the solar system, 4,000 clear and concise entries cover all commonly encountered terms and concepts of physics.

### A Dictionary of Biology

The perfect guide for those studying biology — with over 5,500 entries on key terms from biology, biochemistry, medicine, and palaeontology.

'lives up to its expectations; the entries are concise, but explanatory'

Biologist

'ideally suited to students of biology, at either secondary or university level, or as a general reference source for anyone with an interest in the life sciences'

Journal of Anatomy

# Oxford Quick Reference

**A Dictionary of Psychology**
Andrew M. Colman

Over 9,000 authoritative entries make up the most wide-ranging
dictionary of psychology available.

'impressive ... certainly to be recommended'
*Times Higher Education Supplement*

'probably the best single-volume dictionary of its kind.'
*Library Journal*

**A Dictionary of Economics**
John Black, Nigar Hashimzade, and Gareth Myles

Fully up-to-date and jargon-free coverage of economics. Over 3,400
terms on all aspects of economic theory and practice.

'strongly recommended as a handy work of reference.'
*Times Higher Education Supplement*

**A Dictionary of Law**

An ideal source of legal terminology for systems based on English law.
Over 4,200 clear and concise entries.

'The entries are clearly drafted and succinctly written ... Precision for the
professional is combined with a layman's enlightenment.'
*Times Literary Supplement*

**A Dictionary of Education**
Susan Wallace

In over 1,250 clear and concise entries, this authoritative dictionary
covers all aspects of education, including organizations, qualifications,
key figures, major legislation, theory, and curriculum and assessment
terminology.

# Oxford Quick Reference

**A Dictionary of Sociology**
John Scott

The most wide-ranging and authoritative dictionary of its kind.

'Readers and especially beginning readers of sociology can scarcely do better ... there is no better single volume compilation for an up-to-date, readable, and authoritative source of definitions, summaries and references in contemporary Sociology.'

A. H. Halsey, *Emeritus Professor, Nuffield College, University of Oxford*

**The Concise Oxford Dictionary of Politics**
Iain McLean and Alistair McMillan

The bestselling A–Z of politics with over 1,700 detailed entries.

'A first class work of reference ... probably the most complete as well as the best work of its type available ... Every politics student should have one'

*Political Studies Association*

**A Dictionary of Environment and Conservation**
Chris Park and Michael Allaby

An essential guide to all aspects of the environment and conservation containing over 8,500 entries.

'from *aa* to *zygote*, choices are sound and definitions are unspun'
*New Scientist*

# Oxford Quick Reference

**The Oxford Dictionary of Art & Artists**
Ian Chilvers

Based on the highly praised *Oxford Dictionary of Art*, over 2,500 up-to-date entries on painting, sculpture, and the graphic arts.

'the best and most inclusive single volume available, immensely useful and very well written'

Marina Vaizey, *Sunday Times*

**The Concise Oxford Dictionary of Art Terms**
Michael Clarke

Written by the Director of the National Gallery of Scotland, over 1,800 entries cover periods, styles, materials, techniques, and foreign terms.

**A Dictionary of Architecture and Landscape Architecture**
James Stevens Curl

Over 5,000 entries and 250 illustrations cover all periods of Western architectural history.

'splendid ... you can't have a more concise, entertaining, and informative guide to the words of architecture.'

*Architectural Review*

'excellent, and amazing value for money ... by far the best thing of its kind.'

*Professor David Walker*

# Oxford Quick Reference

**The Kings and Queens of Britain**
John Cannon and Anne Hargreaves

A detailed, fully-illustrated history ranging from mythical and pre-conquest rulers to the present House of Windsor, featuring regional maps and genealogies.

**A Dictionary of World History**

Over 4,000 entries on everything from prehistory to recent changes in world affairs. An excellent overview of world history.

**A Dictionary of British History**
Edited by John Cannon

An invaluable source of information covering the history of Britain over the past two millennia. Over 3,000 entries written by more than 100 specialist contributors.

Review of the parent volume
'the range is impressive ... truly (almost) all of human life is here'
Kenneth Morgan, *Observer*

**The Oxford Companion to Irish History**
Edited by S. J. Connolly

A wide-ranging and authoritative guide to all aspects of Ireland's past from prehistoric times to the present day.

'packed with small nuggets of knowledge'          *Daily Telegraph*

**The Oxford Companion to Scottish History**
Edited by Michael Lynch

The definitive guide to twenty centuries of life in Scotland.
'exemplary and wonderfully readable'

*Financial Times*